A HISTORY OF

MODERN CRITICISM

1750–1950

IN SEVEN VOLUMES

OTHER BOOKS BY RENÉ WELLEK

Immanuel Kant in England

The Rise of English Literary History

Theory of Literature (with Austin Warren)

Concepts of Criticism

Essays on Czech Literature

*Confrontations: Studies in the Intellectual and Literary Relations
  between Germany, England, and the United States
  During the Nineteenth Century*

Discriminations: Further Concepts of Criticism

Four Critics: Croce, Valéry, Lukács, Ingarden

The Attack on Literature & Other Essays

A HISTORY OF MODERN

Criticism: 1750–1950

BY RENÉ WELLEK

VOLUME 6   *American Criticism, 1900–1950*

YALE UNIVERSITY PRESS
New Haven and London

Designed by James J. Johnson
and set in the Baskerville types.
Printed in the United States of America by
Vail-Ballou Press, Binghamton, N.Y.

Library of Congress Cataloging in Publication Data

(Revised for volume 5 and volume 6)

Wellek, René.
  A history of modern criticism.

  Includes bibliographies and indexes.
  Contents: v. 1. The later eighteenth century.—[etc.]
—v. 5. English criticism, 1900–1950.—v. 6. American
criticism, 1900–1950.
  1. Criticism—History. I. Title: Modern criticism.
PN86.W4   801.95'09   85–12005
ISBN 0–300–03378–8 (v. 5: alk. paper)
ISBN 0–300–03486–5 (v. 6: alk. paper)

The paper in this book meets the guidelines for permanence
and durability of the Committee on Production Guidelines for
Book Longevity of the Council on Library Resources.

10 9 8 7 6 5 4 3 2 1

CONTENTS

ACKNOWLEDGMENTS

I use the following articles of mine, sometimes expanded, cut, and changed.

The New Humanists: "Irving Babbitt, Paul More, and Transcendentalism," in *Transcendentalism and Its Legacy*, pp. 185–203. © 1966 by its editors Myron Simon and Thornton II. Parsons.

Outsiders: "The Literary Criticism of W. C. Brownell," *Sewanee Review* 90 (1982): 158–67.

Edmund Wilson: "Edmund Wilson (1895–1972)," *Comparative Literature Studies* 15 (1978): 97–123. Reprinted in *History as a Tool in Critical Interpretation*, ed. Thomas R. Rugh and Erin R. Silva, pp. 63–95.

Lionel Trilling: "The Literary Criticism of Lionel Trilling," *New England Review* 2 (1979): 26–49.

The New Criticism: "The New Criticism: Pro and Contra," *Critical Inquiry* 4 (1978): 28–33. Reprinted in my book *The Attack on Literature and Other Essays* (1982), pp. 87–103.

John Crowe Ransom: "John Crowe Ransom's Theory of Poetry," in *Literary Theory and Structure: Essays in Honor of William K. Wimsatt*, ed. Frank Brady, John Palmer, and Martin Price (1973), pp. 179–98.

Allen Tate: "Allen Tate: Literary Theorist and Critic," in *Englische und amerikanische Literaturtheorie*, ed. Rüdiger Ahrens and Erwin Wolff (1979), 2:557–72.

Cleanth Brooks: "Cleanth Brooks, Critic of Critics," *Sewanee Review* 10 (1974): 125–52. Reprinted in *The Possibilities of Order: Cleanth Brooks and His Work*, ed. Lewis P. Simpson (1976), pp. 196–229.

R. P. Blackmur: "R. P. Blackmur Re-Examined," *Southern Review* n.s. 7 (1971): 825–45. Reprinted in *English Studies Today*, 5th series, ed. Sencer Tonguç (Istanbul, 1973), pp. 453–76.

Kenneth Burke: "Kenneth Burke and Literary Criticism," *Sewanee Review* 79 (1971): 171–88.

Yvor Winters: "Yvor Winters Rehearsed and Reconsidered," *Denver Quarterly* 10 (1975): 1–27.

William K. Wimsatt: "The Literary Theory of William K. Wimsatt," *Yale Review* 66 (1977): 176–92.

1 : CRITICISM BEFORE THE NEW CRITICISM

NATURALISTS, SYMBOLISTS, AND IMPRESSIONISTS

IN THE fourth volume of this *History* Henry James and William Dean Howells were the last American critics discussed as proponents of a theory of a realism. Both James and Howells lived well into the twentieth century. The prefaces to James's New York edition of his novels (1907–17) were, however, hardly noticed in their time. James and Howells were far from dominating the critical scene even in the eighties and nineties of the century. Then, in general, the United States was still ruled by what, in 1911, Santayana labeled the "Genteel Tradition," a variant of Victorianism, of vapid, derivative idealism. The representative figure was Edmund Clarence Stedman (1833–1908), a poet, anthologist, editor of poets, author of *The New York Stock Exchange: Its History* (1905), and a prolific reviewer and critic. In 1891 he delivered a series of lectures on *The Nature and Elements of Poetry* in which poetry is defined romantically as "rhythmical, imaginative language, expressing the invention, taste, thought, passion, and insight, of the human soul" (44). In practice, Stedman praises melancholia (Dürer's woodcut is the frontispiece), rejects "art for art's sake" and exalts both truth, ethical insight and imagination, "the faculty divine." "Poetic expression is that of light from a star, our straightest message from the inaccessible human soul" (259). It is all high-minded, tolerant (even Whitman is praised), vague, eclectic, uncritical, and untheoretical.

The reaction was already under way by that time. It came in several different forms, mostly due to the influx of new ideas and styles from France. Naturalism in the wake of Zola found adherents and imitators. They were novelists and storytellers, hardly critics, though they stated their creed eloquently. Hamlin Garland (1860–1940) invented or borrowed the label "veritist" (similar to Italian *verismo*, possibly suggested by Eugène Véron's use) to describe his kind of naturalism in *The Crumbling Idols* (1908). He hoped to redeem American literature with it. "The present is the vital theme: the past is dead; and the future can be trusted to look after itself" (Brown, 471). The most prominent novelist, Frank Norris (1870–1902), in *Responsibilities of a Novelist* (1903), defended the novel with a purpose recognizing, however, that the novel "preached by telling things and showing things" (Brown, 522) rather than proclaiming a thesis as Zola did in *Fécondité*.

Symbolism came also from France: or rather all the newest French authors and trends found their propagandists in America. There were sympathetic reports on the French movement in magazines very early. T. S. Perry wrote on "The Latest Literary Fashion in France," symbolism, in *The Cosmopolitan* (1892) and Aline Gorren on "The French Symbolists" in *Scribner's* (1893). Vance Thompson (1863–1925), fresh from Paris, edited the oddly named review *M'lle New York* for which he wrote essays collected in a sumptuous illustrated volume *French Portraits* (1900). The essay on Mallarmé (originally 1895) conveys some information on his theories and attempts even an explication of some of his more accessible poems. But the frontispiece is a large photograph of Catulle Mendès, the last of the Parnassians. Thompson preferred Mendès, Jean Moréas, and Albert Mockel to the poets of whom we think most highly today. The book is dedicated to James Huneker (1857–1921), who became the main expounder and importer of recent Continental literature. In 1896 he had defended the symbolist poets against the slurs of Max Nordau's *Entartung* and began to write the long series of articles on Maeterlinck, Laforgue, and many others—not bothering to conceal his dependence on Remy de Gourmont (who was also the model of Vance Thompson). Huneker dedicated his later book of essays, *Visionaries* (1905), to Gourmont and was rewarded by praise for being "one of the best informed of foreign critics, one of those who judge us [French] with the most sympathy and also with the most freedom" (Schwab, 194). This is a true description of Huneker, who must be seen as a reporter, an enthusiastic and uncritical middleman who spread the knowledge of almost any then-current European author, musician, and painter. Huneker is not ideological or exclusive. Almost everybody one can think of in England, France, Germany, Scandinavia, Italy, and even Russia is included and all the arts are combined and confused. In retrospect Huneker himself smiled at his obsession with synaesthesia. "I muddled the Seven Arts in a grand old stew. I saw music, heard color, tasted architecture, smelt sculpture, and fingered perfumes."[1] Though his methods were impressionistic, the style metaphorical and often hectic, the taste indiscriminate, ranging in American literature from *Huckleberry Finn* to *The Wings of the Dove* (Schwab, 129–30), in French from Maeterlinck to Stendhal, in German from Sudermann to Nietzsche, Huneker was free in judging and rating his authors and getting in all kinds of trouble over it. He had praised Shaw lavishly very early. A laudatory review of *Arms and the Man* dates from 1894 but a critical essay in *Iconoclasts* (1905) provoked an insulting letter from Shaw, calling Huneker a "horribly inaccurate ruffian." He berated him: "Your head is full of romantic idolatries and you never observe anything" (Schwab, 168). After that Shaw became Huneker's special *bête noire*. *Promenades of an Impressionist* (1910), the title of one of his books, thus does not describe him fully: he was often a combative, doctrinaire critic freely venting his prejudices. But this belongs to the history of the quarrels of authors rather than to criticism. Still, Huneker fulfilled an important function in his time. Edmund Wilson thought that "it was simply the matter of communicating to the United States, then backward to what seems an incredible degree in its assimilation of cultural movements abroad, the musical and literary happenings of the preceding half-century in Europe" and testified that Huneker "chaotic and careless though he was, made you ravenous to devour his favorite writers."[2]

H. L. MENCKEN (1880–1956)

Vance Thompson, Huneker, and Percival Pollard, who wrote on *Masks and Minstrels of the New Germany* (1911), had all a Bohemian resentment against the commercial and philistine civilization around them, but their remedies were an appeal to so many diverse foreign writers that they could not make a deeper impression: they aroused only curiosity and uneasiness. Only the much younger Henry Louis Mencken was able to give the revolt against the genteel tradition a powerful voice. He was at the height of his influence only after the First World War: in 1927 his *American Mercury* sold 70,000 copies a month. But he had started to write criticism long before. In 1905 he published a small book on *George Bernard Shaw* which was largely a discussion of Shaw's themes much in the manner of Shaw's own *Quintessence of Ibsenism*. Then in 1908, a much larger book on *The Philosophy of Friedrich Nietzsche* followed, a descriptive, summarizing, rather plodding account which puts all the emphasis on Nietzsche's attack on Christianity and its "slave morality" and sees him as a kind of social Darwinist, a propounder of the "survival of the fittest" and of a new aristocracy of amoral "supermen." Mencken also sympathized with his misogyny and his contempt for government and democracy, but the motifs in Nietzsche's thought which would attract us today escaped him entirely. Nietzsche is assimilated to Thomas Henry Huxley, whom Mencken called "the greatest Englishman of all time."[1] These early, sober books were completely overshadowed by Mencken's enormous, indefatigable journalistic activity, since 1908 in *The Smart Set* and since 1923 in *The American Mercury*. Collections of essays, *A Book of Prefaces* (1917), and the six volumes of *Prejudices* (1919–27) established claims to permanence and with the diligently collected, witty, and thorough *The American Language* (1919) Mencken made pretensions to linguistic scholarship in his plea for the independence and vitality of the American variant of English that he insisted on considering a special language. Mencken's influence, briefly interrupted by his pro-German sympathies during the First World War, diminished rather suddenly with the Depression, as Mencken considered politics a farce and thought the poor should remain so. Edmund Wilson, a good judge in such matters, could say that "Mencken was the civilized consciousness of modern America, its learning, its intelligence and taste, realizing the grossness of its manners and mind and crying out in horror and chagrin" (quoted by Stenerson, 219). But "horror and chagrin" seem wrongly chosen terms. Mencken was rather a cheerful, genial satirist who had his fun in ridiculing the American "boob" who had imposed Prohibition, Comstockery, and the Mann Act on a gullible people. Mencken, as Wilson recognized later, "asks for nothing but his Brahms, his beer and his books, and the hilarious spectacle of his neighbors,"[2] the look at the "zoo" of American democracy (a sight he would not have exchanged for that of any other country). Still, below the gay exterior, the high jinks and the bravado, there runs a stream of melancholy, a sense of the "meaningless of life," destroyed by death, a feeling which colors Mencken's literary preferences.

Literary criticism is only a small part of Mencken's activity but it had a strong impact on the change of taste occurring in the country just before and after the First World War, which freed it from the constraints—polite, moral, and upperclass—of the preceding time. Mencken made no pretensions to theory. "Criticism itself," he declares bluntly, "at bottom, is no more than prejudice made plausible" ("A Soul's Adventures," *Smart Set* 48, 1916, 153). In a discussion of J. E. Spingarn, whose Crocean rejection of all classifications and moralizing Mencken welcomed also for its anti-academic tone, he doubted that beauty is "the apparition *in vacuo* that Dr. Spingarn seems to see. It has its social, its political, even its moral implication." "The really competent critic must be an empiricist. He must conduct his exploration with whatever means lie within the bounds of his personal limitation. He must produce his effects with whatever tools will work." Mencken would substitute for Spingarn's "creative criticism" the term "catalytic," explaining it in terms very similar to T. S.

Eliot's chemical metaphor of the poet's impersonal role. The business of the critic is "to provoke the reaction between the work of art and the spectator" ("Criticism of Criticism of Criticism," *PES*, 18–20). The assumption, though not fully pursued, would reduce the critic to a middleman, a catalyzer who at end should discreetly get out of the way. But on a later occasion Mencken rejected the assumption that "the primary motive of the critic" is pedagogical rather than the motive of the artist, "the simple desire to function freely and beautifully, to give outward and objective form to ideas that bubble inwardly and have a fascinating lure in them, to get rid of them dramatically and make an articulate noise in the world." The critic who "lacks the intellectual agility and enterprise needed to make the leap from the work of art to the vast and mysterious complex of phenomena behind it remains no more than a fugleman or policeman to his betters." "But if a genuine artist is concealed within him . . . then he moves inevitably from the work of art to life itself" ("A Footnote on Criticism," *PTS*, 84–86). The critic is swallowed up by the creative artist: "What starts out as a review of a book, becomes a fresh work of art, only indirectly related to the one that suggested it." No critic can stick to his task. He will abandon the criticism of specific works of art and set up shop as "a general merchant in general ideas, i.e. an artist working in the materials of life itself." Mencken believes in "creative criticism." The critic is "first and last, simply trying to express himself"(91). Goethe, Carlyle, Macaulay, Arnold, and Sainte-Beuve are invoked as first-rate artists. "Let us forget all the heavy effort to make a science of Criticism: it is a fine art, or nothing." Truth ceases to matter. "Is Carlyle's Frederick true? Who cares?" (95). Now Mencken also rejects the demand that criticism be "constructive" and doubts whether it ever had an effect on the writer criticized. Nor does the audience apparently matter. "The true aim of a critic is certainly not to make converts" (92). There are no immutable truths in the arts. "Criticism, at bottom, is indistinguishable from skepticism" (97). These extreme positions in the two best-known papers on criticism do not, however, define Mencken's actual practice: he is neither an impersonal catalyst nor an artist oblivious of the truth of his characterizations and judgments, even though he did express a personality and a style of thinking.

In practice, Mencken was a propagandist of the new realistic novel, which sets forth, he hopes, "not what might be true, or what ought to be true, but what actually is true" (*PTS*, 205). Mencken contrasts it with poetry, which he denounces, in a flippant article, as "beautiful balderdash" (154). It consists of denials of either objective or subjective facts. Mencken quotes Browning or rather Pippa saying, "God's in His heaven,

All's right with the world," and Henley saying, "I am the master of my fate: I am the captain of my soul," as examples of poetic untruth and acknowledges only the music of poetry. "Shakespeare ought to be ranked among the musicians, along with Beethoven. As a philosopher he was a ninth-rater" (165). He employed Hamlet "as a convenient spout for some of the finest music ever got into words" (165).

Mencken cared only for the novel and the drama of ideas. Two novelists were his central concern: Joseph Conrad and Theodore Dreiser. The praise heaped on Conrad is hyperbolical. He is "the greatest artist writing in English today" (*Smart Set* 44, 1912, 231), and even "incomparably the greatest artist who ever wrote a novel" (preface to *A Conrad Argosy*, 1942). *The Heart of Darkness* is probably "the best book of imaginative writing that the English literature of the twentieth century can yet show" (*Smart Set*, 241) and "Youth" is "perhaps the best short story ever written in English" (ibid., 96). *Lord Jim* is "the greatest novel in the language" (Nolte, 71). Though Mencken did not discover Dreiser, he became his main champion and originator of his fame. He called *Jenny Gerhardt* "the best American novel," *Sister Carrie* a momentous event in the history of American fiction. These two somewhat incongruous writers share in Mencken's mind a common outlook on life which is also his. "Like Dreiser, Conrad is forever fascinated by the 'immense difference' of things, the tragic vanity of the blind groping that we call aspiration, the profound meaninglessness of life—fascinated and left wondering" (*BP*, 11). In an elaborate comparison Mencken asserts, "Substitute the name of Dreiser for that of Conrad, and you will have to change scarcely a word" (89) in their common creed. "The struggle of man is more than impotent: it is gratuitous and purposeless." "Both novelists see human existence as a seeking without finding; both reject the prevailing interpretations of its meaning and mechanism; both take refuge in 'I do not know' " (88). Still, Mencken sees the difference: "Conrad is far more resolute, and it is easy to see why. He is, by birth and training, an aristocrat." "He has the gift of emotional detachment" (92) while Dreiser "sometimes vacillates perilously between a moral sentimentalism and a somewhat extravagant revolt" (93). The obvious motive force for this dual admiration is a feeling of kinship for the agnosticism and pessimism of the two. But Mencken does, besides, criticize and discriminate among the novels on artistic grounds. The essay on Dreiser is full of harsh judgments on some of the later novels. *The Genius,* for instance, is called "flaccid, elephantine, doltish, coarse, dismal, flatulent, ignorant, unconvincing, wearisome" (107). Later Mencken reviewed *An American Tragedy* unfavorably.[3] The novel is "a shapeless and forbidding monster—a heaping cartload of raw materials for a novel, with rubbish of all sorts inter-mixed—a vast, sloppy, chaotic thing of 385,000 words—at least 250,000 of them unnecessary." Mencken only grants that the book "improves as it nears its shocking climax." Also Conrad, though much more unre-servedly admired, was criticized in some detail. *Victory* is a melodramatic thriller, *Under Western Eyes* is a contrived study of the Russian character, *Chance* is unnecessarily labored. Mencken felt that Conrad needed pro-motion in America while Dreiser had to be defended against the attempts to censor or suppress him. Mencken argued against Stuart Sherman's allegation that Dreiser "imposes his own materialistic philosophy" upon his characters by perversely denying Dreiser's naturalism. "Dreiser's at-titude of mind stems directly not from Zola, Flaubert, Augier and the younger Dumas, but from the Greeks" (Bode, *The Young Mencken*, 555). Mencken also promoted Sinclair Lewis, particularly *Babbitt*, for giving an accurate account of the American hinterland. But he rejected Upton Sinclair very early: In 1908 he accused him of confusing the function of the novelist with those of a crusader. *The Money-Changers* is "a some-what florid treatise in sociology" (ibid., 103). Mencken had no sympathy with socialism.

Mencken's championship of the new American naturalism is accom-panied by his unabashed admiration of quite different writers: James Branch Cabell is the topic of a highly laudatory booklet (1917) and he praised Max Beerbohm's romp, *Zuleika Dobson*, extravagantly (*Smart Set*, 1912, 134–42). Mencken managed to reconcile the admiration for the fantastic utopia of Cabell by arguing that "*Jurgen* is as realistic in manner as Zola's *La Terre*, despite its grotesque fable." Cabell's stature as an artist "depends almost wholly upon his capacity for accurate observation and realistic representation" (*PTS*, 206).

Among the English novelists, Arnold Bennett, admired for his "free-dom from messianic delusion," is seen as being "left empty of passion unable to feel with his characters," paralyzed by his skepticism and irony (*PFS*, 36–37). H. G. Wells, whom Mencken had praised early for *Tono Bungay* and *The New Machiavelli*, disappointed him with his later work. "It shows the absorption of the artist in the tin-pot reformer and profes-sional wise man" (*PFS*, 290). Mencken praised also Somerset Maugham's *Moon and Sixpence*, Aldous Huxley's *Crome Yellow*, but dismissed D. H. Lawrence and Virginia Woolf. Surprisingly, considering Mencken's gen-eral contempt for poetry and feeble interest in it (possibly E. L. Masters and Carl Sandburg excepted); he could praise Ezra Pound's *Provença* for an "arresting and amazing vigor," for its "stark, heathenish music" (*Smart Set*, 1911, 77). But T. S. Eliot's poetry remained a book with seven seals.

Mencken flaunted his descent from a line of German scholars and considered himself the champion of a new national literature freed from the dominance of the "Sassenach" tradition, allowing voices of the new immigrants (Dreiser, Dos Passos, Hergesheimer, Steinbeck) to be heard. He admired Huneker for his opening windows to Continental Europe. "He emancipated criticism in America from its old slavery to stupidity, and with it emancipated all the arts themselves" (*PTS*, 83). But Mencken complained, putting his finger on the difference from himself, that "for all his enterprise and iconoclasm, there was not much of the Berserker in him, and his floutings of the national aesthetic tradition seldom took the form of forthright challenges" (76). Huneker was far too hospitable, "yielding to the hocus-pocus of the mysticists, particularly Maeterlinck" (Bode, *The Young Mencken*, 513). Mencken cared actually little for Continental literature except Nietzsche. The early interest in Ibsen, Hauptmann, and Sudermann is perfunctory. An essay on Strindberg is severe: Mencken detests his interest in spiritualism and theology, "the general looseness and absurdity of his more serious thinking," and concludes by calling him a "second-rate artist" (*Smart Set*, 67).

What shocked most at the time was Mencken's low estimate of the American nineteenth-century literature which appeared to him as dominated by Puritanism, the loose term for vapid idealism and prudish philistinism. Emerson is called "the academic theorist *par excellence*. He inhabited a world of mystical abstractions" (*Smart Set*, 184). "Universally greeted, in his own day, as a revolutionary, he was, in point of fact, imitative and cautious, an importer of stale German elixirs" (*PFS*, 191; similarly, *PSS*, 44) and is blamed for his followers in New Thought and Christian Science. Hawthorne, Mencken complained, "concerned himself with psychological problems that were not only inordinately obscure and labored, but even archaic; his enterprise, in his chief work, might almost be called an attempt to psychoanalyze the dead" (*Smart Set*, 184). Poe is seen as "almost the complete antithesis of a great national artist. In the midst of the most sordid civilization ever seen on earth and in the face of a population of utter literalists, he devoted himself grandly to *héliogabalisme*" (185). Poe hardly interested Mencken as a poet and storywriter. He praised his criticism (333–34, and *PSS*, 60–63) only as a case for the pathology of the country and of his own soul. His writings "are full of strange horrors that beset him; there is little in them else" (Nolte, 162). Whitman was closer to the society but he mistook "the show for a great sacrament, a cheap and gaudy circus for a sort of Second Coming of Christ" (*Smart Set*, 185). Mencken persecuted William Dean Howells as he seemed to him the surviving idol of a detested past. "He really has nothing to say, for all the charm he gets into saying it. His psychology is superficial, amateurish, often nonsensical: his irony is scarcely more than polite facetiousness; his characters simply refuse to live" (*PFS*, 54). Mencken shied away from Henry James. He thought of him as "a sort of super-Howells, with a long row of laborious but essentially hollow books behind him" (*Smart Set*, 13). The only early American writer Mencken admired wholeheartedly was Mark Twain. He showered praise on *Huckleberry Finn*, as "one of the great masterpieces of the world, that is the full equal of *Don Quixote* and *Robinson Crusoe*, that is vastly better than *Gil Blas*, *Tristram Shandy*, *Nicholas Nickleby* or *Tom Jones*" (*Smart Set*, 179), or even more extravagantly: Mark Twain is "the full equal of Cervantes and Molière, Swift and Defoe. He was and is the one authentic giant of our national literature" (181). The pendulum had swung the other way—Mark Twain had been for a long time dismissed as a buffoon. Mencken had read the newly published late writings and welcomed the revelation of Twain's despair and cynicism.

Mencken was an embattled polemicist: he enjoyed what he called demolition jobs ridiculing sentimental novels and poetry and haranguing all the academic critics and the new humanists in particular. He sees them as stodgy, moralistic, archaic; Paul Elmer More is dull, has nothing to say, though he is "perhaps, the nearest approach to a genuine scholar we have in America, God save us all!" (*PTS*, 178). Babbitt is "as much a day-dreamer as Jean-Jacques Rousseau. He wants to return to Buddha and the *bhong* tree, to Socrates and the ilex. . . . He is as sentimental as Bernardin de St. Pierre" (Nolte, 169). The humanists gave tit for tat: Babbitt charged him with "complacent cynicism" (*On Being Creative*, 212) and More labeled him a "brawling vulgarian" (*Demon of the Absolute*, 76).

There is a kernel of truth in these statements. But Mencken fulfilled an important function in his time in liberating the American literary scene from the incubus of complacency and conformity, narrow-minded prudery, blinkering patriotism, and stifling conventions about beauty. There was fervor and some courage in his fight against official censorship and unofficial suppression of the unconventional. Mencken himself later acknowledged that the fight had been won, that the American writer was "quite as free as he deserves to be" (*PFthS*, 289). Also Mencken's advocacy of the new realism and naturalism had its merits, though in retrospect we might feel that he overrated much that was ephemeral and that he remained insensitive to the genuinely great achievements of modernism. His harsh view of the earlier American literary tradition will seem today unjustified, though it served as an antidote to lingering illusions of many in the older generations. But Mencken stuck to his guns.

He disapproved of the rediscovery of American literature. "Historically, there is nothing but folly and ignorance in all the current prattle about a restoration of the ancient American tradition" (19). Only isolated individuals—Emerson, Hawthorne, Poe, and Whitman—deserve attention. Acknowledging all these merits and the gusto, pungent wit, and amusing self-display of much of Mencken's writings, we must still conclude that he cannot survive as a literary critic. He belongs strictly to the past though even today he has kept a large group of admirers, collectors, editors, and most important, devoted readers. Mencken has kept them as he managed to display a picturesque personality with a pungent, energetic style, indulging in amusing comparisons and wisecracks. We have Mencken in a nutshell when he says: "A horse-laugh is worth ten thousand syllogisms. It is not only more effective; it is also vastly more intelligent" (140). It flattered and flatters an audience to feel superior to the "swinish multitude," the "herd," the "booboisie," the professors, politicians, clergymen, and sundry that Mencken professed to despise without the need of theorizing or even too much strenuous thinking.

VAN WYCK BROOKS (1886–1963)

Van Wyck Brooks in his early years belonged, like Mencken, to the harsh critics of American culture and literature. In a mannered dialogue, *The Wine of the Puritans* (1908), he made the Puritans responsible for transcendentalism, idealism, and commercialism. The metaphor of the title is explained: "You put old wine into new bottles . . . the aroma, or the ideal, turns into transcendentalism, and the wine, the real, becomes commercialism" (60). Some years later in *America's Coming of Age* (written 1914, published 1916) Brooks much more straightforwardly and hence much more effectively formulated the same indictment. He did not invent the contrast of "lowbrow" and "highbrow" (the *OED* gives examples from 1911 and 1914) but he made it popular with the first chapter so entitled. It repeats the view that "the Puritan theocracy is the all-influential fact in the history of the American mind" (8) and is the origin of two equally unsocial trends: transcendentalism, which "resulted in the final unreality of most contemporary American culture," and catchpenny opportunism "in the atmosphere of contemporary business life" (9–10). Jonathan Edwards, the highbrow, Benjamin Franklin, the lowbrow, are the two grand progenitors of the American character, creating the duality of desiccated culture and stark utilitarianism (14). The American poets reflect this deadlock. They were 'inadequate, faded, and out of touch." The classical period of American literature was paralyzed by the want of a social background (46). Brooks judges the great figures severely: "Longfellow is to poetry what the barrel-organ is to music" (50). Poe took the romantic bric-a-brac seriously. His world is a "silent world, cold, blasted, moon-struck, sterile, a devil's heath" (59). Hawthorne "models mist as the Greeks modelled in marble." "His gift is meager and a little anaemic" (66). "He was a phantom in a phantom world" (70). Brooks harps on the two extremes. Transcendentalism had "no sense of the relationship that exists between theory and practice, between the abstract and the concrete (71). It made art "an organ of religion" (93). Emerson had an "attenuated voice coming from a great distance, which so often strikes one as a continuous falsetto" (75). Lowell was a "genial ambassador without ideas, without program." The assumption is always the same: American writers lacked integration into a congenial society. They suffered from "unattached idealism," while "the more deeply and urgently and organically you feel the pressure of society the more deeply and consciously and fruitfully you feel and you become yourself" (2). The one exception is Walt Whitman. "He for the first time, gave us a sense of something organic in American life" (112). He "precipitated the American character" (118), gave it "a certain focal center in the consciousness" (119), laid "the cornerstone of a national ideal" (121). Brooks recognizes, however, that Whitman in "accepting everything" accepted "the confusion of things and the *fait accompli*" (123) complacently, "incapable of discipline" (126). European literature "grows closer and denser, while American literature grows only windier and windier" (173). Still, he concludes with a sudden spurt of optimism: "All Americans are good—this is to me an axiom." "Perhaps the dry old Yankee stalk will stir and send forth shoots and burst into a storm of blossoms. And after all humanity is older than Puritanism" (182–83). The conclusion seems incongruous (as is the title, suggested by the publisher; Brooks had called it "A Fable for Yankees") but actually expresses Brooks's main life-long inspiration: "the noble religion of nationalism" (*Sketches*, 185), the hope that a great national literature would be "a stimulus and aid in the evolution of man" (136) and that critics should be "national awakeners" (*Three Essays*, 168). The harmony of society and literature is the ideal: older American literature is criticized for lacking it. The society crippled and thinned out the talents of the writers.

This thesis is the inspiration of Brooks's best-known and best books: *The Ordeal of Mark Twain* (1920) and *The Pilgrimage of Henry James* (1925), both psychological biographies which develop the main theme of the early Brooks: the victimization of the artist by society. Much earlier he had written sensitive though rather thin studies of Sénancour, Maurice de Guérin, and Amiel, entitled *The Malady of the Ideal* (1913), and of *John Addington Symonds* (1914), European writers alienated from their societies, but in the two books on Americans the plight of the artist is ascribed to the particular evils of America. Twain is seen as stunted by the materialism of the Gilded Age but also seduced and corrupted by it and by the pressures of his mother and his wife, who made him conform, outwardly at least, to the upperclass proprieties, inducing a deep repressed despair and cynicism. It had become public with the posthumous *Mysterious Stranger* (1916), *What is Man? and Other Essays* (1917), and *The Letters,* collected by Albert B. Paine (1917). Brooks attempts to account for Twain's "chagrin, that fear of solitude, that tortured conscience, those fantastic self-accusations, that indubitable self-contempt" (26), a "miscarriage in his creative life, a balked personality, an arrested development" (27), with some rather amateurish psychoanalytical theories. He makes much of Twain's sleep-walking on the night of his father's funeral and draws the conclusion that somnambulism indicates a split personality. Twain's preoccupation with twins and doubleness corroborates this diagnosis. Brooks at that time did not know Freud but had read a work by an English psychiatrist, Bernard Hart's *Psychology of Insanity* (1912). But Brooks's dim view of the West of that time and of Hannibal, Missouri, "a desert of human sand!—the barrenest spot in all Christendom surely, for the seed of genius to fall in" (46), caused much resentment: Bernard De Voto's *Mark Twain's America* (1932) chided Brooks for his failure to appreciate the West and Western humor. But worse, in my view, is Brooks's incidental literary criticism which both grossly exaggerates the thwarted potentialities of Twain (an abortive Swift) and underrates his successes, particularly *Huckleberry Finn,* which even much later Brooks considered "a book of boys, for boys, by a boy" (*From a Writer's Notebook,* 102).

The *Pilgrimage of Henry James* (1925) is much more attractive, though it propounds the doubtful thesis that James by moving to England uprooted himself and damaged his art. Brooks belongs to those critics who, like F. R. Leavis, have no appreciation of the late novels: *The Ambassadors, The Golden Bowl,* and *The Wings of the Dove.* In them, says Brooks, "persons had all but ceased to exist for him and 'predicaments' had taken their place" (124). James had lost "a living sense of objective reality" (125), had become "a mind working in the void" (134). But Brooks shirks also an engagement with the novels of the middle period by a lame apology (89) and thus refutes (as he cannot deny their greatness) his own thesis that in leaving America James had cut himself off from the "source of the headsprings of experience" (64). He seems substantially correct in seeing that "in Paris James retained the stamp of his own ancestral Puritan world" (60), that he failed in his siege of London, and that "in spite of his disillusionment, Henry James cherished his original idea of England to the end" (79). His adaptation to the English world showed a loss of "his instinctive judgment of men and things" (105). Brooks sees a "gradual decomposition, more and more marked the more his talent grew, of his sense of human values" (105). The late style shows "the evasiveness, the hesitancy, the scrupulosity of an habitually embarrassed man." Behind his novels, "those formidable projections of a geometrical intellect," he discerns "the confused reveries of an invalid child" (131). The case seems grossly overstated and the reduction to a single cause, expatriation, is surely unprovable and even mistaken. But Brooks in presenting his case by weaving together quotations from James's recollections, letters, and writings evokes the meditative mind of James and the "complex fate" of being an American in Europe with such charm that the unsound thesis is blunted and even nullified. The method of telling in the words of James himself obscures, however, James's irony and complex moral vision.

About the time of publication of *The Pilgrimage of Henry James* Brooks went back to Emerson and became converted to a different view of the American past. He said in a letter: "Everything I have done so far has been a kind of exploration of the *dark* side of our moon, and this blessed Emerson has led me right out into the midst of the sunny side" (Spiller, *Brooks-Mumford Letters,* 33). Much later he said that he "felt consumed with a sense of failure, a feeling that my work had gone wrong and that I was mistaken in all I had said or thought" (*Autobiography,* 739). He started to write a life of Emerson but was unable to finish it: he suffered a severe mental breakdown and struggled for years with depression, emerging in 1932 with the finished *Life of Emerson,* a mosaic of quotations, bland, oddly impersonal, hagiographic in tone. The biographical fact of this "Season in Hell" needs to be told to refute the view that Brooks had a conversion experience after his breakdown. The change preceded the illness. *Emerson and Others* (1927) contains large parts of the later book. Still, the change is undeniable whatever its date. The harsh critic of the American past turned to a *laudator temporis acti.* Not that there was no continuity between these two stages of Brooks's development. Even early he was a romantic nationalist. "The great writer is the voice of the people" (*Pilgrimage,* 51) was his creed and even in his critical days, he wished that the writer's voice would ring out loud and clear and hopeful. His disappointment with the past was a lover's disappointment. America had failed, but later he discovered that when he looked at it more closely he had failed to see it in all its glory.

Brooks devoted most of his later years to a grand history of American literature, *Makers and Finders,* in five volumes, which came out not in the chronological order of events but began with what was the apex of American literature: *The Flowering of New England, 1815–1865* (1936). It was an unprecedented success. It won the Pulitzer prize and sold 12,000 copies in four months. It remains the best volume in the series. *New England: Indian Summer 1865–1915* (1940) followed. *The World of Washington Irving* (1941) went back in time, *The Times of Melville and Whitman* (1947) told about the literature outside of New England, and *The Confident Years, 1885–1915* (1952) brought the story almost up to date. These books have been hailed as "not only the best history of American literature, but as one of the best literary histories in any language" (Carl Van Doren in Hoopes, 198). They do represent an immense amount of reading (Brooks speaks of 4,000 volumes) and especially in the two early books display a gift of evoking atmosphere, costumes, and faces, of drawing miniatures, retelling anecdotes, and describing the life of the writer in America—his personal relationships, his local attachments, his feelings and ideas about many issues—which has attracted many readers. But as literary history the books are a dismal failure. There is scarcely any analysis of actual books, nothing about a continuity of literary themes or forms. Nor is there anything coherent and critical about the world-view of the writers and their relationship to the past or to Europe. The composition is based on purely external divisions and criteria. There is, for instance, a chapter which jumbles together Rowland E. Robinson, who wrote *Uncle Lisha's Shop,* John Dewey, Eugene O'Neill, and Edna St. Vincent Millay, and culminates in a long discussion of Mary E. Wilkins, all for no other reason except that these writers came from New England outside Boston. Only the trite metaphors about "spring time, summer and Indian summer" or a "second March," represented by Edwin Arlington Robinson, Robert Frost, Amy Lowell, John Dewey, and Gamaliel Bradford organize these books. "Withering and rotting," "bursting into bloom," "simulating death," "suspended animation" are a few catchwords on which a continuity is built. Otherwise it is all a picturesque mosaic of names, towns and places, and scattered bits of ideas. The comparisons—Massachusetts a smaller England, Boston another Edinburgh, Cambridge a second Heidelberg, Harvard "a provincial Oxford," Webster resembling Edmund Burke, Edward Everett another Abelard, and Oliver Wendell Holmes an American Pope (*Flowering,* 2, 7,

166, 41, 94, 100, 355)—illuminate nothing. Still, there is merit in Brooks's attempt to place American writers in their localities and to trace their personal relationships in order to prove that there was a genuine literary life in America, even though at times Brooks had to force his evidence and exaggerate the importance of casual encounters. There is truth in Brooks's general view of the urbanization of America. He always looks back to the utopia of a "homogeneous people, living close to the soil, intensely religious, unconscious, unexpressed in art and letters, with a strong sense of home and fatherland," now lamentably uprooted and dispersed (Wasserstrom, *Legacy,* 233). There is, finally, merit in the attention to many forgotten minor writers, though it meant a leveling of distinctions, a flattening out of the landscape, a mistaken egalitarianism, an abdication of criticism.

Alongside these all-inclusive, all-tolerating, nostalgic chronicles Brooks, however, never ceased writing critically in the sense of pronouncing judgments on writers and books of his own time. Only the past was treated with indulgence and even adulation. *The Opinions of Oliver Allston* (1941) thus surprised by its harsh condemnation of much modern literature, of Eliot, Joyce, Pound, the Southern Critics, and many others. The device of reproducing the opinions of a fictitious dead friend was aimed at achieving a double focus, some distance, allowing indulgence in idiosyncrasies under the mask. But the mask is too transparent: the distinction between the two authors is not kept up. It is simply Brooks's notebook which gives him the privilege of not arguing his views but merely stating his own or Allston's opinions, Brooks refers to Allston's "dislike of theorizing." Critics should "abhor theories." "I have no theories and wish to have none" (108). But this is grossly overstated. Actually Brooks adopted a very simple norm of judgment. He wants literature to "contribute to life," to "follow the biological grain," "enhance" and "enrich life," "favor the 'life-drive' " (115), be a "stimulus to life" (133). In such Darwinian or Nietzschean formulas Brooks justifies his distinction between "primary" literature, positive, optimistic, believing in progress and the goodness of man (154–55), written by people who stand for "health, will and courage" and dealing with great themes, "courage, justice, mercy, honor, love" (145). The list of primary writers Brooks offers includes simply all the main classics of literature, optimists or not, Goethe and Dickens, Tolstoy and Dostoevsky (hardly believers in progress), and among the living Thomas Mann, Robert Frost, Carl Sandburg, and Lewis Mumford. The secondary, or "coterie literature," a list of his dislikes, is also long: the French symbolists, Eliot, Pound, Gertrude Stein, Joyce, and the New Critics. The objections to the Southern Critics are based on the patently false view that they wanted to be scientists and that they "evaded the whole world of values" (165). With the years Brooks's attack on "coterie literature" became even more strident and often quite irrational in the expression of his hatred, particularly for T. S. Eliot (see Hoopes, 234) and Joyce, "the sick Irish jesuit." *The Confident Years,* the last volume of his literary history, reasserts his wholesale condemnation of modernism and deplores what he considers the fatal shift from the optimism of William James to acceptance of the pessimism of Henry Adams at the time of the First World War. "Then the great myth of Moby Dick rose in the American imagination and Melville's overpowering sense of the omnipotence of evil blacked out the sunniness and whiteness of Emerson and Whitman" (347).

Brooks, in his later years, wrote many other books, biographies such as *Howells: His Life and World* (1959), the charming *Dream of Arcadia: American Writers and Artists in Italy, 1760–1915* (1958), an elaborate autobiography in three installments (also published in a collective volume in 1961): *Scenes and Portraits: Memories of Childhood and Youth* (1954), *Days of the Phoenix: The Nineteen-Twenties I Remember* (1957), and *From the Shadow of the Mountain: My Post-Meridian Years* (1961), nostalgic in tone, apologetic in intent, urbane and kind, and several collections of notebook opinions, undisguised as such, like *The Writer in America* (1953) and *From a Writer's Notebook* (1958). They contain many sensible and often trite reflections and judgments and continue the attack on new developments. Brooks always wants curative writers who "remind us of the goodness of man, bring back the joy of life and give one a sense of human hope" (*The Writer,* 188). He thus can see a conflict between Faulkner's Stockholm speech on receiving the Nobel Prize and his gloomy novels, can praise Pearl Buck, Trollope, and other solid writers but also vent his anger against the detractors of America and the prophets of doom here and in Europe. In short, Brooks has become a moralist, a preacher, and a glorifier of the usable past of American literature, proclaiming a nationalism made virulent during the Second World War. It had always been his creed.

In his later stages he cannot be taken seriously as a literary critic or historian. The onslaught of modernism is too indiscriminate to carry conviction. The opinion that he is "the American Hippolyte Taine, and Sainte-Beuve and Georg Brandes rolled into one" (Charles Angoff in Wasserstrom, *The Critic,* 201) seems to me grotesque, but he remains a representative figure both for his early diagnosis and illustration of the fate of the writer in America and for the turn to the rediscovery of a glorious American literary tradition.

2: THE NEW HUMANISTS

IRVING BABBITT (1865–1933) AND
PAUL ELMER MORE (1864–1937)

THE humanist or neohumanist movement was an episode in the American debate about culture and literature which, one has the impression, is being forgotten today. Certainly, the issues then debated, though as unresolved as ever, are now discussed in other terms, rarely with reference to the slogans of the humanists: one does not encounter the phrase "inner check" or the contrast between "humanism and humanitarianism," and even "classicism versus romanticism" is not an issue except in historical contexts. The public commotion in 1930, when Irving Babbitt appeared at a large staged debate with Henry Seidel Canby and Carl Van Doren in New York's Carnegie Hall on May 9 and when two collective volumes—one humanist, the other antihumanist—were published, was, after all, ephemeral in its effects. The polemics in the press were from today's perspective on a low level: they were often acrimonious and, as is usual in such cases, often reflected misunderstandings or misinterpretations of the opponents' tenets. There seems to be little point in rehearsing these debates. It would give them a false importance and distort the historical perspective. Anyhow, the movement collapsed under the impact of the Depression and the rise of Marxist criticism. Its social conservatism and its enmity toward recent literary trends ensured its demise.

The year 1930 is not the year that matters for a proper understanding and interpretation of the thought of the two protagonists, Irving Babbitt and Paul Elmer More. Both belong to a much earlier time: to the 1890s, when they formed their basic convictions. Their main writings appeared in the first decade of the century: the first seven volumes of *Shelburne Essays* between 1904 and 1910, *Literature and the American College* in 1908, *The New Laokoon* in 1910, *Masters of Modern French Criticism* in 1912. More and Babbitt must be discussed in terms of the period in which they

17

achieved maturity. It does not help their cause if we focus on the late
years and thus on their reaction to their younger contemporaries after
the First World War. Inevitably, we shall come to the conclusion that
Babbitt indulged in an imperceptive wholesale condemnation of the
whole modern world and modern literature and that More—while willing
to discuss Proust, Joyce, Eliot, and the American naturalists—did so with
little sympathy and understanding.

We might feel today that More's low opinion of many of the prominent
figures of the 1920s, pungently phrased in the essay "Modern Currents
in American Literature" (*NSE*, vol. 1), was, after all, not so far from the
truth, or what we believe today is our more considered estimate. More's
judgments are harshly phrased: Dos Passos's *Manhattan Transfer* is "an
explosion in a cesspool" (63), Edgar Lee Masters's *Spoon River Anthology*
is "only a malodorous flash in the pan" (69), Sinclair Lewis's *Main Street*
"a monotonous tale written in a drab and drizzling style" (69). The author himself obviously "had not risen more than an inch above the aesthetic and ethical level of the people he insults" (70). Dreiser, More
recognizes, is the "most powerful" writer in the group; Clyde Griffiths,
the protagonist of *An American Tragedy*, is "portrayed with a masterly
understanding of the devious ways of a weak untutored nature" (68).
Still, the book is a *"monstrum informe cui lumen ademptum"* (69). The "aesthete" James Branch Cabell hardly fares better. Cabell's method is "a
compound of Maurice Hewlett and Anatole France" (59), and H. L.
Mencken is dubbed a "brawling vulgarian" (76). However, I remain unconvinced that these opinions were arrived at on the right grounds, that
they were judgments of aesthetic sensibility and moral scrupulosity and
not merely deductions from a generalized rejection of naturalistic determinism and a repugnance toward anything ugly and low. The article on
"The Cleft Eliot"[2] confirms this view; the dichotomy between the obscure
poet, the "lyric prophet of chaos," and the solid critic causes only "per-
plexity over some unreconciled paradox." Similarly the essay on Joyce
(*NSE*, vol. 3) simply asserts the "dilemma" of explaining how the sound
view of life expressed in "The Dead" could have changed into the "moral
slough" of *Ulysses*, its "weary and ugly art," its "philosophy of the inane,"
the change in Joyce being in the opposite direction from Eliot's, of
course. The essay on Proust (in *On Being Human*, vol. 3) comes at least
to grips with his general outlook. *A la recherche du temps perdu* seems to
More "one of the gloomiest books ever written" (63) in which Proust
wreaks "his contempt of the world" (43). More quotes Léon-Pierre Quint
to the effect that it leaves "humanity without aim, without joy, without
peace, without outlook of any sort" (56). It affords no relief "in the

promise of a future existence nor in the Progress of Humanity'" (57–58). Predictably More is shocked by "the double theme of hysterical sadism and hysterical masochism" and bored by the story of Albertine, "one of the most maudlin exhibitions of futility ever made in literature" (63). More tries, at least, to describe the "theory of art as an attempt to stay the relativism of Time in the static present of Memory" (65), which for Proust becomes "a factor of despair as memory cannot recreate what is gone." Proust's belief in a supernatural joy derived from art seems to More nonsense: "Art, pure art, art completely severed from actuality, just does not exist" (56). More values only the first half of *Swann's Way*: "Overture" and "Combray" as "the subtlest and finest and most interesting portion of the whole novel. It is highly original, often quaint and exquisite" (47). More uses the occasion to argue against Edmund Wilson's exposition of the symbolist revolt against naturalism in *Axel's Castle*. To More symbolism is only a variant of the broad movement of naturalism. At the end Wilson is reprimanded for "flying distractedly from admiration of Proust to admiration of Marx" (68). The time was 1933. More had in his last years some personal contacts with Eliot and briefly with Edmund Wilson (who described his visit vividly in *The Triple Thinkers*); he had some sense of the mental climate and the literary events of the twenties and early thirties.

One has the impression that Babbitt at Harvard was much more insulated from the new winds of doctrine. Possibly as a deliberate policy, in his published writings at least, Babbitt never tangled with recent or even "modern" literature, if one excepts some slighting allusions to the "advanced stage of psychic disintegration" marked by Joyce's *Ulysses* (*BC*, 132). Even the most prominent names of French twentieth-century literature are missing in the indices of Babbitt's works. When he discusses contemporaries, he singles out only ideologues: Pierre Lasserre, Julien Benda, the Baron Seillière of the French antiromantic polemics, and the Abbé Bremond and Jacques Maritain, more casually, as representatives of Catholic opinion. Babbitt was apparently resolved to remain a historian or at least to draw mainly on historical evidence for his diagnosis of the ills of civilization, while More, possibly because of his long experience as a literary journalist in New York, was paradoxically far less "academic," much more aware of the world around him in spite of his later immersion in the history of the Platonic tradition and his semiretirement to the academic groves of Princeton.

Babbitt's studied silence on concrete works and figures of recent literature and More's somewhat baffled and condescending articles of his last years explain such extravagant judgments as Oscar Cargill's, who speaks of their "almost complete unfamiliarity with the major ideas of their time"[3] and must justify Santayana's phrase, "The Genteel Tradition at Bay" (1931), though one could rather speak of a humanist offensive at that time.

We should then ignore the attempt around 1930 to bring humanism to the general public, to make it a movement and even a kind of religion. Instead, we should try to make the mental experiment of imagining that both Babbitt and More had ceased writing in 1920. By then all their positions had been arrived at long ago. After that date More changed in the direction of a more specific religious commitment, while Babbitt held his creed substantially unchanged all his adult life, even though its formulation and documentation were to stretch over several decades. *Rousseau and Romanticism* (1919) and *Democracy and Leadership* (1924) are implicit in Babbitt's first book, *Literature and the American College* (1908), and that book is in part made up of much older articles; the oldest, "The Rational Study of the Classics," dates back to 1897. More and Babbitt had reached the age of forty in 1904 and 1905 respectively, and by that time most people's minds are made up, solidified and set in a mold. This is certainly true of them: we hear that Babbitt knew his mind perfectly when he met More in Professor Charles Lanman's Sanscrit seminar at Harvard in 1892, and what More often later felt to be his own youthful gropings seemed so only in the perspective of the religious certainty of his last years. Actually, the intellectual position of the two friends was defined very early, and the positions differ as the two differ not only in temperament but in their relation to the intellectual past. The friction between the two came out in the open only late: More found the strongest terms of dissent from Babbitt when he criticized in letters Babbitt's last book, *On Being Creative* (1932), and was upset about his treatment of Wordsworth, so "frightfully one-sided and warped and vindictive" (Dakin, *More*, 317). It is best to discuss the two men separately, as their writings raise different questions and give different answers. They will be remembered as intellectual personalities and not as leaders of an abortive movement (More did not even contribute to the volume *Humanism in America* but merely allowed a section of "The Demon of the Absolute" to be reprinted).

"Brunetière speaks English," said J. E. Spingarn in epitomizing Babbitt's *Masters of Modern French Criticism* (*Journal of Philosophy* 10 [1913]: 693), and from the perspective of a historian of criticism it might be simplest to describe Babbitt as a classicist of the French type. Babbitt wrote two essays on Brunetière which he used in the book; he translated an essay for the *Atlantic Monthly* in 1897 when Brunetière visited Harvard. He shares in general Brunetière's view of the French tradition, his detestation of naturalism, and he wholeheartedly agrees with his attack on critical impressionism. Babbitt was a teacher of French literature at Harvard and was familiar with the classics of the seventeenth century. He admired Racine for "reason, exquisite measure, supreme clearness, delicate sensibility tempered by judgment," quoting Lemaître, the arch-impressionist (*SC*, 95). He defended Boileau vigorously against Saints-bury's denigration and, later in particular, Pascal became the exemplary figure for the conflict of religion and science and the view of the three levels of man: animal, human, and divine. Babbitt saw the immediate ancestry of Brunetière in Désiré Nisard, who was the first to diagnose French decadence and to exalt the seventeenth century in France as the embodiment of the classical spirit and the permanent human mind, in contrast to the eighteenth century. Babbitt, of course, discussed the evolution of Sainte-Beuve's criticism as a happy emancipation from the shackles of romanticism and a discovery or rediscovery of the truth of the classical tradition. The rise of this French nineteenth-century classicism is the central theme of *The Masters of Modern French Criticism*, Babbitt's best organized and most equitable book. *The New Laokoon* assumes the classical doctrine of pure genre, *le genre tranché*, as a starting point for its onslaught on the confusion of the modern arts and their subdivisions. *Rousseau and Romanticism* is intimately related to the French polemics of the early twentieth century about Rousseau—to Lasserre's attack in *Le Romantisme français*, 1907, which Babbitt himself calls "very drastic" (*RR*, 409)—and to the many writings of Seillière and Maurras. Babbitt's relationship is very close, but still it seems a mistake to call Babbitt simply an American Brunetière.

Babbitt could not sympathize with the other side of Brunetière: his evolutionary theory, his attempt to draw an analogy between literary history and biological change (see *NL*, 215). He did not agree with his return to the Roman Catholic Church (*SC*, 145–46, and *MFC*, 330, 334), his "naturalistic pessimism" and "stoic bleakness" (*MFC*, 333, 335).

In spite of all agreement with the antiromantic polemics of the French group around the *Action française*, Babbitt finally shied away from their authoritarian implications and the political consequences of their arguments. Though there was a moment in 1924 when Babbitt preferred a hypothetical "American equivalent of a Mussolini" to the "American equivalent of a Lenin" (*DL*, 312), he disapproved of the Fascist or proto-Fascist forms the antiromanticism had taken in France. He tells us in 1909 that "a year or so ago I chanced to be strolling along one of the narrow streets that skirt the Quartier Saint-Germain, and came on a bookshop entirely devoted to reactionary literature; and there in the window, along with books recommending the restoration of the monarchy, was the volume of M. Lasserre, and other antiromantic publications" (*SC*, 90; exactly the same in *NL*, xii–xiii). Marcus Selden Goldman recalls that, early in 1923 in Paris, he was surprised to find "how deep-rooted was [Babbitt's] objection to the combination of political, religious, and literary aims in a single program like that of *L'Action française*."⁴ Babbitt, one must conclude, remained an American republican and a Protestant, however high may have been his regard for the role of the Roman Catholic Church in history, and however far he was from subscribing to any definite Protestant or even Christian creed.

It will not do to reduce Babbitt to an echo of the French classical tradition. He always looks at it from the outside, welcoming it only as an ally. Something more can, however, be said in favor of seeing Babbitt as a part of the classical revival in English criticism, as a follower of Matthew Arnold. Arnold's early professed classicism, particularly in the 1853 preface to the *Poems*, with its appeal to Aristotle, and Arnold's criticism of the English romantic poets must have shaped Babbitt's outlook significantly. The admiration for Sainte-Beuve and Edmond Scherer, though differently motivated, is shared by both. Babbitt's strong interest in Joubert comes from Arnold and his model, Sainte-Beuve. Babbitt's concept of Goethe, which stresses the sage presented by Eckermann, has much in common with Arnold's view. Arnold's idea of culture, *paideia*, whatever its antecedents, and Arnold's ideal of the total man, with his "imaginative reason," were in Babbitt's mind when he formulated his pedagogical aims. The review Babbitt wrote of Stuart Sherman's book on Arnold (1917 in *SC*) agrees with Arnold's recommendation of the "saving remnant," his qualitative democracy, but ignores the main issues of literary criticism and makes reservations against Arnold's "hope for poetry" as an eventual substitute for religion. He objects that Arnold does not rise "far enough above the naturalistic level, which in his case means the stoical level" (*SC*, 56).

Contrary to the accepted opinion, Babbitt was no admirer of the neoclassical tradition. In *The New Laokoon* the exposition of neoclassical criticism as mere formalism, as a denial of imagination, of the "unconscious and unpremeditated" (*NL*, 52), is as harshly critical as the propounders of the worst romantic clichés could wish. Neoclassicism in France is defined as a "mixture of Aristotle and the dancing master" (66). It "turned the illusion of poetry into a sort of elegant falsehood" (63). Babbitt does, no doubt, condemn romanticism. *Rousseau and Romanticism* is a learned, heavily documented, but also often brisk and even witty attack on some features of romanticism: primitivism and the exaltation of the untutored genius, the yearning for Arcadia or Elysium, and particularly romantic morality conceived as "a denial of a struggle between good and evil in the breast of the individual" (*RR*, 130). Babbitt detests also the sentimental worship of childhood and animals, the glorification of melancholy, and the frenzied nationalism emerging at that time. He likes to choose outrageous examples: Hugo's poem "Sultan Mourad" telling of a monster of cruelty saved by his one-time concern for a pig (*RR*, 143); Hugo's "Ibo" telling of the poet "threatening to outbellow the thunder and to pull comets around by the tail" (*RR*, 392); Wordsworth addressing the child as "Mighty prophet, seer blest" which to Babbitt seems "portentous nonsense" (*NL*, 93) and an "abyss of absurdity" (*RR*, 52), Wordsworth speaking of "One impulse from a vernal wood / May teach us more of man / Of moral evil and of good / Than all the sages can" is condemned as "the most complete denial of culture in Arnold's sense to be found in literature" (*BC*, 60). The Ancient Mariner's redemption by admiring the color of water-snakes is ridiculed as an easy way to salvation: "He obtains subrationally and unconsciously ('I blessed them *unaware*') the equivalent to Christian charity" (*BC*, 120). Browning's poem "Summum Bonum" which ends "Brightest truth, / Purest truth in the universe—all were for me / In the kiss of one girl" elicits the comment: "The supreme good would appear identical with the supreme thrill" (*RR*, 127). Many more of this order, such as Emerson's "The Humble Bee," "yellowbreeched philosopher" "wiser far than human seer" (*BC*, 76), are singled out. Babbitt, often ignoring the occasion and the context, asks always whether this or that saying is true or right if applied today. He cannot tolerate nonsense, whimsy, fancy, hyperbole, and paradox. He allows man only a temporary indulgence in revery "at most as an occasional solace from the serious business of living" (*RR*, 91). This literal-mindedness and censorious tone have earned Babbitt violent condemnations for didacticism, obtuseness, and lack of aesthetic sense but, I think, much should be excused by Babbitt's passionate concern for ideas living, misleading, and corrupting today and by the classroom situation to which these books were originally addressed. He wanted to shock and cure, to make students and readers see the practical consequences of preposterous statements and subvert the easy-going historicism of the time.

These fulminations against romanticism in some way, however, are deceptive. Babbitt actually holds, one could argue, a romantic view of art, of poetry and imagination. He quotes *The Tempest*, "We are such stuff as dreams are made on" (*RR*, xv), and sees man as living in an element of fiction or illusion. "Illusion is the central problem of art" (*RR*, 103);

"art gives the illusion of a higher reality which can be grasped only through a veil of imaginative illusion" (27, also 102). "The illusion of true art" is called "a waking dream" (*NL*, 51) and imagination is praised for "throwing a veil of divine illusion over some essential truth" (*NL*, 100). Babbitt is completely under the spell of romantic formulas when he says that "the imagination must be free and spontaneous. The vital fusion of illusion and insight with the sense of infinitude is found in the true symbol" (*RR*, 101). In agreement with symbolist theory Babbitt can say that "imagination may transform words, and infuse them with a new and active potency" (116). He even approves of "suggestive power" (129), though he thinks that we live in an age "that has gone mad on the powers of suggestion" (178).

The New Laokoon, while in the main a polemic against the confusion among the arts, retreats on essential points. Though Babbitt never questions the desirability of pure genres, he sees, for example, that "music need not be absolute" (*RR*, 171) and admits that there are some virtues in program music. His insistence on classical principles of unity and proportion breaks down when he prefers Ariosto to Tasso, saying that "Ariosto is much nearer to the ancients," judged by the psychological test, "the only test that has value in such matters" (*NL*, 192). He even recognizes that there is a "normal romanticism: a propensity for fiction, for wonder, adventure, surprise" (203). Babbitt's constant stress on measure—proportion—makes him condemn eccentricity, excess, extremes in all forms. He always falls back on the Nichomachean Ethics which could teach us to be "moderate, and sensible and decent" (381). But under this commonsense surface runs a continuum of a deep melancholy, of skepticism and agnosticism or what he calls "positivism," a strong sense of man's ignorance in a mysterious universe which makes Babbitt distrust the cocksureness of a scientist such as Haeckel, who claimed to have solved the riddles of the universe (211), or of the new realists, "flat on their face before science" (*RR*, 371). Babbitt distrusts technical philosophy—epistemology and rational metaphysics. He seems basically an empiricist, though he admits that "humanism cannot get along without religion" (380). But the specific nature of the religion remains obscure. At times it seems to mean little more than a feeling of humility for man's nothingness and helplessness, a sense of his dependence on a higher power (302). At other times Babbitt requires a glimpse of a higher reality of which it remains unclear whether it is an illusion or an insight into an existing realm. Paul Elmer More, who was a firm believer in a clearly articulated Christian creed, brought out this uncertainty very sharply in conversations and letters (Dakin, *More,* 317–18, 341). It affected Babbitt's view of poetry. In criticizing Arnold he missed what he found in Tennyson, "a suggestion, at least, of the pure supernatural light" (*SC*, 56).

This "pure supernatural light"—unimpeded by anything "medieval and narrowly theological" to which Babbitt objected in Pascal (*SC*, 88)— was offered to Babbitt most nearly in the tradition of American transcendentalism. Transcendentalism was all around Babbitt in his youth. But, obviously, Babbitt cannot be described simply as a descendant of the American transcendentalists, and he can only whimsically be described as a New England saint, as he has been by Austin Warren. One could even argue that intellectually he represents an extreme revulsion against transcendentalism. The obvious conflict between Babbitt and his father might support this view. Austin Warren called Edwin D. Babbitt "a physician with a mind open at both ends, a kind of naive and belated Transcendentalist" (*New England Saints*, 144) and surmised that his son considered him a charlatan. Harry Levin described his practice "in the light of hypnotism, spiritualism, phrenology, clairvoyance, massages, sun-baths, electrical treatments, inhabited planets, and utopian socialism." Levin quotes the titles of his pamphlets—*Babbitt's Health Guide, Vital Magnetism, The Fountain of Life*, and *Marriage, with Sexual and Social Up-Building* (in *Irving Babbitt and the Teaching of Literature*, 13). One is tempted to think that Irving Babbitt rejected everything his father stood for, and even without benefit of Freud one could see Babbitt's early development not only as a "temperamental and intellectual hiatus between father and son" (Warren, 145) but as a verbal slaying of the father. But this appearance is deceptive. Austin Warren recognizes that Babbitt did not totally turn away from his father's views but "retained always a qualified respect for Emerson" (145). The relationship to Emerson is not merely respectful. It is certainly a continuity, even a conscious discipleship, as the conclusion to *Masters of Modern French Criticism* shows, in which Emerson is played up as the great counterweight to Sainte-Beuve, the absolutist against the "doctor of relativity." The ideal critic is envisaged as the synthesis of Sainte-Beuve and Emerson.

No doubt Babbitt disapproved of what he must have considered the degeneracy of transcendentalism in the facile optimism of Christian Science, the quackery of his father, and even the pragmatism of his formidable colleague, William James, who seemed to him a preacher of drift and flux, of passive surrender to motion, a glorifier of drunkenness—alcoholic and spiritual (*RR*, 183–84). Babbitt is also uninterested in the minor transcendentalists: he never discusses Thoreau, though More was deeply interested in Thoreau. But Emerson looms large on Babbitt's horizon: he drew from him not only some of his favorite slogans but much of his basic scheme of the mind and soul of man. The term "inner check" comes from Emerson, who in turn derived it from Colebrooke's *Essay on the Vedas* (see Warren, 162). It had been used before Babbitt emphasized it in *The New Laokoon* (201) by More, but Babbitt, of course, had spoken earlier of "self-discipline" (*SC,* 145), which surely supplements and contrasts with Emerson's "self-reliance." The phrases "law for man" and "law for thing" from Emerson's "Ode: Inscribed to W. H. Channing" (*NL,* 200; *RR,* x; *LC,* v) provide a key quotation in support of dualism. But more than such catchwords, Emerson's general enterprise mattered to Babbitt: a reconciliation of the absolute and the relative, of permanence and change, of the One and the Many. Like Emerson, Babbitt assumes some kind of "model" of the human mind, a stratification in which perception is action and manifestation of the will and the individual is transformed into character and finally confronted with the supernatural. Babbitt upholds what could be called abstractly an "intuitive voluntarism." Insight is man's main tool and aim, insight into human nature, which is for Babbitt embodied in tradition, a tradition very similar to the oversoul. Babbitt, for instance, praises Emerson as having "a new sense of the unity of human nature—a unity founded, not on tradition, but on insight" (*MFC,* 346). He approved of what he considered Emerson's genuinely Socratic interpretation of the idea that "man is the measure of all things." Babbitt thinks that "the oversoul Emerson perceives in his best moments is the true oversoul" (362), a realm, one assumes, of spiritual values and not merely the common soul of all men—an "undersoul" in Babbitt's parody of humanitarian identification. Emerson is called "spiritually perceptive," a "wise man," a "true sage" (375, 361), because "he aids criticism in its search for inner standards" and "helps it to see in the present anarchy the potentialities of a higher order." Emerson has a "sense of unity" (391–92), a sense of the absolute which Babbitt defined as "a purely spiritual perception of the light beyond the reason, entirely disassociated from the faith in creeds and formulas" (*SC,* 144). Babbitt sees this as an agreement with Indian philosophy. His own studies of Indian (mainly Buddhist) philosophy could hardly have been undertaken without the initial inspiration of the Orientalism of the American transcendentalists and Emerson's own lifelong concern with the "Wisdom of the Brahmins."

Here is a central point of agreement, even though it is difficult to determine the precise nature of Babbitt's own "spiritual perception." At times he sounds simply like a Puritan who believes in the voice of conscience, which is, however, not simply an inner light but a superindividual obligation, the voice of tradition. But usually what for Emerson is "moral sense" is in Babbitt conceived of as a negative force, a *"frein vital"* (*NL*, 212) as he punned in contrast to Bergson's *"élan vital."* It is recognition of standards and norms, of a "higher will," where "higher" means overriding individual desire, not the will of a higher being. Babbitt seems impatient with any attempt to anchor these standards or norms: the fruits of religion are assumed to be available through work, an inner discipline whose purpose is inner satisfaction, even personal happiness. But at other times the "inner check" is identified with the voice of God or perceived as giving access to the supernatural, the divine, the numinous. It is Babbitt's peculiar aim to combine what seems an ethical rigorism, even asceticism and renunciation, with a glimpse, a hesitant intuition, of the realm of the divine beyond and above reason.

Babbitt was strongly aware of his disagreements with Emerson. In all contexts he suspected him of Rousseauism, of undue optimism, unwarranted trust in the goodness of man and particularly of the common man. Babbitt calls him one of the "sycophants of human nature" (*MFC*, 361). He suspects his "exaltation of genius" (*RR*, 67) and is entirely out of sympathy with his concept of "compensation": he does not believe that spiritual laws parallel physical laws. Babbitt grew up in the atmosphere of mechanistic nineteenth-century science and simply dismissed as "absurd" the many traces in Emerson of *Naturphilosophie* or the even older idea of hieroglyphics of nature. Emerson's fondness for electricity, magnetism, geology, and so on struck him as merely quaint, for he disapproved of the fundamental romantic enterprise in question: the reconciliation of man and nature, the bridging of the gulf between subject and object. We see this in Babbitt's harsh treatment of Coleridge and Wordsworth, who were, after all, among the most important teachers of Emerson.

Babbitt could not sympathize with Emerson's symbolic view of the world: he had himself nothing of the fervently mystical, whimsical tone of Emerson's mind. He did not share the same intellectual ancestry of the neoplatonists, Greek and English, Swedenborg, and Swedenborgians. Babbitt simply did not understand the symbolic view of the world. He could not have made anything of Emerson's saying, "Every solid in the universe is ready to become fluid on the approach of the mind" (*Complete Works*, 7:43).

Ultimately Babbitt, as Austin Warren has argued persuasively (*New England Saints*, 159), must be described as a Buddhist who, without joining in ritual, shared the agnostic, even atheistic view of Buddha with a sense of the world's illusion. More saw that "there was no room for God, in any proper sense of the word, or for Grace in his philosophy" (letter quoted in Dakin, *More*, 341).

More's mind had a quite different starting point and final resting place. More said himself that in his youth he was "steeped in the rankest romantic literature of Germany" (Dakin, *More*, 313) and the essay on "Thoreau's Journal" (*SE*, 5:106–31) shows More's first-hand acquaintance with Fichte, Schelling, Novalis, Friedrich Schlegel, and particularly with Schleiermacher's *Reden über Religion*. At that time (1908) he had long since reacted against this early romanticism. He criticizes the German romantics largely in terms of a contrast between their *Gemüt* and the New England character or conscience. More in his earnestness seems often to misunderstand the Germans' romantic irony and the polemical context and terminology in which they were writing, but he shows a far more correct and more sympathetic understanding of the romantic tradition, and hence also of Emerson, than Babbitt does. More, speaking in later years of his intellectual development, said extravagantly that he had "changed as often as a chameleon" (Dakin, *More*, 323). The set of the *Shelburne Essays* gives him "the impression of a mind groping about and not knowing whither it is bound. The field is too wide and the effect scattered. I seem not to be one intelligence but an unassimilated bundle of impulses and curiosities" (ibid., 371). This may have seemed so to More from the vantage point of his final position, and is supported by the diversity of the topics handled in the *Shelburne Essays*, but it seems unjust to the coherence of the mind approaching all this variety of literature and thought. This is particularly true of More's view of the American tradition, which was traced perceptively by Daniel Aaron in the introduction to his collection of *Shelburne Essays on American Literature*. More's striking emphasis on what has been called "the power of blackness" in American literature, the "gloom, that habitual dwelling on the supernatural significance of life" as the "dominant intellectual tone of the country" (*SE*, 1:64), the emphasis on the continuity from the earliest New England versifiers through Jonathan Edwards to the transcendentalists—all this shows an understanding of the American tradition which seems to me absent in Babbitt. The work of Emerson's generation is lauded by More as the highest and most homogeneous culture this country has yet produced (*SE*, 11:105) in a sweeping commendation which—somewhat uncritically—extends even to Whittier, Longfellow, and Lowell. More had first been impressed by Emerson's essay on "Fate" in 1894. It "contains, he said, such 'wisdom and morality and power and consolation' that 'all the prophets and seers of the world' could hardly surpass it."[5]

In the formal essay on Emerson, which comes as late as 1921, the judgment is hardly changed. Emerson "is the outstanding figure of American
letters" (*SE,* 11:69). His position is not incorrectly described as "romanticism rooted in Puritan divinity" (83) and his philosophy as a "kind of
vanishing dualism" (87). Years before in the first volume of the *Shelburne
Essays* (1904) More had rightly objected, in the essay "The Influence of
Emerson," to the view that Emerson is self-contradictory and incoherent.
"His essays ripple and recoil on the surface, but underneath there is a
current setting steadily to one point" (*SE,* 1:73).

More goes to great lengths to assert the unity of the American tradition. He sees its roots in the England of the seventeenth century: "Out
of it grew the intellectual life of our nation, and even to-day the poverty
of our art and literature is partly due to the fact that our strongest
colonists brought with them only one faction of the endless feud" (*SE,*
1:203) between truth and beauty, the Reformation and the Renaissance.
The continuity of American literature includes also Poe, who appears as
a kind of brother to Hawthorne. Hawthorne's and Poe's vision of evil,
with its awe and terror, is—somewhat too easily if we think of E. T. A.
Hoffmann, Arnim, or even Tieck and certain parts of Jean Paul—contrasted with the pleasant *Waldeinsamkeit* of the Germans, with the "forgotten weavers of moonlight and mysticism" (52, 57). Puritanism, in the
teaching of Jonathan Edwards, gave "an extravagant sense of individual
existence" (48) to the New England man and thus prepared for the utter
solitude of Hawthorne. He had lost the Christian faith, and "overwhelm-
ing superstition" had changed into "shadowy haunting symbolism" (65).
More quotes Hawthorne: " 'We are but shadows, and all that seems most
real about us is but the thinnest substance of a dream,—till the heart be
touched. That touch creates us,—then we begin to be,—thereby we are
beings of reality and inheritors of eternity' " (34). Here More, through
a quotation, formulates best his own basic experience, the illusion of the
world and the ethical substance in man. This is also the main topic of
the essays on Thoreau. Criticizing Santayana, More states bluntly that
"no great poem was ever composed whose author did not have . . . faith
in the reality of the ideal world" (*Harvard Graduates' Magazine* 9 [1900]:
21), and late in life he speaks of "all worthy art" as "mystical initiation"
(*The Catholic Faith,* 1931, 215).

A close examination of More's many essays on English literature would
confirm this conclusion, though More's interest in English literature was
too diversified to be so clearly confined to this symbolist (in the old sense)
tradition. He wrote much on eighteenth-century wits, on poets such as
Crabbe, and on Victorian novelists such as Gissing. But his deepest con-

cern is, after all, with such figures as George Herbert and Henry
Vaughan, whom he prefers to Thoreau, because "he never cut himself
off from the Church and the State, but moved in the greater currents
of tradition" (*SE*, 5:131), and Sir Thomas Browne, whom he commends
for his "religious imagination . . . the faculty, that is, by which we unite
the broken and dispersed images of the world into an harmonious poetic
symbol" (6:167). The Victorian writers who resume this spiritual tradition find his fervent approval: Tennyson for the vision in "The Holy
Grail," which is "nothing else but a sudden and blinding sense of that
dualism of the world and of the human soul beneath which the solid-
seeming earth reels and dissolves away" (7:90), and the now forgotten
Richard S. Hawker, the vicar of Morwenstow (whom Tennyson visited in
Cornwall) for his poem, another "Holy Grail," which More considers "the
most purely spiritual poem in the language" (6:33). The interest in
Shorthouse's historical romance *John Inglesant* falls into the pattern and
so does the admiration for the very different Carlyle, whose sense of the
world's illusion makes him at once a "Hindu seer" and a "Hebrew
prophet" (1:98, 101). The essay on Newman, which disapproves so
strongly of his conversion as to speak of "failure of duty, a betrayal of
will" (8:77), starts with Newman's illusionism, quoting a very early letter,
from 1828: " 'What a veil and curtain this world of sense is: beautiful
but still a veil' " (8:45).

Even when More rejects an author he has the standard of a spiritual
symbolism in mind. Browning's "theory of love," he says, for instance,
"does not expand like Dante's into a great vision of life wherein symbol
and reality are fused together" (*SE*, 3:160–61), while Arthur Symons's
illusion, although attractive to More as any sense of illusion, seems to
him a false illusion and a false disillusion (1:127). More treats Walter
Pater with unusual harshness, because he sees him as a hedonist ending
in "weariness, and satiety, and impotence" (—:114). He must disapprove
of Pater's interpretation of Plato and consider *Marius the Epicurean* as
"only another manifestation of that aestheticism which Pater sucked from
the romantic school of his century and disguised in the phraseology of
ancient faith" (8:96). But More acknowledges that in the past, "I could
not dissociate his Epicureanism from the intellectual and moral dissolution which from the beginning had been so insidiously at work in the
romantic school, and from which, as I thought, I had myself so barely
escaped" (8:83). One feels that he still senses the danger and wants to
ward it off even at the price of injustice. It seems to me false to say that
"Pater was in no proper sense of the word a critic" (8:99) and to see him

purely as the spiritual father of Oscar Wilde and decadent aestheticism (cf. the chapter on Pater in this *History*, volume 4).

Contrary to the gibes against the humanists that they reduced literature to a few great names, More had a broad taste which was far from exclusive and wide reading experience in all manners and ages. He has a genuine historical sense, a "habitual grasp in a single firm vision of . . . the long course of humanity" (*SE*, 9:36). More could enjoy writers who were in no way grist for his intellectual mill. Defending Horace Walpole against the slurs of Macaulay he confesses to an "invincible prepossession in favor of these men of the past who have lived and written for my entertainment" (4:277). He can defend Chesterfield and the advice to his son (5:214) and appreciate Rabelais and Laurence Sterne, rejecting Thackeray's denigration (3:179–80), and admire Byron, particularly his *Don Juan*. He sees that Byron sought "solace and a sense of uplifted freedom. The heroic ideal was gone, the refuge of religion was gone; but passing to the opposite extreme, by showing the power of the human heart to mock at all things, he would still set forth the possibility of standing above and apart from all things" (3:176). The concluding paragraph, which expressed the hope that Byron's point of view will become antiquated with our "learning of the new significance of human life" (3:176), seems almost a rhetorical flourish.

On the whole, More upholds a classical standard. In the essay on Sainte-Beuve praise is given to him as "at bottom from the beginning to the end classical in his love for clarity and self-restraint" (*SE*, 3:62), in his rebuke for excess (63), his "love for the golden mean" (74). It is an occasion to regret that the English did not have, in the Elizabethan age, a Boileau who could have taught Shakespeare "to prune his redundancies, to disentangle his language at time, to eliminate the relics of barbarism in his denouement" (71–72). Arnold's essay on the French Academy must have been in More's mind when he develops the contrast between "the chief glory of English literature [which] lies in the very field where French is weakest, in the lonely and unsociable life of the spirit, just as the faults of the English are due to its lack of discipline and uncertainty of taste" (81). It is still good Arnoldian classicism to speak of "the note of distinction which is concerned more with form than with substance, the reflective faculty which broods over the problems of morality, the questioning spirit which curbs spontaneity, the zest of discrimination which refines the broad effects to the nuance, the power of fancy which transforms the emotions into ideas. In a word the aristocratic element denotes self-control, discipline, suppression" (5:29); the tirade was elicited by Dickens's uncontrolled emotionalism and by Tolstoy's preference for the taste of the illiterate Russian peasant. The classicist preference shows also in an essay which praises Lionel Johnson at the expense of Yeats (1:177), though one must realize that the essay was written in 1904 before Yeats recovered from what to More seemed "wasteful revery" (1:187). Johnson's "firmness and wholesome clearness," "his sternly idealized sorrow" appealed much more. In contrast More could protest against the "super-romantic exaltation of Coleridge's *Kubla Khan* as the supreme type of poetry" (11:161) as it "identifies the inspiration of genius too closely with the automatic creations of the dream-state" (11:161). Similarly Blake's method seems to him "more disastrous to poetry than the most rigid conventions of the [eighteenth] century" (4:229). He could complain then about the preoccupation "with the scattered and blindly working forces that were sapping the very foundation of the structure of eighteenth century life and poetry" (4:216).

More is sometimes an oldfashioned doctrinaire neoclassicist when he condemns Ibsen for "violating the law of tragedy by descending to trivialities and using prosaic language" (*SE*, 2:160), as he still believes in "rules inherent in the medium" (164), and objects to Browning's use of the dramatic monologue as "keeping attention riveted on the individual species or problem" and thus preventing that "escape into the larger and more general vision which makes the transition from prose to poetry" (3:153). For an unargued reason, the dramatic monologue, the Jamesian point of view, and the Joycean stream of consciousness are declared to frustrate the attainment of universality, which to him is the criterion of poetry and genuine art.

More might be exaggerating in a 1917 letter to Babbitt when he acknowledged, "As you know, I owe my whole mental direction to what I have got from you in conversation" (Dakin, *More*, 170n.), but explicit professions of humanism as a creed are rare before 1908, before the preface to the eighth volume of the *Shelburne Essays* and the "Definitions of Dualism" there. But much earlier More had chided Browning for not recognizing "a break between the lower and higher nature of man" (*SE*, 3:163) explaining his popularity, in part, by his "gospel of human passion." The conclusion of *Fifine at the Fair*, "I end with—Love is all and Death is naught—sounds like the wisdom of a school girl" (164), More complains. Browning, in short, is a "false prophet" (165). Similarly Meredith is criticized for his "tendency to confuse things of the body and of the spirit" (2:167). Wordsworth is praised for a "few love poems almost perfect in their restrained beauty" (7:27), for "a great if spasmodic accomplishment" (45), but More puzzles, as many have done before and since, about the contrast between the "inevitableness of the greater work amidst much of sad mechanic exercise" (46), and he chides Wordsworth for "consecrating a life to nature" (42), telling us that "human fate is greater than stocks and stones" (47).

Shelley is criticized for emotionalism, for the absence of an "inner check" (*SE*, 7:13), for his "childlike credulity in believing that religion and political oppression affect a virtuous and innocent humanity." More wants to show that Shelley's political beliefs have literary bearing. They are, he argues, "destructive of that self-knowledge out of which the great creations and magnificent joys of literature grow" (8). More is finally content to grant Shelley "passages of lyrical ecstacy" and to admit that "quite another account might be given than this I am writing" (22). The basic agreement with Arnold's ranking of the English romantic poets is obvious, though More is more hostile to the Rousseauism implied in their trust in nature and human nature. But More is far too aware of intellectual history to see Rousseau as the source of all evil. Ideas of liberty, progress, natural religion, and the innate goodness of man are much older and prevailed in England, in Deism, in the doctrines of Algernon Sidney and many others. More objects that all the eighteenth-century philosophers "excluded that deep cleft within the human soul itself which springs from the bitter consciousness of evil" (6:223).

The essay on Tennyson shows More's attitude best. He criticizes Tennyson's comfortable belief in "one far-off divine event" (*SE*, 7:83) but praises him for showing traces of mysticism, for "feeling himself an entity set apart from the flowing of time" (88). He disapproves of the "official compromise of *In Memoriam*" where "he—not only he, but God himself—is one with the sum of things in their vague temporal progress. In that difference, if rightly understood, lies, I think, the distinction between faith and naturalism" (88). More considers it "a denial of two opposite principles within us, one bespeaking unity and peace and infinite life, the other calling us to endless change and division and discord" (86). Change is the enemy. Evolution, the descent of man, is More's nightmare. In a curious meditation on seeing prehistoric monsters in a museum, his horror at man's animality comes out almost grotesquely.

All this is concerned with beliefs and ideas in literature, More's main interest. But he was by no means oblivious of formal questions. There is an excellent paper on metrics, "The Science of English Verse" (*SE*, 1:103), which appeals to Helmholtz's *Tonempfindungen* and argues sensibly that actual verse is a "compromise between our rhythmic instinct and the normal prose pronunciation" (120). There are scattered comments which could be called "close reading." Thus the forty-fifth stanza of

Shelley's *Adonais* is shown to blend Virgil and Milton. More deplores the vapid phrase "far in the Unapparent" and points to the contrast between the magnificence of the line on Lucan with the "vague allegory of Oblivion shrinking unreproved" in the next verse (7:23–24).

If one looks back at the eleven volumes of the *Shelburne Essays* (and the three of the new series) one cannot but admire the range of topics, the skill of presentation, the knowledge displayed, and the sanity of the judgments if we accept the limits of More's doctrine. The essays are admittedly often mere book reviews, as were, after all, *Causeries du lundi*. But the comparison with Sainte-Beuve's series, though made insistently by those who, like Norman Foerster, called them "the highest accomplishment in literary criticism in the whole of American literature"[6] or called More "the greatest of all American critics, better than a trans-Atlantic copy of a French critic. He stands with Coleridge, Sainte-Beuve, Samuel Johnson and three or four others in the first rank of the critical art,"[7] does disservice to a proper estimate of his achievement. More has not the charm, the ease, and the unsurpassable sense of individuality of Sainte-Beuve. He is not the great personality and authority Johnson was and he has little of Coleridge's philosophical acumen and psychological subtlety. But he has the great merit to have upheld an ideal of judicial and judicious criticism, a personal involvement with ideas tenaciously held, at a time when criticism had become either impressionistic or mired in academic factualism and relativism.

There are serious shortcomings in More's critical writings: a certain tone of smugness and extreme "delicacy" in sexual matters disturbs us today, but these seem minor blemishes in what after all are collections of occasional essays, often extended book reviews, which achieve as a whole a definition of a specific taste and a spiritual position. *Shelburne Essays* can easily be seen as preparation for the later studies in the Platonic tradition, which for More revives in seventeenth-century England in the appealing figures of the Cambridge Platonists. He praises them in reference to Newman because "these earlier theologians, notwithstanding their apparent dogmatism, were in reality akin to the mystics of all ages who find their peace in a faith that needs no surrender [of their mental integrity]" (*SE*, 8:76). On two occasions when I called on More in Princeton in 1929, he lent me, I remember, the *Sermons* of John Smith and *The Candle of the Lord* by Nathaniel Calderwell. He was a Neoplatonist steeped in the symbolic tradition out of which Emerson also grew. Babbitt could not have had a taste for this kind of rarefied spirituality. All More's criticism shows that he was a moralist who, ultimately, appealed to an immediate perception of supernatural truth.

As a *literary* critic Babbitt shows his limitations in aesthetic sensibility and ordinary curiosity. He also was primarily a moralist. But he was, it must be stressed, a forceful and learned historian of ideas: of critical, moral, and political ideas. Though the proliferation of modern scholarship has made many of his studies obsolete, they do within a brief compass trace the history of French criticism, the history of the interrelationship of the arts, the history of the concept of the imagination, the history of primitivism and sentimentalism and many related topics. Unquestionably all these studies are biased by Babbitt's decisive views and sometimes distort their texts—as when Babbitt tries to make Schiller a primitivist (cf. Lovejoy's review of *RR* in *Modern Language Review*)—but they had the great merit of taking ideas seriously at a time when American scholarship was almost exclusively devoted to a factual antiquarianism. Babbitt's point of view, which embraced antiquity, English, French, and German literature with glimpses of the Far East, fostered the cause of comparative literature, a subject he used to recommend emphatically, with a proper sense of its pitfalls (*LC*, 123–25). Appropriately there is now a Chair of Comparative Literature at Harvard University named after him. In the Harvard classroom Babbitt was a commanding personality and his influence on his students left deep traces even when the students turned against him. It is sufficient to allude to T. S. Eliot. Nor can one underrate the effect on a group of students such as Stuart Sherman, Norman Foerster, G. E. Elliott, Newton Arvin, Austin Warren, and Harry Levin or such "renegades" as Van Wyck Brooks and Walter Lippman. Almost single-handed in the academy of the time, Babbitt reasserted the function of literary studies as interpretation and criticism. Whatever his limitations Babbitt deserves praise for defending the liberty of judging: the necessity of criticism.

3: OUTSIDERS

HUNEKER, MENCKEN, AND VAN WYCK BROOKS were essentially journalists: they dominated the critical scene up to the Great Depression. But simultaneously many critics either in the academy or on the fringe of it were active, stating theories often in conflict with the prevailing trends or with each other. There were lonely figures like John Jay Chapman and George Santayana, there was one theorist, Joel E. Spingarn, who wrote no practical criticism, and there was the group of humanists, Paul Elmer More and Irving Babbitt and their younger adherent Norman Foerster.

JOHN JAY CHAPMAN (1862–1933)

John Jay Chapman is a survival from an earlier past: an Emersonian of the purest water, an individualist, and something of a Don Quixote who spent his life, like his admired William Lloyd Garrison to whom he devoted a belated, impassioned book (1913), at "universal reform": in New York politics, on immigration, the persecution of negroes, and so on. He wrote plays for children, closet drama, anti-German pamphlets, and much else. Literary criticism is only a small fraction of his output. It never pretends to any system but does convey some striking insights. Particularly the title essay in *Emerson and Other Essays* (1898) is a strong restatement of the creed of individualism. Emerson is the great rebel, "the arch-radical" (107) against the rule of the masses. "If a soul be taken and crushed by democracy till it utter a cry, that cry may be Emerson's" (106). Emerson is "a Yankee Shelley" (15), whose "works are all one single attack on the voice of the age, moral cowardice" (29). Chapman ignores Emerson's own trust in democracy as he sees the American reality of his own time showing a people "cowed in spirit, illiberal" (103), industrious, narrow-minded, commonplace and monotonous, "so uniform that one man can hardly be distinguished from another, law-abiding, timid, and traditional" (114). Emerson stands above his age like a colossus. But

Chapman knows also Emerson's limitations. He is not a philosopher; he is not a critic as he has "no conception of growth, of development" (43) and lacks historical sense. "Art was a name to him; music was a name to him; love was a name to him" (78). He had no sense of passion or sex. His poetry has too much thought, too much argument. There is an "anaemic incompleteness in Emerson's character" (72).

One would expect Chapman to praise Whitman. But he ridicules the British critics (presumably John Addington Symonds) who exalted him as a representative American poet. He was nothing of the sort: he may be the opposite of the average American, but he is merely "a *poseur*, a horrid mountebank and ego-maniac" (*E*, 121) who has given "utterance to the soul of the tramp" (119). He can be valued only for his "defiance of all men" (128) but his joy of "being in the open air and the joy of being disreputable and unashamed" (117) is not Chapman's idea of individualism, which is always concerned with the health of the body politic, with *Political Agitation, Political Nursery,* the titles of his publications.

Chapman had wide intermittent literary interests—some Italian, as an admiring account of Michelangelo's sonnets and a translation of the fourth canto of the *Inferno* in blank verse show. It reached out, late in his life, to Goethe on whom he wrote a monograph, published only in part, in which he pursued the old charge against Goethe's "Teutonic passion for self improvement" at the expense of the women he loved (Howe, 445–56). Chapman also had Greek interests. His exaltation of Lucian over Plato seems merely perverse. His assault on Gilbert Murray's translations of Greek tragedies predates T. S. Eliot's. Chapman even wrote an essay on Balzac which makes a good point in insisting on Balzac's "absolute benevolence," but the essays on Shakespeare, Browning, Kipling, and Stevenson seem commonplace or predictable. Kipling is condemned for his racism, Stevenson is called derivative: his work is "whipped up literary froth" (Bernstein, 97).

What preserves Chapman as a writer is his power of inventing striking metaphors: thus we are told, "You cannot see Emerson clearly: he is hidden by a high wall but you always know exactly on what spot he is standing. You judge it by the flight of the objects he throws over the wall—a bootjack, an apple, a crown, a razor, a volume of verse" (*E*, 30–31). One may dismiss this as "impressionist" criticism, but in its fanciful way it accurately defines the elusiveness of Emerson as a person, the fixity of his position, and the "democratic" equality of his subject-matter. Stevenson's dependence on older literature is formulated also strikingly: "He is the mistletoe of English literature whose roots are not in the soil but in the tree" (243). Chapman may have learned his method from

Emerson: his life and his lively, opinionated letters testify to his sturdy independence, to something which pejoratively could be called oddity or even crankiness. He did not want, he wrote, to "become a second Sainte-Beuve. His handwriting is all the same size. He is a mill. He is passive. What you want is not a criticism that sizes up the past but stirs up the present" (Howe, 143). But Chapman as a critic did not stir up the present. He remained an outsider who has found admirers like Edmund Wilson only late in his life.

W. C. BROWNELL (1851–1928)

William Crary Brownell seems today not only neglected but forgotten. He is not even mentioned in Alfred Kazin's *On Native Grounds* and in Stanley Edgar Hyman's *Armed Vision,* books written within the living memory of the man. Robert E. Spiller's brief discussion in the standard *Literary History of the United States* refers only to the essay on Matthew Arnold. Since then the silence is complete. In the very full two-volume anthology of *American Literature: The Makers and the Making,* edited by Cleanth Brooks, R. W. B. Lewis, and R. P. Warren, he is not represented at all. Some of this neglect is due to the fact that he did not belong to either of the two main parties of American criticism of the time: he was neither a professor like Irving Babbitt nor a journalist like H. L. Mencken. He began his career as a journalist when he was eighteen but most of his life (since 1888) was spent as an editor and literary advisor of Charles Scribner's, the New York publishers. Edith Wharton, one of his authors, called him gratefully "the most discerning literary critic of our day." He was admired by Stuart P. Sherman, who wrote a laudatory introduction to a new edition of *American Prose Masters* (1923), and there is a thin essay in *John Morley and Other Essays* by G. M. Harper, the biographer of Wordsworth. But that is about all.

Brownell established himself as an author with two books about France. He had spent three leisurely years (1881–84) in Paris and the first two grew out of this formative experience. *French Traits: An Essay in Comparative Criticism* (1888) is a sociological study, somewhat like Emerson's *English Traits* or Taine's *Notes sur l'Angleterre,* which draws a contrast between French social cohesion, respect for institutions, rationality, taste, manners, and disciplined democracy with American individualism, cult of ugliness, and emotional crudity. The balance seems tilted toward the French but at the end Brownell feels that something can be said for the American "zest that accompanies the 'advance on Chaos and the Dark' " (411). The second book, *French Art: Classic and Contemporary Painting and*

Sculpture (1892), is a serious history of French art from the sixteenth century to the time of writing. It must be judged by its date. Brownell admires the realists and impressionists. The newest painter is Monet, but Brownell really warms up only to Rodin, whom he knew personally. The book is dedicated to him and a supplement to a new illustrated edition (1901) pays no attention to new developments except in his work. Based as the book must be on Brownell's Paris observations in 1881–84, it seems unjust to criticize it for ignoring Cézanne and Van Gogh. They were not yet prominent at that time. More serious seems to me the charge of excessive attention to academic sculptors, though Brownell sided with Rodin against the *Institut,* and the predilection for Puvis de Chavannes. The frontispiece of a Corot painting best represents Brownell's own ideal of what painting should be.

As a literary critic Brownell's claims are based on two books, *Victorian Prose Masters* (1901) and *American Prose Masters* (1909), each containing essays on only six authors, which must be supplemented by three small volumes, *Criticism* (1914), *Standards* (1917), and *The Genius of Style* (1924).

Victorian Prose Masters may seem today perverse in its fervent praise of Thackeray and Arnold, the cool handling of George Eliot and Meredith, and the harsh rejection of Carlyle and Ruskin. But the serried argumentation, the often witty and aphoristic formulations, the marshaling of evidence buttressing a general conception, the judicious, detached tone make it a book of rare distinction. There is much to be said, for instance, for Brownell's defense of Thackeray's comments against the dogma of "exit author," then penetrating from France and redefined by Henry James. Brownell argues that the novel is not merely art, and not even a picture of society, but that its effect depends on the personality of the writer. "Thackeray enwraps and embroiders his story with his personal philosophy" (7), and the charge that this intrusion diminishes objectivity and hence illusion is mistaken. Rather Thackeray's subjectivity deepens illusion, attunes the reader to the rhythm of the subject, establishes "a mutuality of relationship" between writer and reader. The comment serves to detach the person from the background and the creator. Thackeray's subjectivity increases the objectivity of his creations. "They are in this way definitely 'exteriorized' " (10). One may not like the nature of Thackeray's commentary and prefer, for instance, Sterne's in *Tristram Shandy* where the characters stand out much more clearly than in many studiously objective novels, but the general defense of the method seems a good one. Wayne Booth in *The Rhetoric of Fiction* says substantially the same thing.

Brownell is deeply impressed by Arnold, his ideal of culture, his concept of criticism, even his slogan defining literature as "criticism of life," his reasonableness, his temper, urbanity, elegance, and severely stoic strain. But he is by no means blind to his limitations. It is an error to call him simply an Arnoldian. Brownell had read Taine and Brunetière and objects that Arnold is not occupied with origins and not much with relations (VPM, 164). Arnold has no interest in history or psychology (165). He lacked the "edge of the aesthetic faculty." When he was in Italy, he was preoccupied with botany (155). Brownell also questions whether Arnold's ideal to "get oneself out of the way and let humanity judge" was ever carried out by him in practice. Certainly Arnold was "prodigiously interested in the process" (158). His motives were didactic, only his method was disinterested (160). In his own name Brownell rejects the common assumption of the inferiority of all criticism to creation. Criticism is not confined to exposition or interpretation. It is "characterization of art as art is a characterization of nature" (169).

Brownell was good at characterization. The essay on George Eliot, curious also as a document of her eclipse around the turn of the century, is not exactly a rehabilitation. But it attempts a judicious balancing of pros and cons, emphasizing her intellectuality, excessively to my mind. A rationalist himself, at least in his critical procedures, Brownell believes that temperament rather than thinking matters in fiction. Thought is universal, impersonal, and often George Eliot "demonstrates that some minds don't repay study" (VPM, 105). George Eliot's world seems to him less concrete than her moral inspiration. "We do not sufficiently feel with George Eliot's personages" (110). Brownell makes good distinctions between the books, vastly preferring the early work. In spite of what he considers her shortcomings as a novelist—a lack of spontaneity, a certain dryness, and even lack of aesthetic sense—he concludes by admiring her immensely for "giving one such a poignant, sometimes such an unsupportable, sense that life is immensely serious" (145). He hopes for her comeback, a hope since amply fulfilled.

Meredith, on the other hand, remains under a cloud today. Brownell admires his imagination, his intellectual eminence and analytic treatment of human nature (VPM, 288). He somewhat wryly accounts for his popularity with the female reading public by his belief in the equality of the sexes but, more insistently than in the George Eliot essay, he rehearses a long list of objections: his lack of temperament, his technical willfulness, his melodramatic plots, his manner of indirection and innuendo. The irony has run to seed. His levity is "elaborately, systematically, awkwardly airy" (261). Most tellingly Brownell argues that his characters, in spite of their whimsical originality, are treated as types. "The psychology dissipates rather than defines their individuality" (247). Meredith has no theme; he has a dozen, a score—as many as he has books (289). He lacks, in short, what Brownell demands of a novelist, "the large rhythm, the sustained note of informing purpose, the deep vibration of some unifying undertone" (288). Oddly enough, Brownell does not even mention Meredith's naturalistic outlook, his ideal of a harmony of blood, brain, and spirit, as he ignores the poetry except for a slighting reference to *Modern Love*.

The essays on Carlyle and Ruskin are harshly dismissive. They ignore much that can be said in their favor but score many points. There is truth in saying that "the only aspect of the French Revolution that pleased Carlyle was not the rise of democracy but the punishment of the *noblesse*. For its ideas he cared not a straw" (*VPM*, 71). Brownell praises only the rehabilitation of Cromwell and the Puritans but condemns Carlyle's politics, his enmity to science, his uncritical treatment of German literature, and the whole tyranny of conscience he personified. Ruskin seems to Brownell a "pure sentimentalist" (208). His art criticism is simply bad. "A bit of botany in a great painter's work was more to him than the loveliest generalization" (219). Brownell does not care for his economics as he never questioned the industrial ideal, and Ruskin's medievalism seemed to him merely weird. That an artisan was reverent and pious in the ages of faith does not say anything in favor of "the absurd embryonic sculpture on St. Mark's" and it is nothing against the "Perseus" that Benvenuto Cellini was a rascal (218).

Brownell did not keep to this insight into the difference between word and man when he wrote *American Prose Masters*. Or was he right in his concern for the mind behind the work, the moral personality, rather than for an analysis of the work? After all, the work is the main source and evidence for the estimate which cannot be drawn purely from biographical sources. Writing on Poe, Brownell cannot forget Poe's squalid life and death, but the essay is still mainly literary criticism. Brownell recognizes Poe's historical importance but is unimpressed by his French fame, dismisses Poe's critical theories and the poetry as mere virtuoso performances. The tales are "tone and nothing else" (*APM*, 181), lack substance, imagination, reality. The common comparison with E. T. A. Hoffmann is mistaken, as in him the weird and the fantastic was always "in affectionate companionship with sentiment and humor," both totally lacking in Poe (406–07). Brownell argues that there is "nothing sinister in Poe, except his desire to produce sinister effects" (215), nothing satanic, nothing sexual or even sensual, except "glitter and tinsel" (201). Poe's lack of moral imagination accounts for the vacuity of his writings

(205). Brownell acutely argues that he cannot be called a Bohemian, an idler and dreamer. He was a hard worker, who wrote ten volumes and went to pieces under the influence of alcohol. He stands out because American literature has no background. "Lacking ancestors and traditions we are without the restrictive influence of a 'stream of tendency,' of an orderly evolution" (220). Brownell shares the view of Henry James and others that America lacked a dense civilization which could produce a great literature.

Hawthorne, one would think, would be Brownell's second example of the isolated artist. He seems like Poe when we are told that his works are "thoroughly original, without literary derivation" (*APM,* 51), and that they lack substance "which has been deemed a quality instead of a defect" (73). But Brownell rejects James's complaint of lack of atmosphere to stimulate initiative, develop talent, and train taste as "art does not reside in material but in treatment" (79). Actually Hawthorne's "environment furnished him material exactly, exquisitely, suited to his genius. His subject was the soul, and for the enactment of the dramas of the soul Salem was as apt a stage as Thebes" (80). Hawthorne was steeped in New England history and *The Scarlet Letter,* his masterpiece, is nourished by it. It is not a story of adultery, not even of sin or the situation of illicit love; it is rather the story of concealment (98). Brownell praises, besides, only *The Blithedale Romance* as "the most artistically articulated and the most naturalistic of his novels," while *The House of the Seven Gables* is "of singular thinness and almost gaseous expansion" (72) and *The Marble Faun* is embroidered by irrelevant information from the Baedeker.

The Emerson essay is similarly ambivalent. He is admired as a fountain of moral wisdom, as a beautiful soul who felt "not so much a delegate of the divine as part of it" (*APM,* 115), but is seen as a "bland angel" (126), as the "most impersonal of individuals," "flooded by light" (122), but lacking in heat, in temperament. Brownell considers his philosophy—circles, polarity, compensation—mere fancy and his rationalization of democracy through the ideal development of the individual mere distaste for "ideas of dominance, dictation, patronage, caste and material superiority" (133). Emerson is concerned only with mind in its creative and not its acquisitive aspect (139). He neglects the furniture of the mind, the historic sense, culture in Arnold's sense as discipline, as effort and tradition. Emerson wanted only to surrender to impulse and intuition (137). Brownell cannot share his optimism, which seems to him "too blithe, too bland, too confident" (151). Judging the actual writings Brownell complains that the *Essays* lack continuity. Emerson's work is "rather a cairn than a structure" (167). The poetry remains abstract while "the

concrete makes poetry an art" (164). But finally Brownell decides that
Emerson belongs with Epictetus, Marcus Aurelius, Montaigne, Pascal,
and Sir Thomas Browne, not bad company, after all.

Poe, Hawthorne, and Emerson suffer from uniqueness, isolation in
their society. Lowell, on the other hand, is representative, average, and
finally mediocre. "He expressed what others think, but with more energy" (*APM*, 226). Brownell dubs him a "jaunty Jeremiah" (224) and
harps on his bookishness. Henry James, however, was quite mistaken,
Brownell argues, when he thought that Lowell was steeped in history.
Brownell quotes Lowell saying: "As Dante tells us, St. Francis took poverty for his bride" and comments with heavy irony, "He does indeed. So
does Francis himself. So for that matter does Giotto" (238). Lowell is only
a philologist. His criticism lacks the supports of literary culture—history
and aesthetics (249). Lowell's essays suffer from the lack of what Brownell
feels to be his own strong point. They have no central conception, they
do not keep "an *ensemble*" in mind (233). His critical work "lacks the unity
of a body of doctrine and even a personal point of view" (262). Its chief
value is exegetical. Brownell thus did not think of him as a forerunner
of humanism. It comes as a surprise that after this slashing attack Brownell praises the poetry. He considers the "Commemoration Ode" 'a "magnificent poem" (279), achieving the "elevation of ecstasy and the splendor
of the sublime." But the stanzas he quotes seem a mere pastiche in the
wake of Collins or Gray.

In contrast to Lowell, the most bookish of authors, Cooper "had not
even a tincture of bookishness. Of the *art* of literature he had perhaps
never heard" (*APM*, 4). He wrote "the most unliterary works of any
writer of eminence in any literature" (6), as he was "first a man and then
a writer. He had no literary standards. He felt no responsibility. He never
thinks of the reader" (8). His books suffer badly from prolixity and can
be tedious. The comparison with Walter Scott limps as Cooper had little
history and wrote of a nature without memories, "with nothing Words-
worthian, nothing pantheistic in his feeling for her" (20). But all these
shortcomings are redeemed by Cooper's power of storytelling and characterization. Brownell thinks that the creation of Leatherstocking alone
"would set him in the front rank of the novelists of the world" (27).
Cooper fused more than any other author "romance and realism" (3).
His characters are "thoroughly realistic and yet imaginatively typical"
(31). Even his women characters, usually considered insipid, are defended as Brownell thinks them based on solid knowledge of an existing
clinging type. Brownell's admiration for Cooper is not, as one may suspect, inspired by childhood memories of the Leatherstocking tales alone.

He knows and praises many of the sea novels, the novels from European history and recent American life. He is apparently in sympathy with Cooper's often harsh criticism of American democracy, New England provincialism, and nonconformity. Brownell, also in his last book, *Democratic Distinction in America* (1927), shared Cooper's attitude of "an advocate of democracy abroad and a critic at home" (44). Like Cooper he thought democracy and distinction compatible, believed in an aristocracy or elite of worth.

The last essay, on Henry James, like the first in *Victorian Prose Masters* on Thackeray, concerns the problems of novel-writing. Brownell's attitude to Henry James is curiously ambivalent. He admires him as a critic, singling out the then hardly known *Prefaces* to the New York edition of his novels as "taken together, constituting a critical cyclopaedia" (*APM*, 292). Brownell sees James's conscious artistry, admires him as the inventor of the "international theme," calling him "the Bopp of the comparative method as applied to fiction" (325), but mostly argues against his theory of the absence of the author and the point of view. Brownell resumes here the argument of the essay on Thackeray. "We see him busily getting out of the way, visibly withdrawing behind the screen of his story . . . making his work, in fine, a kind of elaborate and complicated fortification between us and his personality" (297). Brownell doubts the efficacy of the oblique view through the device of a narrator or reporter. The characters in James's novels seem not to be *his* characters. "The novelist's personages are not sufficiently unified by his own *penchant*, preference, personality, to constitute a society of varied individuals viewed and portrayed from one definite and particular point of view— as the characters of great novelists do" (299). Brownell misses, surprisingly, the unity of the oeuvre he had missed also in Meredith. He thinks James's themes are less concerned with human beings than with "the situation—the 'predicament,' he would aptly say—in which he places them" (307). "Will Densher give a plausible solution to the recondite problem of how to combine the qualities of a cad and a gentleman? Will Maisie decide for or against Sir Claude? . . . Will Chad Newsome go back to Woollett?" (308). Brownell stresses the idiosyncratic, the mannered in James and deplores the decay of "the typical, the representative which constitutes the basis of both effective illusion and significant truth" (305– 06). Finally James is limited by "being altogether of the present time; of the moment." His picture of English society is devoid of a sense of the past (375). Like others before and since, Brownell complains that James "rather pointedly neglects the province of the heart" (310). He asks: "Are we to savor art without experiencing emotion?" (310). A certain coolness in James's temperament makes his report on human nature incomplete. His dominant interest is curiosity. It is disinterested, detached, but "his detachment is enthusiastic. One may say he is ardently frigid" (317). Much of this is well observed and phrased and was at the time of writing the most acute criticism of James and his method. It will appear to our present-day Jacobites sadly unsympathetic.

The twelve essays in the two books are portraits. Nowhere is there a panorama. Nowhere is there continuous theoretical reflection, only asides and digressions. Brownell saw the need of defining his principles and did so in three short books, extended lectures on *Criticism* (1914), *Standards* (1917), and *The Genius of Style* (1924). In the first Brownell argues well for the status of criticism as a "distinct province of literature" (18), as "the classics of aesthetic criticism constitute an impressive body of literature" (13). He comments briefly on the main trends of criticism, mainly in France. He rejects impressionism and the "disproportionate concern for causes" in Taine's theories. His admiration goes to Sainte-Beuve and Edmond Scherer. "Art and letters," he summarizes, "are neither fortuitous phenomena, on the one hand, to be savored and tested, merely by the sharp senses of the impressionist, nor, on the other, technical variants of an isolated evolution" (23), alluding to Brunetière's evolutionism. Brownell finally defends a criticism which judges the relation of art to life with criteria which are realistic, suspicious of the fantastic, but still concerned with the ideal, with ultimate moral and social values. The method, Brownell states, is "statement of the concrete in terms of the abstract" (16). As he rejects or is unconcerned with technique and form as external, he sees the process of criticism as a search for the mind behind the work. "It is the *qualities* of the writer, painter, sculptor, and not the *properties* of their productions, that are [the critic's] central concern, as his function is to disengage the moral value from its material expression" (17). This sounds like old message-hunting, but Brownell means it as searching for the mystery of personality. Solving it would be the "crown of the critical achievement," "the synthetic presentation of a physiognomy, whose features are as distinct as the whole they compose— the whole process interpenetrated by an estimate of value based on a standard of reason" (82). Brownell emphasizes that the critic's equipment must be wider than merely literary: he needs the support of history, aesthetics, and philosophy and of a knowledge of human nature in general. Brownell rejects the appeal to the "strictly consecrated and canonical" as "criticism is a live art, and contemporaneousness is of its essence" (44). Criticism must carry conviction and thus requires an appeal to some accepted standard (42).

In *Standards* Brownell tried to answer this question. But he does not succeed. He only complains about "the wide disappearance of standards altogether" (4) and gives reasons for it: the elective system in the colleges, the spread of education, the self-respect mediocrity has suddenly acquired (65), the "complete cleavage between the generations" (74). Brownell attacks modern art which fails to communicate. "If the artist has not, in popular parlance, 'got it over,' how do we know that he has got it out? He has perhaps had his catharsis, but in secret. Besides we want ours. Ours, indeed, was the the one Aristotle had in mind" (126). Brownell was too much a believer in democracy to assert the claim of a "remnant," the Arnoldian term for minority culture. "The only way the remnant can be increased is by the spread of its standards" (38) is a counsel of perfection but the means to do it remain obscure and so does the exact nature of the standards. Brownell obviously is reluctant to define it in the terms of the new humanists, Babbitt and More, who had cut themselves off from "contemporaneousness" in the arts and the democracy of American society. Brownell's last critical book, *The Genius of Style,* does not further clarify the issues. It is a rambling, often allusive appeal for style, combining order and movement. It contains a sketch of the history of English style with emphasis on what could be called poetic or ornate prose and reflections on the present desire for bald simplicity, for "sensationalism implicit in a naturalistic philosophy" (183). The little book lacks focus and punch. It shows a decline of mental powers.

Still, the two books, to which we can add the lecture on *Criticism,* seem to me a solid achievement: in the quality of mind displayed they seem to me decidedly superior to the books of writers with whom Brownell is usually grouped—G. E. Woodberry, Barrett Wendell, Brander Matthews, Stuart Sherman, and even Babbitt and More, though their range was much greater. Brownell's essays hold firmly to a central insight, attempting always to define the ruling passion, the *faculté maîtresse* of a writer, but in difference from Sainte-Beuve they lack the concrete life of his lavish display of detail and from Taine the passionate colors of his eloquence. Brownell often moves on a plane of abstract generalization which presupposes an intimate knowledge of the authors discussed. Brownell has that knowledge: he alludes to individual books, figures, and scenes with assurance but he always uses them as examples toward his central aim, characterization in intellectual terms, an art of somewhat abstract portraiture. His style goes with it; it is deliberate, often convoluted, even ponderous in its use of recondite Latinisms (titurate, lacustrine). I have, I suppose, read more nineteenth-century criticism in English and French than most people. I cannot think of any model or parallel unless it is Emile Hennequin, whom Brownell does not, I believe, mention. He admired Matthew Arnold, Sainte-Beuve, and the dour Scherer. Today we may see his greatest limitation in the vagueness of his principles: they seem to amount to the old triad of the true, the good, and the beautiful. It is tradition, nineteenth-century convention not properly defined or made articulate. Brownell belongs to what is now a remote past, but he stands out in it amidst appalling mediocrity by the sharpness of his mind, the poise of views, the penetration of his analysis, the judiciousness of his temper, however much we may feel rebuffed by a certain stiffness and old-world dignity, now gone forever, visible also in the photograph prefixed to an anthology of his writings edited by his widow in 1933. But Brownell cannot be dismissed as a "conservative," as a representative of the "genteel tradition," as "too much at ease in a complete and settled world," as Bernard Bandler II phrased it in a sharply critical essay in *The Hound and Horn* (1929). He was an iconoclast in his time, as his criticism of the American and British classics of the nineteenth century shows. He upheld in theory and practice the ideal of a judicial criticism using rational arguments and standards, a rare creed in his and any time.

GEORGE SANTAYANA (1863–1952)

Santayana is a peculiar case. He was a Spaniard by birth but grew up in Boston and never wrote in any other language than English. He said himself, "It is as an American writer that I must be counted, if I am counted at all" (Schilpp, 603), though he remained a Spanish citizen until his death in Rome in 1952; he had left the United States in 1912, never to return even for a visit. He stresses that in all his American years, from his eighth to his fiftieth, he "never had any contact with the deeper layers and broad currents of American Life" (ibid., 602). Still, his book *Character and Opinion in the United States* (1920), the lecture first given at Berkeley, California, on *The Genteel Tradition in American Philosophy* (1911) and its sequel, *The Genteel Tradition at Bay* (1931), his novel *The Last Puritan* (1936), set in Boston, as well as his essays on Emerson and Whitman belie this total aloofness. "Deeper layers and broader currents" seem to exclude the New England intellectual and poetic tradition which Santayana knew intimately. As a member of the Harvard philosophy department under the shadow of Josiah Royce and William James, he had early come to detest the Protestant atmosphere of his surroundings. In 1911 he could tell his half-sister that "I have become almost unconscious of how much I hate it all" here in Boston, not to speak of California and

Canada, which seemed to him "intellectually emptier than the Sahara" (*L,* 110).

The distaste for America (or rather New England) would put Santayana into the company of other American expatriates of the time, though his Catholic sympathies and self-conscious Latinity differ from the usual motivations of exile. What makes Santayana unique in a history of American criticism is the combination of technical philosophy with literary criticism. One can think of Croce and Bergson as possible parallel cases but this is deceptive. Santayana's specific philosophy was developed only after his return to Europe. The elaborate system of the *Realm of Being,* the whole doctrine of the essence, left no trace on his literary criticism and remained quite ineffective as an influence on later developments in America, though Santayana was greatly admired by such diverse critics and poets as J. C. Ransom and R. P. Blackmur, Wallace Stevens and Robert Lowell. Santayana discovered that "the theory of essence was beautifully expounded by Proust" (*L,* 229) but in an essay "Proust on Essences" (*Life and Letters,* 1929, reprinted in *OS*) he correctly pointed out the marked difference: his essence is not the recovery of something in the past (that seems to him only the "well known illusion of the *déjà vu*" [*ELS,* 244]) while his essence is eternal, ideal, and hence out of time (see Schilpp, 544). A 1928 letter even harshly condemns Proust as "too inhuman, idiotically aesthetic, and tediously nonmoral" (*L,* 232). It thus seems preposterous to conclude a study of *Proust and Santayana* by saying: "The appropriate fulfillment of Proust's work was its being read by Santayana."[1]

The literary criticism of Santayana which counts has a philosophical background but it is merely that of naturalism which allows religion to function as a beneficial myth of the imagination. *The Sense of Beauty* (1896) is a book on general aesthetics which in the American context of the time may have been striking for its finely wrought prose but seen from a modern perspective will appear merely a psychological study of aesthetic sensibility of doubtful originality and little theoretical cogency. I have not seen any study of its sources but without trying to pin them down we see that the whole book is clearly dependent on the German psychological aesthetics of the time, on Lotze (on whom Santayana had written his doctor's thesis), on Fechner (though he ignored his experiments), and possibly on a phase of Dilthey. Santayana starts with hedonistic assumptions. Beauty is defined as "pleasure objectified" (*SB,* 52). The problem of the tragic, the comic, and the sublime then has to become an absurd calculus of pleasure and pain as "the element of pain must be overbalanced by an element of pleasure" (225). The effect of art is described as "a power to so synthesize and bring to a focus the various impulses of the self, so to suspend them to a single image, that a great peace falls upon that perturbed kingdom." Two methods of securing this psychic harmony are distinguished: one is to unify all the given elements and another is to reject all the elements that refuse to be unified. "Unity by inclusion gives us the beautiful; unity by exclusion, opposition, and isolation gives us the sublime" (235). The anticipations of I. A. Richards's doctrine are striking in this passage where even the terms "poetry of inclusion" versus "poetry of exclusion" must have their sources, though they are used in Richards quite differently. In Richards "exclusion" means poetry limited to a specific mood or emotion, while "poetry of inclusion" refers to complex poetry, permitting heterogeneity, rivalry, and conflict between feelings. The two terms are also used prominently by Cleanth Brooks.

But these seminal passages are rare: the bulk of the book is vague and bland. The three main divisions of beauty—materials (including sound and color), form, and expression—are impossible to keep apart. Expression is used quite idiosyncratically as "the quality acquired by objects through association" (SB, 193) and in practice is simply a synonym for content. Literature is seen as the middle realm between the plastic arts and music. It culminates for Santayana in the creation of types but even "the greatest characters of fiction are uninteresting and unreal compared with the conception of the gods" (190). The book concludes with gestures toward beauty as "indescribable," as "a consciousness of joy and security, a pang, a dream, a pure pleasure" (267–68), and toward the romantic concept of beauty as "a pledge of the possible conformity between the soul and nature, and consequently a ground of faith in the supremacy of the good" (270). The body of the book has not prepared this conclusion.

The long essay "The Elements and Function of Poetry" in Santayana's next book, *Interpretations of Poetry and Religion* (1900), develops the idea of poetry as the middle realm between sound and meaning. It shows a great awareness of the role of meter and language in poetry. "Verse like stained glass arrests attention in its own intricacies" (IPR, 257) is a good metaphor for the self-reflexivity of poetry though Santayana does not, of course, deny that we can see through the stained glass at the outer world. He rehearses old ideas when he, like Wordsworth, speaks of the poet "disintegrating the fictions of common perception" (260) or "shaking us out of our servile speech and imaginative poverty" recovering "sensuous and imaginative freedom" (266). Still, poetry in his view would not be only relaxation. Santayana wants it rather to be "building a world nearer to the heart's desire" (270), in a phrase from Fitzgerald's *Rubaiyat*. The highest kind of poetry is, however, religion or, at least, the poetry of prophets (214), a company which includes Homer and Dante who express existing religions, and Lucretius and Wordsworth who herald "one which he believes to be possible" (286). Poetry raised to the highest power is identical with religion. Religion then "surrenders its illusions and ceases to deceive" (290). It sounds like Arnold's hope for poetry but is much more directly associated with specific dogmas. In the doctrine of transubstantiation, for instance, religion has rediscovered its affinity with poetry, "for which everything visible is a sacrament, an outward sign of that inward grace for which the soul is thirsting" (286). The unctuous phraseology makes it hard to realize that even then Santayana claimed to be a thoroughgoing materialist.

On the way to this identification of poetry and religion we are told that character creation is not the main task of poetry (*IPR*, 274) and that the substance of poetry is emotion. "The glorious emotions with which [the poet] bubbles must, however, at all hazards find or feign their correlative objects" (277) is a passage which has been claimed as the source of Eliot's "objective correlative."

One would have expected that *Reason in Art* (1905), the fourth volume of the system of philosophy of Santayana's American years, *The Life of Reason*, would have systematized his theory of literature, but the section devoted to it is disappointing. It rehearses the view that "literature moves between the extremes of music and denotation" (*RA*, 260). The magic of poetry "lies in the immersion of the message in the medium" (261). But Santayana considers "absolute language a possible but foolish art" (268). He develops then at length the contrast between poetry and prose. "Poetry has body; it represents the volume of experience as well as its form" (271), while prose is "in itself meagre and bodiless, merely indicating the riches of the world" (279). Prose is, arbitrarily, limited to a mere set of signals, to something merely instrumental, like symbolic logic. "Such a theory of language would treat it as a necessary evil and would look forward hopefully to the extinction of literature" (281), a conception which ignores the many varieties of prose. Santayana concludes by expounding the ideal of a "rational poetry" where the poet would achieve "mastery, to see things as they are, and dare to describe them ingenuously; idealisation, to select from this reality what is pertinent to ultimate interests and can speak eloquently to the soul" (289). This rational poetry will get rid of all "lumber," Santayana's term for what he admits was necessary to the poets: "Homer has his mythology; Dante his allegories and mock science; Shakespeare has his romanticism; Goethe his symbolic

characters and artificial machinery" (280). It seems a dreary ideal, something like "scientific poetry." It is clarified in *Three Philosophical Poets:
Lucretius, Dante and Goethe* (1910).

Lucretius is obviously the poet with whom Santayana sympathizes most
fully. "A naturalistic conception of things is a great work of imagination.
. . . It is a conception of things to inspire great poetry, and in the end,
perhaps, it will prove the only conception able to inspire us" (*TPP*, 21).
Lucretius' melancholy, his view of death and love, and his atomistic cos-
mology find Santayana's approval. Dante, though greatly admired as a
"consummate poet," remains the exponent of the "supernatural" and
hence "too much a man of his own time" (128) who cannot be "a fair
nor an ultimate spokesman for humanity" (131). The essay on Goethe's
Faust (all the rest of Goethe's work is ignored) rings changes on the word
and subject of "romanticism" and incongruously argues that Goethe was
"all his life a follower of Spinoza, a naturalist in philosophy and a panthe-
ist" (139). Santayana sees, however, that Goethe differed from Spinoza:
he did not accept his mechanical interpretation of nature; he believed
in a much more personal immortality; he thought of the world as the
expression of a spiritual endeavor, all ideas totally alien to Spinoza (140).
Instead of concluding that Goethe was no Spinozist (in spite of some
early transient enthusiasm), Santayana complains that Goethe was not a
systematic philosopher (140), a type of mind he vastly prefers to a poet's.
"Philosophers have this advantage over men of letters, that their minds
being more organic, can more easily propagate themselves. They scatter
less influence, but more seeds" (140).

Still, he argues that "the moral of Faust is to be looked for in Spinoza—
the source of what is serious in the philosophy of Goethe" (*TPP*, 189).
Also "the poetic intention of the last scene is altogether Spinozistic" (193).
The salvation of Faust is interpreted by a strained use of Spinoza's *sub
specie aeternitatis*: "The complete biography of Faust, Faust seen under
the form of eternity, shows forth his salvation. . . . To have felt such
perpetual dissatisfaction is truly satisfactory. . . . Your worthiness is
thereby established under the form of eternity" (190). But at the same
time Santayana thinks that Faust has "maintained his enthusiasm for a
stormy, difficult and endless life. He has been true to his romantic philosophy" (187). He has won the wager with Mephistopheles. The last
scene with the *Mater gloriosa*, angels, boys, Paters, and hermits has "nothing Catholic about it" except the names and titles of the personages.
What they say is all sentimental landscape-painting or vague mysticism
borrowed from Swedenborg. Recognizing that *Faust* is not a philosophical
treatise Santayana reflects that the tale was "written to give vent to a

pregnant and vivid genius, to touch the heart, to bewilder the mind with a carnival of images, to amuse, to thrill, to humanize" (141). Incidentally he can be a good literary critic: compare Goethe's *Faust* with Marlowe's and Calderón's *Mágico prodigioso*, reflect on the relation between the Earth Spirit and Mephistopheles, single out the first scene of the second part "where Goethe reaches his highest potency as a poet and as a philosopher" (160), and comment on Goethe's romantic classicism.

Finally he defends his concept of the philosophical poet: "theory, contemplation of all things is imaginative." "A philosopher who attains it is, for the moment, a poet; and a poet who turns his practised and passionate imagination on the order of all things, or anything in the light of the whole, is for that moment a philosopher" (*TPP*, 11). Santayana does not admit a conflict between abstract thought and concrete poetry: he merely denies Poe's view that poetry has to come in spurts, in fleeting moments, must be short-winded or incidental. It *can* have range. After a set comparison of the three poets, Santayana calls for a new comprehensive poet who would hold a realistic Lucretian view of nature, have a Goethean sense of the immediacy of experience, and know the drama of good and evil without Dante's theology. "To correct Dante's error would be to establish a new religion and a new art, based on moral liberty and moral courage. But this supreme poet is in limbo still" (214). He is so even today as Santayana's projected ideal is, after all, an academic fantasy, outside of history and historical reality.

The ideal of rational poetry must have been long in Santayana's mind. It underlies his two essays on Whitman and Browning entitled "The Poetry of Barbarism" (in *Interpretations of Poetry and Religion*). Barbarism is apparently anything which lacks "discipline," "indispensable to art" (*IPR*, 209), any "failure of reason" which is a "failure of art and taste" (210). Browning lacks "love of form for its own sake which is the secret of contemplative satisfaction" (194). He is a purveyor of raw emotion, a portrayer of passion. Browning's lovers "extinguish sight and speech, each on each; sense, as he says elsewhere, drowning soul" (200). Browning's art is "still in the service of the will" (194), proclaims a criterion derived from Schopenhauer, who was for a time Santayana's favorite philosopher. Whitman comes off even worse. He is "all surface without an underlying structure" (179). "He has gone back to the innocent style of Adam, when the animals filed before him one by one and he called each of them by its name" (178). He is a primitivist and that is why he can never become a "poet of the people," as "nothing is farther from the common people than the corrupt desire to be primitive" (185). His sentimental glorification of the brotherhood of man seemed to Santayana outmoded. "What Whitman seized upon as the promise of the future is in reality the survival of the past" (183). But then Santayana had become critical of the whole American tradition descended from Puritanism through Emerson and Whitman to philosophical idealism imported from Germany. Actually his attitude toward Emerson was ambivalent. An early prize essay (1886) calls him "a mystic turned dilettante" but professes to be charmed "by so much sweetness and serenity."[2] No wonder Santayana did not win the prize. The essay in *Interpretations of Poetry and Religion* repeats the astonishment at Emerson's "beautiful soul" (217) and then states that Emerson "at bottom had no doctrine at all" (218). "Reality eluded him. Imagination was his single theme" (220). "All Nature is seen as an embodiment of our native fancy" (225). All minds are unified "in the single soul of the universe," "evil evaporates in the universal harmony of things," notions which to Santayana seemed merely fanciful nonsense. Emerson's obsession with the spectacle of necessary evolution entails, Santayana complains, the surrender of the "category of the better and worse, the deepest foundation of life and reason" (228). This optimism is a legacy of a pious tradition. Emerson remains a "Puritan mystic" "with poetic fancy and a gift for observation and epigram" (230). Though in entire sympathy with the national ideal of democracy and freedom, Emerson's heart was fixed on eternal things. Thus he cannot in any sense be called "a prophet of his age and country" (233). A centenary address (1903) is much more favorable in tone.[3] Emerson's synthesis of faith and reason, its projection of "beauty and mind" into all forms of matter, seems to be accepted but the suppression of criticism may have been due to the festive occasion.

Santayana's criticism of the New England tradition which had to include Emerson became harsher with the years. In 1911 he delivered a lecture on "The Genteel Tradition in American Philosophy" (first in *University of California Chronicle,* reprinted in *WD*) which found this damaging label for transcendentalism conceived as attenuated Calvinism. Emerson is included in the condemnation of what now seems to Santayana "sheer subjectivism" (*WD*, 194). He is characterized in the terms of the earlier essay as a "cheery, childlike soul, impervious to the evidence of evil" (197), as preparing the way to Whitman and William James, who left the genteel tradition behind. Whitman is described as embracing an "unintelligent, lazy, self-indulgent pantheism" (203). The lecture to the California audience ends with an appeal to throw off the yoke of the genteel tradition, favored by the primeval solitudes of the West, and, in an odd reversal, "to live in the imagination, in an inner landscape, in the mind in which alone happiness can be found" (214–15).

The return to Europe and the long stay in England after the outbreak of the First World War brought a shift in Santayana's interests. He composed a little book, *Egotism in German Philosophy* (1915), a sweeping attack on German idealism as mere solipsism and moral egotism. There is a chapter entitled "Hints of Egotism in Goethe" which draws a picture of Goethe as a "lordly observer, a traveller, a connoisseur, a philanderer," the type of an immoral aesthete. "Absolute egotism in Goethe, as in Emerson, summoned all nature to minister to the self" (*ELC*, 182). "Faith in absolute Will" is considered "a deep element of his genius" as in that of his country (185). Santayana sees it proved by the war and even draws a witty, malicious parallel to Goethe's love affairs. "Every pathetic sweetheart in town was a sort of Belgium to him; he violated her neutrality with a sigh; his heart bled for her innocent sufferings, and he never said afterwards in self-defense, like the German Chancellor, that she was no better than she should be. But he must press on" (183). In a preface to a reprint, dated August 1939, Santayana defended the book against the common charge that he took "an unworthy advantage of public resentment against particular acts of the German government in order to justify his prejudice against German Philosophy" by arguing that he was not attacking "something exclusively German but rather the universal prepotency of will and ambition in man." He admits "an obvious animus pervading these pages which it was a pleasure to vent. I had chafed for years under the pressure of a prim academic idealism derived from the Germans" (vi–vii).

In a calmer mood, after the war, Santayana gave an account of *Character and Opinion in the United States* (1920), the moral background, the academic environment, and the Harvard philosophers, venting again his distaste for the atmosphere of moralism, vague idealism, and commercial materialism. Still, the portraits of his two teachers and later colleagues, William James and Josiah Royce, while highly critical of their teachings, are tempered by fine human sympathy. Santayana finally returned to the topic in a booklet, *The Genteel Tradition at Bay* (1931), provoked by the new humanist movement which he saw as a revival of the genteel tradition. But none of the new humanists is mentioned by name and only one passage asks a direct question: "What is the supernatural sanction they evoke?" and gets no answer. "I can find little in their recommendations except a cautious allegiance to the genteel tradition. But can the way of Matthew Arnold and of Professor Norton be the way of life for all men for ever?" (69). The booklet does not come to grips with any specific issue raised by Babbitt and More. It rather ineffectually moves about in loose generalities concerning the "four R's": the Renaissance, the Ref-

ormation, the Revolution, and Romance, defending traditional humanism in order to come down heavily on absolutism in morality which
"smells of fustiness as well as of faggots" (74).

American literature understandably receded from Santayana's sight in
the later years in Italy, though his novel *The Last Puritan* (1936) is full of
literary discussions and opinions. But as they are put into the mouths of
fictional characters they should not be assumed to be Santayana's own,
however close they come to other personal pronouncements. Occasionally
Santayana reacts in letters to new readings. Emerson, he thought now,
was "a fanatic at bottom, a radical individualist" and even "a cruel physical Platonist" (Cory, 186). He read Faulkner's *Sanctuary* and Robert Lowell's *Lord Weary's Castle*, commenting on them with some puzzlement. But
he never could get through *Moby Dick* (*I.*, 312–13, 366, 229).

English literature was inevitably one of Santayana's main educational
legacies. He often quotes or alludes to Wordsworth, Keats, Shelley, Byron, Fitzgerald, and Tennyson. Shakespeare was early relegated to a
lower place in his pantheon of the great: Homer, Lucretius, Virgil, Dante,
Cervantes, Goethe. An essay, "The Absence of Religion in Shakespeare"
(originally in *New World* 5 [1896], reprinted in *IPR*), makes the point that
"for Shakespeare, in the matter of religion, the choice lay between Christianity, and nothing. He chose nothing" (*IPR*, 152), a falsely put dilemma
which ignores the conditions of the secular Elizabethan stage. Nor can
one take seriously the argument that Shakespeare "leaves life without a
setting and consequently a meaning" and that "the cosmos eludes him"
(154–55). As Santayana takes Macbeth's speech "Tomorrow and tomorrow" to be the sum of Shakespeare's wisdom, he can accuse him of
"philosophical incoherence" and find him "still heathen" and even "morose and barbarous in its inmost core" (156). "Unity of conception," to
Santayana, "is an aesthetic merit no less than a logical demand" (164).
The argument anticipates T. S. Eliot's view of Shakespeare's "rag-bag
philosophy."

An essay on *Hamlet* (originally an introduction to the Harper edition,
1908, reprinted in *OS*) rehearses the common view, expounded by J. M.
Robertson, that there is an incongruity between the inherited plot and
Shakespeare's imposed characterization in order to sketch Hamlet's character as a contrast between his "intelligence and courage" and the lack
of "practical conviction and sense of reality" (*OS*, 65; *ELC*, 134). At the
end Santayana returns to a version of his complaint about the absence
of religion in Shakespeare. Here is "no necessary human tragedy, no
universal destiny or divine law. It is a picture of incidental unfitness, of
a genius wasted for being plucked unripe from the sunny places of the

world" (*OS,* 67; *ELC,* 135). The demands for unequivocal anwers, even for a coherent philosophical system, is again implicit in saying "How blind to him [Shakespeare] and to Hamlet, are all ultimate issues, and the sum total of things how unseizable" (*OS,* 57; *ELC,* 130).

A late essay, "Tragic Philosophy" (*Scrutiny* 4 [1936], also in *ELC*) shows a change of mind. Santayana discusses there T. S. Eliot's contrast between the despairing speech of Macbeth and the passage in *Paradiso* where Piccarda accepts God's will: "E' la sua voluntade è nostra pace" (III, 85). He thinks them rightly "incommensurable" (*ELC,* 270) but then he contrasts "the rich and thick medium" of Macbeth's speech with the transparent reasoning of Dante's verse fancifully evoked. "Each word, each rhyme, files dutifully by in procession, white verses, three abreast, like choristers, holding each his taper and each singing in turn his appointed note" (272). But then Santayana, while still saying that "Macbeth's philosophy is that there is no philosophy, because, in fact, he is incapable of any" (268), considers Dante's whole universe "childishly unreal. We can understand why Mr. Eliot feels his to be 'superior' philosophy; but how can he fail to see that it is false?" (274). Seneca, whom Eliot considered the main source of Shakespeare's views, and Shakespeare "stuck fast in the facts of life" (275). Santayana approves stating the truth, which he sees in conflict with inspiration, his term for imagination. This is to him tragedy and the tragedy of religion is its defeat by Truth (276). Truth is Santayana's own skepticism tempered by animal faith. It is hardly a philosophy of tragedy or even a tragic philosophy.

An essay on Shelley (1913, in *WD,* also in *ELC*) puts the question of "the poetic value of revolutionary principles." Santayana disapproves of revolution. "The life of reason is a heritage and exists only through tradition" (*WD,* 156; *ELC,* 187). He dislikes the "theoretical destructiveness," "the wantonness of Shelley's invectives" (*WD,* 164; *ELC,* 193), accuses him of not understanding "the real constitution of nature," of "ignorance of this world," and of a "very unintelligent view of evil" (*WD,* 168, 174, 173; *ELC,* 195, 199, 198). "His sympathies are narrow as his politics are visionary, so that there is a certain moral incompetence in his moral intensity" (*WD,* 172; *ELC,* 197). Still Santayana admires and defends Shelley. "He really has a great subject matter—what ought to be," he has "a vehement sense of wrong," a "vivid love of ideal good" (*WD,* 158, 164, 165; *ELC,* 188, 193, 192). "It was the purest, tenderest, richest, most rational nature ever poured forth in verse" (*WD,* 175; *ELC,* 199), but Shelley's Utopianism expecting paradise on earth just round the corner, his metaphysical Platonism, pantheism, and atheism remained "too hazy in its sublimity" (*WD,* 181; *ELC,* 204). Thus his poetry lacks solidity, remains lyrical, visionary, "quite unrealisable in this world of blood and mire." "The realm of eternal essences rains down no Jovian thunderbolts, but only a ghostly Uranian calm" (*WD,* 185; *ELC,* 207). In spite of some criticism of Arnold's formula, Santayana implicitly endorses Arnold's dubbing Shelley a "beautiful and ineffectual angel."

When he was in England during the war, Santayana read Dickens as a solace and escape, finding confirmation of his love for the English. The essay (in *Dial* 71 [1921], then in *Soliloquies in England,* 1922) is far from uncritical, however. Dickens is described as insensible to "religion, science, politics, art. He was a waif himself and utterly disinherited" (*ELC,* 211). He had "no *ideas* on any subject; his one political passion was philanthropy." In his novels "we may almost say there is no army, no navy, no church, no sport, no distant travel, no daring adventure." Unfortunately, he "inherited the most terrible negations. Religion lay on him like the weight of the atmosphere, sixteen pounds to the square inch, yet never noticed nor mentioned. He lived and wrote in the shadow of the most awful prohibitions" (212). Santayana then describes the world Dickens presented, the simple life worth living, the glow of the hearth, the charm of humble things, the nobleness of simple people, his concern for the deformed, the half-witted, the abandoned, all redeemed by a "sense of happy freedom in littleness" (216). Santayana defends then Dickens's caricatures. There *are* such people. "The most grotesque creatures of Dickens are not exaggerations or mockeries of something other than themselves, they arise because nature generates them, like toadstools" (220). Santayana admires Dickens's morality, his sense of the distinction between good and evil, his distrust of idealists who "do not wish mankind to be happy in its own way, but in theirs." "Love of the good of others is something that shines in every page of Dickens with a truly celestial splendor" (222). Dickens "is one of the best friends mankind has ever had." In conclusion Santayana exhorts "parents and children, in every English-speaking home, in the four corners of the globe, to read Dickens aloud on a winter's evening" (223), a patriotic and sentimental admonition out of tune with Santayana's usual detachment and air of superiority.

This survey of Santayana's comments on poetic theory and individual poets and writers does not, I must confess, bring out the personality of the man and philosopher so beautifully examined in his own three volumes of autobiography and defended eloquently in "Apologia pro mente sua." It does not convey the charm of his precise style which freed itself from early preciousness nor a feeling for the equanimity and justice of his mind. But I have not, I think, been unjust in my criticisms of individual theories and opinions. They are admittedly only a small fragment of his mental life, as criticism, at least literary criticism, was only a marginal or even inferior activity for him. In a 1922 letter to George Lawton, who urged him to give up metaphysics and devote all his time to literary criticism, Santayana answered: "Criticism is something incidental—talk about talk—and to my mind has no serious value except perhaps as an expression of *philosophy* in the critic. When I have been led to write criticism it has never been for any other reason" (*L*, 195–96). Then Santayana, appealing to Plato's "contempt for an image of an image," compares criticism to "poor original tea-leaves in their fifth wash of hot water." "And you are drinking slops."

In a less irritable mood, in a context not particularly limited to literary criticism, Santayana could see the function of criticism. He even admits that "a critical habit is perhaps more spontaneous in me than a constructive one. I like to lean on the works and opinions of others. . . . The secondary place of criticism, like that of reflection in general, has its prerogative. The critic gains a certain comprehensiveness, and the spontaneity of taste, without being suppressed, is challenged and enlightened. It clarifies our allegiances" (Schilpp, 549). "Criticism, by a transcendental necessity, is thus internal to each logical organism or rational mind," but "criticism," he concludes, "is necessarily relative to presuppositions which must be accepted on faith" (551, 553). This is, I fear, the sum of his wisdom: the appeal to the personality and to the authority of a critic established by his total life-work. Santayana must stand high in any general verdict, though paradoxically his strictly literary criticism remains fragmentary and marginal and often does not seem illuminated by the light of his philosophy.

4 : ACADEMIC CRITICISM

THE WAY criticism invaded and sometimes even took over the college and university teaching of literature in the United States differs considerably from the English story. There it was mainly a conflict between the traditional classical training and the new subject, English. English was often defended with nationalistic and social arguments. It fostered pride in the past and the Empire; it helped to educate the masses which had no access to Latin and Greek. English had to justify itself by imposing subjects and methods requiring rigorous and intense study: Anglo-Saxon, Germanic philology; biographical and bibliographical studies and editions were stressed throughout the nineteenth century. Only in the early twentieth century did criticism capture the academy, even though the figure of Matthew Arnold had loomed in the background, neglected at first but then taken up as an inspiration, if not a model, by much later critics, I. A. Richards and F. R. Leavis.

In the United States the situation was very different. Criticism in the colleges survived in the terms of eighteenth-century rhetoric and oratory. Hugh Blair's *Lectures on Rhetoric and Belles Letters* (1782) were adopted as textbooks by Yale in 1785, by Harvard in 1788, and were reprinted many times in the early nineteenth century. Scholarship in English literature and the modern languages was almost nonexistent, except at Harvard College. George Ticknor (1791–1871), a diplomat by profession, for a time a Harvard professor, wrote a *History of Spanish Literature* (3 vols., 1849) which was a well-documented firsthand account, surpassing the early books by Friedrich Bouterwek and Jean-Charles-Leonard Sismondi and preceding serious Spanish work. Francis James Child (1825–1896) edited *The English and Scottish Popular Ballads* (1857–58, new edition in 5 vols.), which for the first time collected all versions on sound editorial principles. The situation changed rapidly with the founding in 1876 of Johns Hopkins University, which provided graduate instruction on the German model and the founding of the Modern Language Association in 1883. The explosion of English and to a lesser extent French and

German scholarship which followed did not, however, help the cause of criticism. It was primarily antiquarian and philological with emphasis on Old English, Middle English, and Shakespeare. It was, in part at least, inspired by a nostalgia for Teutonic roots and the Middle Ages and by a hardly compatible desire to emulate the natural sciences in hunting for facts and looking for causes in literary and historical sources. Teutonic racism, the original inspiration of *Germanistik* which included Old English, was for obvious reasons an artificial growth in America, and so was romantic medievalism, which had no roots in a largely Protestant and commercial society. American colleges and universities were far more isolated from their cultural surroundings than the metropolitan universities on the European Continent (Paris, Berlin, Vienna). They encouraged withdrawing to the academic ivory tower, the enhancing of the professors' self-esteem and social status by indulgence in "mysteries" incomprehensible and useless outside the university—useless even to the majority of students who went out to teach composition, language, and literature in the small colleges and large state universities where they had taken over the old function of rhetorical instruction. The separation between academic scholarship and the practice of literature became even wider when the genteel tradition was replaced by naturalism and regionalism, with the descent of American writers into the slums and stockyards, farms and mines, and with growing distrust of "Europe," the intellect, tradition, and learning in general.

This antiquarian scholarship dominated American universities and colleges well into the twentieth century. It has many achievements to its credit: editions, biographies, historical studies, investigations of sources, and so on, but failed to live up to an ideal of humane learning as well as to the practical demands of teachers. I remember meeting a professor, the late Carlton Green, at the University of Hawaii, who with wry humor complained how well he had been prepared to teach his students for forty years by his Harvard thesis on "Placenames in the Venerable Bede." Still, there is a good argument for a place—at least in the best universities, equipped as they are today with splendid libraries—for preserving and cultivating even the remotest corners of literary history, as there is a place for classical and Oriental studies even of the most esoteric kind. But the imposition of this specialized learning on all and sundry interested in literature as a living force became intolerable.

The revolt came first from the teachers who felt the effects of the English aesthetic movement and thus offered "appreciation," a romantic enthusiasm for the good and the beautiful, sweetness unaccompanied by light. The memoirs of men who have described their years of study around the turn of the century—Bliss Perry's *And Gladly Teach* (1935), Henry Seidel Canby's *Alma Mater* (1936), and William Lyon Phelps's *Autobiography with Letters* (1939)—voice deep discontent with the prevailing system. Phelps was the first teacher at Yale to offer a course on the contemporary novel (1895–96), promptly dropped at the insistence of his superiors who threatened him with dismissal, and the first American scholar to write on *The Russian Novelists* (1911). The book opens with the statement, "Russian fiction is like German music—the best in the world." But the love of literature which Phelps and comparable teachers elsewhere instilled in their students was without critical standards and intellectual rigor. Phelps was drawn more and more into reviewing which became hardly more than gushing advertising for books. One can exempt Lewis E. Gates (1860–1924), a Harvard professor whose *Studies and Appreciations* (1900) gives a reasoned defense of "Impressionism," "the individual bliss of the hearer." "The critic," he argues, "must have much of the dilettante's fine irresponsibility, perhaps even the cynic's amused aloofness from the keen competitions of daily life" (232). While this and similar passages stress enjoyment against explanation and judgment, Gates constantly acknowledges that "there is something objective in a work of art" (214), that the critic "must be alive to a work of art" as "a delicate transparent illustration of aesthetic law" (233). Gates has interest, unique at that time and place, in Dilthey referring to *Die Einbildungskraft des Dichters* (215) and in an article on "Taine's Influence as a Critic" (1893), welcomes even his materialism "as healthy as sea-air" (204). Unfortunately Gates produced little. His selections from Jeffrey, Arnold, and Newman with good introductions are hardly innovative.

Then Joel Elias Spingarn attempted to introduce the aesthetics and critical principles of Benedetto Croce.

JOEL ELIAS SPINGARN (1875–1939)

In 1910 J. E. Spingarn, then Professor of Comparative Literature at Columbia University, gave a public lecture, "The New Criticism," which attracted a good deal of attention. Spingarn used the term as Benedetto Croce used it to refer to his own theories. The lecture[1] is little more than an exposition of some of the rejections stated in Croce's *Estetica*. It very quickly disposes of impressionism, "the adventures among masterpieces," historical criticism in the sense of background studies, psychological criticism, dogmatic criticism (judgment by rules), aesthetic criticism (speculations about art and beauty), all "shifting the interest from the work of art to something else" (*CC*, 7). Spingarn suggests by contrasting Scaliger and Aretino, Boileau and Saint-Évremond, that the conflict between dogmatists and impressionists pervades the whole history of criticism which he finds, since Madame de Staël, dominated by the idea of "expression." He rephrases it in the terms of Goethe's review of Manzoni: "What has the poet tried to do, and how has he fulfilled his intention? What is he striving to express and how has he expressed it?" Spingarn then simply expounds Croce's rejections, content to describe his basic view as "expression is art" without making any attempt to explain its very special meaning in the context of the whole Crocean system of the moments of the spirit. The result is a mere list of things the new critic "has done with": the rules, the genres, concepts such as the comic, the tragic, the sublime; style and all rhetorical terms such as metaphor and simile; the confusion to drama and theater, technique, versification, the history and criticism of poetic themes, concern for race, time and environment, the evolution of literature, and finally the old rupture between genius and taste. Its overcoming is considered "the final achievement by modern thought on the subject of art" (37).

Not surprisingly these rather bald rejections gave rise to misgivings and protests. Spingarn developed some points in later articles: "Notes on Dramatic Criticism"[2] asserted the independence of drama and theater, rejecting the history of the theater as irrelevant to criticism. "All these external conditions are merely dead material which have no aesthetic significance outside of the poet's soul" (CC, 87). The identification of taste and genius, the recommendation of "creative criticism" evoked the ghost of Oscar Wilde and lent support to the charge of "aestheticism" and "impressionism." H. L. Mencken, who was delighted with Spingarn's anti-academic sallies, doubted the idea of "creative criticism" and wanted to substitute "catalytic" criticism.[3] Paul Elmer More accused Spingarn of impressionism and Spingarn later tangled with Irving Babbitt. Spingarn reviewed *Masters of French Criticism* severely, criticizing Babbitt as a "moralist of considerable power" but not "a critic or student of criticism" (CC, 189). In the original review (in *Journal of Philosophy* 10 [1913]: 693–95) he spoke of Babbitt as "Brunetière speaking English" but in the reprint (in *Creative Criticism*, 1931) Spingarn professed to see "a much closer parallel to Thomas Rymer," the seventeenth-century critic whom Macaulay had called "the worst critic that ever lived." An article, "Scholarship and Criticism," in Harold E. Stearns's iconoclastic *Civilization in the United States* (1922) depicted the American university as being "created for the special purpose of ignoring or destroying scholarship" (95). Ticknor's *History of Spanish Literature* and some Dante scholarship are the only achievements which find favor in Spingarn's eyes. "Of the general level of our French and German studies I prefer to say nothing and silence is also wisest in the case of English" (96). The state of criticism seems to Spingarn equally deplorable. The dominance of moralistic criteria and the absence of any concern for aesthetics are the main charges: sensibility, training in taste, a "wider international outlook" are Spingarn's wishes.

Spingarn, however, never practiced what he preached. He had been an eminent student of the history of criticism. His *History of Literary Criticism in the Renaissance* (1899) was praised by Croce and is still a standard work. Spingarn pursued the topic further in an edition of *Critical Essays of the [English] Seventeenth Century* (3 vols., 1908–09) with an elaborate introduction. He helped to found the *Journal of Comparative Literature* and always kept comparative views in his mind. He caused a sensation by a review of a huge French thèse (Magendie's *La Politesse mondaine et les théories de honnêteté en France au XVIIe siècle*, 1926) in which he showed that the neglect of Italian antecedents and sources had vitiated the whole argument. The history of the idea of the gentleman had been one of Spingarn's own projects. He abandoned historical scholarship which was his actual strength, when he was, in 1911, fired from Columbia University by President Nicholas Murray Butler, largely because he had defended a colleague who had been expelled for getting involved in a breach-of-promise suit. Spingarn had to leave academic life and devoted the rest of his life to founding the National Association for the Advancement of Colored People, of which he was president until his death, to the organizing of the publishing house, Harcourt, Brace and Company, and to horticultural pursuits: he became an authority on the clematis. These biographical details are needed to explain the fact that Spingarn's role as theorist of literature remained a short episode. There is no evidence that he "more than anyone else of his generation" supplied "rationale and method for the analytical criticism of Eliot and the critics of the thirties and forties," as Robert Spiller asserts in the *Literary History of the United States* (1155). Allusions to Spingarn are very rare and J. C. Ransom would have never entitled his book *The New Criticism* (1941) if he had even known about Spingarn's lecture. Spingarn did valuable work as a historian of critical ideas and did something to draw attention to Croce. But Croce need not to have been filtered through Spingarn: he was read in Douglas Ainslie's clumsy translation of the early *Estetica* while the bulk of his work was and is being ignored.

THE CHICAGO ARISTOTELIANS

The debate about the role of criticism in the university was revived when John Livingston Lowes, a Harvard professor, author of a justly admired source study of Coleridge's *Ancient Mariner* and *Kubla Kahn* called *The Road to Xanadu* (1926), proclaimed in his presidential address to the Modern Language Association that the "ultimate end of our research is criticism in the fullest sense of an often misused word" (*PMLA* 48 [1933]: 1399–1408). Howard Mumford Jones, author of the impressive study *America and French Culture, 1750–1848* (1927), replied that literary scholarship should be "historical, not aesthetic" (*English Journal* 23 [1934]: 740–58). This gave occasion to Ronald Salmon Crane (1886–1967), a learned and acute historian of ideas, mainly of the eighteenth century, a severe reviewer of shoddy scholarship, to proclaim a sharp distinction of "History versus Criticism in the Study of Literature" (*English Journal* 24 [1935]: 645–67, reprinted in *IH*, 2:3–24). History was to be kept and even made immune from inroads of criticism. "Narratives of literary history must remain indifferent to questions of literary values" (2:8) while literary criticism is "simply the disciplined consideration, at once analytical and evaluative, of literary works as works of art" (2:12). Crane emphasized justly the need for theory and its grounding in general philosophy and the need for concentrating on an analysis of works of art apart from their origins in the minds of the authors and their causes in society and history. Finally the introduction of criticism into the university was strongly advocated. The article did not commit itself to any specific critical method at that time but in the next years, under the influence of Richard McKeon, Professor of Philosophy at the University of Chicago, Crane developed a theory which has become known as "Chicago Aristotelianism." Besides a group at the University of Chicago— Elder Olson, Norman Maclean, R. W. Keast, Bernard Weinberg—the doctrine has made only a few converts and has never spread beyond the confines of the university and its organ, *Modern Philology*. In 1952, however, the group brought out a large volume, *Critics and Criticism,* which collected expositions of the theory, criticism of rival theories, historical studies, and some interpretations of texts written over a number of years.

The group, one should stress, asserts the plurality of distinct critical methods (*CC,* 9) and calls its commitment to Aristotle "hypothetical, and not dogmatic" (11). A relativism, even universal tolerance, seems to be proclaimed but actually the group was convinced that its method is the only right and legitimate method for an analysis of literature and condemned, often in the harshest terms, all alternative approaches. One can even say that the group made its strongest impact with the destructive articles on I. A. Richards (R. S. Crane), Cleanth Brooks (R. S. Crane), William Empson (Elder Olson), R. P. Warren (Elder Olson), and Robert Heilman (W. R. Keast), to which we must add the wholesale condemnation of all modern criticism in Crane's lecture series, *The Languages of Criticism and the Structure of Poetry* (1953). Conviction of one's own rightness is inevitable, even though the proclamation of universal tolerance sounds unnecessarily hypocritical. One should grant that the group scored many points against the incriminated critics: Richards is guilty of psychologism, Cleanth Brooks has a narrow concept of poetry as irony, Robert Heilman sees *King Lear* as a mere pattern of imagery, Empson juggles with his types of ambiguity, R. P. Warren pressed the symbolism of the *Ancient Mariner* far too hard. Some of the criticisms are simply appeals to common sense and the laws of evidence, but underlying it all is the claim that all modern critical theory has gone astray since it deserted the teaching of Aristotle. It has become "dialectical," a pejorative term for any theory which is suspected of being Platonic. Aristotle is considered the only theorist who devised a scheme to study poems as a class of objects, as concrete artistic wholes (*CC*, 14), while all later criticism beginning with Longinus considered poems as a mode of discourse. Criticism instead of studying concrete works concerned itself with general poetic qualities or with what the Chicago group calls "dialectics," the differences between poetry in general and other activities of man: the other arts and sciences in particular. The recommended method is to use Aristotle's "parts" of Greek tragedy, plot, the imitation of human action, character, thought, diction, spectacle, in this order, with emphasis on plot and pleasure, the result of catharsis, as the end of art. It remains unclear why modern methods have not succeeded in analyzing concrete works as wholes by their methods and why "plot" and "pleasure" have to be considered the central problems of poetics. Imitation was refuted by the German romantics and Coleridge. In McKeon's very learned and wide-ranging account of literary theories which mentions almost every name of the history of criticism, neither Friedrich Schlegel nor F. W. J. Schelling are even referred to. "Pleasure" is a meaningless description of the effect of poetry. Croce was right when he said that defining art by pleasure is like defining fish by the water they swim in. Pleasure and displeasure are ubiquitous and catharsis, purgation of pity and fear, is obscure and hardly relevant to most poetry. Also, the whole preoccupation of the Chicago group with rigid genre distinctions seems mistaken. Genres flow into each other: there is epic in drama, drama in epic, epic in the lyric, lyric in the epic and the drama and so on in all variations. One need not accept Croce's total rejection of the concept and can recognize the role of genre as a formal model in history to see that the Chicago group's belief in rigid genre distinctions leads to unprofitable dilemmas. Thus we are told that there is a sharp distinction between mimetic and didactic poetry, with the conclusion that Dante's *Divine Comedy* is declared to be didactic and not mimetic (*CC*, 590). It is wrong to consider action and symbol in the *Divine Comedy* as if the poem had not plenty of action and was full of symbols and still could advocate a doctrine. The order of the "parts" in Aristotle's discussion of Greek tragedy requires the Chicago group to downplay the language of poetry which they conceive, more like Scaliger than Aristotle, as the inert matter on which the poet imprints his form. This is why Crane can call Cleanth Brooks a "materialist monist" (93) and why the group shows no interest in modern linguistics or in close reading, understood as attention to contextual semantics, to ambiguity, paradox, and irony.

The Chicago group are learned historians of criticism with the impractical ideal of complete objectivity and completeness of evidence. One should recognize and admire McKeon's many contributions to the history of ancient and medieval criticism, the erudition and analytical acuteness of Crane's reflections on eighteenth-century criticism as well as his classification of recent critical trends in the Alexander lectures. He also wrote a valuable schematic survey, "Critical and Historical Principles of Literary History" (*IH*, 2:45–156), which has been, I believe, totally ignored, and a history of "The Idea of Humanities" (1:3–170) which traces the shifting definitions and evaluations of the humanities from the Renaissance to seventeenth- and eighteenth-century ideas but has a yawning gap. The name of Goethe is not even mentioned, and the whole phalanx of Germans (Winckelmann, Herder, Schiller, Wilhelm von Humboldt) who did so much to revive the idea of humanity and the humanities is ignored, an omission possibly explainable by the date (1943) of the original lectures. One also must admire the learning with which Bernard Weinberg, in his *History of Literary Criticism in the Italian Renaissance* (2 vols., 1961), disentangled the controversies of the time and earlier in *French Realism: The Critical Reaction: 1830–1870* (1937) examined all the evidence.

Acknowledging all the learning which went into the Chicago enterprise, we must ask whether they were able to demonstrate the fruitfulness of their theory by a study of concrete texts of literature. There were several attempts to do so with what seems to me meager results. The first was Olson's analysis of Yeats's "Sailing to Byzantium" which replaces the Aristotelian "plot" with the "argument" of a lyrical poem, tracing it in bald language, step by step (*Kansas City University Review* 8 [1942]: 209–19). Crane analyzed the plots of Jane Austen's *Persuasion* and of two Hemingway short stories, "The Killers" and "The Short Happy Life of Francis Macomber." Each time he tries to establish a dominant theme.

Thus in discussing "The Killers" he argues that Ole Anderson waiting passively for the killer is the theme of the story and not Nick Adams's initiation into the reality of evil, as Brooks and Warren had argued in *Understanding Fiction. Persuasion* has, Crane tells us, a "plot of internal action," Anne Eliot's recognition of Wentworth's intelligence and goodness of heart while all the other business in Lyme and with the Musgroves remains mere "occasions," mere "treatment."

Crane's most elaborate and longest paper on the "Concept of Plot and the Plot of *Tom Jones*" (*IH*, 2:616–47) propounds a concept of plot which is more than a series of events but includes considerations of character and thought and of general effect. In a note Crane concedes that "some other word than 'plot' to designate the formal principle I have been attempting to define" (*CC*, 632n.) should be found. This "plot" is a function of three variables, the nature of the events, the moral character and deserts of the hero, and the degree of responsibility of what happens to him (632). Crane then argues (assuming that catharsis and our pleasure in it is the end of art) that the events are invented and told to make us feel "comic pleasure" (635), as our pity and fear is greatly attenuated by Fielding's concepts of Tom's impulsive generosity and gallantry and the pervasive irony of the telling. Some of the devices of the plot are minutely rehearsed and some minor criticisms are made, but, at the end, Crane confesses, honest and straightforward as he is, that we have to go beyond "formal" criticism of his kind and need other terms and distinctions "if we are to talk discriminatingly about the general qualities of intelligence and feeling in *Tom Jones*" (646) and thus be able to defend Fielding against Leavis's "somewhat insensitive judgement" (646). Here and elsewhere, for instance, in his comments on Gray's "Elegy on a Country Churchyard" (*LCSP*, 175–76), it becomes obvious that within Crane's system every poem must be perfect, as there is no standard by which to judge it. As Yvor Winters remarked in *The Function of Criticism*, "Criticism would be forestalled at the outset" (21).

The Chicago Aristotelianism remained a strictly local, academic affair and left few traces though a younger man, Wayne Booth, who later wrote a persuasive refutation of the dogma of "objective" fiction, *The Rhetoric of Fiction* (1961), professed allegiance to the creed. Criticism, however, triumphed in the academy only with the New Criticism, which also had to struggle for recognition. It succeeded because its pedagogical weapon, "close reading," popularized mainly by Brooks and Warren in *Understanding Poetry* (1938), caught on in the 1940s. Yale adopted it as a classroom text in 1940 and in 1946 called Cleanth Brooks from Louisiana. At Harvard F. O. Matthiessen expounded *The Achievement of T. S. Eliot*

(1935) and the *American Renaissance* (1941). At Princeton Allen Tate was brought in for the writing program and his successor, R. P. Blackmur, managed to move into the English Department as a full professor though he never had finished high school. At Stanford Yvor Winters struggled for years for recognition. J. C. Ransom stayed at a quiet little Ohio college but exercised wide influence as editor of the *Kenyon Review.* Robert Heilman moved in 1948 from Louisiana to the University of Washington in Seattle. Even Robert Penn Warren, primarily a novelist and poet, has been since 1950 a number of years in loose association with Yale, and Kenneth Burke, though one of the few critics who shunned the academy, taught intermittently at Bennington College, Vermont, and made guest appearances elsewhere. These fates of the original New Critics concern only the early years and a few institutions. The establishment of the New Criticism in the academy was a much longer process and slowly covered the whole country. The old violent conflict between history and criticism all but vanished, though it must be still smouldering and may reappear in the future.

MORE SCHOLAR-CRITICS

Not only the Chicago Aristotelians and later some of the New Critics combined scholarship and criticism. But also conventional literary historians began in the twenties to step beyond strictly positivist academic scholarship. When I was a graduate student of English at Princeton University in 1927–28, John Livingston Lowes's *Road to Xanadu* (1927) was felt like a breath of fresh air. The Harvard professor (1867–1945) had studied Coleridge's reading, which shaped the making of *The Ancient Mariner* and *Kubla Khan,* with prodigious learning and detective skill. He wrote an elaborate, often precious prose describing his hunt for sources as an exciting story and set it all within an ambitious framework of a psychology of the creative process. On second thought, however, one must conclude that the psychology consists only of a few easily manipulated metaphors about the deep well, the hooked atoms, and the "sea-change," an image from Ariel's song in *The Tempest,* which has since become a hackneyed bore. The book could be condensed to a list of possible parallel passages tucked away in an edition of these poems.

The book is rent by the conflict between the associationist psychology Lowes employs throughout which would make these poems examples of mere "fancy" and the constant gestures toward some ultimate mystery: "We may only marvel and bow the head" (428). At the same time Lowes dismisses Coleridge's "metaphysical lucubrations" and his "nebulous theories" on imagination and fancy, questioning the distinction (103) and thus preventing an understanding of *Kubla Khan* which is reduced to an incoherent dream "in which 'thinking' abdicated its control" (413). In spite of its impressive scholarship and appealing narration, the book is an example of theoretical confusion.

Other attempts to see literature not as a social picture but as an art came from students of genres and devices. Elmer Edgar Stoll (1874–1959) in many books, particularly *Shakespearean Studies* (1927), *Poets and Playwrights* (1930), *Art and Artifice in Shakespeare* (1932), *Shakespeare and Other Masters* (1940), and *From Shakespeare to Joyce* (1944), argues against treating drama as a transcript of life and on behalf of the importance of stage conventions, stock figures, and situations as crucial for critical interpretations. Stoll has done much to put Shakespeare firmly back on the stage and to refute the pseudoproblems of modern Shakespearean scholarship, such as Iago's "motiveless malignity" or Falstaff's "courage." He has shown that there is much archaic technique in Shakespeare, who must not be judged with the standards of Ibsen or Shaw. He has argued persuasively that Restoration comedy is not "a 'real society,' not a faithful picture even of the 'fashionable life'; evidently it is not England, even 'under the Stuarts,' whether since or before the Revolution or the Great Rebellion" (*From Shakespeare to Joyce,* 63). Still, the salutary emphasis on convention and tradition cannot completely discharge the relations between literature and society. Even the most abstruse allegory, the most fanciful pastoral, the most outrageous farce, properly interrogated, tells us something of the society of a time. Actually, the limits Stoll puts on the interpretation of Shakespeare by arguing that everything that was not comprehensible to the contemporary audience must be excluded from Shakespeare's meaning lands him in a historicism that assigns the scholar an impossible task: reconstructing a vanished theater audience and its reactions and also forbidding him to find (and not only invent) riches in a text that may have been invisible to a contemporary. It asks us to forget three hundred years of history; it impoverishes works that have attracted and accumulated meanings since their inception. We simply cannot avoid judging ourselves from our present-day point of view, as Stoll did himself in condemning wholesale all allegorical, symbolical, and psychoanalytical interpretations.

Stoll's younger colleague at Minnesota, Joseph Warren Beach (1880–1957), was the first American student of the technique of the novel. Inspired by Henry James, on whose method he wrote a perceptive book (*The Method of Henry James,* 1918), and later influenced by Percy Lubbock's *Craft of Fiction,* he traced the evolution of novelistic technique in American and European fiction (*The Twentieth Century Novel: Studies in Technique,* 1932, and *American Fiction, 1920–40,* 1941) from the Victorian novel to the novel he calls "well-made" when Flaubert enforced the idea of "exit author" to what Beach calls expressionist novel writing: Gide, Dos Passos, Joyce, D. H. Lawrence. "Narratology," as it is now called, has since become an industry on the confines of criticism and historical scholarship. Its American pioneer should not be forgotten.

Even stylistics had at least one distinguished practitioner among American scholars before the impact of the German *Stilforschung* imported by Leo Spitzer and Erich Auerbach. Morris W. Croll (1872–1947) wrote a series of subtle analytical papers on Latin, French, and English prose style from Lyly's *Euphues* to Sir Thomas Browne. Particularly the paper on "The Baroque Style in Prose" (1929) is a masterpiece of observation and classification: the Euphuistic, Senecan, Tacitean, and Libertine trends are clearly distinguished and sensitively analyzed. Unfortunately, it took many years before Croll's essays could be collected after his death.[1]

It seems to be an act of justice to point out these three scholars (there may be others) who early cultivated an intense study of works of art before the methods of the New Criticism caught on and apart from the cross-fertilization of the new "history of ideas," as it was defined by Arthur O. Lovejoy (1873–1962), the eminent philosopher and historian of philosophy. Lovejoy formulated a concept of intellectual history that would be set off both from the usual history of philosophy and the German *Geistesgeschichte.* It differs from the history of philosophy by studying "the repercussions of ideas outside the great technical systems" (*EHI,* 8), particularly in literature. The systems of philosophy are broken up into "unit-ideas," which can be traced in their ramifications in the diverse disciplines, as Lovejoy demonstrated magisterially in *The Great Chain of Being* (1936). The philosophical systems are examined for their contradictions and internal tensions. Lovejoy rejects the German *Geistesgeschichte,* which tries to construe a unitary *Zeitgeist* as irrational, and examines key terms, catchwords such as Nature or Romanticism, with the jaundiced eye of a nominalist. "Semantic history" is central to Lovejoy's method and practice. An appendix to his and George Boas's *Primitivism and Related Ideas in Antiquity* (1935) contains a table of sixty-five meanings of the word "Nature," and the word "romantic" seems to him so ambiguous and contradictory that it "has come to mean so many things that by itself it means nothing" (*EHI,* 232). He suggests that we should learn to use the word "romanticism" in the plural and that the "romanticism of one country has little in common with that of another." Romanticism is described as holding "ideas in large part heterogeneous, logically independent and sometimes essentially antithetic to another in their implications" (see *Journal of the History of Ideas* 2 [1941]: 261). I have tried to show[2] that this extreme skepticism is unwarranted, that all the main romantic movements show close affinities, and that romantic ideas form a tightly coherent whole. The romantic concept of imagination, symbol, myth, and organic nature implicate each other. While Lovejoy recommends discarding the concept and the word, he is in several papers preoccupied with describing the great historical change from the Enlightenment to romanticism. Several items in *Essays in the History of Ideas* (1948) trace individual phases of this process. "The Chinese Origins of a Romanticism," "The First Gothic Revival and the Return to Nature," and others on Herder, Schiller, Friedrich Schlegel, Coleridge, and Kant are concerned with these shifts in terms reconcilable with older conceptions. Both in *The Great Chain of Being* and in later papers Lovejoy operates with concepts such as organism, dynamism, and what he calls "diversitarianism," which are descriptive of what is usually called romantic. One paper, "The Parallel of Deism and Classicism," raises the problem central to German *Geistesgeschichte*. Lovejoy shows that deism, a radical heterodoxy, and neoclassicism, an orthodox literary theory, have many assumptions in common. The parallel is drawn so cautiously and persuasively that we must be convinced that we are getting at the "time spirit" of the eighteenth century, which Lovejoy would prefer to call the "unconscious mental habits" or the "diverse kinds of metaphysical pathos" prevalent at that time. Lovejoy's enterprise must be welcomed: his immense learning, wide historical perspective, which includes classical antiquity and the classical period of Germany, and his analytical acuteness make him a great figure not only in American scholarship. Still, some misgivings remain. The concept of "unit-ideas" is atomistic: they are conceived as something almost fixed, which enters only into external relations with different systems or areas of thought. They change only because of their place in a system and not in their internal nature. They somehow precede the shifting verbal labels that were attached to them in the course of history. This course is conceived as an almost self-sustaining process of movement of ideas apart from the general context of political history and social change. This excessive intellectualism becomes a danger when the "History of Ideas" is offered as a substitute for literary history. Lovejoy himself does not force his criteria on the history of literature. The paper "Milton and the Paradox of the Fortunate Fall" illuminates a passage in *Paradise Lost* but is not offered as literary criticism, rather as exegesis in terms of its theological background. Nor are the passages from Pope, Akenside, and others quoted in *The Great Chain of*

Being offered otherwise than as examples of the spread of philosophical ideas to didactic poetry. But in the introductory chapter to *The Great Chain of Being,* Lovejoy draws a distinction between the study of literature chiefly for its thought-content and the enjoyment of it as art. "The interest of the history of literature is largely a record of the movement of ideas . . . and ideas in serious reflective literature are, of course, in great part philosophical ideas in dilution" (*GCB,* 16–17). If we ignore the reservation of "largely" and "in great part," we must conclude that Lovejoy conceives of literature as the water added to philosophy. We all should then give up studying the diluted product in favor of the genuine article of philosophy. Imposing philosophical standards on the world of imagination, which must not only be enjoyed but contemplated and studied, would constitute another reductionism parallel to the doctrines of Marxism and psychoanalysis.

This happened, often quite independently of Lovejoy, particularly in the study of American literature, which in its early stages has little to offer to a taste for art. Vernon L. Parrington's (1871–1929) *Main Currents of American Thought* (1927–30) became the standard account of American literary history. The title speaking of "thought" is modified by the subtitle, "An Interpretation of American Literature from the Beginnings to 1920." In practice, the books are mainly a history of American political thought as reflected in literature. An uneasy compromise is achieved: political ideas, Parrington tells us in his introduction, are "anterior to literary schools and movements, creating the body of ideas from which literary culture eventually springs" (*MC,* 1:111). This may be true of the early United States but seems an unproven generalization for many other literatures. The emphasis on political ideas is somewhat modified by attention to economic, social, and theological ideas, but in practice Parrington has little to say concretely about economic and social conditions and ideas. Parrington has been called a Marxist and was certainly welcomed in the Depression years as a Marxist, but there is no evidence that he actually used a Marxist method or approach. He had socialist sympathies, had read William Morris, and learned from Charles A. Beard about the economic interpretation of the American Revolution and the Constitution, but he is right in asserting that he "holds no brief for a rigid scheme of economic determinism" (3:xx). He is a straightforward historian of ideas, who does little to explain their origins. Georg Brandes, from whom he drew the title and whose liberal pathos he shared, is the nearest comparable figure rather than Taine. He has nothing of Taine's Hegelianism or attention to climate and race, except for one passage that reflects on the influence of Melville's mixed English and Dutch ancestry (2:210).

Parrington's own bias for Jeffersonian democracy is openly declared. His cast of mind is eighteenth-century, rationalistic, utilitarian, realist, and thus unsympathetic to the old Puritans and to any theology. Parrington, who was born in Aurora, Illinois, was a self-conscious Westerner who taught English Literature for years in Kansas and Oklahoma and only became prominent as a Professor of English at the University of Washington in Seattle. He had spent an unhappy year at Harvard and ever since resented what he felt to be the condescending snobbery of New England. He had, however, a surprising sympathy for what he called "the mind of the Old South." The books impressed by their vivid, first-hand accounts of many minor figures, by the skill of character-drawing, and the often rhetorical pathos of his political allegiance, which is strongly anti-English, egalitarian, "liberal" in the peculiar American sense.

Considered as literary history, the books are, however, disappointing. Parrington has contempt for what he calls the "belletristic," though he recognizes occasionally that literary standards have to be used. Thus Hamlin Garland's *A Spoil of Office*, he notes, is "a social tract rather than a work of art" (*MC* 3:298). He makes it easy for himself by declaring "the problem of Poe, fascinating as it is," to be "quite outside the main current of American thought," to be left "with psychologist and belletrist with whom it belongs" (2:50). He can disparage Henry James as "aloof from the homely realities of life," as "shut up within his own skull-pan," "concerned only with *nuances*" (3:241). Similarly, Hawthorne is relegated to a world "forever dealing with shadows" (2:446). There is in Hawthorne "no suggestion of interest in the creative ideas of the time, in metaphysics or politics or economics or humanitarianism" (2:447), hardly a convincing accusation of the author of a campaign biography of President Franklin Pierce. Hawthorne's work "slides into symbolism and allegory" (2:446), terms used interchangeably and pejoratively. Hawthorne, Parrington concludes, "was the extreme and finest expression of the refined alienation from reality that in the end palsied the creative mind of New England" (2:450). Consistently, Parrington disparages James Russell Lowell as a "bookish amateur of letters" from whom "history remained a blank" (2:461). "For twenty one years he wandered with Norton and Longfellow and Child in the Sahara of medieval scholarship" (2:465). Also, Longfellow's "door shut securely against all intrusion. The winds of doctrine and policy might rage through the land, but they did not

rattle the windows of his study to disturb his quiet poring over Dante"
(2:440). Though the sections on Emerson, Thoreau, and Melville are
more sympathetic, they deplore the mysticism of the transcendentalists
and the pessimism of Melville. Still, unexpectedly, Emerson, "a Puritan
of the Puritans," is praised in conclusion as a "free soul," as "the flowering of two centuries of spiritual aspiration—Roger Williams and Jonathan Edwards come to more perfect fruition" (2:399), and Thoreau is
somewhat obscurely termed "a Greek turned transcendental economist"
(2:401). It is not surprising that Whitman appears to Parrington "a great
figure, the greatest assuredly in our literature" (3:86), the "completest
embodiment of the Enlightenment—the poet and prophet of a democracy that the America of the Gilded Age was daily betraying" (3:69). One
would expect Parrington to welcome the rise of realism, but Howells gets
only lukewarm praise. He appears as a "specialist of women's nerves, an
analyst of the tenuous New England conscience, a master of Boston
small-talk" (3:250). The last volume of Parrington's *Main Currents,* "Beginnings of Critical Realism in America," remained unfinished and was
not improved by reprinting with it an earlier essay about "The Incom-
parable Mr. Cabell" (1921). There was a residue of aestheticism in Parrington's taste for James Branch Cabell and Hergesheimer that clashed
with his ideological preoccupations. Important as Parrington's history
was, *Main Currents of American Thought* deflected studies of American
literature into concerns with political ideology.

The situation was rectified by F. O. Matthiessen's *American Renaissance*
(1941), the first book that gave a close reading and an aesthetic evaluation
of the great American authors around 1850: Emerson, Thoreau, Hawthorne, Melville, and Whitman. Matthiessen's enormously ambitious long
book (672 pages) had grown out of his studies of T. S. Eliot and Henry
James but was again affected by political ideology. Matthiessen was a
Socialist and saw his five authors he had studied sensitively and intently
finally as reducible to a common denominator: "their devotion to the
possibilities of democracy" (ix), a trivial conclusion obsessively repeated.
But we must see Matthiessen's book as the culmination of a distinguished
career as scholar and critic.

Francis Otto Matthiessen (1902–50), a native of Pasadena, California,
studied English literature as an undergraduate at Yale, as a Rhodes
scholar in Oxford, and as a graduate student under J. L. Lowes at Harvard. He wrote a thesis, *Translation: An Elizabethan Art* (1931), a close
examination of the translations from Castiglione, Plutarch, Montaigne,
Livy, and Suetonius. The highest praise goes to Philemon Holland for
his translation of Livy and Suetonius in terms clearly derived from T. S.

Eliot's concept of "unified sensibility." Holland possessed "the direct sensuous apprehension of thought." Saying that his thought "came to him with the same immediacy as the odor of a rose" (226) echoes the very phrasing of Eliot. But Matthiessen is not only persuaded of Holland's preeminence by the accuracy and colloquialism of his style, but praises his patriotic motivation. Holland thought of Livy and Suetonius not as ancient classics, but as "men with something to say that might be vital to England's destiny" (181). Even here, in this school work, Matthiessen's concern to make the past serve a present purpose is anticipated. *American Renaissance* was to be vital to America's destiny. The publication of the thesis was preceded (in 1929) by a monograph on the Maine author Sarah Orne Jewett (1849–1909). Matthiessen writes of her with the nostalgia for a vanished world. But it is not quite right to accuse him of sentimentality. He clearly sees her limitations and says expressly: "There is a stark New England Sarah Jewett does not show, sordid, bleak and mean of spirit" (149).

But the mature Matthiessen emerged with *The Achievement of T. S. Eliot* (1935). It shows that he had learned the lesson of the New Criticism that form and content are inseparable and that what matters "is not what a poem says but what it is" (vii). Matthiessen expounds and accepts Eliot's theory of literature, the impersonality of the author, the objective correlative, the dissociation of sensibility, the emphasis on visual imagination and colloquial language in order to show that "his criticism steadily illuminates the aims of his verse while his verse illustrates many aspects of his critical theory" (99) and to refute "the fallacy that there is no harmony between his 'revolutionary-creative' work and his 'traditionalist' criticism" (178). The book was written after Matthiessen had met Eliot during his stay at Harvard in 1933–34, when he delivered the lectures published as *The Use of Poetry and the Use of Criticism*. The lectures themselves disappointed Matthiessen as he thought that Eliot had "little aptitude for the historical method" (153), but he took to the man, his poetry, and his literary theories, though he even then distanced himself sharply from Eliot's turn toward orthodoxy and political conservatism. Matthiessen accepted the view that "for an appreciation of Eliot's poetry our acceptance or rejection of his doctrine remains irrelevant" (109), appealing to I. A. Richards's discussion of belief. The second edition (1947) added chapters on Eliot's plays and *The Four Quartets* and a preface that asserts his "growing divergence from Eliot's view of life" and proclaims himself a "political radical" (ix).

American Renaissance (1941) remains the star example of the reconciliation of literary history and criticism in American literary scholarship.

The scholarship itself is impressive. We can only smile that a printer's error, "soiled fish" instead of "coiled fish," seduced Matthiessen to look for a "metaphysical conceit" (392), for a *discordia concors*. We may wonder why Hegel's formula that "freedom is the recognition of necessity" should be ascribed to Engels (591), and whether it can be right to call Kafka "the almost pure example of the Freudian novelist" (313). But these are details which do not impair the exposition of his five authors, their styles, their "conception of the function and nature of literature and the degree their practice brought out their theories" (vi), their ethos, their political and philosophical views, and whatever seemed relevant of their biographies and their relations both to contemporaries, such as the Hawthorne-Melville friendship, or to models and antecedents. Melville's use of Shakespeare is the most striking and possibly too hard-pressed example.

A critical system or at least scheme is implied. Matthiessen firmly embraces the organic point of view, the identity of form and content. He appeals for its formulation not to the German sources, but to Croce, who in turn endorsed De Sanctis's concept of "form." Matthiessen read Croce's brief introduction to the English translation of De Sanctis's *History of Italian Literature* (1931). The identity of form and content allowed him to study both language and ideas, sometimes coming to surprising conclusions. Matthiessen can say that "Emerson, Thoreau and Whitman all conceived of themselves as poets, though judged strictly by form, none of them was" (*AR*, 55). It seems in flat contradiction to the drift of the book, which culminates in Whitman and praises his language experiment as well as his whole view of life. "The fusion of word and thing" is envisaged as the goal of art: Matthiessen quotes Whitman, "Nature will be my language full of poetry,—all nature will *fable*, and every natural phenomenon be a myth" (628). Organic form in Matthiessen leads to metaphor, to image—primarily visual—and finally to symbol and myth. The difference between symbol and allegory is for Matthiessen the main critical standard. He appeals again to Croce, quoting the *Aesthetics* (249), but again ignoring the sources in Goethe and Coleridge. As in Croce, allegory is disparaged and symbol exalted. A sharp line is drawn between the two: allegory is intellectual and has no aesthetic value. Symbol and symbolism imply the right merger of thought and passion (248). The distinction is turned against Hawthorne, "in whose writing there is none of the amalgamation of sense and thought that places both Melville and Thoreau in the metaphysical strain" (232). "Metaphysical" is used here in two different senses: it implies a continuity with metaphysical poetry and the seventeenth-century style. Thoreau and Melville show a kinship with the seventeenth century; both "felt close to the work of Sir Thomas Browne" (98). Compared to them, Hawthorne has an eighteenth-century taste and mind. "Hawthorne, alone of the five writers who have been the subject of this volume, did not conceive of his work in any relation to myth" (630). Matthiessen buttresses this by a list of Hawthorne's reading (230n.) and by emphasizing his distrust of the worship of nature. Thoreau, in contrast, has an "unswerving confidence that man could find himself by studying nature" (238). "Metaphysical," however, can also mean T. S. Eliot's much wider and looser concept of Henry James as a "metaphysical novelist" (232). The ideal is always that of unified sensibility, the total integrated man. The very last sentence of Matthiessen's book is a quotation from Coleridge, who "held to be the major function of the artist" to have "brought the whole soul of man into activity" (636). This is, after all, a very old ideal. Even Addison wanted man to be whole; Schiller, Jean Paul, and many others exalted it. It allows Matthiessen to construe a deep split between intellect and heart in Hawthorne and to dismiss Emerson's "double consciousness." He quotes Emerson: "The two lives of the understanding and of the soul, which we lead, really show very little relation to each other" (30) and exalts, in contrast, Melville, who "wanted nothing less than the whole of life." The whole of life means here "the primitive and enduring nature of man," "the hidden antiquities beneath the Hotel de Cluny" that reminded Melville on a visit to Paris of "the darker, deeper part" of Ahab (466). Matthiessen sees in the symbol of the whale—which he refuses to pin down to an allegory of evil—a triumph of the myth-making imagination, which points ahead to Joyce and the *Magic Mountain* of Thomas Mann rather than back to Jean Paul and E. T. A. Hoffmann (291). All these concepts hang together as application of the organic theory: the identity of form and content, the series ascending from metaphor to image to symbol, and the low status of allegory and of any dualism in man.

This critical conception is supplemented and, I think, contradicted by Matthiessen's concept of tragedy. Emerson is obviously not tragic: he "lacks the vision of evil" (*AR*, 181). He is bland, accepts himself complacently, lacks humility (75). Whitman is not tragic either; he even can say "there is, in fact, no evil" (625). Thoreau is also not concerned with tragedy. Only Hawthorne and Melville are. Matthiessen considers the recognition of evil in the world as the essence of the tragic attitude, which he sometimes defines in Keats's terms as "the love of good and evil" (349). In *The Scarlet Letter*, the acceptance of fate is crucial as well as the recognition of guilt. Hawthorne's "protagonists finally face their evil and know it deserving of the sternest justice, and thus participate in the purgatorial movement, the movement towards regeneration" (350). Matthiessen recognizes that purification through suffering (such as Lear's and Samson's), *catharsis*, not of the audience alone but of the hero, is essential to tragedy. But Matthiessen greatly prefers *Moby-Dick* to Hawthorne's work and thus embraces an alternative concept of tragedy, which he considers peculiarly Shakespearean, but which seems to me rather that of romantic titanism as it was first formulated by Schiller. It puzzles me why Matthiessen considers a line from Melville's "Battle Pieces," referring to the "double-face image of life" (512), as "one of the most comprehending perceptions ever made of the essence of tragedy" (513). Ahab, Matthiessen's admired tragic hero, is a titan, a Prometheus rebelling against God or the order of the universe. There is no recognition of guilt, no purgation, and Matthiessen has to admit that "catharsis is frustrated" (456), or, I would say, simply absent. "His tragedy is that of unregenerate will." He suffers but "is not purified by suffering." He remains, like Ethan Brand, damned (457). Thus, the constant parallel Matthiessen draws between Ahab and Lear—however strong the verbal echoes—limps badly. I do not see how Matthiessen can say that "Shakespeare's conception of tragedy had grown into the fibre of Melville's thought" (435). He rightly calls "Ahab's tragedy a fearful symbol of the self-enclosed individualism" (459). The final chase of Moby-Dick may be "the finest piece of dramatic writing in American literature" (421), but it is not a tragedy, as it lacks any ethical conflict. Ahab goes down to death in his pride; one cannot say of him what Matthiessen says of Melville, "though good goes to defeat and death, its radiance can redeem life" (514). Ahab does not represent good, and there is no radiance after his end. Also in *Pierre*, Matthiessen states, there is no purgation. "If the man destined to fail will fail despite any effort he makes, tragedy tends thereby to be robbed of catharsis" (417). But tragedy without catharsis is not anymore tragedy. The attempt to exalt Melville as a tragedian must fail.

All these literary standards are then encompassed by "the devotion" of these writers "to the possibilities of democracy" (*AR*, ix). No doubt, all these writers and practically every American of the mid-century were democrats (what else? monarchists?), though only Hawthorne was a committed Democrat who held government offices. But the "possibilities of democracy" formula allows Matthiessen to include any criticism of industrial capitalism and any scheme for social reform and to identify these hopes with that "unshackled, democratic spirit of Christianity in all things" (270) that Melville found to be the essence of Hawthorne's greatness. Matthiessen makes then a tortuous effort to see Hawthorne's joining Brook Farm as an escape from "all the fopperies and flummeries which have their origin in a false state of society" (240) and to minimize the relation of *Blithedale Romance* to Hawthorne's experience during his stay there. Oddly enough, even the conclusion of *The House of the Seven Gables* is seen as anti-property declaration buttressed with a quotation from Engels (336). The marriage of Phoebe and Holgrave is "meant finally to transcend the old brutal separation of the classes," though Matthiessen objects that the "reconciliation is somewhat too lightly made." Hawthorne overlooked the fact that "he is sowing all over again the same seeds of evil" (322). No allowance is made for the happy ending conventional in a novel of that time; a fictional situation is solemnly examined for its presumed distant economic consequences. Still, Matthiessen concludes, "The novelist has helped free us from our reckless individualism in pointing to the need for a new ethical and cultural community" (343). The chapter on English poverty in the *English Notebooks* shows "at least a faint perception of the need for collectivism" (336), though elsewhere Matthiessen quotes Hawthorne stating that "the real Me was never an associate of the community" (241). Hawthorne was an isolated, alienated man, and it seems forcing the texts to see him as propagandist for a new community.

Melville's "unshackled, democratic spirit of Christianity in all things" became Matthiessen's favorite quotation, repeated at least three times (*AR*, 376, 414, 442), and buttressed by the peroration in the chapter "Knights and Squires" in *Moby-Dick* addressing God, "the centre and circumference of all democracy . . . Spirit of Equality . . . Thou great democratic God!" (444). Melville evokes Bunyan, Cervantes, and Andrew Jackson, an odd trio, as his heroes and the crew of the Pequod are motley enough racially to illustrate the equality of mankind. But it is hard to see what social hope is held out in Melville's quarrel with God and the order of nature.

It is easy to think of Whitman as a socialist; he certainly had sympathies for the socialism of Pierre Leroux mediated by George Sand. Matthiessen quotes him on the gloomy future of America growing "vast crops of poor, desperate, dissatisfied, nomadic, miserably-waged populations" (*AR*, 589) and draws a parallel to G. M. Hopkins, the English Jesuit poet, writing, "I'm afraid some great revolution is not far off. Horrible to say, in a manner I am a Communist" (588). Matthiessen feels this the issue of the day and sees Dreiser (the subject of his last book) to be "the chief heir of the qualities the poet [Whitman] liked most to dwell on: sympathy, solidarity" (625).

This overriding political theme becomes literary when Matthiessen concludes his book with a plea for a new mythology whose principal function would be the symbolizing of the fundamental truths found in Melville's Christian belief in equality and brotherhood, as poured out in his praise to "the great God, absolute, the centre and circumference of all democracy." Melville "wrote the enduring signature of his age" (*AR*, 656), an estimate hardly justified by the effect of Melville either in his time or even in his renewed afterfame and modified by Matthiessen himself when he recognizes that "Melville did not achieve in *Moby-Dick* a *Paradise Lost* or a *Faust*" (656).

American Renaissance established a view of the history of American literature that seems to be accepted, though the very claim of a "renaissance" is untenable. What rebirth and of what? one may ask. The term is used vaguely as the equivalent of flowering, climax, peak, or something similar. The book, undoubtedly a great achievement in its scope and penetration, bursts at its seams; the combination of social pathos, close reading, and critical theories about tragedy, allegory, and symbolism set in the tradition of the Coleridgean aesthetics of organic form holds together with difficulty. The excursions into the assumed parallel sister arts seem often to go astray. The conventional genre pictures reproduced do not illuminate the texts, and the account of the theories of the American sculptor Horatio Greenough, while new and interesting, brings in a different theoretical tradition: functionalism derived from Gottfried Semper.

Just in these last years of the war and its aftermath, when Matthiessen was active in leftist politics, he turned to an intensive study of Henry James. In 1943 he edited *Stories of Writers and Artists* with an introduction on the theme of the artist in James and wrote an essay on "James and the Plastic Arts" (in *Kenyon Review* 5:533–50). In 1944 a study of the revisions of *The Portrait of a Lady*[3] argues effectively that James's "ambiguity was not unintentional," not "the obscurantism of a man who could not make up his mind" (*HJ*, 169). The paper interprets the conclusion persuasively: Isabel in returning to Rome submits to the "discipline of suffering" (183) and gives "meaning and value to renunciation" (186). The book *Henry James: The Major Phase* (1944) pursues then the argument that Henry James was "a very deliberate and unconfused moralist" (*AR*, 476). Matthiessen tries to rehabilitate James's last three long novels, silently rejecting their dismissal by Leavis and openly criticizing Van Wyck Brooks for seeing Henry James's life in England as "flight, frustration, and decline" (*HJ*, xiii). In *The Ambassadors*, Matthiessen argues, Strether is awakened to a wholly new sense of life. "Yet he does nothing at all to fulfill that sense" (*HJ*, 389), while Madame de Vionnet "has learned from life that no real happiness comes from taking. The only safe thing is to give" (41). *The Wings of the Dove*, Henry James's masterpiece in Matthiessen's estimate, is dominated by the pathos of the death of a beautiful woman, "a peculiarly recurrent American theme" (50). But Densher is "the problem figure." He "has been transformed by the dead girl's hovering presence. Like the hero of any great tragedy he has arrived at the moral perception of the meaning of what has befallen him" (77). Matthiessen, true to his profession that "aesthetic criticism, if carried far enough, inevitably becomes social criticism" (xiv), sees the book as striking the chords of "renunciation, of resignation, of inner triumph in the face of outer defeat," which he feels "was not in keeping with the spiritual history of his American epoch" (80). It is an elegy for the past, Henry James's and America's, which Matthiessen also finds in Sarah Orne Jewett, Emily Dickinson, and Mark Twain's *Huckleberry Finn*. It seems a forced association, as *The Wings of the Dove* is quite remote even chronologically, not to speak of subject matter, form, and tone. *The Golden Bowl* presents then real social, moral, and psychological difficulties. Matthiessen is much troubled by Mr. Verver's innocence, which seems to him to contradict his success as a recent multimillionaire. Verver's hold on Charlotte is considered "as nothing short of obscene" (100), and Maggie "seems to get an unnatural knowledge of evil once she keeps her innocence intact" (101). Matthiessen judges finally that the book is "decadent" or rather simply a romance "with all its magnificence hollow of real life" (102, 104). He then comments on the late stories and the unfinished novel, *The Ivory Tower*, and ends by meditating on Henry James's concept of degrees of consciousness or awareness both as a measure of human worth and, hardly convincingly, as guarantor of personal immortality (146). But Matthiessen cannot be content with individual spiritual growth and hopes to have the degrees of consciousness translated into terms of social consciousness, which he finds in his own peculiar combination of Christianity, democracy, and socialism (151). Concern for the characters and their behavior as if they were people in real life dominates, though Matthiessen also pays attention to James's use of iterative imagery, distinct in the three novels, and to the *Notebooks* (1947), which Matthiessen was (along with Kenneth Murdock) to edit.

The book was followed by a huge anthology, *The James Family, including Selections from the Writings of Henry James, Senior, William, Henry and Alice James* (1947). The ample sensitive comment brings out the differences and tensions in the family circle, compares William and Henry James, and discusses the "American in Europe" theme that was to dominate Matthiessen's own experience at the first seminar of American Studies at Salzburg and as Visiting Professor at the University of Prague in 1947. *From the Heart of Europe* (1948) gives his rose-colored report.

Matthiessen's interests in American literature were not confined to the five writers of *The American Renaissance* and his old loves, T. S. Eliot and Henry James. He was invited to contribute to *The Literary History of the United States,* edited by Robert Spiller, William Thorp, Thomas H. Johnson, and H. S. Canby in three volumes (1948), a collaborative enterprise by fifty-five authors. It inevitably turned out a collection of individual essays—excellent, good, and in a few cases mediocre—held together by an all-inclusive plan to discuss any writing done on the soil of the United States, including philosophy, theology, and political and scientific thought, as well as a sketchy social and political history of the country. One can learn from it what R. G. Collingwood argued: there cannot be any cooperative history except as an inventory, inasmuch as historical imagination and judgment must be one and personal. Matthiessen's contributions are just that, though the chapter on Edgar Allan Poe tries hard to be an objective, sober account of his life and literary career. Matthiessen oddly leaves it to the reader to decide whether "Poe's work is merely a meretricious fabrication" or "a completely imaginative creation" (1:330). Matthiessen leans obviously to the first alternative but makes much of Poe's influence in France and thus tries to refute Parrington's view that Poe was "remote from the currents of American thought. It can be argued that the materialism of so many of Poe's interests, his fondness for inventions and hoaxes, and his special flair for journalism make him more 'representative' than Emerson or Whitman of ordinary Americans." Even more important, he fostered the trend to a more analytical, intellectual literature, and "his investigation of the roots of Gothic horror in morbid states of mind has been part of American fiction from Brockden Brown and Poe through Ambrose Bierce and William Faulkner." Matthiessen concludes: "He stands among the very few great innovators in American literature" (1:342).

The chapter on recent "poetry" is also mainly expository. It includes a treatment of Ezra Pound that hints at "human emptiness" (2:1338) and gives an account of his politics as a "catastrophic instance of what can happen when the artist loses all foothold in his society" (2:1340). But the account of the Southern fugitives, particularly J. C. Ransom, to whom he had devoted a laudatory review (reprinted in *R,* 40–49), is entirely sympathetic, as are short accounts of Hart Crane, E. E. Cummings, W. C. Williams, Wallace Stevens, Conrad Aiken, and others. Only Stephen Benét's *John Brown's Body,* then a great success, elicits mild disapproval. Matthiessen's overriding social concern is shown in his comment on Howard Baker's "Ode to the Sea": "It cuts to the heart of our age when it proclaims, 'Man is collective. Change is sure' " (2:1353). Still, the chapter ends with praise for Eliot's *Four Quartets*.

More can be learned of Matthiessen's view of American poetry by looking at the *Oxford Anthology of American Verse* (1948) he compiled and its short introduction. He deplores the rhetoric of the nineteenth century, Lowell and Longfellow in particular, but otherwise shows an extremely tolerant and catholic taste, not only in the choice of poems reprinted, but in a number of generous reviews (reprinted in *R*) and in the comments and accounts of lectures and readings Matthiessen gave at Salzburg and Prague. At a conference at Alpbach, Matthiessen chose poems by Sandburg, Frost, and Eliot to illustrate the extremes of American poetry and apparently felt that his admiration for Eliot was not incompatible with praise for Karl Shapiro, just as he had no trouble passing from James to Theodore Dreiser, to whom he devoted his last unfinished book (published in 1951). The motivation is primarily political. Matthiessen even defends Dreiser's late (summer 1945) joining of the Communist party, as "a symbolic act affirming his adherence to international solidarity" (202, 250). Dreiser thought it not incompatible with partaking in the Congregational Communion Service and meditating about "My Creator" (249, 241). But Matthiessen also admires his novels, though he recognizes their shortcomings—the clumsiness of the writing, the absurdities of some of the plots, the tastelessness of much of the dialogue, the primitive reasoning of the commentary full of "chemisms," and the other stock-in-trade of nineteenth-century materialism—but always finds some redeeming features. Matthiessen has to strain very hard to defend the title of *An American Tragedy*. It is, he admits, only "a pathetic story of a cornered animal . . . not a tragedy but written out of a profoundly tragic sense of man's fate" (207). Though the accounts of the novels are often perceptive and far from uncritical, the book is still an anticlimax to Matthiessen's work: strangely flat and forcedly apologetic, not only about Dreiser's politics and philosophy, but also about Matthiessen himself, his commitments and the changes in him. His speech "The Responsibilities of the Critic," delivered at the University of Michigan in May 1949, is his last and best defense. He reproves the New Critics (or rather their imitators) for regarding "literature merely as a puzzle to be solved" (*R*, 5) and concentrates then on the fear of the widening gulf between "minority culture and mass civilization." The critic must know the past. "A good critic of Goethe must know Mann, a critic of Donne or Dryden, Eliot" (6) repeats the insight of Allen Tate. Matthiessen defends Parrington for "insisting on the primacy of economic factors in society," though he denies being a Marxist. He argues rather that the "principles of Marxism can have an immense value in helping us to see and comprehend our literature" (11) and appeals to the example of Christopher Caudwell in England: it shows the "wide gap that still exists between America and Europe" (12). But then the lecture returns to the old plea that the critic "must judge the work as work of art: judgment of art is unavoidably both an aesthetic and social act" (150). The critic must have "the double quality of experiencing our own time to the full and yet being able to weigh it in relation to other times" (18) is the Eliotic conclusion. It shows that Matthiessen in spite of his fervent commitment to what he called "the possibilities of democracy," but in practice were the politics of Henry Wallace, remained true to his insight into the nature of art and kept his sound aesthetic judgment. He remains the most impressive figure among American scholar-critics in this decade.

In 1942, a year after *American Renaissance,* Alfred Kazin (born in 1915) published *On Native Grounds,* a history of American prose literature since the rise of realism in the 1890s—a book, like Matthiessen's, animated by faith in the possibilities of American democracy, tracing "our alienation" from the business civilization "on native grounds" (ix). Like Matthiessen, Kazin rejects the purely aesthetic approach, though he recognizes that criticism begins with "workmanship, talent, craft" (xi). His history is a "moral history, which is greater than literary history" (x). While Matthiessen's and Kazin's ideologies converge, Kazin came from a very different background. As his much later autobiographies, *A Walker in the City* (1952), *Starting Out in the Thirties* (1966), and *New York Jew* (1978) tell us, he grew up among Polish-Jewish immigrants in New York and moved in Marxist or at least radical circles in the Depression years, though he never joined the Communist party. The book sees American literature as "born in protest, born in rebellion" (31). It has a clear scheme of threefold periodization: before the First World War (1890–1914), the period before the Wall Street Crash and the Depression (1918–29), and finally the Depression years almost up to Pearl Harbor (1930–40). Kazin thus distinguishes three waves of realism: the first (today called naturalism) includes Dreiser, Norris, Upton Sinclair, and others. The realism of the second period is milder: Sherwood Anderson and Sinclair Lewis were the leading novelists. Finally there is the new naturalism of the thirties: Dos Passos and Farrell in particular, disturbed by maverick figures—Faulkner and Thomas Wolfe. Kazin writes with impetuous verve, combining often vague and unprovable generalizations, sometimes in whole series of interrogative sentences, with allusions to

specific details in the books discussed. He has a great gift of characterization. For instance, Thorstein Veblen's gloomy point of view, his satire
of American business civilization, his grotesque humor, his contempt for
optimistic Marxism is well integrated with a sketchy biography and an
account of his style of "witty pomposity" (132), "wringing academic jargon to death" (138). The hostile chapter on Faulkner, which, Robert
Penn Warren acknowledged, "puts the argument against Faulkner more
fully and effectively than any other critic,"4 draws a sharp contrast between furious expression and dull and commonplace content while acknowledging "a really fantastic virtuosity of mind, a virtuosity and ready
inventiveness unsurpassed in modern American writing" (456). Kazin
sees "a power almost grotesque in its lack of relation to the situation or
character . . . it is a greatness moving in a void" (459). In his optimism
he surely overdraws "the monotonal despair" (469) of Faulkner. The
whole chapter contains a rare, explicit value judgment while Kazin usually shows a very wide sympathy for all manners of writing: for Willa
Cather as well as Dos Passos and Thomas Wolfe. The remarks on Steinbeck's naiveté or the condemnation of *For Whom the Bell Tolls* (338) are
rare exceptions, except in the chapters on criticism, which engage Kazin's
intellectual convictions directly. They are built on contrasts of the liberals
with the new humanists and the Marxists with the New Critics in a chapter called "Criticism at the Poles." The condemnation of Babbitt is excessively harsh. To call him "narrow and censorious and patronizingly
vulgar" (295) can be argued, but to say that "spiritually Babbitt was not
superior to Mark Hanna" (297) or to speak of "his lack of ethical conviction" (299) seems blatantly false. A Marxist like Granville Hicks is
charged with "shrewish moralism" (421) and "monumental naiveté"
(420), while the New Critics are all lumped together and accused of
"unrelieved bitterness and rage and contempt" (433), surely quite in-
applicable to such sweet-tempered minds as John C. Ransom or Cleanth
Brooks. Blackmur is accused of a "voracious passion for the critical process itself which becomes monstrous—an obsession with skill, criticism
driven to technical insights" (440), but the quotation substantiating this
indictment merely reflects on the effect of the decay of religion on Shelley, Swinburne, and Hardy. The chapter with its emphasis on the New
Criticism combining formalism with "scientism" (432) must have helped
to establish the current legend about the New Criticism, which is neither
formalist nor, even less, scientist. Kazin's last chapter "America! America!" tells of the new nationalism, mainly Van Wyck Brooks's celebration
of the American past and his wholesale condemnation of modern liter-

ature in *The Opinions of Oliver Allston,* with some distaste but also resignation. "The pressure of the times is too great; it beats upon all of us" (517).

Kazin's chapters on criticism are anticipated by Bernard Smith (born 1909) whose *Forces in American Criticism: A Study in the History of American Literary Thought* (1939) is a straightforward Marxist account. "The esthetic nihilists" are disparaged. He rejoices in the termination of Eliot's *Criterion*: Eliot had nothing to fight for anymore. "But those who believe in scientific methods, in realism, a social equality and democracy are hopeful and are fighting" (387) are Smith's last words. But it would be unjust to reduce the book to the last pages of polemics. Actually it is a solid, well-informed, and even-tempered account of the history of American criticism with a bias for the socially aware, "progressive" authors and attention to class situations and attitudes. The carefully balanced chapters on Emerson, Poe, and Henry James are not simple denunciations of aestheticism. The accounts of Parrington and Granville Hicks show well the divisions and contradictions in their minds. There are rare lapses in a sober history. It is wrong to describe Spingarn as "rootless cosmopolitan upperclass" (285) or to speak of Croce's "mysticism unashamed" (283).

Then, in 1948, Stanley Edgar Hyman (1919–70) wrote a lively conspectus of modern criticism, mainly English and American, in *The Armed Vision: A Study in the Methods of Modern Literary Criticism.* Its emphasis is the opposite of mine: while I see modern criticism as an attempt to study the aesthetic, moral, and social essence of literature, Hyman sees the achievement of modern criticism in the importation of concepts and methods from the social sciences: from psychoanalysis, sociology, mainly Marxism, and anthropology. Marx, Frazer, and Freud are the great models and the ultimate aim is to achieve a science "with a formal methodology and a system of procedures" which would be "capable of repetition by anyone with the requisite interest and ability" (9). Evaluation and appreciation are banished to a purely subjective area. But the body of the book fortunately belies this plodding scientific ideal. It actually culminates in a glorification of Kenneth Burke, who is seen as the great synthesizer who "has done almost everything in the repertoire of modern criticism" (461), erected "the most embracing critical system ever built" (394), following his own advice, "Use All There is to Use" (375). He is the ideal critic, accepted wholesale with only mild complaint about his "anachronistic resistance to progress" (397).

All the other chapters, each headed by a name as representative of a trend or method, are arranged in a scale from disapproval to mild endorsement up to hymnical praise. Hyman begins with a chapter on "Edmund Wilson and Translation in Criticism." Wilson is described as an "introductory critic" who "makes skillful use of other men's researches and insights, sometimes without credit" (21) and denounced for commercialism, chauvinism, and obsessive sexuality. Only the psychoanalysis of *The Wound and the Bow* finds favor in Hyman's eyes. The grossly unfair section was wisely dropped from later editions. The next chapter on the scale, "Yvor Winters and Evaluation in Criticism," rehearses some of his extravagant and even ridiculous opinions to characterize him to be "an excessively irritating and bad critic of some importance" (72). "T. S. Eliot and Tradition in Criticism" is at least taken seriously, though the distaste for his religion and politics is obvious. It concludes that "despite all Eliot's protests to the contrary, the *man* Eliot is of course the clue to both the poetry and the criticism, just as in the last analysis the 'tradition' seems to be reducible to a personal need" (103). Hyman thus disposes of the validity of Eliot's conceptions far too easily. The next chapter on "Van Wyck Brooks and Biographical Criticism" makes predictable points against the abuse of biography while the next on "Constance Rourke and Folk Criticism" praises the *Roots of American Culture* (1942) devoted to folk art very highly. The sixth chapter, entitled "Maud Bodkin and Psychological Criticism," praises her *Archetypal Patterns in Poetry* (1934) as "to have made probably the best use of psychoanalysis in literary criticism" (142). But Bodkin's book is strictly Jungian, as Hyman recognizes. The relation of Freud to Jung allows a not uncritical discussion of Freudian psychoanalysis and of Gestalt psychology. Hyman expects more from the special version (topology) of Kurt Lewin: "From it literary criticism can expect the greatest invigoration it has had since Coleridge first attempted to turn formal scientific knowledge on poetry" (163), an odd prophecy based on false historical knowledge: Coleridge never used science except in the sense of Schelling's *Naturphilosophie* while severely criticizing the Associationist psychology of his time, and one has not heard of any literary criticism from Kurt Lewin or his few followers.

The next chapter, "Christopher Caudwell and Marxist Criticism," centers on *Illusion and Reality* (1937), a crude mixture of diluted vulgar Marxism and anthropology, as it it were "the foremost work of Marxist literary criticism" (168). Caudwell, a young Englishman who died fighting in Spain against Franco, is called "the most genuinely important Marxist cultural thinker of our time" (174). Hyman takes seriously his theory about the origins of poetry in rites to grow crops as the ideal union of poetry and production that will be achieved in different form under socialism. He admires a chart, "The Movement of Bourgeois Poetry," that lists parallels between economic conditions and literary movements in a quite dilettantish and often erroneous manner. "Caroline

Spurgeon and Scholarship in Criticism" follows on the scale. Her *Shakespeare's Imagery and What It Tells Us* (1935) is highly praised, though Hyman sees the comic results of her biographical deductions from imagery. The next chapter on "R. P. Blackmur and the Expense of Criticism" admires him as "probably the subtlest and most distinguished close reader in American criticism" (244). But to praise his linguistic proficiency, his wide learning, and humble honesty (244) seems a misreading of his character and gifts. "Willliam Empson and Categorical Criticism" emphasizes Empson's *Some Versions of Pastoral*. "Categorical" means simply genre criticism. The piece on *Alice in Wonderland* is praised as "probably the most completely successful brief Freudian analysis of literature yet written" (283). The next to last chapter on "I. A. Richards and the Criticism of Interpretation" is a veritable hymn to his "learning in almost every area of knowledge." He appears as "the greatest and most important of practicing professional literary critics. Perhaps more than any man since Bacon Richards has taken all knowledge as his province, and his field is the entire mind of man" (319). Richards, according to Hyman, "created modern criticism in the most literal sense" (317). With him begins "objective criticism" (315).

Then follows the enthusiastic praise of Burke and a curious conclusion that puts hope in teamwork in criticism and favors attention to "the movies, the detective stories, the radio, and the comic book" (407). Every one of these chapters is full of references to polemics and scattered periodical articles and contains sandwiched-in excursions into the history and background of the different approaches. These seem to me the weakest spots in a lively book: the sketch of biographical criticism since Walton's *Lives*, the account of the English anthropologists since Frazer, the histories of psychoanalytical criticism and of Marxist criticism, also in Russia, suffer from often surprising lacunae of knowledge, particularly in matters beyond America and England. It is, for instance, simply wrong to call De Sanctis a follower of Taine (180) or to praise Soviet criticism for having improved in the thirties just when the dogma of Socialist realism was promulgated, and it is strange to banish the New Critics and F. R. Leavis to occasional mention in the excursions into background. The book seems to me out of focus, or rather its focus is predominantly psychoanalytical and Marxist with interest in the new Richardsian semantics: the rare combination best represented by Hyman's idol, Kenneth Burke.

Whatever the shortcomings of the books discussed—Parrington's, Matthiessen's, Kazin's, Bernard Smith's, and S. E. Hyman's—they accomplished the rediscovery of American literature and criticism.

5 : MARXIST CRITICISM

MARXIST criticism is supposed to have dominated the years of the Great Depression, the "Red Decade." But "Marxist" is a misnomer even when the author is claimed to be a Marxist. Marxism usually did not mean an actual grasp of the Marxist doctrine but merely a generalized anticapitalism, sympathy for the working classes, and admiration for the Russian Revolution. Much of what was called literary criticism had hardly anything to do with strictly literary matters, beyond debates about such hoary topics as literature and propaganda. Most of the issues raised belong rather to a history of the radical labor movement and the history of the Communist party and the struggles within the party between the orthodox faction following the Moscow edicts and those proclaiming themselves Trotskyites. The purges and the Ribbentrop-Molotov pact caused defections, and one can speak of the demise of the movement with Pearl Harbor and the war. But Marxist motifs in literary criticism remained prominent in such diverse critics as Edmund Wilson, Kenneth Burke, Lionel Trilling and F. O. Matthiessen, who cannot be labeled Marxists. I have no intention to follow the sinuosities of the party line or to define the exact relationship of the writers to the party or the fervor of their commitment when they remained mere fellow travelers. There is an excellent detailed account, Daniel Aaron's *Writers on the Left* (1961), which should satisfy every student of the time. As usual I shall single out the figures of most interest to concrete criticism and leave the polemicists aside.

Max Eastman (1893–1967) is the oldest of the radical group: he was for a time John Dewey's assistant at Columbia University, became the editor of *The Masses* (1912–17) and the *Liberator* (1918), went to Russia for two years, later sided with the exiled Trotsky, and finally completely abandoned Communism, writing for the *Reader's Digest*. Eastman is a split personality: his fervent belief in the Russian Revolution went hand in hand with writing sentimental poetry and with a theoretical interest in the status and technique of poetry. In 1913 he published his first book,

The Enjoyment of Poetry, based on his Columbia lectures which profess to be a contribution to psychology. The poetic is there contrasted with the practical. Lovers of poetry are "lovers of the quality of things" (*EP,* 4). They are possessed by the impulse to realize (5). Poetry "heightens consciousness" (144), a phrase Eastman derived from Edith Sitwell's *Poetry and Criticism.* Though poetry as such is not concerned with conduct and the conveyance of meaning, it may be of value, he argues, to "purposive conduct and adjustment for the future" (130). All this is Bergsonian and possibly simply pragmatist and empiricist in its stress on the contrast between science and concrete experience. It is then developed by a miscellaneous collection of verbal devices in poetry: Eastman gathers instances of names, comparisons, figures of speech, before presenting us with what amounts to an anthology of English poetry with commentary illustrating the realization (or simply poetic representation) of action, of things, of emotions, and finally of pure poetry, meaning melodious, onomatopoetic poetry dependent on rhythm and verse. Eastman even gives advice on how to compose poetry by surrendering to "a flow of waves" in the mind (127). It is all dilettantish, persuading to the "Enjoyment of Poetry."

Though the conception of poetry as "realization" has remained the same, the emphasis in Eastman's *Literary Mind: Its Place in an Age of Science* (1932) has shifted. Poetry is now seen as completely pushed into the corner by the victorious march of science. The new humanists are attacked as reactionary scholars-gentlemen and modern literature is chided for its cult of unintelligibility in Cummings, Joyce, and T. S. Eliot, for its striving for pure poetry, and for its whole esoteric exclusiveness. A chapter is called "Poets Talking to Themselves." One should expect Eastman to welcome I. A. Richards's psychological approach, saying "critical remarks are merely a branch of psychological remarks" (*LM,* 297), but Eastman rejects Richards's solution. Eastman complains, "Accepting the inevitable division of labor between poetry and science Richards nevertheless proposes to restore poetry to her position of sovereignty. The *coup d'état* of Ogden and Richards consists in cutting off knowledge from life and then declaring poetry once more the mistress of life" (301). The fundamental error is "trying to cut off the organization and control of practical activity from science and bring it into poetry" (303). Eastman rejects the concept of pseudostatements and the whole hope for poetry, the idea that poetry is capable of saving us, that it is a means of overcoming chaos. Eastman remained for a long time a believer in the progress of science and the Russian experiment, though he soon disapproved of the cultural politics of the Soviet Union. *Artists in Uniform: A Study of*

Literature and Bureaucratism (1934) is a firsthand account of the suppression of the Russian avantgarde, well informed for the time. The suicides of Esenin and Mayakovsky, the humiliation of Boris Pilnyak, the framing of Evgeny Zamyatin, the silencing of Isaak Babel, the whole imposition of a new dogmatism by fiat from above is well documented. Eastman had no sympathy for what he considered the German nonsense of dialectics as he remained all his life a good pragmatist and empiricist and finally shed his belief in the Communist utopia.

If we understand Marxist criticism as an acceptance of the class struggle, as hope for a radical social revolution and for a new proletarian art, we can speak of Marxist criticism only since the early twenties. The earliest manifesto "Toward Proletarian Art" in *The Liberator* (February 1921) is touchingly optimistic. "When there is singing and music rising in every American street, when in every American factory there is a drama group of the workers, when mechanics paint in their leisure and farmers write sonnets, the greater art will grow and only then" (*MG*, 70). This sentimental utopia was signed by Irwin Granich (1893–1967), who had just begun to use the name Michael Gold. He continued to recommend *Proletkult* as a model and praised Trotsky's *Literature and Revolution* in *The New Masses* (1926) fulsomely. Trotsky is to him a new Leonardo da Vinci (*MG*, 131). Dismissing Mencken, Van Wyck Brooks, and company he calls impatiently for a great literary critic. "Life! send America a great literary critic. . . . Send an artist, Send a scientist. Send a Bolshevik, Send a man" (139). But the "Messiah" did not arrive. Gold could only cause shock waves by his rude attack on Thornton Wilder (in *New Republic*, 1930), as "Prophet of the Genteel Christ," for the "vapidity of his little readings in history" (*MG*, 199), and later in 1935 by his indignant rebuttal to Dreiser's antisemitic outbursts (*MG*, 223). In 1941 Gold devoted a whole book, *The Hollow Men*, to a denunciation of the "renegades" from Communism. He spared nobody: Hemingway, Steinbeck, Dos Passos, and his fellow critics, Eastman and Granville Hicks. Gold remained faithful to his death.

Granville Hicks (1901–82) resigned from the party after the signing of the Ribbentrop-Molotov pact and slowly distanced himself from his earlier critical principles. In the afterward to a reprint (1969) of his best known book, *The Great Tradition: An Interpretation of American Literature since the Civil War* (1933), Hicks himself made the obvious criticism: "If, I was arguing, artists would study Marx or join or at any rate support the Communist party, they would be better artists. What nonsense!" (318). He sees that "Marxism was a useful instrument of the explaining of literary phenomena but had nothing to do with evaluating them"

(309), and he recognizes his youthful personal limitations: his lack of interest "in either metaphysical or psychological problems" (310) and in poetry. But in his actual judgments Hicks finds little to correct. *Winesburg, Ohio* was "the book which shaped his mind" and there was, "of course, Dos Passos" (317, 320). *The Great Tradition* as printed in 1933 propounds a simple thesis: American literature in the acquisitive age was necessarily escapist, remote from the life of the nation, insubstantial like Hawthorne, Melville, Thoreau, and Emily Dickinson, or conformist like Lowell and the Brahmins and hence second-rate. Whitman was the "founder of the new American literature" (30) but he was entangled in the contradictions of individualism and collectivism he could not resolve. Mark Twain is dismissed as "merely an entertainer" (41). Only Howells is admired, though his limitations are found not only in his prudishness but in his "failure to emphasize the major movement in the life of the nation" (88). He did not "strike to the center of American life," Hick's euphemism for saying that he did not write about the working class. It is easy to guess what Hicks says about Henry James, the "fugitive" from America. Still, he admires his subtlety and makes moral observations. He criticizes *The Golden Bowl* because it "depends on the reader's granting James's assumption that Maggie is a person of unusual simplicity and innocence, though her every thought and deed reveal falseness besides which Charlotte's so-called duplicity is positively admirable" (119). The standard applied to these earlier writers is always the same: they don't exemplify the ideal artist "for whom self-expression is also the expression of the society of which he is part" (130).

Hopes for American literature pick up with the muckrakers and naturalists. Upton Sinclair is a major author and Dreiser's "six massive novels are built on the rocks of honesty and pity" (*GT,* 229) in spite of innumerable faults. Sinclair Lewis seems to Hicks "the most satisfying of our authors, if one wants a detailed, accurate record of the way people live" (230). Hicks is very severe to James Branch Cabell, "a fraud, a sleek, smug egoist" (221) and cool to Willa Cather, objecting to her "sweet sentiment and vague nostalgia" (225). Hicks is at his worst when he lectures Edwin Arlington Robinson on his concern with eternal problems. "The only problems we really know are those posed by our own age. There are no eternal problems; each age has its own dilemmas, and, though some of these recur, they take their character from a particular situation" (244). All recent authors are unsatisfactory: Hemingway escaping into drink (277), Faulkner "in danger of mechanically manufacturing thrills in the Grand Guignol manner" (267). The book culminates in a peroration asserting that the "central fact in American life is the class struggle" and urging writers to "give their support to the class that is able to overthrow capitalism" (306). If this is social explanation or Marxism, it can be summed up quickly. The enemy is capitalism: it has pushed American writers either into isolation and alienation or into opposition, which can be mild and timid or determined and open. The open position is preferred. It is an ingenuous, even naive book which is considered the classic of American Marxism. It has at least the courage of judging: it is criticism.

James T. Farrell's *A Note on Literary Criticism* (1936) sounded then the death knell of Marxist dogmatism, without renouncing commitment to the cause. Farrell, with his credentials as the author of the proletarian novel *Studs Lonigan,* argued simply that literature is a branch of the fine arts *and* an instrument of social influence (*NLC,* 11). Farrell surveys recent criticism, impressionism, humanism, and Marxism. He criticizes Hicks and others for the view that "literary artists of the past were propagandists" (41), for the assumption that literature always follows economics (60), and for the prohibition of any writing about the past and history decreed by Gold against Thornton Wilder (98–99). Farrell produces the passages in Marx which acknowledge an indirect relationship between literature and society. He concludes that "functional extremism [his jargon for art as propaganda] rampantly leads to one-sided formulae, to rationalization of prejudices and the concoction of meaningless recipes for the novelist of the classless society of the future" (85). Farrell argues that the attempt to set up a proletarian art, cut off from the past, ignores the inevitable carry-over from the tradition. He also doubts the possibility of a collective novel and does not see how Dos Passos's *42nd Parallel* differs substantially from individualistic novels in the way he seeks to establish character (114). He illustrates his point of view when discussing *The Possessed* by Dostoevsky. We can refute him (which Farrell thinks easy), we can explain his views by telling the story of his life and thus stow Dostoevsky away in a museum as a historical curiosity, or we can do "our real duty as literary critics—devote ourselves to the assimilation of Dostoevski's values in and for our time" (208). This was, Farrell thinks, the approach of Marx in his estimate of Balzac and of Lenin in his article on Tolstoy. But "this functional approach, necessary in an age of social crisis, should not preclude other values and meanings." Farrell wants to recognize "the existence of pluralism in literature" (289), teach a lesson of tolerance.

A year after Farrell's sensible book, the *Partisan Review* was revived as an independent periodical. It had been founded by William Phillips and Philip Rahv in 1934 under the auspices of the Communist party but

languished because of internal dissensions. The new periodical an-
nounced a conscious policy of combining Marxism with an advocacy of
modernism. Revolution in society demanded revolution in literature,
while in Russia the revolution when in power condemned and persecuted
modern art. This combination inspired the eminent critic who emerged
from the group, Philip Rahv (1908–73), born Ivan Greenberg in the
Ukraine. He had begun as a radical polemicist who wrote for the *New
Masses* and the *Daily Worker,* hailed Gorky as "a great leader of the cultural
revolution," and dismissed Joyce and D. H. Lawrence as "tangential to
the concrete course of history" (*ELP,* xii) with good Marxist phraseology. Rahv remained a staunch Marxist, despite his contempt for Stalin-
ism, until his death, sharply antireligious, totally convinced of the Marxist
concept of history.

Rahv was no theorist unless one considers his formula for the two
traditions of American literature, "Paleface and Redskin" (in *Kenyon Review,* 1939), more than a bright aperçu. Henry James contrasts with Whitman, Melville with Mark Twain, patrician with plebeian, allegory and
symbolism with naturalism, highbrow with lowbrow. The idea is then
developed and modified in "The Cult of Experience in American Writing" (*Partisan Review,* 1940). Lambert Strether's advice to little Gilham,
"Live!" in *The Ambassadors* is used to show that even James shares this
cult and thus "represents a momentous break with the then dominant
American morality of abstention" (*ELP,* 9). The cult of experience is to
Rahv the "basic theme and unifying principle" of a "truly national body
of experience" (10), bridging the gap between the two traditions. They
were, after all, "historically associated in the radical enterprise of sub-
verting the puritan code of stark utility in the conduct of life." "Whitman
and James are the true initiators of the American line of modernity"
(14). Cooper, Hawthorne, and Melville were "romancers" rather than
novelists. Hemingway, Sherwood Anderson, and Faulkner exemplify the
cult of experience and the anti-intellectualism of American literature
which he formulated in Marxist terms: "This superstructural level is
seldom reached by the typical American writer of the modern era" (19).
The note of regret of an intellectual who thought of New York as an
outpost of Europe is obvious.

The strength of Rahv's long career is in discussions of particular
works. He does what critics do and should do: he characterizes and
judges. He writes well in difference from the often colorless, stodgy style
of his allies and he has an aesthetic sensitivity which overcomes ideological barriers unsurmountable to others. He is, admittedly, limited in taste
and historical range. Literature begins with Hawthorne in America and

Gogol in Russia and ends with Rahv's own American discoveries: Saul
Bellow, Randall Jarrell, John Berryman, Bernard Malamud. Poetry is
beyond his ken but he is a keen commentator on contemporary criticism.
Eliot, who is to him "the finest literary critic of this century in the English
language" (*ELP*, 82), is handled gingerly with obvious reservations about
his religion and politics. F. R. Leavis is admired for his "robustness, firmness, downrightness" (264) but trounced for his glorification of D. H.
Lawrence. Leavis created a "Lawrence who never really existed" (270).
Leavis's own beliefs "positively disallow his solidarity with Lawrence"
(271) and Leavis is wrong in praising Lawrence as a critic. *Studies in
Classic American Literature* is "not the masterpiece it is reputed to be"
(267). Rahv consistently rejects the New Criticism for the "self-induced
dullness of the narrow textual-formalistic method" and for its "unacknowledged and unanalyzed commitment to an obscurantist social and
historical ideology" (*MP*, 66). Rahv particularly objects to Ransom's attempt to see fiction as poetry, arguing against the overrating of style and
diction. Fiction for Rahv is "character creation, the depth of life out of
which a novelist's moral feeling springs, the capacity of constructing a
plot . . . to invest the contingencies of experience with the power of the
inevitable" (50). Rahv equally rejects the myth criticism which became
fashionable in the fifties. "To take the fact that myth is the common
matrix of many literary forms as an indication that myth is literature or
that literature is myth is a simple instance of the genetic fallacy" (9) seems
to me true, while to say that "what this craze for myth represents most
of all is the fear of history" (7) is a doubtful Marxist conclusion. He is,
however, right in pointing out that "identifying a mythic pattern in a
novel or a poem is not tantamount to disclosing its merit—an assumption
patently false, for the very same pattern is easily discoverable in works
entirely without merit" (21).

Rahv played a role in bringing back Henry James into prominence.
"Attitudes toward Henry James" (1943) is an excellent rejection of the
then current negative attitudes toward James, while shunning the other
extreme of the Henry James cult then developing. He praises *The Golden
Bowl* as "among the half dozen great novels of American literature" (*II*,
67) and characterizes well the contradiction in James's work: "a positive
and ardent search for 'experience' and simultaneously a withdrawal from
it, or, rather, a dread of approaching it in its natural state" (69). He is
surely right in saying, "There never was a writer so immersed in personal
relations, and his consistency in this respect implies an anti-historical
attitude." "Europe is romance and reality and civilization, but the spirit
resides in America" (70). The essay is buttressed by a study of James's

women, "The Heiress of All the Ages" (1943) (*ELP*, 43–61). Much later in "Henry James and His Cult" (1972; in *ELP*) Rahv somewhat recanted. He objects to what he considers the incense of Leon Edel's biography and argues that in "the literature of the world James is not a figure of the first order" (97), comparing his fate to Nikolai Leskov's, Adalbert Stifter's, and Gottfried Keller's, underrating the mere difficulties of translating James. Rahv concludes that in spite of "a certain kind of psychological lyricism James cannot be regarded as a truly modern writer" (103) such as Kafka, to whom Rahv devoted a good introductory essay (250–62).

Rahv's best criticism is, however, devoted to Russian literature, which he knew in the original language. His articles on Dostoevsky were preparations for a book which never materialized. The two essays on Tolstoy seem to me inferior.

An early essay, "The Death of Ivan Ilyich and Joseph K." (1940), draws a strained parallel between Tolstoy's story and Kafka's *Trial*. Tolstoy's story is allegorized in Marxist terms: "as to the mysterious catastrophe which destroys Ilyich, what is it in historical reality if not the ghost of the old idealism of status returning to avenge itself on its murderer? Through Ilyich's death the expropriators are expropriated" (*LSS*, 46,50). Fortunately Rahv soon outgrew this kind of Marxism. A later essay on Tolstoy, "Tolstoy: The Green Twig and the Black Trunk" (1946), preserves the Marxist slant: Tolstoy's "attack on civilization is essentially an attack on the conditions that make for alienation" (*ELP*, 212). His doctrine of Christian anarchism has little religious content but is rather a "formulation of a social ideal and a utopian program" (221).

The essays on Dostoevsky are much more perceptive. The one on *The Possessed* (1938) analyzes the ideological issues well and formulates what has been said before: "Reactionary in his abstract content . . . Dostoevsky's art is radical in sensibility and subversive in performance" (*ELP*, 128). Rahv suggests interestingly that "Dostoevsky had a prodigious appetite for people, but is insensitive to texture and objects. . . . It is this quality which permits his narrations their breakneck pace—there is no need to stop, when there is nothing to look at" (126).

The article on "The Legend of the Grand Inquisitor" (1954) formulates the debate most clearly. "Dostoevsky so represents the truth of history . . . that we see it as patently belonging to the Inquisitor, not to Christ. Dostoevsky nonetheless takes his stand with Christ" (*ELP*, 147). "If Dostoevsky rejects the wisdom of the Inquisitor, it is solely in the terms of the desperate paradox of his faith in Christ" (148).

The discussion of *Crime and Punishment* (1960) rejects any simple motivation of the crime, singling out Dostoevsky as the first novelist who "fully accepted and dramatized the principle of uncertainty or indeterminacy in the presentation of character" (*ELP*, 155). Rahv rejects all allegorizing which would make Svidrigailov a double of Raskolnikov instead of a character in his own right with "no affinity of the mystical order" with the protagonist (160). The epilogue is disparaged as "implausible and out of key with the work as a whole" (172). Rahv puts his finger on the weakness of the antiradical polemics of the book. "The novel depends on the sleight-of-hand of substituting a meaningless crime for a meaningful one" (173).

The article "Dostoevsky: The Descent into the Underground" (1972) makes a paradoxical defense for the suppression, by the censors, of the passage in chapter 10 of *Notes from the Underground* about "faith and Christ" (*ELP*, 177). "They were acting like genuine literary critics" (180), and Dostoevsky acknowledged it implicitly: he never restored the cut passage. Dostoevsky "denounced the quite concrete social and political freedoms demanded by his radical contemporaries in the name of an 'absolute freedom' devoid of any experimental basis in the real life of man—a freedom whose absolute character is metaphysically contrived, purely imaginary, abysmally utopian, and historically inconceivable" (182).

Actually Rahv's last paper, "The Other Dostoevsky" (1978), makes much of the utopian Dostoevsky dreaming the dream of the golden age which, in its secularism and implied atheism, contradicts the Christian vision. Rahv insists on the conflict between "the extreme sceptic and the extreme believer" (*ELP*, 189) which embodies the contradictions of the historical moment in which Dostoevsky lived. In the discussion of "The Dream of a Ridiculous Man" Rahv dismisses the ending as "factitious" and tries to show that Dostoevsky accomplished a double aim. "He exhibits the splendor of the longed-for golden age while simultaneously exhibiting the innate evil of our nature which brings about its disintegration. This procedure fully expresses his own basic duality" (190). Dostoevsky because of his pessimism about human nature cannot fully commit himself to his utopian vision. Rahv uses images from Wallace Stevens's poem "Sunday Morning" to conclude that "Dostoevsky never put out of his mind the 'dominion of the blood and sepulchre,' but at times, however equivocally, he came close to discovering his paradise in the 'balm and beauty of the earth' " (202). Rahv here strongly supports the case for a Dostoevsky seen as an almost erotic poet, celebrating the earth and human brotherhood, as the foremost Czech critic, F. X. Šalda, argued in 1929 (*Šaldův zápisník* 3 (1929): 337ff.).

Looking back at the Marxist criticism, one should praise the attention to the social sources and implications of literature which had often been neglected before, but the actual criticism rarely developed this approach systematically. The best criticism was written when a critic like Rahv emancipated himself from the framework of the dogmatism even though he still professed adherence to the general creed.

6: EDMUND WILSON (1895–1972)

EDMUND WILSON is the one American critic most widely known and read in Europe. In the United States he is (or rather was) a dominant figure: the man of letters, a general critic of society. Many of his writings, such as *The American Jitters* (1932), *To the Finland Station* (1940), *The Scrolls from the Dead Sea* (1955), *Apologies to the Iroquois* (1959), and *O Canada* (1965), range far beyond the province of literature. Wilson also wrote fiction, plays, and verse, recorded impressions of his travels to Soviet Russia, Israel, Haiti, and the main countries of Europe, and in several autobiographical writings left a full record of his development and views on all possible subjects. The diaries and notebooks which Leon Edel has edited and the collection of letters constitute an account of a man's most intimate feelings and a chronicle of his involvement in his time from his first trip to Europe in 1908 to his last illness.

Thus some injustice is done if I limit myself strictly to the literary criticism. Focusing on it we are immediately confronted with two difficulties. Wilson himself disclaimed being a literary critic. "I think of myself simply as a writer and a journalist. I am as much interested in history as I am in literature," he said in 1959.[1] Then, as a good empiricist, Wilson refuses to be pinned down to a theory. In introducing his anthology, *The Shock of Recognition* (1943), Wilson states expressly that "the best way to understand the general is, in any case, to study the concrete" (foreword). There are only two essays in the enormous corpus of Wilson's writings which can be considered deliberate pronouncements on the theory of criticism and literature: "Marxism and Literature" (1937) and "The Historical Interpretation of Literature" (1941) (*TT*, 197–212, 257–70). One must look to casual remarks and the implications of opinions and observations in order to discover the theories and standards that underlie his critical activity. One must be aware of the changes or at least the shifts of emphasis in his critical preoccupations, which run parallel to his political commitments, changing in turn with the social history of the United States.

99

It might be best first to define Wilson's position in a history of American criticism. Clearly he precedes the New Criticism, even though his career overlaps its heyday. Wilson never discusses any New Critic in detail. We find only perfunctory allusions, say, to Allen Tate's "finding fault with Keats for giving in to the emancipatory views of his time" (*TW*, 426), or to Ransom's question about Shakespeare's reference to "dusty death" (*CC*, 518), where even the name of Ransom is omitted, or Empson's "interesting study of the Alice books" (*SL*, 546). Only in 1962 did Wilson comment on Leavis. He professes not to have read his books, "and when I have read him, he was always railing against somebody. He is the kind of dogmatic person who inevitably antagonizes me." "Why try to cast an anathema on somebody who doesn't like George Eliot? I detested *Silas Marner* and *Adam Bede* when I had to read them for school, and I've never got around to *Middlemarch*. And why regard Max Beerbohm as trivial?" Still, Wilson recognizes that Leavis's "interest in literature is passionate and moral" (*BBT*, 535–36).

In the interview in which he speaks of the Leavis-Snow controversy about the two cultures without committing himself on the issue, Wilson tells of a plan to write "a sort of farce-melodrama of academic life." "The villain is a New Critic, who methodically takes Yeats's poems apart and discovers homosexuality in the 'Wild Swans at Coole'—note the 'Wilde' swans, and of course the swans are really young men" (*BBT*, 546). Without mentioning names Wilson voices elsewhere his disapproval of "finding religious symbols and allegories in even such extremely nonreligious writers as Henry James and Stephen Crane," and he must be alluding to Leslie Fiedler's *Love and Death in the American Novel* (1960) when he complains about the assumption that "the sexual situations described in American fiction could only have taken place in America" (553). A similar passage refers to the "vast academic desert of the structure of *The Sound and the Fury,* the variants in the texts of *The Scarlet Letter* and the religious significance of *The Great Gatsby*" (576). He compares the present fashion of interpretation with the "technique of Jewish *pilpul,* that purely intellectual exercise which consists in explaining some passage from Scripture in a fantastically farfetched way" (553). But these remarks seem off target. Neither strained psychoanalytical nor religious allegorizing is characteristic of the main New Critics and they, of course, had no sympathy for the minute pedantries of textual criticism which Wilson attacked in his pamphlet *The Fruits of the MLA* (1968). There seems a deliberate gingerly shrinking in Wilson's complete silence abut I. A. Richards, Kenneth Burke, Yvor Winters, R. P. Blackmur, Cleanth Brooks, F. O. Matthiessen, to mention only the most obvious names. He reviewed only Lionel Trilling's first book on *Matthew Arnold,* praising it but shirking a discussion of literary criticism (*New Republic* 98 (1939): 199–200).

There is one exception, and that is T. S. Eliot, if we consider him a New Critic. Wilson early recognized that Eliot "has now [in 1929] become perhaps the most important literary critic in the English-speaking world" (*SL,* 436) and showed some surprise at the extent of Eliot's influence. "It is as much as one's life is worth nowadays, among young people, to say an approving word for Shelley or a dubious one about Donne." Wilson speaks, I think mistakenly, of Eliot's "scientific study of aesthetic values" (*AC,* 115, 116–17) and recognizes that Eliot's criticism is "completely nonhistorical. He seemed to behold the writing of the age abstracted from time and space and spread before him in one great exhibition, of which, with imperturbable poise, he conducted a comparative appraisal" (*SL,* 713–14). In *Axel's Castle* Wilson wrote a whole page parodying Eliot's critical method: ridiculing his name-dropping and what to Wilson seemed irrelevant linkages and comparisons (*AC,* 124). Wilson felt that the antiromantic reaction induced by Eliot is "leading finally into pedantry and into a futile aestheticism" (122).

Much later (in 1958) in a review of *The Sweeniad,* a satire on Eliot by "Myra Buttle," the pseudonym of Victor Purcell, a Cambridge classical don, Wilson defended Eliot. "It is silly to be outraged by his criticism of Shakespeare, Milton and Shelley." He agrees with Eliot that Dante's *Divine Comedy* "transcends any of Shakespeare's plays," that Milton's imagination is auditory rather than visual, and that Shelley writes loosely (*BBT,* 372–73), but he dislikes Eliot's impersonations of the "formidable professor," or of a revived Dr. Johnson who tries to instruct us "which poets of the past, and to what extent, it is permitted [us] to read and admire." He is irritated by Eliot's talk about the "Main Stream" of poetry which seems to exclude Auden and even Yeats (384–86). The dislike of Eliot's airs of a literary dictator is of course part and parcel of Wilson's disapproval of Eliot's politics and religion.

Wilson's distaste for the American new humanists, Irving Babbitt and Paul Elmer More, is even stronger. The humanists excited much public attention around 1929 but their doctrines were formulated much earlier, even in the 1890s and the first decade of this century. Wilson, in "Notes on Babbitt and More" (1930) and an article "Sophocles, Babbitt and Freud" (1930), comments sharply disagreeing with Babbitt's interpretation of *Antigone.* Wilson had adopted a view of Greek tragedy which rejects the usual view of Sophocles's serenity, emphasizing rather the horror and violence of his plots, and objects particularly to the attempts, going back to Goethe, to play down Antigone's abnormal devotion to her brother (*SL*, 451–67, 468–75).[2] Wilson in his polemics against Babbitt and More defends even "art for art's sake" as justified in its time and argues for freedom of experimentation with such new techniques as the "stream of consciousness" in Joyce against More's uninformed sneers. More, he concludes, is "really an old-fashioned Puritan who has lost the Puritan theology without having lost the Puritan dogmatism" (460, 463, 466), and Babbitt is called "an old-fashioned snob and pedant," "a fanatical literary moralist" who propounds an "aesthetically stupid philosophy" (*BBT*, 384, 535, 397). Wilson had called on More in Princeton in December 1929 before his public attack and had written a somewhat satirical account of his visit which he published only after More's death in 1937, in a toned-down version (*TT*, 3–14).

Thus Wilson is clearly set off from the two main trends of American criticism in the first half of this century. He has rather affinities with the group of critics who, around 1920, revolted against the "genteel tradition": with H. L. Mencken and Van Wyck Brooks. Wilson tells us how in 1912, at the age of seventeen, he came across *The Smart Set,* and was "astonished to find audacious and extremely amusing critical articles by men named Mencken and Nathan, of whom I had never heard" (*DCB*, 92). Mencken is later praised in extravagant terms: "He is the civilized consciousness of modern America, its learning, its intelligence and its taste, realizing the grossness of its manners and mind and crying out in horror and chagrin."[3] With him "the whole perspective of literature in the United States was changed" (*BBT*, 30). Wilson, however, came to recognize Mencken's unpleasant features: his contempt for the common man, "the great American boob," his pseudo-Nietzschean worship of the superman and later his "tenderness to Nazis." Wilson admits that he can be "brutal, obtuse," that as a thinker he is "brash, inconsistent and crude," but he continued to admire him as "our greatest practicing journalist" since Poe, defending his "using a bludgeon on a society that understands nothing but bludgeons." Wilson particularly valued *The American Language* and praised his prose style for its "personal rhythm and color." He was "a poet in prose and a humorist" (*SL*, 296; *BBT*, 33, 32, 31; *SL*, 159; *DCB*, 104).

In an invented dialogue between Scott Fitzgerald and Van Wyck Brooks, Wilson has Fitzgerald address Brooks: "You were almost alone, when you first began to write, in taking American literature seriously. . . . You were among the first to stand for the romantic doctrine of experience for its own sake and to insist on the importance of literature as a political and social influence." Brooks understood that the failing of our literature was "the timidity of the 'genteel tradition' " (*SL*, 143).

"America's new orientation in respect to her artistic life was inaugurated in 1915 by Brooks's *America Coming of Age* and two years later more violently promoted by Mencken's *A Book of Prefaces*" (164). When Brooks turned later into a sentimental, indiscriminate chronicler of American literary history with the series of books beginning with *The Flowering of New England* (1936), Wilson continued with his almost unstinting praise of Brooks, though he himself had a far more critical view of the past of American literature. As late as 1963 Wilson called Brooks "one of the top American writers of our time," "the first modern literary historian to read through the whole of American belles letters," comparing him, extravagantly to my mind, to the greatest literary historians, Francesco De Sanctis and Hippolyte Taine (*BBT,* 554–55). Wilson reviewed every one of Brooks's books favorably, though he came to see that Brooks is not "really a literary critic because he is not interested in literature as an art and lies under serious suspicion of not being able to tell chalk from cheese. . . . Van Wyck Brooks concerns himself with literature mainly from the point of view of its immediate social significance." Still, he has "the historical imagination." He can "show us movements and books as they loomed upon the people to whom they were new" (*CC,* 13, 15). Even the *Opinions of Oliver Allston* (1941), a deplorable book which divides writers into "primary," optimistic writers and the lesser breed of pessimists, is handled very gently by Wilson. It "revealed that [Brooks's] own standards of excellence are still more or less those of an enthusiastic young man in his twenties in the heyday of H. G. Wells, a young man for whom Tolstoy and Ibsen, on the one hand, and Victor Hugo and Browning, on the other, all inhabit the same empyrean of greatness" (227). Wilson sees the change in Brooks from the "somber and despairing" early writings to the "chortling and crooning" *Flowering of New England* (10–11) and its successors, but he cannot bring himself to acknowledge Brooks's sell-out to a bumptious nationalism, to the "nativism" which has since inflated the study of American literature.

Wilson sided with these critics of American business civilization in the twenties, but he differed from them as a critic in two crucial respects: he had a sure, well-defined taste, and he acquired tools for the analysis of literature from nineteenth-century historicism, particularly Marxism, and from Freud. He learned (if such a thing can be learned) his sense of quality in his school, Hill School in Pottstown, Pennsylvania, very early. He speaks gratefully of his classical training, particularly of one teacher, Alfred Rolfe (*TT,* 233–56), and of his early acquaintance with the writings of James Huneker, whose *Egoists* (1909) gave "a stimulating account of the excitement to be derived from the writings of Stendhal, Flaubert,

Huysmans and Baudelaire."[4] As an undergraduate at Princeton, class of 1916, Wilson studied French literature under Christian Gauss (1878–1951), with whom he established a lifelong, almost filial relationship. Gauss was, in Wilson's estimation (which lacks, I think, public documentation), "a brilliant critic—by far the best, as far as I know, in our academic world of that period" (*SL*, 36).[5] In the dedication to Wilson's first critical book, *Axel's Castle* (1931), Wilson says that "it was principally from you that I acquired then my idea of what literary criticism ought to be— a history of man's ideas and imaginings in the setting of the conditions which have shaped them." The published correspondence in *The Papers of Christian Gauss* shows how Wilson deferred to Gauss's advice and how his taste was formed by an early immersion in French literature. Wilson spent almost two years in France (from November 1917 to July 1919), first as a wound-dresser and then in intelligence. The war shook his aestheticism and what might be called his upperclass consciousness. (His father was a lawyer who had been attorney general of New Jersey for a brief period.) He realized that "I could never go back to the falseness and dullness of my prewar life again. I swore to myself that when the War was over I should stand outside society altogether."[6] After the Armistice he sent to friends a manifesto "indicting the institutions of the Western world and suggesting a way out in the direction of socialism" (*A Prelude*, 268). When he returned he plunged into the life of Greenwich Village and into journalism, first as managing editor of *Vanity Fair* and later as drama critic and associate editor of the *New Republic*. He became a declared dissenter, a "radical," a Bohemian, violently opposed to the reigning business temper of the time. He welcomed thus the stockmarket crash of 1929 with some glee as an exposure of the "stupid gigantic fraud" of capitalism (*SL*, 229). In the worst winter of the Depression (1930–31) Wilson went on extensive trips through the country investigating poverty, strikes, and racism such as the Scottsboro case vividly described in *The American Jitters* (1932). Early in 1931 he studied Marx seriously for the first time, and he moved more and more toward communism, signing, for instance, a manifesto calling for the election of William Z. Foster for president in 1932. In 1935 Wilson made a trip to Russia for several months and wrote an account which, while showing some signs of disillusion, still asserted that "you feel in the Soviet Union that you are living at the moral top of the world" (*RB*, 375). But Wilson very soon got into conflict with the orthodox communists, for he could not help being shocked by the great purges. Still, in 1940, he published *To the Finland Station*, a glowing account of the rise of socialism and communism, of the lives and teachings of Marx, Engels, Trotsky, and

Lenin. Lenin is particularly admired as the propounder of "one of the great imaginative influences of our age—a world-view which gives life a meaning and in which every man is assigned a place." But Stalin is now called "a bandit-politician" (FS, 452). That year Wilson broke with the *New Republic*: he opposed the pro-Allied policy of its owners. He retired from public life almost completely, considering the war simply a struggle between two greedy imperialisms. In the summer of 1945 he made a trip to Europe as a reporter, which he then described in *Europe without Baedeker: Sketches among the Ruins of Italy, Greece and England* (1947). The book is a strange display of Wilson's American nationalism and feeling of superiority over the little nations of Europe (England and France included). Despite all the criticism of American policies Wilson had remained a strong nationalist. As early as 1928 Wilson said that it "is our high destiny to step in and speak the true prophetic words to declining Europe" (*TW*, 245). Even in 1956 Wilson could assert that "for myself, as an American, I have not the least doubt that I have derived a good deal more benefit of the civilizing as well as the inspirational kind from the admirable American bathroom than I have from the cathedrals of Europe," though in the same book of reflections, *A Piece of My Mind*, he could also declare: "When, for example, I look through *Life* magazine, I feel that I do not belong to the country depicted there, that I do not even live in that country."⁷ Wilson did not file income tax returns from 1946 to 1955 and defended this lapse in a pamphlet entitled *The Cold War and the Income Tax* (1963) with a violent attack on American bureaucracy and policies. He accepted all the clichés of the opposition: Roosevelt lured the United States into the war, the Cold War was started by the Americans, it was just a struggle between two greedy seaslugs or gorillas. Just at the time when he felt most strongly opposed to American policies and had almost stopped commenting on contemporary American literature, he was widely honored. In 1963 he received the Presidential Medal of Freedom, and later the National Medal for Literature. He enjoyed the rewards of the Establishment with the privilege of rebelling against it. In academic circles his reputation had been low since Stanley E. Hyman's unfair chapter in *The Armed Vision* (1948), but it rose again in the last years of his life when Sherman Paul, Charles P. Frank, and Leonard Kriegel published sympathetic monographs and Frank Kermode, John Wain, Alfred Kazin, Norman Podhoretz, and others wrote laudatory articles.

It seemed necessary to trace Wilson's political opinions because his criticism reflects these changes very accurately. Long before the dedication to Gauss, Wilson must have been aware of the historical setting and even conditioning of literature. He tells us that at the age of fifteen he had read Hippolyte Taine's *History of English Literature* in translation and that his "whole point of view about literature was affected by Taine's methods of presentation and interpretation." Later he read him in French and admired particularly the comparison between Tennyson and Musset (*BBT,* 2). Wilson's admiration for this passage (which confronts the audience of Tennyson—the family circle, the world travelers, the connoisseurs of antiquity, the sportsmen, the lovers of the countryside, the wealthy Victorian businessmen and their ladies—with that of Musset—the intellectuals, the Bohemian artists, the earnest specialists, the hectic women of leisure), survived the cooling-off that we feel in the chapter on Taine in *To the Finland Station,* in which Wilson disagrees with Taine's hostile view of the French revolution. Wilson deplores here the "monotonous force" of his style, the "cocksure and priggish tone." Taine "manages to combine the rigor of the factory with the upholstery and the ornamentation of the nineteenth-century *salon*," but Wilson still admires Taine's scientific program, which he sees modified by "strong moral prepossessions." From Taine and, I assume, many other historians Wilson drew general concepts of determinism, or at least genetic causation (*FS,* 44–45, 49; cf. *TT,* 260–61). He frequently refers to the racial ancestry of authors. Thus, in the case of Oscar Wilde we must take into account his Italian blood "in considering his theatrical instincts and his appetite for the ornate" (*CC,* 333). Wilson makes much of the moral genius of the Jews. "It was probably the Jew in the half-Jewish Proust that saved him from being the Anatole France of an even more deliquescent phase of the French belletristic tradition" (*FS,* 306–07). He even appeals to the elusive inheritance of the character of a grandfather when he explains Ronald Firbank's passion for perfection by the slogan of his grandfather, a big railroad contractor: "I value as nowt what I gets for nowts" (*CC,* 492, 487). As in Taine great importance is sometimes assigned to climate and weather: we are told that Genevieve Taggard was born in the state of Washington and taken as a baby to Honolulu and are asked "whether the moods and the emotions of lyric poetry are not, to a considerable degree, the products of varying weather. In countries where the seasons change, our feelings also run to extremes." In California even poetry becomes equable and bright as the climate (*SL,* 346–47). Wilson seems to believe in a linguistic determinism when he says that "our failure in the United States to produce much first-rate lyric poetry is partly due to our flattening and drawling of the vowels and our slovenly slurring of the consonants" (749) and makes much of the Russian aspect of verbs to conclude that Russians lack a sense of time which then explains even the lengths of their novels and plays (*RB*, 413–18). He can even establish a link between the progress of technology and a literary genre. The ghost story was killed by electric light. "It was only during the ages of candlelight that the ghost story really flourished" (*CC*, 172). Once he makes the odd statement that value is determined by demand: "If Manet cannot possibly be considered so great a painter as Titian, it is partly because, in his lifetime, there was so much less demand for his work" (*BBT*, 146).

More convincingly, throughout his career Wilson would point to the social origins of a writer such as Ben Jonson or Max Beerbohm (*CC*, 431).[8] He would try to reconstruct the background, for example, in the politics of upstate New York during the Civil War in order to explain the stories of Harold Frederic (*DCB*, 59ff.) or treat the novels of Harriet Beecher Stowe as "a great repository which contains solid chunks of history,"[9] drawing from literature a social picture of the time. More boldly he would generalize on the spirit of an age or time. Thus Dorothy Parker's poetry belongs to the "general tone, the psychological and lit- erary atmosphere of the period," to the twenties, "when people were much freer" than in the thirties, when "they began to have to watch their pockets" and their politics. He looks back at the twenties, when "the idea of the death of a society had not yet begun working on people to paralyze their response to experience" (*CC*, 169–70). Wilson's first book of criti- cism, *Axel's Castle* implies such generalizations about succeeding time- spirits. Wilson himself acknowledges that the scheme of Alfred North Whitehead's *Science and the Modern World* (1926) suggested the plan of his own book (*AC*, 3, 5). Just as romanticism as interpreted in Whitehead's book reacted against the Newtonian science of the eighteenth century, so symbolism reacted against the naturalism, Darwinism, and positivism of the nineteenth century. As early as 1926 Wilson conceived the idea of an international symbolist movement which, I believe, was new at that time.[10] The grouping of Yeats, Valéry, Eliot, Proust, Joyce, and Gertrude Stein was an insight which has been developed only much later. It was 1933 before Valery Larbaud proclaimed Proust a symbolist.[11] This con- cept of the unity and continuity of the international movement and the selection of the great names was Wilson's. We may, however, have doubts about the inclusion of Gertrude Stein and note Wilson's blind spot: his ignoring of the Germans—George, Rilke, and Thomas Mann. We may doubt Wilson's success in attempting to stress the concepts of space-time and relativity implied in Proust and Joyce as being the equivalent of the metaphysics of Whitehead. "As in the universe of Whitehead, the 'events,' which may be taken arbitrarily as infinitely small or infinitely comprehensive, make up an organic structure, in which all are interdependent, each involving every other and the whole; so Proust's book is a gigantic dense mesh of complicated relations." Joyce is assimilated to Proust in these terms: "Like Proust's or Whitehead's or Einstein's world, Joyce's world is always changing as it is perceived by different observers and by them at different times" (AC, 158, 221–22). But the claim that these symbolists (in Wilson's sense) reflect or incorporate the most advanced insights of modern physical science and even point to an ultimate union of art and science can hardly be sustained. Oddly enough, instead of endorsing Valéry's similar hope, Wilson disparages Valéry as a philosopher. "Most of Valéry's reputation for profundity comes, I believe, from the fact that he was one of the first literary men to acquire a smattering of the new mathematical and physical theory." "He never seems to have gotten over his first excitement at reading Poincaré" (79).

This whole concept is in conflict with the side of symbolism that Wilson cannot help stressing: "a sullenness, a lethargy, a sense of energies ingrown and sometimes festering." Wilson calls A la recherche du temps perdu "one of the gloomiest books ever written," evokes the aridity and dreariness of Eliot's The Waste Land, and even says of Yeats that his poetry is "dully weighted, for all its purity and candor, by a leaden acquiescence in defeat." Joyce, however, is exempted. "It is curious to reflect that a number of critics . . . should have found Joyce misanthropic" (AC, 283, 164, 218–19).

Axel's Castle is, however, dominated by other motifs: Wilson's view that verse is a dying technique, that poetry is a thing of the past, and that symbolism will be or should be replaced by a new naturalism. There seems to be a shift in Wilson's view during the writing of the book. The first chapter on "Symbolism," originally published as "A Preface to Modern Literature" in March 1929, gives a sympathetic account of the French symbolist movement, whereas the last chapter, "Axel and Rimbaud," originally published in February and March 1930, after the stock-market crash, has a tone of disapproval.[12] We are told that "the only originality of the Symbolists consisted in reminding people of the true nature and function of words" (AC, 245), that is, their power of suggestion. We are then treated to a contrast between the fictional Axel (in Villiers de l'Isle-Adam's tragedy) who says "Live? our servants will do that for us" (263) and the life-story of Rimbaud, told with the embellishments then current, concluding that "Rimbaud's life seems more satisfactory than the works of his Symbolist contemporaries" (283). He hopes now that we shall live to see Valéry, Eliot, and Yeats displaced and points suddenly to Russia as "a country where a central socio-political idealism has been able to use and to inspire the artist as well as the engineer" (293). Wilson has been converted to Marxism.

But has he become a Marxist literary critic? The question cannot be answered by a simple "yes" or "no." Wilson certainly becomes conscious of the class concept and the economic conditions of literature. When Michael Gold, a Marxist critic, attacked Thornton Wilder as a typical bourgeois, Wilson, though a friend of Wilder, defended Gold for raising the class issue, in "The Literary Class War" (1932) (*SL*, 535). Occasionally, Wilson engaged in Marxist allegorizing. Thus, referring to the fact that we are told at the end of the novel that Madame Bovary's daughter is sent to a cotton mill after her mother's suicide, Wilson remarks: "The socialist of Flaubert's time might perfectly have approved of this: while the romantic individualist deludes himself with unrealizable fantasies, in the attempt to evade bourgeois society, and only succeeds in destroying himself, he lets humanity fall a victim to the industrial-commercial processes, which, unimpeded by his dreaming, go on with their deadly work" (*TT*, 77). But even here Wilson does not quite endorse this interpretation put into the mouth of a socialist of Flaubert's time: Wilson must have been aware that the fate of poor Berthe is quite incidental to the meaning of the book. At most, it adds one more cruel touch. In the same paper, "The Politics of Flaubert" (1937), the liaison between Rosanette, the daughter of poor silk-mill workers, with the hero of *L'Éducation sentimentale*, Frédéric Moreau, is considered "a symbol of the disastrously unenduring union between the proletariat and the bourgeoisie, of which Karl Marx had written in *The Eighteenth Brumaire*" (80). But this paper is an exception.

In 1938 Wilson discussed "Marxism and Literature," expressly quoting some of the standard texts: Engels's letter to Starkenburg, in 1890, admitting a reciprocal interaction between the economic base and the superstructure, the letter of Engels to Minna Kautsky disapproving of overtly tendentious novels, the Sickingen debate with Lassalle which Wilson reduces to Marx chiding Lassalle for mistaking the role of his hero, and the passage that praises Greek art and grants that "certain periods of highest development of art stand in no direct connection with the general development of society, nor with the material basis and the skeleton structure of its organization" (*TT*, 199).[13] Wilson sees this passage only as an inconsistency without discussing the issue itself and continues briefly to expound Lenin's essays on Tolstoy, accepting their thesis that Tolstoy represents the psychology of patriarchal peasantry. Wilson is most impressed by Trotsky's *Literature and Revolution* (1924), agreeing with him that there cannot be a proletarian literature and that a work

of art must first be judged as a work of art. Wilson sees that the identification of literature with politics is liable to terrible abuses and he
deplores developments under Stalin such as the damning of the music
of Shostakovich. He concludes that "Marxism by itself can tell us nothing
whatever about the goodness or badness of a work of art": a conclusion
that rejects, in principle, all the efforts of Marxists such as Lukács to
develop a specific Marxist aesthetics. "What Marxism can do, however,
is throw a great deal of light on the origins and social significance of
works of art" (204). Wilson seems to allude to a view like that of Lukács
(though I know of no evidence that he had read or could have read him
at that time) when he denies that "the character of a work of art" must
be "shown engaged in a conflict which illustrates the larger conflicts of
society." What matters is the moral insight. Wilson cites the death of
Bergotte in Proust's novel and, rather incongruously, Thornton Wilder's
Heaven's My Destination and Hemingway's story "The Undefeated," as examples of apparently trivial subjects widening into universal significance.
Narrowly prescriptive requirements such as Granville Hicks's that the
author's point of view must be "that of the vanguard of the proletariat"
are rejected, as is the doctrine of "socialist realism" as a futile attempt
"to legislate masterpieces into existence" (205–07). Wilson distinguishes
between "short-range and long-range" literature (like Ruskin's "books
for the moment" versus "books for the ages"), recognizing that art can
be and has been a political weapon. But what remains of Dante is not
his commitment to the Emperor Henry or of Shakespeare to "Elizabethan imperialism." In general, Wilson argues, revolutionary periods were
not periods of great creative upsurge in literature. Wilson can think only
of Chénier and Blok, and they hardly prove the opposite: Chénier was
guillotined and Blok died in despair with the revolution in Russia. But
at the end of the article Wilson embraces the most utopian side of Marxist
doctrine. "It is society itself, says Trotsky, which under communism becomes the work of art." Wilson knows that "this is to speak in terms of
centuries, of ages; but in practicing and prizing literature, we must not
be unaware of the first efforts of the human spirit to transcend literature
itself" (*TT,* 208, 209, 212). The odd ideal of a humanity which can and
should dispense with art—apparently beginning to be realized in Soviet
Russia—is evoked somewhat hesitantly. I believe that this passage,
though anticipated in the recently published notebooks (*TW,* 421, 129),
is unique in Wilson's public writings.

The Princeton lecture on "The Historical Interpretation of Literature"
(1940), which followed the paper on Marxism three years later, rehearses

the same topics under a different title and in a markedly subdued tone. Wilson glances at the origins of the historical approach in Vico (a figure briefly discussed also in connection with his discoverer, Michelet, in *To the Finland Station*), Herder, Hegel, and Taine. Taine and Michelet, Wilson observes, paid attention to the influence of social classes before Marx. Marx and Engels as literary critics were "tentative, confused and modest." Again the passage on Greek art is singled out as giving Marx "a good deal of trouble." Bernard Shaw and Franz Mehring are mentioned as "the great critics who were trained on Marx," and Trotsky's *Literature and Revolution* is called "brilliant and valuable" (*TT*, 262, 263, 265). But now a new motif is introduced: psychoanalysis, or simply "the interpretation of works of literature in the light of personalities behind them." Wilson thinks of Freudian psychoanalysis merely as an extension of the biographical interpretation as practiced by Dr. Johnson and Sainte-Beuve. He praises Van Wyck Brooks's *Ordeal of Mark Twain* (1920) as a model. "The attitudes, the compulsions, the emotional 'patterns' that recur in the work of a writer are of great interest to the historical critic." Freudian, individual psychology is assimilated to the historical method which in turn has absorbed the Marxist approach. Wilson advocates such a combination but sees that the historical or better simply the genetic approach does not solve the problem of criticism as value judgment. He repeats the argument stated in the Marxism paper. "No matter how thoroughly and searchingly we may have scrutinized works of literature from the historical and biographical point of view, we must be ready to attempt to estimate . . . the relative degrees of success attained by the products of the various periods and the various personalities. We must be able to tell good from bad, the first-rate from the second-rate. We shall not otherwise write literary criticism at all, but merely social or political history as reflected in literary texts, or psychological case histories from past eras" (266–67).

Wilson solves the question of value judgment to his satisfaction by an appeal to an emotional reaction which he considers the Kantian solution as he learned it from his Princeton teacher, Norman Kemp Smith. Attempts to define standards such as "unity, symmetry, originality, vision, inspiration, strangeness, suggestiveness, improving morality, socialist realism," do not impress him: "you simply shift the emotional reaction to the recognition of the element or elements" and still might not have a good play, a good novel, a good poem. This reliance on taste leads Wilson to accept a self-appointed and self-perpetuating elite of "genuine connoisseurs who establish standards of taste" and "will compel you to accept their authority." Wilson trusts, far too easily, that "imposters may try to put themselves over, but these quacks will not last" (*TT*, 267–70). He believes in the verdict of the ages.

The appeal to taste is nothing new. For instance, in 1927 he is content to say: "I do not pretend that my own primary judgments as to what is good poetry or what is not are anything other, in the last analysis, than mysterious emotional responses" (*SL*, 210), and he can even endorse the silly criterion for poetry proposed by A. E. Housman, tongue-in-cheek, that "the most intense, the most profound, the most beautifully composed and the most comprehensive works of literary art . . . are also the most thrilling and give us most prickly sensations while shaving" (*TT*, 28–29). Wilson preserved an admiration for the "gusto" of Saintsbury, the intensity of the poetic effect propounded by Poe. Saintsbury is called the "sole full-length professional critic, who is of really first-rate stature," "a gourmet and something of a glutton" for whom "the enjoyment of literature [is] somehow a moral matter" (*CC*, 306, 368–69). Wilson here seems to define his own attitude and prevalent practice: conveying the joy of literature by describing, evoking, or often simply summarizing the books he has read. As he said himself: "There are few things I enjoy so much as talking to people about books which I have read and they haven't, and making them wish they had—particularly a book that is hard to get or in a language that they do not know" (*SL*, 376). Many times Wilson deplores the decline of "appreciation" in favor of purely technical or philosophical or sociological treatment of literature (*BBT*, 49). The bulk of his criticism is undeniably that of an "introductory critic," a middleman, an expositor and chronicler of literary events, a role which we should not underrate in its effects on several generations of readers nor underrate for the sheer abilities it requires in the skill, say, of retelling Proust's series of novels or the numerous memoirs of the Civil War in *Patriotic Gore*. But Wilson's ideal of the critic goes of course beyond this function. A reviewer-critic should know "the past work of every important writer he deals with and be able to write about an author's new book in the light of his general development and intention. He should also be able to see the author in relation to the national literature and the national literature in relation to other literatures" (*SL*, 603). In "A Modest Self-tribute" (1952) Wilson quite rightly claims to have "tried to contribute a little to the general cross-fertilization, to make it possible for our literate public to appreciate and to understand both our Anglo-American culture and those of the European countries in relation to one another" (*BBT*, 5).

Though Wilson detested the American humanists he arrives at a humanism of his own: "the belief in the nobility and beauty of what man as man has accomplished, and the reverence for literature as a record of this." Since his school years "humanism had continued to serve me when the religion had come to seem false. The thing that glowed for me through Xenophon and Homer in those classrooms of thirty years ago has glowed for me ever since" (*TT*, 254–55).

Marxism remains firmly relegated to being a variety of the historical approach. As the discussion of Marx in *To the Finland Station* shows, Wilson, though deeply impressed by Marx's personality, devotion, and moral fervor in criticizing the industrial society of his time, came away from a study of his writings totally unconvinced by two crucial Marxist doctrines: surplus value and the dialectic. The labor theory of Marx is rejected as "the creation of the metaphysician," fallacious because of its narrow concept of human motivation, and the dialectic is dismissed as a "religious myth disencumbered of a divine personality and tied up with the history of mankind." Dialectic is simply the "old Trinity": "the mythical and magical triangle . . . which probably derived its significance from its correspondence to the male sexual organs," a hoary joke of antitrinitarian polemics (*FS*, 298, 194, 190). History in Marxism is "a substitute for old-fashioned Providence" (436). Wilson consistently criticized overt propaganda art. "There is no sense," he says in discussing "Communist Criticism" (1937), "in pursuing a literary career under the impression that one is operating a bombing plane" (*SL*, 650). Marxist criticism does not recognize that "there are groups which cut through the social classes, and these tend to have an independent existence. The writers make a group of their own; the painters make a group of their own; the scientists make a group. And each of these groups has its own tradition, its own craft and body of doctrine which has been brought down to the present by practitioners that have come from a variety of classes through a variety of societies. . . . A Communist critic who, in reviewing a book, ignores the author's status as a craftsman is really, for purposes of propaganda, denying the dignity of human work" (501). In quite a different context Wilson illustrates this idea, admitting that Virgil was not possible without Augustus: but also without Apollonius Rhodius, his Alexandrian predecessor, the poet of the *Argonautica* (*FS*, 187). Wilson had learned from Marxism that "economic and social forces do play a much larger part in molding people's ideals, and consequently in coloring their literature, than most people are willing to admit" (*SL*, 501), but he did not adopt either the concept of history or the commitment to the cause of a literature futhering the aims of Marxism. Proletarian literature does not and cannot exist, just as "there could not be proletarian chemistry or prole-

tarian engineering." "When the proletariat learn to appreciate the arts
. . . they will appreciate and understand them in the same way as anyone
else." "There are already great proletarian names among the arts and
sciences, but they are the great names of artists and scientists, not of
proletarians."[14] The involvement of art in ideology and class is denied:
a universal art and even universal human nature is assumed here. Marxism is rejected.

Actually, Wilson's interest in psychoanalysis grew, and the book *The
Wound and the Bow* (1941) is expressly devoted to the problem. Not that
Wilson had not known of psychoanalysis before. One of his earliest papers, "The Progress of Psychoanalysis," dates back to 1920.[15] Wilson's
interest in an author's psychology was not merely biographical. He assumes, in the discussion of Proust, that "the real elements, of course, of
any work of fiction, are the elements of the author's personality: his
imagination embodies in the images of characters, situations and scenes
the fundamental conflicts of his nature of the cycles of phases through
which it habitually passes. His personages are personifications of the
author's various impulses and emotions" (*AC,* 176). But only in *The Wound
and the Bow* is the connection between psychic disease and artistic accomplishment stated as a thesis. The title essay, the last in the book, uses the
Philoctetes story from Sophocles's play. "The victim of a malodorous
disease . . . is also the master of a superhuman art" (*WB,* 294). But one
could object that the Philoctetes story does not lend itself as a model for
the "conception of superior strength as inseparable from disability" or
the idea "that genius and disease, like strength and mutilation, may be
inextricably bound together" (287, 289), as Wilson seems to claim. Philoctetes had the miraculous bow before he was bitten by the snake. The
story does not imply that the bow may not be owned or drawn without
the wound. But we must not press the parallel; we should be content
with the Philoctetes story simply as an allegory of the situations described
in several essays of the book. "Dickens: The Two Scrooges" emphasizes
the shock of the six months the boy of twelve spent laboring in a blacking
warehouse; "The Kipling Nobody Read" exploits the degrading experiences of Kipling as a little boy with foster-parents in England, slightly
fictionalized in the story "Baa Baa Black Sheep," and his further bru-
talizing at the United Services College, oddly glorified in *Stalky and Co.*
The other essays in the volume hardly fit the formula of the title. But
even the pieces on Dickens and Kipling cannot be reduced to mere ex-
emplifications of the theory. They are also essays using the traditional
methods of criticism. In the Dickens essay Wilson is looking for the
darker side of Dickens at the expense of his humor. Dickens's interest in
criminals and rebels, thieves and murderers, in scenes of violence such

as hangings or the burning of Newgate prison in *Barnaby Rudge,* his general revolt against the institutions and the temper of the age and its representative, the Queen, whom he studiously avoided meeting, is skillfully expounded. In his last unfinished novel, *The Mystery of Edwin Drood,* "Dickens has turned," Wilson claims, "the protest against the age into a protest against self." Wilson sees Dickens accepting the verdict that "he is a creature irretrievably tainted" (102–03), a conclusion which seems warranted only if we assume that the murderer Jasper somehow embodies the submerged mind of Dickens himself.[16] But the essay was deservedly influential in changing the accepted image of the jolly Christmas Dickens, though Wilson's own picture seems overdrawn in the other direction.

Similarly, the essay on Kipling, though it makes much of the boy's tribulations as explaining how "the work of [his] life is to be shot through with hatred," soon becomes straight literary criticism. *Stalky and Co.* is the worst of Kipling's books, "crude in writing, trashy in feeling" whereas *Kim* is almost a first-rate book (*WB*, 111, 114, 123). But psychological criteria are used on occasion. The concept of overcompensation seems to be invoked when we are told that it is "proof of Kipling's timidity and weakness that he should loudly overdo this glorification" of his motherland. It seems hard, however, to understand why "the ferocious antagonism to democracy which finally overtakes him must have been fed by the fear of that household in Southsea which tried to choke his genius at its birth" (138, 143). It assumes that the boy Kipling saw the principle of democracy in the ferocious tyranny of his guardians and that he knew of his genius at that time. Even *The Light that Failed,* Wilson argues, shows that "the theme of anguish which is suffered without being deserved [that is, the going blind of the hero] has the appearance of having been derived from a morbid permanent feeling of injury inflicted by his experience at Southsea." The whole attempt to derive every theme from these childhood experiences seems often forced: thus, "Mary Postgate," the story of a soldier killed in an airplane, is considered to illustrate the "theme of the abandoned parent" (actually a plain and dull companion who stood in a maternal role to the soldier) as "reflecting in reversal the theme of abandoned child" (166). As often in psychoanalysis, it is "Heads or tails, you lose."

We must look beyond *The Wound and the Bow* for Wilson's use of psychoanalytical insights. "The Ambiguity of Henry James" in *The Triple Thinkers* is the best-known essay which tries to interpret *The Turn of the Screw* as "a neurotic case of sex repression." The ghosts are not real ghosts but hallucinations of the governess (*TT*, 88). Wilson's view is easily refuted not only by Henry James's express declaration in the *Notebooks* (published after Wilson's essay) but by the obvious fact (which Wilson tries to dispute, however) that "Mrs. Gross, the housekeeper, recognizes the dead valet in the highly specific description of the sinister intruder given by the governess, who had never before heard of Peter Quint."[17] While the paper seems mistaken in the attempt to psychoanalyze James's ghost story, it does perceptively discuss James's preoccupation with the "conception of a man shut out from love, condemned to peep at other people's activities," "dramatizing the frustrations of his own life" (100– 01). In a postscript to the essay (1948) Wilson accepts the psychoanalytical interpretation by Dr. Saul Rosenzweig of James's accident during a fire at Newport, Rhode Island, in 1861 (when he was eighteen) but backs away from its full implication when he disowns the idea of "reducing the dignity of these stories by reading into them the embarrassments of the author" (129, 130n.). Much of the paper is straight literary criticism. Thus Wilson singles out the first volume of *The Tragic Muse* as "solid and alive," as James's "best novel," and condemns *The Awkward Age* "for combining a lifeless trickery of logic with the equivocal subjectivity of a nightmare" (106, 111). Wilson won a prize as a Princeton undergraduate with an essay on Henry James[18] and preserved for him a lifelong affection and not uncritical admiration. Unlike Van Wyck Brooks (and F. R. Leavis) Wilson cherishes the last novels of Henry James. They are not, "as Mr. Leavis asserts, fundamentally unreal and weak. Intellectually, they are perhaps the most vigorous, the most heroically conceived, of his fictions" (*SL*, 220).

Wilson became technically psychoanalytical only when he used Freud's article "Charakter und Analerotik" (1908) or some of its derivatives to characterize Ben Jonson. He finds in Ben Jonson the three traits, pedantry, avarice, and obstinacy, ascribed by Freud to childhood attitudes toward excretatory processes. Avarice appears in literature as a hoarding of words. Wilson, however, suddenly retreats from his commitment to the Freudian approach. "I am not qualified to 'analyze' Jonson in the light of this Freudian conception, and I have no interest in trying to fit him into any formulation of it. I am not even sure that the relation between the workings of the alimentary tract and the other phenomena of personality is, as Freud assumes, a relation of cause and effect; but I am sure that Freud has here really seized upon a nexus of human traits that are involved with one another and has isolated a recognizable type" (*TT*, 219). Thus "anal eroticism" in Wilson has come to mean nothing more than a psychological type, a pattern of character traits exhibited in the life and writings of Ben Jonson and apparently also in Gogol and

Joyce (*CC*, 216–17). But I cannot see that the recurrent themes of Ben
Jonson's plays, "miserliness, unsociability, a self-sufficient and systematic
spite," prove anything about Ben Jonson as a person or why a character
like Morose (the man pathologically and comically afraid of noise in *The
Silent Woman*) shows Ben Jonson "tormenting himself for what is negative
and recessive in his nature" (*TT*, 221). Ben Jonson, to my mind, has fun
at the expense of a miser and wants his audience to laugh at his plight
and gloat over his falling into a trap. Wilson underestimates the role of
genre, of stage stereotypes and theatrical conventions.

Wilson defends the interest in individual psychology as compatible
with the historical method and with Marxism. "The attitudes, the compulsions, the emotional 'patterns' that recur in the work of a writer are
of great interest to the historical critic. These attitudes and patterns are
embodied in the community and the historical moment, and they may
indicate its ideals and its diseases as the cell shows the condition of the
tissue. The recent scientific experimentation [I am not sure what Wilson
can be referring to] in the combining of Freudian with Marxist method,
and of psychoanalysis with anthropology, has had its parallel development in criticism." While welcoming this combination Wilson always sees
the limits of any genetic approach. "Freud himself emphatically states in
his study of Leonardo that his method can make no attempt to account
for Leonardo's genius. The problems of comparative artistic value will
remain after we have given attention to the Freudian psychological factor
just as they do after we have given attention to the Marxist economic
factor and to the racial and geographical factors" (*TT*, 266–67).

Only rarely can we discover Wilson's criteria for artistic value. It is
clear that poetry is judged by Wilson quite inadequately: he inherited,
possibly from Saintsbury, a distinction between content and form which
made form largely mean conventional versification and euphonious
sound-effects. Poetry is to him "a technique," and a "dying technique"
at that.[19] He rejects the narrowing of the concept of poetry to lyrical
verse, protesting Valéry's view that poetry is "absolutely different in kind
from prose," that it is "all suggestion, while prose is all sense" (*AC*, 82).
He argues that historically verse was used for all kinds of purposes. In
antiquity Lucretius and Virgil used it for philosophical argument or instruction in agriculture; Victorians like the Brownings wrote novels in
verse; in recent times the use of poetry is confined to the description or
expression of emotion (*AC*, 118–20; *TT*, 16–18). But Wilson draws from
this specialization of the concept of poetry, which parallels the "purification" of the other arts, the unwarranted conclusion that poetry is destined to disappear. This is justified by a theory that verse, being "a more

primitive technique than prose," is losing its early association with music and has become "ocular." One can understand that Wilson disliked the blank verse of Maxwell Anderson (*TT,* 26–28) and had his doubts about the success of modern verse drama as advocated by T. S. Eliot, but surely his forecast of the disappearance of verse is not likely to be fulfilled, considering the enormous output even in industrialized societies, not to speak of other countries and languages where verse has kept its dominance. Wilson reviewed many poets and wrote poetry himself, much of it humorous and parodic, but his relation to it remains unsure, awkward, even hostile, and his vocabulary in dealing with it is often vague and imprecise. He quickly slides into a discussion of theme and ideology and makes many egregious blunders in his estimates.

Emily Dickinson seems to him "a little overrated" (*PG,* 489), Robert Frost is "excessively dull and he certainly writes very poor verse" (*SL,* 240). E. E. Cummings is an "eternal adolescent," "as half-baked as a schoolboy," expressing "familiar and simple emotions," but at least he is not like Wallace Stevens "insulated or chilled; he is not indifferent to life." Stevens suffers "from a sort of aridity" but remains "a charming decorative artist" (50, 53, 49, 241). Auden has "arrested at the mentality of an adolescent schoolboy," though later Wilson recognized him as "an incredible virtuoso" (*SL,* 669; *BBT,* 362). Pound's poems are "a pile of fragments." "In spite of the parade of culture and the pontifical pretenses, Ezra Pound is really at heart a very boyish fellow and an incurable provincial" (*SL,* 45). No doubt, some of these jibes have their measure of truth, but even in the sympathetic discussions Wilson's limitations as a critic of poetry are glaring. The chapter on Yeats in *Axel's Castle* manages to ignore such poems as "The Second Coming" (1921) or "Sailing to Byzantium" (1928). Wilson criticizes him for what in recent jargon has been called "elitism," his "dignity and distinction" "becoming more and more impossible in our modern democratic society," for his aloofness from the "democratic, the scientific, the modern world," "from the general enlightened thought of his time," and Wilson is comprehensibly impatient with *A Vision,* which he contrasts with the so much more sensible *Intelligent Woman's Guide to Socialism and Capitalism* by Bernard Shaw (*AC,* 39, 40, 47, 59). The essay on T. S. Eliot in the same book excels in suggesting the personal sources of Eliot's views. *The Waste Land* illustrates "the peculiar conflicts of the Puritan turned artist, the horror of vulgarity and the shy sympathy with the common life, the ascetic shrinking from sexual experience and the distress at the drying up of the springs of sexual emotion, with the straining after a religious emotion which may be made to take its place" (105). A diary entry is even more perceptive in saying that *The Waste Land* is "nothing more nor less than a most distressing moving account of Eliot's own agonized state of mind during the years which preceded his nervous breakdown." "It is certainly a cry *de profundis* if there ever was one—almost the cry of a man on the verge of insanity" (*TW*, 247–48). Wilson, however, never tried to say anything about the *Four Quartets*. In poetic taste Wilson remains an incurable imagist who admires the music of smooth verse and the vividness of visual metaphors in Edna St. Vincent Millay, Elinor Wylie, or Genevieve Taggard, poets he greatly overrated, and not only for personal reasons. Music and image somehow combined or fused are his ideal of poetry.

He is much more satisfactory and much more concrete when he speaks of the novel. A great novelist "must show us large social forces, or uncontrollable lines of destiny, or antagonistic impulses of the human spirit, struggling with one another" (*WB*, 126–27). The idea, old enough, of the need of contraries in art is developed also as an argument against propaganda art. "One of the primary errors of recent radical criticism has been the assumption that great novels and plays must necessarily be written by people who have everything clear in their minds. People who have everything clear in their minds, who are not capable of identifying themselves imaginatively with, who do not actually embody in themselves, contrary emotions and points of view, do not write novels or plays at all— do not, at any rate, write good ones. And—given genius—the more violent the contraries, the greater the works of art" (*TT*, 180). Somewhat surprisingly this criterion of violent contraries, apparently not necessarily reconciled, is used to put down *War and Peace* as not "quite one of the very summits of literature" because of its "idyllic tendency," for "a certain element of the idealization in which we are all disposed to indulge in imagining the lives of our ancestors" (*CC*, 448). One could argue that *War and Peace* shows violent contraries: war and peace, age and youth, good and evil, and so forth, more than most novels, but Wilson has a point in feeling the nostalgia that permeates many scenes. In all of these passages nothing suggests anything but a clash of contraries. But when Wilson reads Pushkin's *Evgeny Onegin*, which he admires almost beyond any other work of literature, he feels as if he were watching the process "by which the several elements of [Pushkin's] character, the several strands of his experience, have taken symmetry about the foci of distinct characters." Pushkin's "serenity, his perfect balance of tenderness for human beings with unrelenting respect for reality, show a rarer quality of mind than Stendhal's" (*TT*, 46).

Balance, equipoise is not quite resolution, reconciliation. But in a few passages Wilson thinks of art in these terms. "That was the paradox of literature: provoked by the anomalies of reason, by its discord, its chaos, its pain, it attempted, from poetry to metaphysics, to impose on that chaos some order, to find some resolution for that discord, to render the pain acceptable" (*SL*, 271). Sometimes Wilson conceives this ordering and consoling function of literature in crass utilitarian terms: "All our intellectual activity, in whatever field it takes place, is an attempt to give meaning to our experience—that is, to make life more practicable; for by understanding things we make it easier to survive and get around among them." Immediately afterwards the function of literature is again defined as curative: "We have been cured of some ache of disorder, relieved of some oppressive burden of uncomprehended events" (*TT*, 269–70). It sounds almost like Wordsworth speaking of the "lightening of the burden of the mystery." In the upshot, Wilson seems to require some basic optimism from a writer. Thus he prefers Steinbeck to Aldous Huxley because of Steinbeck's "irreducible faith in life." Referring to *After Many a Summer Dies the Swan*, Wilson says: "We shall become more likely to find out something of value for the control and ennoblement of life by studying human behavior in this spirit than through the code of self-contemplation that seems to grow so rootlessly and palely in the decay of scientific tradition which this latest of the Huxley's represents" (*CC*, 44). Similarly Wilson complains about the stories in Angus Wilson's *The Wrong Set* that "we end by being repelled and by feeling that it is not quite decent to enjoy so much ugliness and humiliation. There ought to be some noble value somewhere" (*BBT*, 272). On occasion Wilson seems, however, to consider this idealizing function of literature simply a fraud. He can say that "art has its origin in the need to pretend that human life is something other than it is, and, in a sense, by pretending this, it succeeds to some extent in transforming it" (*SL*, 62). But in a discussion of Dostoevsky we are told that "the work of art has only the dignity of any other self-protective movement." Dostoevsky "has falsified life, because he has pretended to harmonize something." "The work of art is therefore an imposture."[20] But this imposture, this beautiful lie is ultimately seen as a noble necessity. Wilson wrote a crude and obtuse essay, "A Dissenting Opinion on Kafka" (1947), which argues that it is impossible "to take him seriously as a major writer," but the objections to his presumed pessimism and religious mysticism come from a deep core of Wilson's nature. When he quotes in conclusion Kafka's aphorism "one must not cheat anybody, not even the world of its triumph," Wilson protests. "But what are we writers here for if it is not to cheat the world of its triumph?" (*CC*, 392). This is why he was so impressed by André Malraux's *Voices of Silence*, "one of the really great books of our time":

Malraux believes that modern Western art "has a tremendous philosophical and moral importance, because it represents, for the first time,
a deliberate declaration by man of his will to master the world, to create
it in conformity with his own ideals" (*BBT,* 137, 139). Wilson felt the
same. Art is consolation, and expression of faith in life. Paradoxically he
sounds like Arnold or Keble, who speak of poetry as the *vis medica,* the
healing power in a time of unbelief.

I have tried to show that Wilson cannot be simply dismissed as lacking
a coherent point of view. He early adopted a version of Taine's determinism and when he was converted to Marxism assimilated the Marxist
approach, deprived of its dialectic, to a general historical view of literature and literary study. Marxism became a variety of genetic explanation
alongside psychoanalysis. Judicial criticism, the decision of what is good
and what is bad in art, remained reserved to a judgment of taste independent of history.

I am aware that Wilson cannot be judged merely a theorist. On many
questions he has nothing to say, for he has not thought them worthy of
his attention. He is, and never claimed otherwise, a practical critic who
has fulfilled his aims in reporting and judging books and authors from
many countries on an enormous variety of subjects. He has opened windows, and not only to Russia. His human sympathy is almost unlimited.
It extends, as he just remarked, "even to those [manifestations of the
American literary movement] of which, artistically, he disapproves" (*SL,*
229) because he wanted to assert the dignity of the literary vocation in
America. This sympathy seems, on occasion, too indiscriminate when we
think of his weakness for such trivial authors as Ronald Firbank or shallow raconteurs such as Casanova, whom Wilson prefers to Rousseau (*WB,*
192),[21] or for eccentrics such as J. J. Chapman. Still, we might find his
hero-worship for teachers such as Mr. Rolfe or Dean Gauss touching,
and I for one make no complaints about his contempt for detective fiction
and historical romances.

Still, there are definite limits to the reach of his mind. I am not thinking only of his obvious lack of technical skill in analyzing narrative modes
or poetic structures. More disturbing is the coarseness and even sentimental vulgarity of his dominant interest in sex, displayed in some of
the fiction and, obsessively, in the notebooks. He shows hardly any interest in the fine arts or music. He lacks understanding not only for
religion, which he treats as a "delusion," but also for philosophy. The
early enthusiasm for Whitehead, his "crystalline abstract thought" (*TW,*
290), seems to be based on a misunderstanding. It supported Wilson in

his limited sympathies for symbolism and made him discount the "two divisions of mind and matter, body and soul,"[22] also in his polemics against the neohumanists. But he could not share Whitehead's neoplatonic idealism or his concept of God and soon abandoned him for Marxism. But as Wilson's Marxism discarded the dialectics, it meant rather a return to a basic positivism and pragmatism, a commonsense attitude to reality. One sees this also in the comment on existentialism, which Wilson ridiculed for its assumption that "the predicament of the patriotic Frenchmen oppressed by the German occupation represents the condition of all mankind" (CC, 399). Wilson seems not to know that Sartre had formulated his views by 1936 and that existentialism goes back to Heidegger and ultimately to Kierkegaard. Wilson thus could not escape from the limitations of a world view fundamentally akin to his early masters, Bernard Shaw and H. G. Wells, however much he transcended their provincialism. In spite of his cosmopolitanism, the wide range of his interests, there is a closeness and even crudity about his self-assurance and air of authority. But as public critic he dominates the early twentieth century with a resonance unmatched by any of the New Critics.

7: LIONEL TRILLING (1905–1975)

IT IS NOT easy to focus on the literary criticism of Lionel Trilling if literary criticism is understood strictly as comment on literature: theories about it, principles, and specific texts. Trilling belongs, with Edmund Wilson, to critics of culture, in particular American culture, and he is often concerned with questions of politics, pedagogy, psychology, and self-definition, which are only remotely related to literature. Still, all these concerns involve literature at least marginally, illuminate his literary criticism, and thus require some discussion.

Even the development of his politics needs to be sketched. Trilling started to write stories and book reviews for the *Menorah Journal* in 1925, a journal concerned with the "sense of identity of the Jews" which would be neither religious nor Zionist (see "Young in the Thirties," *Commentary* 41 [1966]: 47). Later, however, Trilling rejected the importance of Jewishness for his work. He grants that "it is never possible for a Jew of my generation to 'escape' his Jewish origin," but, he says, "I cannot discover anything in my professional intellectual life which I can specifically trace back to my Jewish birth and rearing. I do not think of myself as a 'Jewish writer.' I do not have in mind to serve by my writing any Jewish purpose. I should resent it if a critic of my work were to discover in it either faults or virtues which he called Jewish" (*Contemporary Jewish Record* 7 [1944]: 15). When Trilling was asked to become a member of the advisory board of *Commentary,* he declined on the grounds that joining a Jewish magazine "would now" for him "be only a posture and a falsehood."[1] We must take these disclaimers at face value. When in "Wordsworth and the Rabbis" (1950) Trilling recalls his early reading of *Pirke Aboth,* a second-century rabbinical tract, he does so only to engage in an exercise in the history of ideas. "The Judaic quality" (*OS,* 123) he tries to demonstrate in Wordsworth turns out to be stoicism and some motifs of mysticism and quietism to which the Jewish fathers present only a remote analogy. Trilling does not claim more. He does not serve a Jewish purpose.

In 1930 he started to contribute to the *Nation* and *New Republic,* joining the left-wing intelligentsia during the years of the Depression. He says himself that "we were a group who, for a short time in 1932 and even into 1933, had been in a tenuous relation with the Communist Party through some of its so-called fringe activities."[2] He must have been disillusioned early not only with the party he never joined but also with Marxism. There is little Marxism in his writings unless we consider simply historicism and determinism or a strong interest in class relations and in the problem of "alienation" as Marxist. But all these ideas predate Marx and are not used by Trilling in a specifically Marxist framework. Politically Trilling preserved his "liberalism," the term oddly used in the United States which, in economic convictions, means the opposite of what in England and on the continent of Europe had been the creed of liberalism: laissez-faire, free enterprise. Here it rather favors socialism or at least the welfare state. But liberalism for him means also a belief in progress, in humanitarianism, in human and civil rights, in equality for the negro and, of course, the Jew, still discriminated against in the academy, as Trilling's slow advancement at Columbia was to show. But Trilling must have early become suspicious of the utopianism of his fellow liberals. Much later he spoke of his "thoroughly anti-Utopian mind" ("Paradise Reached For," *MCR* 5 [1959]: 21), and he distrusted all hopes for the malleability of human nature. Freud must have been the decisive influence, though Trilling did not write about him expressly before 1940. (The book on Arnold [1939] contains only one brief suggestion of a Freudian interpretation, see p. 130.) From Freud he learned to stress "a given of biology, definitive of man's nature," "the essential immitigability of the human condition" (*SA*, 156). The panaceas of the thirties seemed to him naive. His only novel, *The Middle of the Journey* (1947), finely written but too schematic and argumentative to be a good novel, presents this conflict within the intelligentsia. With the growth of the Communist threat after the Second World War, Trilling spoke of himself as an "anti-Communist" (*Commentary* 44 [1967]: 76), and during the student unrest in the late sixties he came to see the students' revolt as mistaken in its assumption of "dealing with the university as if it were perfectly continuous with the society, or as if it were the microcosm of the society" (*PR*, 35 [1968]: 392). The Jefferson lecture, *Mind in the Modern World* (1972), shows Trilling's unhappiness about "the ideological trend which rejects and seeks to discredit the very concept of mind" (30), the new extreme irrationalism which advocates intoxication, violence, and madness (35). But even at this late stage one cannot speak of Trilling's "conservatism" as Joseph Frank did in a well-known essay, "Lionel Trilling and the Conservative Imagination," if we take "conservatism" in any current political

sense accepted either in England or in the United States. Trilling remained, undoubtedly, committed to the principles of liberalism and to
its criticism of the American business civilization as well as to the ideals
of equality, justice, and freedom. He became, at most, disillusioned with
politics and the hope of literature influencing politics (*BC*, 83). He rejected the Soviet version of "progress" and any other millenianism, but
that should not earn him the label of "reactionary" or "Establishment
figure" or even "conservative."

Trilling's political development, which is typical of his time and place—
the early involvement with radicalism, even fellow-traveling, the disen-
chantment with Soviet Russia, the growing apprehension of the dangers
of a new totalitarianism, a revulsion from the mindless destructiveness
of the students' revolts—would be of little relevance here if it had not
been a theme of Trilling 's literary criticism. Certainly the conflict between the artist and his society dominates much of Trilling's thinking.
He constantly assumes the "adversary intention, the actually subversive
intention, that characterizes modern writing," the belief that "a primary
function of art and thought is to liberate the individual from the tyranny
of his culture" (*BC*, xii–xiii), that the poet has to destroy a world of
"specious good" (quoted from Wallace Fowlie, in "Rimbaudelaire," *MCR*
34 [1961]: 4). In the description of a course on the antecedents of modern literature, Trilling selected only texts that exemplify the subversion
of traditional attitudes: Frazer's *Golden Bough,* which provided "a bridge
to the understanding and acceptance of extreme mental states, rapture,
ecstasy, and transcendence, which are achieved by drugs, trance, music
and dance, orgy, and the derangement of personality" (*BC*, 18),
Nietzsche's *Birth of Tragedy* with its celebration of the orgiastic state, Conrad's *Heart of Darkness,* depicting the compelling attraction of savage life,
Dostoevsky's *Notes from the Underground,* rejecting all the assumptions of
modern civilization, and other texts, all illustrating the rise of irrationalism. Even Mann's *Death in Venice* is chosen for its dream of the goat-orgy,
and *The Magic Mountain* is interpreted, very selectively if one thinks of
Hans Castorp and Joachim, in the light of Mann's pronouncement that
"all his work could be understood as an effort to free himself from the
middle class," which to Trilling seems insufficient: the end is not merely
freedom from the middle class but freedom from "society itself," what
he calls "beyond culture," the title of his last collection of essays (1965).
The doctrine of alienation, which Trilling defines in Marxist terms (*EL*,
467), is for him "an act of criticism" (*BC*, 230).

What worries Trilling in particular is that this adversary relation of
the artist (of which he obviously approves) has been most successfully

stated by writers who do not criticize their society from the point of view of American liberal democracy but often hold illiberal and reactionary opinions. He is upset by the "discrepancy that exists between the political beliefs of our educated class and the literature that, by its merit, should properly belong to that class" (*LI*, 97), whatever "belonging" could mean here. He complains that "no connection exists between our liberal educated class and the best of the literary minds of our time" (98–99). Trilling cites Proust, Joyce, Lawrence, Eliot, Mann ("in his creative work"), Kafka, Rilke, and Gide (98) in support of this view, though these writers held very different political opinions, often quite irrelevant to the American situation. One can doubt, for example, that Proust, a *dreyfusard*, Joyce, and Gide were so indifferent to liberal ideas.[3] Trilling was attracted by most of these writers, particularly by Joyce, but his main love was reserved rather for Jane Austen, the Victorians, Henry James, and E. M. Forster. The general tendency of his first book of essays, *The Liberal Imagination*, is a plea that the liberal class be reconciled with modern literature. It is the program of *Partisan Review* as reconstituted in 1937; political radicalism is to be combined with modernism at a time when modernism was ostracized in Russia in favor of socialist realism. Trilling wanted a link "between the political ideas of our educated class and the deep places of the imagination," a link for which he found the odd phrase "the liberal imagination," which is surely meant not "pejoratively"[4] but as the ideal he hoped for. In practice, as an exchange with William Barrett clarifies, Trilling wanted the ideals of liberalism (which he recognized as derived from the Enlightenment) criticized, modified, and revised by the tradition that could vaguely be called romantic: Rousseau, Blake, Burke, and Wordsworth. Trilling complains that "contemporary liberalism seems incapable of responding to the realistic values of Romanticism which, equally with the idealistic values of the Enlightenment, are properly part of its heritage" (*PR*, 16 [1949]: 654), "idealistic" meaning here "utopian" and not "idealism" in a philosophical sense. He alludes to John Stuart Mill's essays on Coleridge and Bentham in which Mill proposed to correct Bentham by Coleridge, utilitarianism by idealism, and he hails Freud for having achieved the right synthesis.

Freud is the key figure in Trilling's thinking. He is seen as the culmination of "Romanticist literature" (*LI*, 35), even though Trilling knows Freud's system to be militantly rationalistic and positivistic (40). Trilling accepts Freud's view of the self, his whole topography of the mind (ego, super-ego, and id), the crucial role of the Oedipus complex (chiding, for instance, Enid Starkie for dismissing it in her biography of Baudelaire; see "Rimbaudelaire" in *MCR* 34 [1961]: 5), and he particularly extols

Freud's later writings. *Civilization and Its Discontents* is his favorite, and from *Beyond the Pleasure Principle* he derives a theory of tragedy which, he thinks, corrects Aristotle's, which gives "a show of rationality to suffering" (*GF,* 35). Trilling reads into Freud a theory of the "mithraditic function" of tragedy; "the homeopathic administration of pain is to inure us to the greater pain which life will force upon us" (*LI,* 56), a revival of the old commonplace idea formulated, for instance, by Corneille, that tragedy is a training in stoicism. But elsewhere, in a discussion of *King Lear,* Trilling rejects the view that the sufferings of Lear and Gloucester are "redemptive" and almost accepts Jan Kott's interpretation, which would make *King Lear* sound like *Endgame,* grotesque, absurd, merely horrifying. Trilling sees that the theme of *King Lear* is not only "the decay and fall of the world" and simply nihilism. Shakespeare rather "took for granted a rational and moralized universe but proposed the idea that this universal order might be reduced to chaos by human evil" (*EL,* 133). Trilling does not share Shakespeare's view. Tragedy invites us to find in it some pedagogic purpose, but for Trilling "the invitation cannot really be thought to be made in good faith" (*SA,* 83). Tragedy, he argues, negates life, "celebrates a mystery debarred to reason, prudence, and morality" (84). Thus it seems not so odd that Trilling thought of Tertan, the young man who ends in madness in his story "Of This Time, of That Place," as an "impressive, even heroic figure" who "made the demand on me that I come as close as I could to tragedy" (*EL,* 783). One can argue as Robert Boyers does, that Trilling failed, but one can hardly deny that this concept of tragedy, basically identical with Schopenhauer's, is much on his mind and tallies well with his acceptance of Freud's death instinct, though he recognizes that its existence is not proved clinically. Freud formulated for Trilling his personal and cultural pessimism, his "vision of necessity in our biological heritage and long cultural history" (*GF,* 58), mitigated only by "the grandeur, the ultimate tragic courage in acquiescence to fate" (*LI,* 56). Freud as a person is Trilling's hero: misunderstood, neglected at first, rejected, persecuted, exiled, and finally dying of cancer, stoically refusing medication which would have impaired his autonomy.

But this exaltation of Freud to "one of the very greatest of humanistic minds" (*BC,* 91) and even the claim that "Freud ultimately did more for our understanding of art than any other writer since Aristotle" (*LI,* 161) should not obscure the fact that Trilling is very critical of Freud's own views on literature and art. "Freud speaks of art with what we must call contempt. Art, he tells us, is 'substitute gratification,' and as such is 'an illusion in contrast to reality' " (42). Freud sees art as "almost exclusively hedonistic" (45). Art for Freud is a narcotic, "the artist is virtually in the same category with the neurotic," while Trilling appeals rather to Lamb's essay on "The Sanity of Art." He quotes Freud admitting that the psychoanalytical method "can do nothing toward elucidating the nature of the artistic gift, nor can it explain the means by which the artist works—artistic technique" (47). Trilling accepts the reading of *Hamlet* in terms of the Oedipus complex and even the interpretation of the three caskets. He praises in general the technique of looking for latent meanings but reserves his highest praise, besides the concept of tragedy, for Freud's "making poetry indigenous to the very constitution of the mind." The mind with Freud is "exactly a poetry-making organ" (52), an interpretation of Freud's emphasis on symbol-making that approximates him, illegitimately I think, to Vico or Hamann or the Schlegels, who all knew about the metaphorical workings of the mind. But as in his use of Marx, so with Freud: Trilling shies away from using Freudian techniques in his literary criticism. Though general Freudian concepts occur occasionally, I do not recall a single instance of psychoanalytical interpretation anywhere in his criticism. One possible exception is the use of "oceanic" in explaining lines in stanza 9 of Wordsworth's "Immortality Ode," for which Trilling quotes Freud (144), omitting, however, to tell us that Freud drew the term from Romain Rolland and said that "I myself cannot discover this 'oceanic feeling' in myself " (see *Studienausgabe* 4: 198). Trilling in passing praises Franz Alexander's essay on *Henry IV* (51), Ferenczi's *Thalassa* (147n.), and Norman O. Brown's chapters on Swift and Luther (*MCR* 5 [1959]: 21), but when confronted with psychoanalytical reading such as Saul Rosenzweig's of Henry James, he rejects it outright (*LI*, 165–66). He raises doubts about Edmund Wilson's use of the Philoctetes story. "It is not an explanatory myth at all" (180). Trilling cannot be called either a Marxist or a Freudian critic.

Trilling's literary criticism may be best defined by situating it in relation to the New Criticism. Trilling obviously was not a New Critic in any sense of belonging to the group, but his outlook was profoundly shaped by the New Criticism and was, in many ways, not so dissimilar as widespread preconceptions assume. Trilling had personal and even organizational contacts with the New Critics: he was a Senior Fellow of the Kenyon School of Letters (though he never taught there), he took an active part in the English Institute, which, in its early years, was a forum of the New Criticism, and he was on the board of editors and contributed to the *Kenyon Review,* the journal edited by John Crowe Ransom. His own anthology, *Literary Criticism* (1970), contains an ample selection from the New Critics. Trilling welcomes the reaction against the positivistic, pseu-

doscientific study of literature, a reaction that he thinks was first formulated by John Jay Chapman in 1927 (though Irving Babbitt's cogent
Literature and the American College dates from 1908 and J. E. Spingarn
had started his campaign as early as 1904). In a speech at Cornell University, *The Scholar's Caution and the Scholar's Courage* (1962), Trilling acknowledged that "only by overcoming the virtual dominance of the
historical point of view has the graduate study of literature made any
advance toward that humanistic actuality which is properly desired for
it . . . and certainly it is true that the history of literature can stand like
a lion in the path that leads to literature itself—and did stand so until a
very few decades ago, when it was challenged by the critical movement
. . . which affirmed the autonomous interest in literature itself " (13). In
an article entitled "The Farmer and the Cowboy Make Friends" (*Griffin*
5 [1956]: 4–12), Trilling tells an anecdote about a Yale professor who
spent the whole lecture hour on the biography and political career of
Andrew Marvell but at the end could say about his ostensible subject,
the poem "To His Coy Mistress," only: "As for the poem, gentlemen—a
gem—a gem!" (7). Trilling thus endorses the main point of the New
Criticism when he says, "Criticism, we know, must always be concerned
with the poem itself " (*LI*, 129; also *LC*, 11). The aim of criticism, he
argues, is to get beyond the simulacra, that is, the false interpretations,
the legends accumulated around it, to get at the "poem as it really is"
(*LI*, 129). In commenting on *Kubla Khan*, he can say that "we admit the
possibility that a work of art can exist in its own right, without reference
to us, like a tree, or a mountain, or an animal" (*EL*, 874). He even can
say that "literary study, if it is to fulfill its implied promises, must sooner
or later be a study of language" (*SR* 66 [1958]: 379). Alluding apparently
to T. S. Eliot's Minnesota speech on the lemon-squeezer school of criticism, Trilling argues that "one may not surrender one's right to press
each work as hard as one can in order to make it yield the full of its
possible meaning" (*BC*, 193), though in another context, overtly referring
to Eliot's speech and recognizing the reaction against the New Criticism,
Trilling takes a cautious middle ground. "I have no wish to be involved
in the issue of this reaction. I am aware that modern critical practice has
sometimes gone to extravagant lengths in interpretation, yet I find that
there really is a good deal of difficulty to be encountered in literature,
often where it is least suspected, and it seems to me profitable and interesting to press harder upon a work of literature than my temperament
naturally inclines me to. In short, I am concerned neither to attack nor
to defend the modern criticism" (*SR* 66 [1958]: 375–76). In general Trilling welcomes a collaboration between literary history and criticism. He

considers the conflict as "entirely factitious if we conceive of literary history and criticism in their ideal forms" (*Griffin* 5 [1956]: 7). In 1962 he could look back at the New Criticism as something that has "by now lost its chic, and its force is abated" but that is so "because it has in large part been incorporated in the graduate system," and "we cannot doubt that it has had a liberalizing—perhaps even liberating—effect" (*The Scholar's Caution*, 6).

Trilling, however, disagreed with the New Critics on several crucial points. In an essay entitled "The Sense of the Past" (1942) Trilling charges that "in their reaction from the historical method [the New Critics] forget that the literary work is ineluctably a historical fact, and what is more important, that its historicity is a fact in our aesthetic experience" (*LI*, 184). Trilling acknowledges that the "New Critics' refusal to take critical account of the historicity of the work" is motivated by "the impulse to make the work of the past more immediate and real" but argues, paraphrasing T. S. Eliot, the supposed initiator of the New Criticism, that "it is only if we are aware of the reality of the past that we can feel it as alive and present" (186). He criticizes Cleanth Brooks and Robert Penn Warren's college anthology *Understanding Poetry* (1938) for not asking the question, "What effect is created by our knowledge that the language of a particular poem is not such as would be uttered by a poet writing now?" (187), going so far as to say that if Wordsworth's "Immortality" ode "were offered to us now as a contemporary work, we would not admire it" (186). But then Trilling recognizes that the preference of the New Critics for the poetry of the seventeenth century meant that "they were involving their aesthetics with certain cultural preferences, they were implying choices in religion, metaphysics, politics, manners" and thus "were exercising their historical sense" (187). Trilling has taken back or at least modified his charge of their lacking a sense of the past.

He also profoundly disagreed with the New Critics, or rather T. S. Eliot, about the role of personality in literature. He disapproves of the view that "the poet is not a person at all, only a *persona*" and that to "impute him a personal existence is a breach of literary decorum" (*SA*, 8). He resents being forbidden "to remark the resemblance between Stephen Dedalus and James Joyce" and thinks it cannot be "wholly fortuitous" that "the hero of Proust's novel is named Marcel" (8). He welcomes Donald Davie's plea for "the immediate exhibition of the self " in recent poetry (9). Biography and the relation between life and work was always one of Trilling's concerns; his thesis on Matthew Arnold (1939) is primarily an intellectual biography, and the slighter book on E. M. Forster (1943), while inevitably at that time deficient in biographical information, tries to relate his writings constantly to the man. Trilling argues that in reading "Lycidas" "we cannot dismiss from our minds the fact that the young poet who speaks so proudly of the profession of poetry and of his noble desire for fame is to become one of the world's great poets, as famous as ever he could have wished." We cannot ignore that a poem by Emily Dickinson is "based upon the femininity of the poet": no man could have spoken about "sweet Thermopylae" (*El*, 918–19). Sometimes Trilling looks for models in real life for fictional figures, though he admits the critical irrelevance of the comparison—"an awareness of the relation between an actual person and a created character can have no part in our assessment of a work of fiction"—but proceeds then to tell about the models in real life for the two students in his own story, "Of This Time, of That Place," saying that this information is "useful in helping us understand the interplay between actuality and imagination" (781). Discussing Henry James's *Princess Casamassima*, which he calls "intensely autobiographical" (*LI*, 78), he draws a strained parallel between Paul Muniment and William James, and Paul's sister Rosy and Alice James. *The Bostonians* is also considered to "bear in an important way upon the personal problems of Henry James's own life which are implied, we must inevitably suppose, by Ransom's fears" (*OS*, 115). But at other times Trilling rejects simple biographical explanations: he disapproves of reducing the decline of Wordsworth's poetic powers in later life to any single cause, be it remorse for his treatment of Annette Vallon, disappointment with the French Revolution, or the quarrel with Coleridge (*LI*, 130).

Trilling's fundamental disagreement with the New Criticism concerns, however, the role of ideas and of moral and political aims in literature. The disagreement goes back to a different conception of the nature of literature. Trilling is one of those who do not think that literature is primarily an art analogous to painting or music. "Literature," he argues, "doesn't easily submit to the category of aesthetic disinterestedness—so much of it insists '*De te fabula*—this means *you*' and often goes on to say, 'and you'd better *do* something about it quick.' " Literature is thus persuasion, rhetoric, propaganda, and "will involve important considerations of practicality and thus of cogency, relevance, appositeness, logicality, and truth" (*GF*, 136). He emphasizes that "art [and he means here literature] is not a unitary thing." "We must not make reference only to its 'purely' aesthetic element requiring that every work of art serve our contemplation by being wholly self-contained and without relation to action" (*LI*, 289). In my own terminology Trilling upholds the view that a work of literature is an assembly of values, some of them aesthetic, others moral and intellectual, and that it is designed to have effects in real life: to convey information, to shape moral and intellectual attitudes, to stir to action. Trilling is thus disturbed by what he considers the anti-intellectual, antiphilosophical attitude of much modern criticism, quoting T. S. Eliot's notorious pronouncements that neither "Dante nor Shakespeare did any thinking of his own" and that Henry James had "a mind so fine that no idea could violate it" (284). He argues against my and Austin Warren's attempt, in *Theory of Literature* (1948), to show that ideas in literature become effective only if "they cease to be ideas in the ordinary sense and become symbols, or even myths" (283). Trilling disputes this, at least for the novel, for which he claims "the right and the necessity to deal with ideas by means other than that of the 'objective correlative,' to deal with them directly as it deals with people or terrain or social setting" (274). As examples of the American novel of ideas Trilling produces Hemingway and Faulkner, surely the two writers of the time who were furthest from making overt philosophical statements; and when Trilling appeals to another witness for the novel of ideas, Stendhal, he says himself that Stendhal expresses ideas "in terms of prisons and rope ladders, pistols and daggers" and concedes that "it is in the nature of ideas to be so expressed" (274). He knows very well the difference between a philosophical statement and its use in a work of literature. "Kafka does not exemplify Kierkegaard; Proust does not dramatize Bergson" (292). All that Austin Warren and I argued was that ideas change in an aesthetic context. Even the witty exaggerations of T. S. Eliot want to say no more than the obvious: Dante and Shakespeare were no philosophers and Henry James did not embrace a specific ideology.

Much of this disagreement is due to Trilling's almost exclusive attention to the novel. He considers it always in terms of conflict between realism and romance, the conditioned and the free self, the mimetic and the didactic. The novel is, he often emphasizes, referential, reportorial. "Reality still remains one of the great effects toward which literature directs itself" (*Griffin* 2 [1953]: 5). "The novelist is the artist who is consumed by the desire to know how things really are, who has entered into an elaborate romance with actuality. He is the artist of the conditioned, of the impingement of things upon spirit and of spirit upon things, and the success of his enterprise depends as much upon the awareness of things as upon the awareness of spirit" (*GF*, 93). Trilling thus can, at times, defend the realism of the commonplace, exemplified by Howells, "the actuality of the conditioned, the literality of matter, the peculiar authenticity and authority of the merely denotative" (*OS*, 93).

He disapproves of speaking of money in Dostoevsky's novels as "symbolic": "as if one never needed, or spent, or gambled, or squandered the stuff—and as if to think of it as an actuality were subliterary" (93n.). The mere pleasure in reality, even in the trivialities that Howells enumerates—"the family budget, nagging wives, daughters who want to marry fools, and the difficulties of deciding whom to invite to dinner" (92)—adds to Trilling's sense of what he calls the "denseness" of the modern realistic novel. But he is of course aware of its limitations and the current disapproval of "literal reality": "Having admitted the existence of literal reality, we give it a low status in our judgment of art. Naturalism, which is the form of art that makes its effects by the accumulation of details of literal reality, is now in poor repute among us" (94). Trilling, while accepting and even praising lifelikeness, accurate social picture-taking, thinks of it mainly as a means toward a social and moral end. The novel is not only mimetic but also didactic, critical, incitory, providing ideals and models for life. Trilling praises the novel as "the most effective agent of the moral imagination." "Its greatness and its practical usefulness lay in its unremitting work of involving the reader himself in the moral life." "It taught us, as no other genre did, the extent of human variety and the value of this variety. It was the literary form to which the emotions of understanding and forgiveness were indigenous, as if by the definition of the form itself" (*LI*, 222). The novel Trilling has in mind is primarily the English novel of the nineteenth century, the novel of manners based on "the tension between middle class and aristocracy" (260), and more generally "the huge, swarming, substantial population of the European novel" (262), a "product of class existence" (262), which presumably includes Tolstoy and the great French novelists, particularly Flaubert.

The European novel is constantly preferred to the American. Trilling spoke even of his "quarrel with American literature" (*F,* 3), and in many contexts he elaborated the contrast between the English and the American novel, much to the disadvantage of the latter. The conflict of classes, the social struggle, is absent in the American novel. The famous complaint of Hawthorne and Henry James about "the disadvantage under which the American novelist labored because he lacked a historical past and a strongly structured society has been generally thought to have been bewailing the lack of interesting details, of variety and color in American life, and no doubt they did mean just that." But, Trilling argues, "more essential was their sense of the difficulty—the virtual impossibility—of making the American novel an expression of the will, of directing it against something, of making it serve some deep or unnamed moral-political intention, as the European novel did" (*MCR*, 10 [1960]: 10). The only early American novel that satisfied Trilling's requirements is Mark Twain's *Huckleberry Finn*, "one of the world's great books and one of the central documents of American culture" (*LI*, 105). It has "the power of telling the truth," has "the truth of moral passion: it deals directly with the virtue and depravity of man's heart." It is "a hymn to the older America forever gone . . . not yet enthralled by money" (106, 114). But the modern American social novel seems to him an almost total failure, though he grants that life in America has "thickened" since the time of Hawthorne's and James's pronouncements. The first essay in *The Liberal Imagination*, "Reality in America," accuses the critics of American society, V. L. Parrington, Charles Beard, and the Marxist Granville Hicks, of a crude conception of reality and criticizes Dreiser sharply for his "bookish diction," for his "dim, awkward speculation, his self-justification, his lust for 'beauty' and 'sex' and 'living' and 'life itself,' " and his "showy nihilism" which at the end turned into "blank pietism" at the very time he joined the Communist party (18–19). Trilling questions whether any American novel since Sinclair Lewis's *Babbitt* has told us "a new thing about our social life" (263). Sherwood Anderson belongs with Dreiser. He lacks mind. "His affirmation of life by love, passion, and freedom had, paradoxically, the effect of quite negating life, making it gray, empty, devoid of meaning" (28). His work shows no "real sensory and social experience" (29), has no wit, no specific idiom. The characters are simply not there. The mysticism is crude, the populism facile. Only *Winesburg, Ohio* has "a touch of greatness" (25). Also the newest writers fall short of Trilling's demands. Dos Passos "lacks humility and wisdom" (299). Hemingway is immature: "a strongly charged piety toward the ideals and attachments of boyhood and the lusts of maturity is in conflict with the imagination of death" (298). Faulkner remains "provincial" (213) though saved by his "awareness of the inadequacy and wrongness of the very tradition he loves" (298). "A Rose for Emily" is trivial in its horror. *Sartoris* is mere melodrama. Even *The Sound and the Fury* and *As I Lay Dying* "are essentially parochial" (*Nation* 133 [1931]: 491–92). Thomas Wolfe displays "a single, dull chaos of his powerful selfregard" (*LI*, 296). Only two writers escape the general condemnation: F. Scott Fitzgerald is "the last notable writer to affirm the Romantic Fantasy" (249), "a moralist to the core" who has "warmth and tenderness, gentleness without softness" (244), and surprisingly John O'Hara, whose "passion for verisimilitude" and preoccupation with social distinctions is appreciated so highly that his "metaphysical fear of society" is oddly enough considered "to bring him close to the author of *The Trial*."[5]

The English novels of the nineteenth century that Trilling discusses in some of his best and best-known essays are always praised for the balance between the acuteness of social observation and the moral issues they pose. Jane Austen's *Emma* embodies the ideal of "intelligent love" in a setting that Trilling describes as a "pastoral idyll." Jane Austen is for Trilling "the first novelist to represent society, the general culture, as playing a part in moral life" (*OS*, 228). Also *Mansfield Park* is seen as a story in which Jane Austen "puts the question of literature [that is, the theatricals] at the moral center of the novel" (219), and Mary Crawford is considered the first figure in fiction to represent insincerity (220). Even Fanny Price, prudish, timid as she is, appears to him as a "Christian heroine" like Milly Theale in *The Wings of the Dove* (213), and the rich, smooth, fat, dull Lady Bertram is allegorized to make the book speak "intimately to our secret inexpressible hopes" (230). Dickens's *Little Dorrit*, "one of the most significant works of the nineteenth century" (50), is "more about society than any other novel that is about society in its very essence" (51). He recognizes, however, that "the novel at its best is only incidentally realistic" (65) and treats it as a Dantesque allegory with the theme of incarceration running through it. But Trilling defends Henry James's *Princess Casamassima* as giving a "substantially accurate picture of the anarchist underground of the time" (*LI*, 68), centered on the theme of the "dispute between art and moral action, the controversy between the glorious unregenerate past and the regenerate future." (77), a conflict very much on Trilling's own mind. Similarly Trilling defends *The Bostonians* as a "representation of American actuality" which like *The Princess Casamassima* and most of James's other fiction represents "the conflict of two principles: energy and inertia; spirit and matter of spirit and letter; force and form, creation and possession; Libido and Thanatos." James's mind is nothing if not "dialectical": "the values assigned to the two opposing principles are not permitted to be fixed and constant" (*OS*, 108). James thus belongs to the tradition of the English novel with its balance of what Trilling calls "moral realism," while the American novel is either naturalistic, mired in inert matter, or unconditioned, spiritual, existing precariously in a rarefied air.

The sharp contrast between the English and the American novel seems overdrawn. To say that "Americans have not turned their minds to society" (*LI*, 212) assumes a specific narrow definition of what society means. Even in the nineteenth century there was a society and even a class structure in America: alternative distinctions such as ethnic or regional conflicts could have been an inspiration for the novel, and Trilling, of course, knows that the American "romance" flourished with Poe, Melville, and Hawthorne, all of whom may have been, as Trilling thinks, "quite apart from society" and may demonstrate the "lack of social texture" in America but cannot and are not to be dismissed as writers. Actually in a late essay called originally "Our Hawthorne," Trilling defends Hawthorne while granting that his "world is thinly composed," arguing that "whatever its composition lacks in thickness is supplied by an iron hardness" (*BC*, 199). Hawthorne, "our modern Hawthorne," is seen as "our dark poet, charged with chthonic knowledge," who can be compared to Kafka, though he may be inferior in power. Henry James's little book on Hawthorne is deficient in appreciating this side of Hawthorne: "It is touched with Philistinism of his epoch" (196). This revised view of Hawthorne must, however, be seen in the context of Trilling's prognostication for the future of the novel.

Trilling does not agree that the novel is dead, as it has often enough been declared to be. He grants that it is now at a standstill: it has "to compete with sociologists, psychologists, the cinema, and television" (*GF*, 125). It may be simply exhausted as a genre just as the poetic drama is exhausted. The interest in class, manners, and money which gives density to the English novel has declined. Optimism and a belief in human goodness have dwindled since Belsen and Buchenwald (*LI*, 264–65). The novel, Trilling argues, deals with "will," an elusive concept in Trilling which does not mean anything like the voluntarism of Nietzsche or Schopenhauer but something much more pragmatic, a psychological drive as in William James or Bergson. It seems to mean simply some aim, some purpose, some commitment to "action and moral judgment" (289). Today, this will, "the religious will, the political will, the sexual will, the artistic will—each is dying of its own excess." If I understand this, Trilling is saying that the artist or rather novelist had excessively engaged in social purpose or even propaganda and now, in 1946, has withdrawn within himself. But Trilling thinks that a turnabout is necessary: "The great work of our time is the restoration and reconstitution of the will" (267). It cannot be achieved, however, by the apocalyptic remedies proposed by prophets such as D. H. Lawrence. Suddenly, Trilling appeals to the concept of Romance. In a murky passage, rare in the usually lucid Trilling, he comes up with the curious notion that "romance" is a "synonym for the will in its creative aspect, especially in its aspect of moral creativeness." Trilling appeals to Henry James's preface to *The American,* which, however, on inspection does not support this view: will or moral creativeness is not even mentioned. But Trilling must have the preface in front of him, for he uses phrases from it on the very same page: "the beautiful circuit of thought and desire" and "the things we cannot possibly not know." Trilling reads into James the view that "the novel has had a long dream of virtue in which the will . . . learns to refuse to exercise itself upon the unworthy objects with which the social world tempts it, and either conceives its own right objects or becomes content with its own sense of its potential force—which is why so many novels give us, before their end, some representation, often crude enough, of the will unbroken but in stasis." While the precise meaning and the allusion to specific novels eludes me, I understand what follows: "It is the element of what James calls 'romance,' the operative reality of thought and desire, which, in the novel, exists side by side with the things 'we cannot possibly *not* know,' that suggests to me the novel's reconstitutive and renovating power" (269). Realism is not rejected, "the things we cannot possibly *not* know," but it must be combined with romance, which is the other name for imagination, ideas, wishes, desires, hopes. The English and the American novel are reconciled: romance and realism are one.

In looking at the present state of the novel, Trilling must deplore "the banishment of the author from his books, the stilling of his voice which reinforced the faceless hostility of the world and [has] tended to teach us that we ourselves are not creative agents and that we have no voice, no tone, no style, no significant existence" (*LI*, 270). The whole trend of the modern novel since Flaubert, with its dogma of "exit author," seems rejected. But Trilling also disapproves of the art novel in which "the personality of the author is consciously displayed—nothing could be more frivolous" (271), though it seems unclear where to draw the line for the proper tone and voice recommended before. But what Trilling mainly hopes for is a new novel of ideas (274). He insists that he does not want to establish a new genteel tradition as his praise of the English nineteenth-century novel was by some understood. His concept of the novel includes *The Iliad, The Possessed,* and Farrell's *Studs Lonigan* (259). Trilling does not like two new developments. He criticizes "elaborately styled fantasies" in the manner of Djuna Barnes's *Nightwood*. Joyce, he feels, is no counterargument. "When the prose of *A Portrait of the Artist* becomes what we call poetic, it is in a very false taste" (272n.), and *Ulysses* is not an art novel but is basically prosaic, even "one of the most delightful and charming books of the age," "one of the kindest books in the world, one of the most loving and forgiving" (*Griffin* 6 [1957]: 6), a deliberate challenge to the usual view of Joyce's pessimism and misanthropy. Nor can Trilling sympathize with the "drastic reduction in the status of narration" which seems to him a symptom of the lack of faith that "life is susceptible of comprehension and thus of management." He chides

Sartre for speaking about "the foolish business of story-telling" (*LI*, 270) and recognizes "how uneasy [the novel] is with the narrative mode, which once made its vital principle, and how its practitioners seek by one device or another to evade or obscure or palliate the act of *telling*" (*SA*, 134–35).

Thus the "novelist of the next decades will not occupy himself with questions of form" (*LI*, 272), predicts Trilling in 1949, and he seems to approve. Trilling is preoccupied with ideas, with social purpose, with moral intention. He constantly returns to the view that literature has "a nasty unaesthetic tradition to insist about some degree of immediate practicality" (*GF*, 136). He repeats: "Strange and sad as it may be to have to say it again, 'art is really a criticism of life' " (78). He had defended the Arnoldian formula in his first book as referring to the function of literature rather than to its nature (*A*, 196), and he defended it once more against Eliot's adverse comment. "Arnold meant, in short, that poetry is a criticism of life in the same way that the Scholar Gipsy was a criticism of the life of an inspector of elementary schools" (*OS*, xiii). Trilling remained committed to Arnold's view that "literature is an agency, depending upon and supplementing other social agencies" (*A*, 371).

But Trilling's position and practice are misrepresented if we think only of pronouncements such as "the novel achieves its best effects of art often when it has no concern with them, when it is fixed upon effects in morality, or when it is simply reporting what it conceives to be objective fact." He immediately continues: "The reverse is of course also true, that the novel makes some of its best moral discoveries or presentation of fact when it is concerned with form, when it manipulates its material merely in accordance with some notion of order or beauty" (*LI*, 277). He varies this elsewhere: "The novelist was to impose upon the harsh, resistant reality of life a unifying form. . . . He paid tribute not only to art but to the life upon which he imposed form—reality, even verisimilitude, was best achieved through the strictness of conscious art" ("The Wheel," *MCR* [1962]: 5). Trilling does not think much about form and the use of the term with him is often contradictory. He can say that "form is not the result of careful 'plotting'—the form of a good novel never is—but is rather the result of the necessities of the story's informing idea" (*LI*, 252). Applied to the drama, form is again identified with idea: "Its idea *is* its form. Form, even in [the abstract arts], is no less an idea" (284). He can say also, shifting from the Platonizing idea-form, that "dialectic is another word for form" (283). Trilling is uninterested in or suspicious of aesthetics, though he praises L. A. Reid's *A Study in Aesthetics* (1931):

he feels that the Beautiful has fallen into disrepute and disapproves the tendency of aesthetics, which he ascribes to the example of Aristotle's discussion of tragedy, "to suggest that the elements of harshness and pain in a work of art are present only that they may be overcome in reconciliation and peace and that the perfect aesthetic effect is repose" (*GF,* 134). Trilling obviously does not believe in disinterested contemplation and rejects aestheticism, but it is not true that he has no aesthetic standards. If we examine his interpretations of individual books not only in the collection of essays but in uncollected reviews scattered over many periodicals and even book-club magazines such as the *Griffin* and the *Mid-Century Review* and particularly if we read his extensive commentaries on plays, short stories, and poems in the bulky college anthology *The Experience of Literature* (1962), we discover that Trilling consistently uses the same standards as the New Criticism did, which, of course, in their turn are rooted in the organistic tradition of English criticism—in Coleridge in particular. Trilling constantly judges with the primacy of the whole in mind. "As with many poems," he comments on Wordsworth's "Immortality" ode, "it is hard to understand any part until we first understand the whole of it" (*BC,* 131). This whole is understood, and the New Critics would agree, as often contradictory, tensional. He looks, like them, for ironies and paradoxes. The irony of Jane Austen, he argues, is not moral detachment but "an awareness of the contradictions, paradoxes and anomalies" of the world (*OS,* 206). Keats's "Ode to a Nightingale" presents us in its seventh stanza "with a curious and deeply moving paradox" (*EL,* 896). Flaubert's *Bouvard et Pécuchet* appeals by reason of its ambiguity (*OS,* 197, 183). Babel's story "Di Gratto" culminates in the irony of a contrast between the pure and peaceful contemplation described in the last paragraph and the violence of the actor's leap (*EL,* 715). Hawthorne's story "My Kinsman, Major Molineux" "owes its new fame" to "its brilliant, bitter, ambivalent humor" (*BC,* 193). A poem by Robert Frost, "Neither Out Far nor In Deep," which he had described as "the most perfect poem of our time" (*PR* 26 [1959]: 451), is interpreted quite in a New Critical manner as owing its charm and power "to the discrepancy between, on the one hand, its tone and ostensible subject, and, on the other, its actual subject" (*EL,* 944). The shifts in the meaning of the word "look," occurring five times in the poem, are elaborately commented upon, though usually, one must grant, Trilling pays little attention to such details. But he can comment perceptively on the diction of a poem by E. E. Cummings which deliberately violates the parts of speech ("My father moved through dooms of love," *EL,* 949–50).

We must conclude that Trilling's position in a history or map of American criticism is extremely complex. He is clearly committed to the social and moral function of literature, particularly the novel. He defends a realism which, at the same time, is a moral realism, meaning an expression of purpose to interpret and change society. He himself described his method: "Since my own interests lead me to see literary situations as cultural situations, and cultural situations as great elaborate fights about moral issues, and moral issues as having something to do with literary style, I felt free to begin with what for me was a first concern, the animus of the author, the objects of his will, the things he wants or wants to have happen" (*BC,* 13).

But, in other contexts and with increasing frequency in later years, the stress in Trilling's writings moves from the "will," the purpose of literature, to "mind" coupled with a growing suspicion of the importance of literature. As early as 1940 he can say that "literature is inadequate if asked to do the work of the will and earn its living by constructive activity" (*KR* 2 [1940]: 436). When he complains that literature is seen as "the recording barometer of the weather history" which implies that "a living thing is transformed into a dead datum," "a merely mechanical response to economic and social events" (439), he has Marxism in mind. But even later Trilling obviously draws on literature as the great reservoir for evidence of our civilization, morality, and sensibility, as "the summary and paradigm of our cultural life" (*LI,* 266). But then, more and more, he comes to doubt whether art really tells the truth about its age, whether the *Zeitgeist* is really expressed by it and whether we do not overrate the role of literature in society. He recognizes that literature can be just play, "fortuitous and gratuitous, beyond the reach of the will alone" (280). In a discussion of the Leavis-Snow controversy about the "two cultures," Trilling chides Leavis for having "no recognition of those aspects of art which are gratuitous, which arise from high spirits and the impulse to play" (*BC,* 151). In the year before his death Trilling asked the question, "following my great master Rousseau, whether art is what people say it is—totally a benefit in our life," and he answers it in the negative, agreeing that "it keeps us from looking at the object directly, it keeps us from experiencing things directly" (*Salmagundi* 41 [1978]: 105–06). In some pronouncements Trilling prefers philosophy to poetry, quoting as his star witness a letter of Keats saying that "poetry is not so fine a thing as philosophy," "an eagle is not so fine as a truth" (*BC,* 233), a lame, purely metaphorical flourish at the end of his book, *Beyond Culture.* At times, Trilling can recommend the "authority, the cogency, the brilliance, the hardness of systematic thought" (*LI,* 290), even in criticism, but when pressed he calls himself "a pragmatist in the precise and conditioned sense in which William James defends the position." Trilling refers to a page in *Some Problems of Philosophy* ([1948], 60) where James defines the pragmatic rule: "The meaning of a concept may always be found, if not in some sensible particular which it directly designates, then in some particular differences in the course of human experience which its being true will make." We are back at praxis, at the particular, the concrete effects in life. Nor do we get further when Trilling says, "I consider myself a committed naturalist if I formulate views on such matters" (*PR* 16 [1949]: 655). Trilling, in spite of an early distaste, shows some sympathy for the philosophical position of Santayana, though he does "not pretend to understand Santayana's doctrine of essences, not having read the works in which he expounds it" (*GF*, 153). Trilling is simply not interested in technical philosophy: he confesses his impatience with Descartes and Spinoza; the references to Kant, oddly enough considered to belong to "Romanticism" (*LI*, 194), are quite perfunctory; and the more frequent quotations from Hegel do not inspire confidence when Trilling misreads him as making the aesthetic the criterion of the moral, an error pointed out by Joseph Frank (*Widening Gyre*, 258). Trilling has a professional command of the main currents of thought in the nineteenth century, particularly in England, as his book on Arnold amply demonstrates, but his excursions into the history of ideas in earlier ages seem to me often deficient in a knowledge of the texts and the literature about them, particularly outside England. Thus the lectures *Sincerity and Authenticity* (1972) grossly overrate the newness of the idea of selfhood and the issue of sincerity: he pays no attention to Socrates or Aristotle, Marcus Aurelius or St. Augustine, not to speak of the mystical tradition. To say that "at a certain point of history men became individuals," that "in the late sixteenth and early seventeenth centuries, something like a mutation in human nature took place" (*SA*, 24, 19), seems to me as unprovable as Virginia Woolf's view that human nature changed in 1910.

Actually, Trilling was of two minds about this issue: on the one hand he believes in distinct period styles, distinct "moral idioms" (*SA*, 2), in the *Zeitgeist* in some Hegelian or Marxist sense, and thus in the necessity of what he calls "the cultural mode of thought," culture used here as the broad anthropological term (*BC*, 175), but on the other hand he cannot quite deny that "human nature never varies, that the moral life is unitary and its terms perennial" (*SA*, 2). In discussing his own book on *Sincerity and Authenticity*, Trilling admits a conflict between what he calls the categorical and the dialectical modes of thought and suggests that the two are not irreconcilable. "In judging one's own conduct one does best to stay with the categorical mode" assuming "a fixed and permanent law"

(*Salmagundi* 41 [1978]: 88), while, I suppose, in studying history one must embrace a form of cultural relativism. There is in Trilling in spite of his historicism and relativism a strong yearning for absolutes, if not religious or transcendental in any way, then for moral and aesthetic absolutes.

Still, he did not find these absolutes: as a pragmatist and naturalist, he could not. He rather considered "openness and flexibility of mind" "the first of virtues" (preface to 2nd ed. of *Matthew Arnold* [1949]). He often says "on the one hand" and "on the other," or both sides are right or both are wrong. Thus those who see art as amoral and those like Ruskin who think that only a good man can be a good artist (*EL*, 320) are both mistaken. Trilling found for this suspension of judgment, for this large tolerance, ideal confirmation in Keats's concept of "negative capability": "when a man is capable of being in uncertainties, mysteries, doubts, without an irritable reaching after fact and reason" (*OS*, 32). "In an ideological age such as ours the faculty of Negative Capability is a rare one." Trilling claims it for himself: "Only the self that is certain of its existence, of its identity, can do without the armor of systematic certainties" (37). He seems to have been very certain of this self, the "shaped self" he misses in his contemporaries, an impression that established and enhanced his authority as wise man, I think rightly so: there is sanity in his seeing all sides of a question, wisdom in "the awareness of the qualities of things" which "in the aesthetic realm we call style and in the realm of morals character" (*KR* 2 [1940]: 442). It seems thus unfortunate that this very quality exalted him in his own eyes and in those of his surroundings into the role of a spokesman who uses the term "we," not simply as a *pluralis majestaticus* but in conscious identification with a group that has been called the New York intellectuals. He recognized the truth of the criticism that the "we" in his writings shifts from "just people of our time as a whole; to Americans in general and most often to New York intellectuals" but insists on the validity of his generalizations. They are valid for this group often enough as when he says "we hate and fear the general culture" (*BC*, 83), but are we or they prepared to say that "we have a predilection for violence" (*OS*, 132), that "we are in love with death" (*OS*, 144), that "we are ashamed of our lives" (*SA*, 105)? "We all," he says, "believe that there is no crime" (*EL*, 484). "Duty grates upon our moral ear" (*OS*, 216). "Adultery is an archaic word. *Unfaithful* begins to sound quaint, inappropriate to our modern code" (*Encounter* 11 [1958]: 17). "Very old people, we feel, have no personal being, no Identity" (*OS*, 138), etcetera, etcetera. And how do "we all participate in the existence of William Blake" (*BC*, 206)? This identification with fashionable views of a small group makes Trilling vulnerable to such fads as the views of R. D. Laing and Norman O. Brown about "madness as health." Both the lectures *Sincerity and Authenticity* and *Mind in the Modern World* conclude with a worried rejection of these absurdities. Trilling recognizes that they "foster a form of assent which does not involve actual credence" (*SA*, 171) and that a divinity is postulated, "each one of us a Christ," "with none of the inconveniences of undertaking to intercede, of being a sacrifice" (172). Finally, Trilling the spokesman has seen through at least the extreme advocates of irrationalism and has come back to a concept of mind that implies, as he says himself, the "idea of order, even of hierarchy" (*Mind*, 30).

8: THE NEW CRITICISM

TODAY THE New Criticism is considered not only superseded, obsolete, and dead, but somehow mistaken and wrong. Four accusations are made most frequently. First, the New Criticism is an "esoteric aestheticism," a revival of art for art's sake, uninterested in the human meaning, the social function and effect of literature. The New Critics are called "formalists," an opprobrious term used first by Marxists against a group of Russian scholars in the twenties. Second, the New Criticism, we are told, is unhistorical. It isolates the work of art from its past and its context. Third, the New Criticism is supposed to aim at making criticism scientific or at least "bringing literary study to a condition rivaling that of science" (*Critics and Criticism*, ed. R. S. Crane, 45). Finally the New Criticism is being dismissed as a mere pedagogical device, a version of the French *explication de texte*, useful at most for American college students who must learn to read and to read poetry in particular.

I want to show that all these accusations are baseless. They can be so convincingly refuted by an appeal to the texts that I wonder whether current commentators have ever actually read the writings of the New Critics. Inevitably one must ask what the reasons are for this ignorance and these distortions, and one will have to come up with answers that allow a statement of the limitations and shortcomings of the New Criticism. Still, I think that much of what the New Criticism taught is valid and will be valid as long as people think about the nature and function of literature and poetry.

Before we enter into the merits of the case we must come to an agreement as to whom we should consider New Critics. The term itself is old. The Schlegel brothers, early in the nineteenth century, called themselves "neue Kritiker," and Benedetto Croce, when he did not want to use the pronoun, "I," referred to his own views as "la nuova critica." Joel E. Spingarn, the historian of Renaissance criticism, took the term from Croce when he expounded Croce's theories in a little book, *The New Criticism*, in 1911. E. E. Burgum edited an anthology with this title in

1930, and finally John Crowe Ransom, the founder of the *Kenyon Review,* wrote a book, *The New Criticism,* in 1941 which seems to have established the term in common usage, even though the book was far from being a celebration of the New Criticism. Ransom discusses there not contemporary American criticism in general but only three critics: I. A. Richards, whom he criticizes sharply; T. S. Eliot, against whose views on tradition he makes many objections; and Yvor Winters, whom he rejects in the strongest terms. It earned him a virulent reply in Winters's *Anatomy of Nonsense.*

In 1941 when Ransom's book was published the views and methods of the New Criticism were long established. One can best observe their gradual emergence by thinking of them as reaction against the then prevalent trends in American criticism. Without too much simplification we can distinguish four main trends in American criticism before the advent of the New Critics. There was, first, a type of aesthetic impressionistic criticism, of "appreciation," ultimately derived from Pater and Remy de Gourmont, prevalent in the first decade of this century. James G. Huneker may stand here as the representative figure. Then there was the humanist movement, of which Irving Babbitt and Paul Elmer More were the acknowledged leaders. In 1930 there was a great public commotion around them, but this date is misleading. The main writings of both Babbitt and More appeared in the first decade of the century: the first seven volumes of More's *Shelburne Essays* between 1904 and 1910, Babbitt's *Literature and the American College* in 1908, *Masters of Modern French Criticism* in 1912. Then there was the group of critics who attacked the "genteel" tradition, the American business civilization, the "bouboisie," and propagated the naturalistic novel, Dreiser in particular. H. L. Mencken and the early Van Wyck Brooks were in the limelight in the twenties. Finally there were the Marxists who flourished during the Great Depression in the early thirties. Granville Hicks is their best-known spokesman, but the much more versatile critic Edmund Wilson was also deeply affected by Marxism, though his actual methods were rather revivals of appreciation or of historicism in the wake of Taine. None of these critics can be mistaken for New Critics.

The new methods, the tone, and new taste are clearly discernible first in the early articles and books of John Crowe Ransom, Allen Tate, R. P. Blackmur, Kenneth Burke, and Yvor Winters, and somewhat later in Cleanth Brooks, Robert Penn Warren, and William K. Wimsatt. A date such as 1923 when Allen Tate spoke of a "new school of so-called philosophic criticism" (in Thomas Daniel Young, *Gentleman in Dustcoat,* 152) cannot be far off the mark for the earliest stirrings in the United States.

The influence of T. S. Eliot was obviously decisive, to which later that of I. A. Richards should be added. Eliot's *Sacred Wood* dates from 1920, Richards's *Principles of Literary Criticism* from 1924.

If we look at this list of names we soon discover that the group was far from unified. Ransom, Tate, Cleanth Brooks, and R. P. Warren may be grouped together as Southern critics. Burke and Blackmur stand apart, and Yvor Winters was a complete maverick. I could collect and quote a large number of their pronouncements violently disagreeing with their supposed allies and show that they hold often quite divergent and even contradictory theories. Even Ransom, the teacher in different years of Allen Tate, Cleanth Brooks, and R. P. Warren, holds views very different from those of his pupils. Burke and Blackmur later rejected the New Criticism in strong terms, and Winters never was happy with the association. The view that the New Criticism represents a coterie or even a school is mistaken. With the evidence of disagreements among these critics—which it would take too much time to develop in detail—it may seem wise to conclude that the concept and term should be abandoned and these critics discussed each on his own merits.

Still, something tells us that there is some sense in grouping these critics together. Most obviously they are held together by their reaction against the preceding or contemporary critical schools and views mentioned earlier. They all reject the kind of metaphorical, evocative criticism practiced by the impressionists. Tate, Blackmur, Burke, and Winters contributed to a symposium highly critical of the neohumanists and others voiced their rejection elsewhere. They all had no use for Mencken and Van Wyck Brooks, particularly after Brooks became a violent enemy of all modernism. Furthermore, they were almost unanimous in their rejection of Marxism, with the single exception of Kenneth Burke, who in the thirties passed through a Marxist phase and after his first book moved away from his neocritical beginnings anyway. What in the American situation mattered most was that they were united in their opposition to the prevailing methods, doctrines, and views of academic English literary scholarship. There, in a way the younger generation may find it difficult to realize, a purely philological and historical scholarship dominated all instruction, publication, and promotion. I remember that when I first came to study English literature in the Princeton Graduate School in 1927, nearly sixty years ago, no course in American literature, none in modern literature, and none in criticism was offered. Of all my learned teachers only Morris W. Croll had any interest in aesthetics or even ideas. Most of the New Critics were college teachers and had to make their way in an environment hostile to any and all criticism. Only Kenneth Burke was and remained a freelance man of letters, though he taught in later years occasionally at Bennington College and briefly at the University of Chicago. But he very early deserted the New Criticism. It took Blackmur, Tate, and Winters years to get academic recognition, often against stiff opposition, and even Ransom, R. P. Warren, and Cleanth Brooks, established in quieter places, had their troubles. Ransom's paper "Criticism, Inc." (1937) pleaded for the academic establishment of criticism, and thanks to him and others criticism is now taught in most American colleges and universities. But it was an uphill fight. I still remember vividly the acrimony of the conflict between criticism and literary history at the University of Iowa, where I was a member of the English department from 1939 to 1946.

The New Critics with one voice questioned the assumptions and preoccupations of academic scholarship with different degrees of sharpness. The wittiest and most pungent was Allen Tate. In a lecture, "Miss Emily and the Bibliographer" (1940), Tate exposed the vain attempts to emulate the methods of science by tracing influence conceived in terms of forces, causes and effects, or biological analogies of growth and development, or by applying psychology, economics and sociology to literature. They all shirk, Tate argues, the essential of criticism, "the moral obligation to judge," for "if we wait for history to judge," as they plead, "there will be no judgment." We must also judge the literature of our own time. "The scholar who tells us that he understands Dryden but makes nothing of Hopkins or Yeats is telling us that he does not understand Dryden" (*Essays of Four Decades* [1969], 153). As early as 1927 Tate said that "the historical method has disqualified our best minds for the traditional functions of criticism. It ignores the meaning of the destination in favor of the way one gets there" (*New Republic* 41 [1927]: 330). Winters argues similarly. The superstition of a value-free literary history ignores the fact that "every writer that the scholar studies comes to him as a result of a critical judgment" (*The Function of Criticism*, 24). The professors who engage in "serious" literary study—bibliography, philology, textual criticism, and related disciplines—not only hold criticism in contempt and do their best to suppress it in the universities, but also, Winters tells us bluntly, "were fools and where they still flourish they are still fools" (17). Blackmur also rejected the methods of what I call "extrinsic" criticism. Scholarship, he grants, is useful in supplying us with facts but becomes obnoxious when "it believes it has made an interpretation by surrounding the work with facts" (*The Lion and the Honeycomb*, 181). The mild-mannered Ransom could become caustic at the expense of "the indefensible extravagance in the gigantic collective establishment of the English faculties" that fail to teach criticism (*Kenyon Review* 2 [1940]: 349–50). Many more voices could be added to a revolt against the positivism of nineteenth-century scholarship, which in the United States was vigorously stated as early as 1908 by Irving Babbitt in *Literature and the American College* and was widespread and effective on the continent of Europe, especially in the twenties.

Still, one should understand that this rejection of academic historical scholarship must not be interpreted as a rejection of the historicity of poetry. Cleanth Brooks has, in many contexts, mostly in interpreting seventeenth-century poems, shown that the critic "needs the help of the historian—all the help he can get" (*English Literature Annual* [1946], 155). "The critic," he argues, "obviously must know what the words of the poem mean, something which immediately puts him in debt to the linguist (or rather lexicographer, the OED, I might add); and since many of the words are proper nouns, in debt to the historian as well" (134). In order to interpret the "Horatian Ode" of Andrew Marvell correctly we must obviously know something of Cromwell and Charles I and the particular historical situation in the summer of 1650 to which the poem refers. But historical evidence is not only welcomed as a strictly subordinate contribution to the elucidation of a poem.

Brooks and all the other New Critics reinterpret and revalue the whole history of English poetry. It was an act of the historical imagination (however prepared before) to revise the history of English poetry: to exalt Donne and the metaphysicals, to reinstate Dryden and Pope, to sift and discriminate among the English romantic poets, preferring Wordsworth and Keats to Shelley and Byron; to discover Hopkins, to exalt Yeats, and to defend the break with Victorian and Edwardian conventions as it was initiated by Pound and Eliot. Brooks's "Notes for a Revised History of English Poetry" (1939) sketch the new scheme clearly. Winters's books, particularly his last, *Forms of Discovery* (1967), do the same, with a different emphasis, more dogmatically. But it is not enough to refute the allegation of lack of historical sense by pointing to the interest in historical elucidation and even in literary history properly conceived. Rather I would argue that the New Criticism embraces a total historical scheme, believes in a philosophy of history, and uses it as a standard of judgment.

History is seen substantially in the terms of T. S. Eliot. There used to be once a perfectly ordered world which is, for instance, behind Dante's poetry. This world disintegrated under the impact of science and skepticism. The "dissociation of sensibility" took place at some time in the seventeenth century. Man became increasingly divided, alienated, specialized as industrialization and secularism progressed. The western world is in decay, but some hope seems to be held out for a reconstitution of the original wholeness. The total man, the undivided "unified sensibility" which combines intellect and feeling, is the ideal that requires a rejection of a technological civilization, a return to religion or, at least, to a modern myth and, in the Southern critics, allowed a defense of the agrarian society surviving in the South. The basic scheme has a venerable ancestry: Schiller's *Letters on Aesthetic Education* (1795) were the main source for Hegel and Marx. In the American critics, particularly in Tate and Brooks, the scheme is drawn from Eliot's view of tradition. In Eliot the "unified sensibility" comes from F. H. Bradley, who knew his Hegel. Brooks is confident in focusing on Hobbes as the villain; Tate singles out Bacon, Gibbon, and La Mettrie as the destroyers of the old world view. Ransom puts out a different version, blaming "Platonism," which means presumably any generalizing abstracting view of the world. Tate praised Spengler's *Decline of the West* (*Nation* 122 [1926]: 532) and gave the scheme a peculiar twist in his practical criticism. He was most interested in poets who come at the point of dissolution of the original unity, who dramatize the alienation of man: Emily Dickinson and Hart Crane, in particular. Tate sees poems always within history and echoes Eliot saying, in 1927, "My attempt is to see the present from the past, yet remain immersed in the present and committed to it" (*The Literary Correspondence of Donald Davidson and Allen Tate* [1927], 189).

The role of criticism is great for the health of poetry, of the language, and ultimately of society. The charge of rejecting history, of having no "sense of the past" (voiced even by Lionel Trilling, in *The Liberal Imagination*) is easily refuted. Its refutation has already answered the other main accusation, that of aestheticism, of an art-for-art's-sake view of literature. It is based on the insistence of the New Critics that the aesthetic experience is set off from immediate practical concerns: from rhetorical persuasion, bare doctrinal statement, or mere emotional effusion. The aesthetic state of mind can be induced only by the coherence and unity of a work of art. These views have an ancient lineage long preceding the art-for-art's-sake movement. The distinctions among aesthetic contemplation, scientific truth, morality, and practical usefulness were most elaborately drawn in Kant's *Critique of Judgment* (1790), and the idea of the coherence, unity, and even organicity of a work of art is as old as Plato and Aristotle. It was modified and amplified by the German critics around 1800, from whom Coleridge drew his formulas, and Coleridge is the immediate source for English and American critics. One may raise doubts (as Wimsatt has) about the metaphor of organism applied to a work of art if it is pushed too far, but there seems to me a simple truth in the old view that a successful work of art is a whole in which the parts collaborate and modify one another. Much of the "close reading" practiced by Cleanth Brooks and followers demonstrates this truth even on recalcitrant material. But this insight is grossly distorted if it is supposed to lead to the conclusion that poetry is cut off from reality, is merely self-reflexive, and that it is thus only an inconsequential play of words. When Brooks combats the "heresy of paraphrase" he objects to reducing a work of art to a statement of abstract propositions, or to a moral message, or to any literal verifiable truth. But this emphasis on the specific "fictionality" of all art, its world of illusion or semblance, cannot mean a lack of relation to reality or a simple entrapment in language. Tate, for instance, emphatically condemned "that idolatrous dissolution of language from the grammar of a possible world, which results from the belief that language itself can be reality, or by incantation can create reality: a superstition that comes down in French from Lautréamont, Rimbaud and Mallarmé to the Surrealists, and in English to Hart Crane, Wallace Stevens, and Dylan Thomas" (*Essays*, 406). Poetry is turned to the world, aims at a picture of reality. It cannot be absolute or pure. It remains impure, like anything human, a theme eloquently developed in R. P. Warren's essay "Pure and Impure Poetry" (1942).

Both Brooks and Ransom uphold a version of imitation, of mimesis. Brooks asserts that the poem, if it is a true poem, is a "simulacrum of reality" (*Well-wrought Urn*, 194) or "a portion of reality as viewed and valued by a human being. It is rendered coherent through a perspective of valuing" (*Literary Criticism*, 737–38). In Ransom poetry is a display, a knowledge and restoration of the real world: a celebration of the beauty of nature, even a "representation of natural beauty" (*Poems and Essays*, 171). None of the New Critics could have believed in the prisonhouse of language. This supposed consequence of any view of the unity, self-reflexiveness, and integration of a work of art has been debated thoroughly, for example, by Murray Krieger in *The New Apologists for Poetry* (1956) and by Gerald Graff in *Poetic Statement and Critical Dogma* (1970), but it poses a false dilemma. A poem may have coherence and integrity without losing its meaning or truth. The very nature of words points to the outside world. In *A Window to Criticism* (1964) Murray Krieger speaks of a "miracle," but such a gesture toward the irrational seems unnecessary unless we consider the reference of almost every word a "miracle." It points to or may point to an object in the outside world and at the same time is part of a sentence, of a phonemic and syntactical system, of a language code. The parallel to painting is obvious: a painting is enclosed in a frame, is organized by a relation of colors and lines, but simultaneously may represent a landscape, a scene, or the portrait of a real man or woman.

In the writings of the New Critics the coherence of a poem is not studied in terms of form, as the label "formalism" suggests. Actually the New Critics pay little attention to what is traditionally called the form of a poem. Brooks and Warren in their textbook, *Understanding Poetry,* inevitably pay some attention to the role of meter and stanzaic forms, and Winters expounded his view on "The Audible Reading of Poetry" (in *The Function of Criticism,* 79ff.). But the New Critics reject the distinction of form and content: they believe in the organicity of poetry and, in practice, constantly examine attitudes, tones, tensions, irony, and paradox, all psychological concepts partly derived from Richards. Irony and paradox is used by Brooks very broadly. It is not the opposite of an overt statement "but a general term for the kind of qualification which the various elements in a context receive from the context" (*Well-Wrought Urn,* 191). It indicates the recognition of incongruities, the union of opposites that Brooks finds in all good—that is, complex—"inclusive" poetry. Brooks has most consistently held a strictly organic point of view. Other critics desert it. Thus Ransom draws a distinction between structure and texture which reverts to the old dichotomy of content and form. A poem, he says strikingly, is "much more like a Christmas tree than an organism" (*Kenyon Review* 7 [1945]: 294), with the metaphors thought of as ornaments. Winters comes to a similar conclusion with a different emphasis. A poem is for him "a statement in words about a human experience" (*In Defense of Reason,* 11). The charge of formalism in any sense that is valid for the Russian school is completely off the mark. The New Critics are overwhelmingly concerned with the meaning of a work of art, with the attitude, the tone, the feelings, and even with the ultimate implied world view conveyed. They are formalists only in the sense that they insist on the organization of a work of art which prevents its becoming a simple communication.

The allegation that the New Critics want to make criticism a science seems to me even more preposterous. It might have emanated from those who felt hurt by their attack on "appreciation," on loose impressionism and mere self-indulgence in "adventures among masterpieces." More recently it often comes from defenders of a hermeneutics that assumes a mysterious identification with the author's cogito or rejects interpretation in favor of an "erotics of art," as Susan Sontag does in *Against Interpretation* (1964). Actually the New Critics are enemies of science.

Science for Tate is the villain of history which has destroyed the community of man, broken up the old organic way of life, paved the way to industrialism, and made man the alienated, rootless, godless creature he has become in this century. Science encourages utopian thinking, the false idea of the perfectibility of man, the whole illusion of endless progress. Tate says bluntly: "Poetry is not only quite different from science but in its essence is opposed to science" (*This Quarter* 5 [1932]: 292). In Ransom, in particular, poetry is conceived as the supreme antidote against science. He makes the conflict of art and science the leading theme of history. "In all human history the dualism between science and art widens continually by reasons of the aggressions of science. As science more and more reduces the world to its types and forms, art, replying, must invest it again with body" (*The World's Body,* 198n.). The investment with body, the reassertion of the particularity of the world against the abstractions of science, is Ransom's leading theme: the restoration of what he calls the "thingness" (*Dinglichkeit*) of the world is the aim and justification of poetry. None of the New Critics has any sympathy for the mechanistic technological views of the Russian formalists. The New Critics have completely shunned modern linguistics, such as the use of phonemics or of quantitative methods, and if they sometimes spoke of criticism as a systematic, rational discipline they could not mean a modern value-free social science, for they always stressed the necessity of judgment, the qualitative experience poetry gives us. In the attempt to defend poetry against the accusation of irrelevancy they put forward claims for the truth of poetry, for the knowledge conveyed which is conceived as superior to that of science. Over and over again Tate says that literature provides "the special, unique and complete knowledge" (*Essays,* 202), "knowledge of a whole object, its complete knowledge, the full body of experience" (105). It is not a claim like that of the romantics for some visionary power, some special insight into a world beyond, which might lead to an obscurantist theory of double truth. It is rather a view of knowledge as "realization," as full awareness in the sense in which we can say, "You don't really know what it is like until you have lived through it." It is ultimately a version of the unified sensibility of T. S. Eliot, the union of feeling and intellect achieved in poetry. Criticism cannot be neutral scientism: it must respond to the work with the same totality of mind with which the work is created. But criticism is always subordinated to creation. Its humility contrasts precisely with the aggressions, the impositions of science.

None of the New Critics would have thought that their methods of close reading are "scientific" nor would they have identified criticism with "close reading." Ransom, Tate, Blackmur, Winters, and Burke had developed their theories of poetry and their general point of view long before they engaged in anything like close reading. Tate's first excursion into close reading is the essay "Narcissus as Narcissus" (1938), a commentary on his own "Ode to the Confederate Dead." The examination of a poem apart from biography and conventional literary history became, no doubt, an important innovation in the teaching of literature in American colleges and universities. The turn to the text was mainly accomplished by the success of *Understanding Poetry* (1938) by Cleanth Brooks and Robert Penn Warren, which invaded the strongholds of philological scholarship in the early forties. The method of close reading became the pedagogical weapon of the New Criticism. One should grant that the proliferation of "explications" became later a dreary industry, but it is a mistake to consider close reading a new version of *explication de texte*. Close reading as practiced by Cleanth Brooks differs from *explication de texte* by offering critical standards, leading to discrimination between good and bad poems, resolutely pursued in the textbook and in many other articles since. The aim is understanding, "interpretation." The now fashionable term "hermeneutics" refers to the theory of understanding developed first in Bible studies. The method of the New Critics may differ from the intuitive identification proposed by the phenomenologists in the wake of Poulet or from the fusion of horizons in the mode of Gadamer, but the aim is the same. It is hard to see how a study of literature can get along without interpretation of individual works and how one can be "against interpretation," as Susan Sontag entitled her book, or declare "interpretation" to be "the real enemy" (Jonathan Culler, in *Comparative Literature* 28 [1976]: 250). The view voiced by Richard E. Palmer, in his book on *Hermeneutics* (1969), that the New Criticism has "a technological concept of interpretation" (7) mistakes its aim of suppressing irrelevant subjective preconceptions or biographical explanations for an indifferent scientism. It seems to me far-fetched to bring in T. S. Eliot's belief in original sin as Gerald Graff does (in "What Was New Criticism? Literary Interpretation and Scientific Objectivity," in *Salmagundi* [1974]: 72–93) to explain the New Critics' emphasis on impersonality. It comes rather from Flaubert's and Joyce's desire for an objective art, "impersonality" meaning a rejection of overt didacticism and confessional display. The New Criticism surely argues from a sound premise, that no coherent body of knowledge can be established unless it defines its object, which to the New Critic will be the individual work of art clearly set off from its antecedents in the mind of the author or in the social situation, as well as from its effect in society. The object of literary study is conceived of not as an arbitrary construct but as a structure of norms which prescribes a right response. This structure need not be conceived of as static or spatial in any literal sense, though terms such as the well-wrought urn, or Joseph Frank's spatial form, or Wimsatt's verbal icon suggest such a misinterpretation. All these metaphors aim at a genuine insight: although the process of reading is inevitably temporal in criticism, we must try to see a work as totality, a configuration, a gestalt, a whole.

I hope I have succeeded in refuting the common misconceptions about the New Criticism, but I have studied the history of criticism long enough to know that there must be reasons for the fact that the New Criticism is currently in such disfavor that, for instance, Geoffrey Hartman could not only entitle a book and an essay *Beyond Formalism* (1970; the essay dates from 1966) but quote there Trotsky, of all people, attacking the very different Russian formalists from his Marxist point of view and conclude that "there is good reason why many in this country, as well as in Europe, have voiced a suspicion of Anglo-Saxon formalism. The dominion of Exegesis is great: she is our Whore of Babylon, sitting robed in Academic black on the great dragon of Criticism and displaying a repetitive and soporific balm from her pedantic cup" (56) and says that "explication is the end of criticism only if we succumb to what Trotsky called the formalist's 'superstition of the word' " (57). Hartman and others have tried to overcome this superstition either by appealing to a purely intuitive identification with the author behind the work or by advocating a complete liberty of interpretation in an attempt to exalt criticism to the status of art, to obliterate the distinction between criticism and creation for which Roland Barthes invented the convenient common term "écriture."

But the objections to the New Criticism do not come only from this new apocalyptic irrationalism. They are much older and more serious. The New Critics were immediately attacked from two sides long before the new movements were imported from France. The Chicago Aristotelians, who exalt plot, character, and genre, strongly disapproved of the New Critics' concern for language and poetic diction. Language, according to the Chicago school, is merely inert matter, a material cause of poetry, a view which seems to go back rather to the Renaissance scholar Scaliger than to Aristotle himself. The New Critics fared badly in their hands. R. S. Crane attacked Cleanth Brooks's "critical monism," deploring his preoccupation with paradox and his conclusion that the structure of poetry is the structure common to all literary works (*Critics and Criticism*, 95). Crane also criticizes the New Critics for their "morbid obsession with the problem of justifying and preserving poetry in an age of science" (105) as this was no problem for Crane and his group. Crane accepts pleasure as the aim of art and imitation as its procedure in which we find pleasure and instruction. One must admit that the Chicago critics scored many points against the overreadings in R. P. Warren's study of *The Ancient Mariner* and the attempts of Robert Heilman to read *King Lear* as an almost spatial pattern of images. Yet the Chicago Aristotelians were on some points the allies of the New Criticism. Crane was one of the first to defend and to recommend the study of criticism in the university ("History versus Criticism in the Study of Literature" [1935], reprinted in *The Idea of the Humanities* [1967]). The whole group advocates a rational systematic study of poetics, even though their insistence on strict genre conventions and neutral analysis was unacceptable to the New Critics concerned with the nature of poetry in general and with criticism as evaluation.

The next, much more effective rejection of the New Criticism came from the so-called myth critics. Myth as a system of metaphors or symbols is a central device in much of the New Criticism, but in the myth-critics it becomes the one overriding concern. Poetry is simply (and I think wrongly) identified with myth, and myth is used so broadly that it includes any theme, any story you can think of: Huck Finn floating down the Mississippi with Jim is a myth. Myth-criticism allows a discussion of content apart from the poem: it often became mere allegorizing. Every work of literature is a quest, or a version of the death of God and its rebirth. Still, one should recognize that Northrop Frye in his *Anatomy of Criticism* (1957) has not entirely discarded the achievements of the New Criticism, though he rejects criticism as judgment in theory (though hardly in practice).

The New Criticism was then totally rejected by the critics of consciousness, the so-called Geneva school and its followers in this country. Georges Poulet, their most articulate spokesman, does not want to analyze a single work of art, is uninterested in its form or specificity, for he is searching for the author's cogito behind his total oeuvre. The other French group—which must not be confused with the Geneva school— the structuralists, who come from Saussure's linguistics and from Lévi-Strauss's anthropology, have some affinities with the New Criticism in their concern for a microscopic analysis of texts and a general poetics. Roman Jakobson was the link between the Russian formalists and the Paris structuralists, and all his recent work, hailed by I. A. Richards as the fulfillment of his own ambitions, demonstrates his concern and skill in interpreting individual poems. But his methods are linguistic, attentive to the grammar of poetry, and pointedly ignore criticism as judgment or ranking. Nevertheless, there is one trend in Parisian structuralism, particularly the acute analyses of fiction or symbol practiced by the Bulgarian Tzvetan Todorov and by Gérard Genette, which is not incompatible with the ambitions of the New Criticism. Many others in France and in the United States aim at an all-embracing structure of universal poetics and finally at a science of semiotics: an ambition beyond the ken of the New Critics. Their ethos, unlike the often religious motivation of the Geneva school, is scientific; the philosophy, implied positivistic or materialistic: some of the French group have embraced Marxism. The distance from the New Criticism is obvious.

Surely one of the reasons for the demise of the New Criticism is the distrust many feel toward the political and religious views of the main New Critics: toward T. S. Eliot's Anglicanism, which is shared for instance by Cleanth Brooks, or toward the Roman Catholicism of Allen Tate (a convert) or William K. Wimsatt, as well as toward the participation of three of the Southern critics (Ransom, Tate, R. P. Warren) in the so-called agrarian movement, formulated in the symposium *I'll Take My Stand* (1930). But the New Critics—unlike the later Eliot and the early Richards—never tired of rejecting the amalgamation of poetry and religion. Tate says expressly that "literature is neither religion nor social engineering" (*Essays,* 619), and Brooks and Wimsatt always kept the two realms rigorously apart in their critical practice. But one cannot deny that ultimately poetry with several of the New Critics turns out to be, if not religion, then a preparation for religion: it is assigned a role comparable to the imagination in Wordsworth and Coleridge. The poet and his reader are each brought back to the totality of their beings, are restored to their original humanity.

If one rejects this version of history, one can see the justification of a new turn in poetic taste. The revival of the English romantics as the visionary company centered in Blake, and the current attempts to dismiss T. S. Eliot both as poet and critic, and to reduce the role of all modernism, imply a rejection of the New Criticism also in the everyday matters of selection and ranking of poets and poems.

Still even more profoundly the New Criticism is affected by the general revolt against aesthetics per se, by the whole rejection of any distinction between the aesthetic state of mind and any other activity. It goes back to the German theory of empathy, even to Benedetto Croce, wrongly suspected of aestheticism, though he abolished the distinction between art and any act of intuition, and to John Dewey's *Art as Experience* (1934), which denies all distinction between aesthetic and other experiences of heightened vitality; and paradoxically to the literary criticism of I. A. Richards, who had such an influence on the American New Critics with his book on *Practical Criticism* but propounded a behavioristic theory which ignores the difference between aesthetic and other emotions completely. Thus the very basis of any concern with poetry or literature as an art is undermined. The New Criticism has become a victim of the general attack on literature and art, of the "deconstruction" of literary texts, of the new anarchy which allows a complete liberty of interpretation and even of a self-confessed "nihilism."

One limitation of the New Critics seems to me serious, possibly because of my commitment to comparative literature. They are extremely anglocentric, even provincial. They have rarely attempted to discuss foreign literature or, if they have done so, their choice has been confined to a very few obvious texts. Dante is discussed by Allen Tate; he comments on passages in *The Idiot* and *Madame Bovary*. Winters admires the poems of Paul Valéry. Blackmur, late in his life, did write, often vaguely and obscurely, on Dostoevsky, Tolstoy, and Flaubert. A recent excursion of Kenneth Burke into Goethe seems most unfortunate. That is about all. The justification of this preoccupation with texts in English is presumably the conviction of the critics that poetry is implicated closely in the language; and lyrical poetry, the nature of poetry in general, was their first concern. Still it *is* a limitation, considering the inexhaustible wealth of the world's literature speaking to us in many tongues, crying to be interpreted and judged.

I will not conceal my own conviction that the New Criticism has stated or reaffirmed many basic truths to which future ages will have to return: the specific nature of the aesthetic transaction, the normative presence of a work of art which forms a structure, a unity, coherence, a whole, which cannot be simply battered about and is comparatively independent of its origins and effects. The New Critics have also persuasively described the function of literature in not yielding abstract knowledge or information, message or stated ideology, and they have devised a technique of interpretation which often succeeded in illuminating not so much the form of a poem as the implied attitudes of the author, the resolved or unresolved tensions and contradictions: a technique that yields a standard of judgment that cannot be easily dismissed in favor of the currently popular, sentimental, and simple. The charge of elitism cannot get around the New Critics' assertion of quality and value. A decision between good and bad art remains the unavoidable duty of criticism. The humanities would abdicate their function in society if they surrendered to a neutral scientism and indifferent relativism or if they succumbed to the imposition of alien norms required by political indoc-trination. Particularly on these two fronts the New Critics have waged a valiant fight which, I am afraid, must be fought over again in the future.

The differences between the so-called New Critics are so great that it will be best to characterize them individually. In the following chapters an effort is made to bring out the individual traits of each of these critics. The emphasis in the chapters will differ: sometimes it is on the theoret-ical and philosophical implications, sometimes on polemical issues, some-times on the judgment on individual writers and works of literature. In one or the other chapter an attempt is made to discuss all the writings of the critic; in others I have deliberately passed over books which seem of little relevance to the main issues. In some cases I have voiced my strong disagreement, in others my approval is evident, but I always try to preserve a certain distance and detachment. I refuse to be lumped together with the New Critics, though I cannot and do not want to deny my sympathy for many of their positions, just as I agree with critics of quite different times and countries. My basic position was formulated before I knew anything about American New Criticism and hardly much about the English developments. My paper "The Theory of Literary History," 1936 (in *Travaux du Cercle Linguistique de Prague,* vol. 6) is suf-ficient evidence. Beyond specific points of disagreement I want to state my misgivings about the concept of "dissociation of sensibility" and the whole historical scheme implied. I cannot agree with the divorce between propositional and emotional language. I realize that there are many con-tradictions and obscurities in their language on crucial issues: particu-larly the relation between the autonomy of literature and the representation of reality. In expounding the ideas of these critics it will be inevitable to return to some discussion of the issues of this chapter and, in a few cases, even to repeat the most striking quotations in the context of the single critic's work.

9: JOHN CROWE RANSOM (1888–1974)

In "Philosophy and Postwar American Criticism" (1962, reprinted in *Concepts of Criticism*, 1963), I tried to relate the main contemporary American critics to their explicit or implicit philosophical backgrounds. I classed Ransom confidently with Bergsonism, stressing his isolation among the New Critics who could be called rather Coleridgeans. On second thought, after reexamining Ransom's books and reading many of his scattered uncollected writings for the first time, I have come to the conclusion that this alignment must be modified and his position defined differently.

It is true that Ransom sympathizes with Bergson's attack on scientific abstraction (*GT*, 219), with his defense of qualities (259), with his rejection of psychophysics (229), and that in a review of Wyndham Lewis's *Time and Western Man* (*SR* 37 [1929]: esp. 358–59) Ransom defends Bergson's idea of flux and of nature's invincible contingency. But Ransom wanted to have Bergson go much further: "I am sorry to say that Bergson has not been interested in defending the particularity of physical objects. He has devoted himself to defending the particularity of living organisms and of states of mind." He might, continues Ransom out-Bergsoning Bergson, "just as well have saved the inorganic objects, too." For "a thing is of inexhaustible variety and its concrete energy will never submit to determination. . . . The things too are whole and free" (*GT*, 218–19).

This is Ransom's primary insight, his point of departure both as a philosopher and aesthetician. The world is a loose assembly of objects, particular, individual, concrete, dense, but also contingent, heterogeneous, and diffuse. With obsessive frequency Ransom varies this one motif: "A real thing is a bundle of complementary qualities and an inexhaustible particularity" (*SR* 37 [1929]: 361). "The object appears to us as a dense area of contingency, that is concretion" (*KR* 7 [1945]: 284). The world has body, is made of objects which have "a qualitative density, or value-density" (*NC*, 293).

At a crucial point of *The World's Body* Ransom uses the German word

Dinglichkeit, which he translates as "thinginess" (*WB*, 121, 124), for this primary insight. It is a most unusual term, which points to a German source. It does not figure in any German dictionary with the single exception of Grimm's *Wörterbuch*. A word list dating from 1482 translates it *entitas, Wesentlichkeit*, a sense which would be about the opposite from Ransom's. The term does not occur in Kant, Schelling, or Schopenhauer. Hegel uses *Dingheit* in *Die Phänomenologie des Geistes*[1] and so does Heidegger in his famous lecture on "Das Ding" (1950).[2] As far as I have been able to ascertain, Nietzsche first uses *Dinglichkeit* in *Götzendämmerung* (1889) in the context of a discussion of Heraclitus who, Nietzsche tells us, recognized "die Lüge der Einheit, die Lüge der Dinglichkeit, der Substanz, der Dauer."[3] It occurs again in an aphorism included in the posthumous miscellany *Der Wille zur Macht* (1901). Nietzsche asserts there: "Wir haben nur nach dem Vorbilde des Subjekts die Dinglichkeit erfunden und in den Sensationen-Wirrwarr hineininterpretiert."[4] Thomas Mann, an avid reader of Nietzsche, uses it again in *Der Zauberberg* (1924). Mynheer Peeperkorn is said to be averse to theoretical discussion: "Peeperkorns Verlangen nach Dinglichkeit entsprang aus anderen Gründen."[5] Here the pejorative use in Nietzsche takes on a more favorable turn, remote, however, from a clearly philosophical use. The passage in Johannes Volkelt's *System der Aesthetik*[6] in which he contrasts poetry and painting with architecture and music according to "Dinglichkeit und Undinglichkeit des Gehaltes" is also different. Husserl's term is closest to Ransom when in 1907 he gave a whole lecture course on the "thing" and called his theme in a notebook "Versuch einer Phänomenologie der Dinglichkeit und insbesondere der Räumlichkeit," but this entry was not printed until 1950.[7] Recently, presumably under the influence of phenomenology, *Dinglichkeit* has become common in German philosophical and critical writing, for example, Käte Hamburger, in her *Philosophie der Dichter* (1966), discussing Rilke uses the word as many as four times on a page (202). Thus it seems possible that Ransom invented the term himself, forming it on the analogy of such words as *Zärtlichkeit, Männlichkeit*, and so on, to judge from a letter (dated October 29, 1971) which he wrote me in answer to an inquiry about the word's source.

But why did Ransom make up or pick up a German term? He seems not to have been aware of the great role which "thing" played in the works of two contemporary poets: in Rilke, who celebrated things in his speech on Rodin (1907) and wrote a whole series of famous *Dinggedichte*; and, more recently, in Francis Ponge, who since *Parti pris des choses* (1942) writes his poems about things including pebbles and soap. Sartre, in an

essay on Ponge, "L'Homme et les choses" (1944)[8] developed the theme
in terms of Husserlian phenomenology.

Ransom's *Dinglichkeit* must have been inspired by his study of German
philosophy: of Kant, Hegel, and Schopenhauer. Kant particularly is invoked as "his mentor" (*PE*, 159), and he includes himself among "Kant-
ians" (185). This seems puzzling, as he had realized very early that Kant
is a "rationalist of the sternest order" (*GT*, 274). Ransom could not approve either his view of religion (78) or his view of "sentiment as moral
weakness" (*WB*, 219), though recently Ransom agreed with Kant "not
daring to make images of the Unknown God" (*So R*, n.s. 4 [1968]: 596).
Kant, quite differently from Ransom, had changed the dogmatic concept
of things to a purely logical system of relations and conditions of knowledge. The explanation of Ransom's "Kantianism" must be sought not in
any philosophical allegiance but in Kant's aesthetics.

In spite of his complaint against Bergson's failure to defend the freedom of inanimate objects, the world of things is for Ransom not only a
world of sticks and stones but of "precious objects," objects beyond price,
anything to which our affective life is attached: father and mother, hus-
band or wife, child, friend; one's own house, but also the sun and moon,
sky, and sea; and even such objects as one's nation, church, God, business,
"causes," and institutions (*KR* 9 [1947]: 643). The love of a shabby old
place, an old horse, or an old wife, of anything which is cherished irra-
tionally, "exempted from the fair or market valuation" (*WB*, 213), constitutes this world of precious objects.

Ransom calls a knowledge of this world of things "ontology," in a sense
very different from the historical meaning of the term which was invented by the Calvinist theologian Rudolf Goclenius (1547–1628) and
adopted by Christian Wolff. Wolff, the dominant German philosopher
before Kant, understood ontology to mean the study of the nature of
the real in abstraction from its specific embodiments, in contrast to cos-
mology and psychology. Ontology is concerned with the general formal
characteristics or categories—a conception which is almost the opposite
of Ransom's concern with the qualitative particularity of the world. Kant
substituted "the modest name of Analytic of pure understanding for the
proud name of ontology" (*Kritik der reinen Vernunft*, B 303) and demolished the so-called ontological argument for the existence of God.

In Ransom "ontology" is often used as a synonym for any concern with
actual reality. The term is grossly misunderstood if it is equated with
"aesthetic" or "formalist." Ontology, on the contrary, is knowledge of
being, which is not to be understood as the highest abstraction and not

at all in the sense of Heidegger and existentialist thought, but as the assembly of real things, as "nature." One must admit that in *The New Criticism* Ransom uses the term in almost any combination, often very loosely. There is ontological "speculation" (327), "consideration" (318), "interest" (302), "principles" (293), "argument" (290), "question" (288), "law" (327), "efficacy" (336), "intimations" (330), "brief" (331), "sense" (331, 335), "triumph" (333), "competence" (333), "density" (335), and possibly more. Still, in many cases "ontological" means Ransom's conception of particular being, as when he tells us that science has no "realistic ontology" (*NC*, 80).

All this amounts to a conception of a pluralistic universe, realistic rather than Platonic and idealistic (*IC*, 124). Ransom speaks of his "Platonic and metaphysical days" as a thing of the past (*KR* 5 [1943]: 280) and shows considerable sympathy with naturalistic points of view: "naturalism" in a biological sense, as shown by his interest in Freud, dating back as far as 1924,[9] in Dewey and Santayana. A review of Maritain's *Dream of Descartes* says expressly, "Of religion one is obliged to think that we need a better anthropology, a better psychology, to define this kind of experience and accord to it its rights—not a more ingenious metaphysics." He even concludes, "It does not seem immoderate to say that there is no hope of understanding religion unless it can receive a modern and therefore a secular description" (*SR* 54 [1946]: 154, 156).

Thus Ransom's surprising declaration of being a Kantian is by no means an endorsement of idealism. Ransom expressly disapproves of "the hole of subjectivism" (*So R* 7 [1942]: 534). He characterizes Coleridge as "a not always intelligible adapter of German idealism, cloudy and rhetorical and insistently metaphysical" (*WB*, 163). He considers Hegel "Plato's pious and dutiful successor" (*LC*, 33), upholder of "an extravagant monism" (*KR* 6 [1944]: 119), and dismisses the dialectics as mere "wordplay" (117). The admiration for Kant seems largely limited to the aesthetics "which I took, and take, to be of the highest human authority" (*So R*, n.s. 4 [1968]: 587), and thus to the *Critique of Judgment*, "the foundation of systematic aesthetics" (*LC*, 31), which is interpreted mainly as an exposition and defense of two ideas Ransom embraces as his own. Kant is seen in contrast to Hegel as a defender of "natural beauty" (*PE*, 171) whose view of nature as "free and purposive" supports Ransom's feeling that the natural world is our home. Kant also teaches that "the meaning of beauty is an effect that external nature accomplishes, not man" (*KR* 26 [1964]: 254). He also answers the question of what is poetry? "Kant's view is simple, and for all except the new 'symbolist' critics (who covet for poetry a 'creativity' upon which there are to be no limits) it will be adequate: Poetry is the representation of natural beauty" (*PE*, 171). Thus Ransom can praise Wallace Stevens as "a nature poet according to Kant," "a very good Kantian" (*KR* 26 [1964]: 239, 231). One other idea struck Ransom in the *Critique of Judgment*, the view that "it did not matter to poetry whether the world it set up has real existence or was only imaginary" (*SR* 74 [1966]: 399) or that "the aesthetic judgment is not concerned with the existence or non-existence of the object" (*WB*, 131). Kant thus appears as "the most radical and ultimate spokesman for poetry that we have had" (*PE*, 169).

Kant is thus called upon to authorize a very old theory of poetry: a version of mimesis. The poet presents or represents the world of objects and thus makes us know it. The poet makes this knowledge explicit in a work of art (*WB*, 231), articulates what may have remained inarticulate. He makes us realize the world, brings home to us what we may have known either dimly or abstractly. The poet does not impose an alien, superior mind on an inert world, but he discovers and liberates what had been hidden in the objects. This knowledge of the poet obviously implies a claim for the truth of poetry. Ransom speaks of the "cognitive integrity—the truthfulness of poetry" and asserts that poetry has "more truth than science cares to tell" (*NC*, 93) and that poetry at least "seeks truth" (*WB*, 155).

This truth of poetry is insistently set off against the truth of science. As early as 1923 Ransom told us that art "fishes out of the stream what would become the dead abstraction of science, but catches it still alive'" (*Literary Review* of the *New York Evening Post*, July 14, 1923) and in 1929 he spoke of works of art as "psychic exercises which are just so many rebellions against science" (*Sat R*, September 14, 1929, 125). Most strikingly, in a footnote tucked away in *The World's Body*, the conflict of art and science is put into a historical perspective. "In all human history the dualism between science and art widens continually by reason of the aggressions of science. As science more and more completely reduces the world to its types and forms, art, replying, must invest it again with body" (*WB*, 198n.). Art, in a paradoxical reversal of ordinarily assumed chronology, is "considered late, post-scientific, rebellious against science. . . . Back of art, there is the embittered artist, whose vision of the real has been systematically impaired under the intimidations of scientific instruction" (*SR*, 37 [1929]: 362). Art "comes after science." It "attempts to restore the body which science has emptied." Quoting a simple observation, "the trees stood up against the sky," Ransom argues that "the

line, and the poem have improvised a successful immunity which preserves the object, a 'total situation,' from suffering siege and reduction"
by science (*KR* 1 [1939]: 198–99).

Ransom conceives of science almost always as utilitarian, practical, applied, identical with technology. The speculative scientist is never considered. "Science," he says, "belongs to the economic impulse and does not
free the spirit" (*WB*, 49). Art differs in being disinterested, an idea
known mainly in the Kantian formula of *interesseloses Wohlgefallen*, which
Ransom, however, quotes several times in Schopenhauer's version: "Art
is knowledge without desire" (*GT*, 315; *WB*, 45, 325; *IC*, 103), while he
alludes to Kant's teaching only once (*WB*, 307). Obviously he preferred
Schopenhauer's "knowledge" to Kant's "satisfaction." The odd reversal
of the succession of art to science can be defended by extending the
concept of science to include any and all practical activities.

How does Ransom concretely envisage this special knowledge conveyed by poetry? How, in practice, is this investing of the world with
body to be accomplished by poetry? Sometimes he draws distinctions
between the assertions poets make. They either observe the world as
particularity when they say something as simple as "the trees stood up
against the sky." Or they animate the inanimate; they commit what Ruskin called "the pathetic fallacy"—no fallacy to Ransom—or they even
animate "abstract qualities" (*WB*, 158–59). At other times Ransom describes the process of knowing as a series of identifications: "Images are
perceptions, and perceptions are assertions; perceptions are as true and
as false as propositions." He appeals to the "Neo-Hegelians" from whom
"he received his fullest understanding of what is implied in a perception"
(156–57). As far as I could discover, there is no authority for the statement that "perception *is* assertion" in either Green or Bosanquet, while
Bradley does teach that simple assertions about our feelings (for example, "this hurts, I am hot") imply an analytic judgment of sense. But
whatever Ransom's exact source may be, the progression—images, perceptions, assertions, propositions—allows him to argue for the truth of
poetry, for poetry as a true knowledge of the world. Knowledge, we could
object, must mean here something like "realization," "awareness." It is
the function assigned to poetry by the Russian formalists or by Max
Eastman who, differently from Ransom, uses realization or awareness to
relegate poetry to a lowly place below science. While one can hardly
refuse the use of the term "knowledge" in Ransom's sense, it will not
satisfy those who have a more systematic, rational, and coherent ideal of
truth in mind.

But what is meant by "investing with body," "restoring the concrete

world," or in an alternate phrase, "recovering the denser and more re-
fractory original world which we know loosely through our perceptions
and memories" (*NC*, 281)? These transactions seem to reduce poetry to
the humble function of somehow tightening or sharpening our everyday
perceptions, of reminding us of the actual world of manifold qualities.
They seem to make poetry a dispensable luxury for the man of vivid
perceptions and acute awareness.

Greater claims for poetry are made intermittently. Whimsically, Ransom can draw on the old microcosm-macrocosm parallel. "Is it not splendid if it is true that a small book of small poems contains just so many
miniature or local editions of the cosmos itself, the whole bookful being
of a size to go into a coat pocket, and any one of them of a size to go
into a pocket of the brain?" (*Texas Quarterly* 9 [1966]: 191). Elsewhere an
appeal is made to Wordsworth's "spots of time" and the "timeless moment" of Eliot's *Four Quartets*, to an epiphany which establishes a communion with God. It is an aesthetic moment which "seemed to bring us
into the presence of the unknown God who gave us the sense of beauty
and caused beauty to appear in his creation, establishing at least a moment of communion." "Beauty," says Ransom referring to his earlier
views, "ranked even above morality, and was our highest natural faculty"
(*So R*, n.s. 4 [1968]: 587–88).

In an unargued transition Ransom shifts the function of poetry from
the display, knowledge, and restoration of the real world or from a sudden contact with the supernatural to an adoration and glorification of
this world. Art celebrates the concrete, the highly sensible (*GT*, 22). The
poet's piety is "natural piety." "In romantic art"—and Ransom prefers
it to classical art, differing from his fellow critics—"we revel in the particularity of things, and feel joy of restoration after an estrangement from
nature. The experience is vain and aimless for practical purposes. But
it answers to a deep need within us. It exercises that impulse of natural
piety which requires of us that our life should be in loving *rapport* with
the environment" (*Sat R*, September 14, 1929, 127). "The poet's faith, I
should say, is that this is 'the best of all possible worlds' " (*PE*, 183). Poetry
is not only festal, not merely a celebration of the beauty of nature, but
also, in a slight contradiction, nostalgic, commemorative, "in the past
tense," even the pluperfect (*WB*, 250). Once it is conceived as yearning
for the lost paradise. "The little world [poetry] sets up is a little version
of our natural world in its original dignity, not the laborious world of
affairs. Indeed, the little world is the imitation of our ancient Paradise,
when we inhabited it in innocence" (*PE*, 100).

The religious implications and motives are obvious in the late passages as they are in the early book *God without Thunder.* I would not want to decide how they can be reconciled with the strong naturalistic statements quoted before, with the view that poets are "prodigious materialists" (*WB,* 326), or that "to the theologian the poet might want to say, One world at a time" (*PE,* 184). Transcendence seems expressly denied in these pronouncements.

Some corollaries for a theory of poetry follow from Ransom's concept of poetry. Ransom plays down the personality of the poet, a motif well worn in modern theories since Flaubert and Mallarmé. "Anonymity is a condition of poetry. . . . A good poem, even if it is signed with a full and well-known name, intends as a work of art to lose the identity of the author" (*WB,* 2). "By the doctrine of expressiveness art is disreputable" (308), presumably because it would be self-indulgence.

It follows also that Ransom has little use for affective theories of poetry. Ransom argues that there is "no emotion at all until an object has furnished the occasion for one," as "emotions are correlatives of the cognitive objects" (*NC,* 201). Feelings are "calls to action, and always want to realize their destiny, which is to turn into actions and vanish" (*WB,* 290) and thus presumably are not aesthetic. But elsewhere Ransom can say that "the human importance of the art-work is that it 'touches the heart' " (*KR* 12 [1950]: 202), and sentiment (obscurely different from emotion and feeling) is sometimes equated with the aesthetic experience. The sentence "Sentiment is aesthetic, aesthetic is cognitive, and the cognition is of the object as an individual" (*WB,* 216) sounds almost like Croce, though elsewhere Croce is chided—wrongly, I think—for assuming that art is "simple child's play" (*SR* 37 [1929]: 362). His "aesthetics denied him a criticism" (*SR* 52 [1944]: 558), says Ransom, in defiance of Croce and almost all of Italy.

Precious objects are prized by our affections, but there is, for Ransom, a difference between the genuine artist who distances and thus overcomes sentiment and the sentimental artist who has "the right sentiment for the object, but articulates the object no better than a man who has merely the sentiment" (*WB,* 231). Art feels cold, not hot.

Consistently, Ransom has little use for Aristotelian catharsis. In the traditional interpretation as "a gross physiological metaphor," it seems to him "inept" and in the refined version of S. H. Butcher merely "an agent of moral improvement" (*WB,* 179). "Its object is to intensify the aesthetic moment in order to minimize and localize it, and clear the way for the scientific moment" (211), "scientific" meaning here something like practical or even civic. Aristotle wanted to purge the Greeks of their sense of cosmic evil. He wanted them to be good citizens (187).

"Art gratifies a perceptual impulse and exhibits the minimum of reason" (*WB*, 130). But criticism, in contrast, is conceived as rational and scientific, if we mean by science not any imitation or claim for the method of the exact sciences but a systematic approach toward a general theory of poetry and the arts. "Criticism is a science, and a science must know what it is doing" (*Sat R*, March 24, 1934, 574). "Criticism must become more scientific, or precise and systematic" (*WB*, 329). It must be based on theory and ultimately on aesthetics. "Theory, which is expectation, always determines criticism and never more than when it is unconscious" (*WB*, 173). "The authority of criticism depends on its coming to terms with aesthetics" (*IC*, 92). Criticism must concentrate on the "objective literature itself " (*NC*, 75) and must be distinguished from interest in biography, literary history, and sociology. Ransom can be caustic at the expense of the pedants in the English departments, on the "indefensible extravagance in the gigantic collective establishment of the English faculties" who fail to teach criticism (*KR* 2 [1940]: 349–50). He is quite explicit in rejecting the Marxist approach of Bernard Smith's *Forces in American Criticism* (in *Free America* 4 [1940]: 19–20), though much later Ransom says casually that "at any rate, the social conscience [of the Marxist critics] influenced him very deeply" (*KR* 12 [1950]: 208). I am not aware of any public evidence for this influence, at least on Ransom's literary criticism.

The advocacy of systematic criticism induced Ransom to support criticism in American universities and colleges as an academic subject. Particularly the essay "Criticism, Inc." (1937) and the book *The New Criticism* (1941) gave Ransom a commanding, elder statesman's position in the movement he had named. Ransom's book is highly critical of the critics there considered. It is far from a celebration of the New Criticism, as Ransom sharply criticizes Richards for his psychologism, for "very nearly severing the dependence of poetic effect upon any standard of objective knowledge or belief " (*IC*, 95). He makes many objections to Eliot's criticism, its emotionalism, and its concept of tradition. A review of Eliot's *Use of Poetry and the Use of Criticism* (*Sat R*, March 24, 1934, 574) criticizes him for disdaining theory, just as he was later to charge him with "theoretical innocence" (*NC*, 145). Quite as sharply Ransom rejects Yvor Winters's moralism.

The other critics to whom the label has stuck are by no means immune from Ransom's criticism, even though he may have seen them as allies in the general cause. Empson is praised as "the closest and most resourceful reader that poetry has had" (*NC*, 102), but even the Richards chapter in *The New Criticism*, which endorses some of Empson's gross misreadings, recognizes the "overreading" of the "bare ruined choirs" passage in Shakespeare's sonnet. An earlier essay, "Mr. Empson's Muddles" (*So R* 4 [1938–39]: 322), more stringently criticizes his "almost fanatical devotion to puns" (326). Empson's interpretation of Marvell's "The Garden" seems to Ransom "the most extreme example of what I regard as Mr. Empson's almost inveterate habit of overreading poetry" (331). Empson is "a solipsistic critic, because he has much to say about anything, and not the strictest conscience about making what he says 'correspond' with what the poet says" (333). His ambiguity is rather multiplicity. The meanings may be irrelevant to each other, inconsistent, or at the worst contradictory (336). He and Richards admire "all possible complications, all muddles, indiscriminately" (337).

Similarly Cleanth Brooks is praised as "the most forceful and influential critic of poetry that we have" (*PE,* 148), as "the most expert living reader or interpreter of difficult verse" (*KR* 2 [1940]: 247), but Ransom disagrees with Brooks's preoccupation with paradox, wit, and irony. Paradoxes must be resolved (*KR* 9 [1947]: 437). "Opposites can never be said to be resolved or reconciled merely because they have been got into the same poem" (*NC,* 95). Irony in poetry should occur only occasionally. Paraphrase, condemned by Brooks, is "a critical function" (*KR* 9 [1947]: 442). The defense of poetry "must be of its human substance and on the naturalistic level" and not by some "fairly impenetrable esoteric quality" postulated by Brooks (438).

Of the two prominent critics more loosely associated with the New Criticism, R. P. Blackmur and Kenneth Burke, Ransom admires Blackmur more. Quoting him on Shelley and Emily Dickinson, he praises these passages as "in depth and precision at once beyond all earlier criticism in our language" (*NC,* x). *Language and Gesture* is called "the official classic in exegesis of the poetry of an age" (*PE,* 102). But neither does Blackmur live up to Ransom's ideal of a critic. He remains a formalist. He forgets "that there are substantive as well as formal values in the poem" (108). "Substantive" must here mean something like Ransom's "ontological."

Ransom admires Kenneth Burke as "of all our critics philosophically the subtlest, temperamentally the most ironic" (*New Republic,* February 18, 1946, 257), as "a master of innovations even upon the most modern forms of Dialectic" (*Texas Quarterly* 9 [1966]: 191). But Burke is said "to play too near the rational surface of the poem and the reason it does not go deeper is that he is no lover of nature" (*KR* 14 [1952]: 231). Poetic metaphor is not to be identified with scientific analogy (*So R* 7 [1942]: 530n.) as Burke tries to do. Burke, "the most bristling with modern technicalities," drawn from psychology, anthropology, sociology, and linguistics, is on the side of modern rationalism (*KR* 10 [1948]: 684, 687) and thus fails to understand poetry.

Of all English and American critics of the recent period only Allen Tate seems to have commanded Ransom's complete assent. Tate's essays "Three Types of Poetry" and "Poetry as Knowledge" move on the lines of Ransom's thought. It might be difficult to establish priorities between teacher and pupil.

Thus Ransom differs sharply from the other New Critics (with the exception of Tate) in his concern for the world of nature, for what he calls "ontology." *The New Criticism* concludes with a chapter "Wanted: An Ontological Critic" (279 ff.), that is, a critic who would be concerned with the relation between the words of the poet and "the world beyond words," "that dense, particular, individual world of objects." The final desideratum is an "ontological insight" (*IC,* 112), an insight into nature, an aim shared by criticism and poetry. Criticism is then "pure speculation" (91), not distinguishable from aesthetics and ultimately from philosophy.

I have deliberately postponed the discussion of Ransom's most widely known and criticized idea, the dichotomy of structure and texture. "A poem is a logical structure having a local texture" (*IC,* 110) is the main formula, in which "structure" is used not in the sense of linguistic structuralism as totality or system but as rational argument (which Ransom somewhat confusingly calls "logical"), while "texture" is the presentation of the qualitative density of the world. "The texture is ubiquitous; and to put it simply it consists in interpolated material which does not relate to the argument" (*KR* 5 [1943]: 286). This dichotomy has been called a revival of the ancient form-content duality and has been seen even as a relapse into the view of poetry as decoration: images, metaphors, and so on embellishing the rational or moral content. Ransom later saw a parallel to his structure-texture dualism in Freud's ego-id contrast. "The thought-work in the poem" is the ego's, while "the play upon substance" is the id's (*KR* 9 [1947]: 655). This contrast would assume that the texture of a poem is somehow arrived at unconsciously, hardly a view which can be defended, as Ransom's other reflections assume a conscious working-out of the metaphorical and metrical texture of the poem. Nor can one be convinced by his attempt to relate structure to Eliot's emotions and texture to feelings, as structure is always defined as a logical or rational argument (*NC,* 156).

Mostly Ransom makes the structure-texture dualism so sharply distinct that texture appears as "redundant," "irrelevant," "adventitious" in relation to structure. But on the other hand, there is the prose argument which is equally indispensable. We are told, "No prose argument no poem" (*KR* 5 [1943]: 286) and that "a poet who argues badly is a reproach to poetry" (*Hika* 5 [1939]: 10), a standard which is used to disparage poems Ransom considers poorly argued, such as Joyce Kilmer's "Trees," or poems which are only strings of images or scenes, such as *The Waste Land,* severely criticized as incoherent in 1923 (*Literary Review* 3 [1923]: 825–26).

Metaphor is the main element of texture. The abandonment of metaphor would mean the abandonment of poetry (*PE,* 181). Metaphor serves to "remove the object from classification and disposition, as a particular always qualitatively exceeds the universal" (*LC,* 23). Metaphor "serves to obscure the pointer relation of prose language or serves to densify the imagery and to increase 'naturalism' " (*SR* 52 [1944]: 568). "Naturalism" here must mean "ontology," mimesis and not naturalism as it is understood in Zola's sense, which Ransom always condemned when he discussed the modern American novelists (see *American Review* 7 [1936]: 301–18). Metaphor is "one militant way of defending nature" (*PE,* 181), as it is "a going to the Concrete of nature for its analogy" (180).

Ransom rejects the version of metaphor, expounded by I. A. Richards, as an "interanimation of tenor and vehicle." "The profits of the transaction do not amount to much in themselves" (*NC,* 77). He doubts Richards's account of Coleridge's example of imagination from *Venus and Adonis* as a case of modification or interanimation between Adonis and the shooting star. He shows that Richards can mistake the vehicle for the tenor in a well-known passage comparing the Thames with the flow of the mind in Denham's *Cooper's Hill* (*NC,* 68–72). Metaphor for Ransom is simply "a sort of second poem attached to the given poem" (77). "The vehicle must realize itself independently and go beyond its occasion" (85). Antony (in a scene with Eros in *Antony and Cleopatra*), comparing the change in himself with the changing shapes of clouds, is an example that proves to Ransom that "few of the images have anything to do with Antony's own situation" (85). They live their own life. They are importations, or "importers" (*KR* 12 [1950]: 505).

The independent life of the metaphor is one of the reasons for Ransom's preference for the poetry of the metaphysicals. "The conceit," he argues, "has no explicit tenor, but only a 'vehicle' covering it. . . . The tenor of a metaphysical poem is," at most, "conventional and generalized, while the texture is thick and odd" (*NC,* 188–89). Ransom even states that a metaphysical poet makes "the whole poem, or some whole passage of it, out of the single unit metaphor" (185). He can, however, produce only "The Exequy" of Henry King and the compasses passage from Donne's "Valediction: Forbidding Mourning" as examples. But there are many genuinely metaphysical poems such as "Twicknam Garden" which do not fulfill this supposed requirement. It is simply not true that "a single extended image bears the whole weight of the conceptual structure" (*So R* 1 [1936]: 10) in a metaphysical poem.

Beyond the metaphor there is myth. "Myths are conceits, born of metaphor" (*WB,* 140). Poets are "constantly creating little local myths" (*GT,* 66) with their metaphors. The great myth, religion, has decayed and has made myth unavailable to the modern poet. Yeats, however, "disproved" this (*KR* 1 [1939]: 311). He alone among modern poets created a new myth, though, in other contexts, Ransom dismisses "the phases of the moon" as "a private system: the work of a prose thinker" (*So R* 7 [1941–42]: 526). Also, "the Ossianic and Irish mythology produced nothing that is worthy of his ultimate stature as a poet" (*KR* 1 [1939]: 314).

Ransom argues mostly for the structure-texture dichotomy. "Texture is the thing that peculiarly qualifies a discourse as being poetic; it is its differentia" (*NC,* 220). Sometimes, he considers meter either to be a third equal element making a triad of the poetic transaction—comparing the head with structure, the heart with texture, and the feet with the meter (*KR* 16 [1954]: 560), or he makes meter and "the phonetic effect" serve as "a sort of texture to the meaning" (*NC,* 318). He defends meter as "bringing about the abdication of prose" (*WB,* 258) and providing the poet with a mask (257), thus supporting the anonymity and impersonality of poetry. Ransom, however, does not believe in the expressiveness of meter. He frequently ridicules the usual assumptions about sound symbolism (95–97). He "cannot discover a fixed scheme" in free verse (*NC,* 262). He opts thus for a bold, rhythmical reading of poetry in preference to a reading emphasizing the spoken prose rhythm. The chanting Yeats, we might add, was a better reader of poetry than the subdued, prosy Eliot.

It all comes to a rejection of organicism, of what for Ransom is the superstition of totality, coherence, unity, *gestalt.* A poem, he says memorably, is "much more like a Christmas tree than an organism" (*KR* 7 [1945]: 294–95), or with different metaphors, a poem is like a democratic state and not a totalitarian government (*IC,* 108), or a poem is like a house with the paint, paper, and tapestry comparable to the texture, and the roof and beams to the structure (110–11). Once, he seems to admit that a work of art is an organism with parts functionally attached to each other, producing a whole. However, he immediately withdraws this apparent concession, insisting that this view of totality would apply also to a machine or to a scientific operation (*KR* 7 [1945]: 289–91). Ransom finds it odd that literary critics, "so many of them," should claim "that this same rigorous organization obtains within a poem; that the Universal or logical plan of the poem is borne out perfectly in the sensuous detail which puts it into action" (*PE*, 164). Still, after arguing as usual for the concrete and particular, Ransom concludes that "it would be wrong to give the impression that in a poem, necessarily, the intellectual Universal has always disappeared from sight and now exists only in the Concrete." Rather, "it is my impression that as often as not a poem will recite its two versions, side by side" (174). We are back to the unresolved dichotomy. The idea of a reconciliation or synthesis presented by the Hegelian Concrete Universal (revived by Bosanquet in the second lecture of *The Principle of Individuality and Value* [1912]) is finally rejected as "a gaudy paradox" (*KR* 6 [1944]: 121). There is no "resolution," no "fusion" in poetry (*IC*, 109). In unusually strong terms Ransom asserts that "it is a lie to say that contradictories may not coexist, for they do it in poetry" (*So R* 4 [1938–39]: 338). "We must not become fools of the shining but impractical ideal of 'unity' or of 'fusion' " (*NC*, 183). The reconciliation of opposites formulated in a famous passage by Coleridge, endorsed by Cleanth Brooks, is rejected. "I cannot but think that the recent revival of Coleridge's involved critical language has been obfuscating" (*KR* 9 [1947]: 439). There is also no identification of subject and object, no such integral experience as propounded by Dewey (*KR* 7 [1945]: 286). The work of art as Dewey describes it becomes "too fluid for human identification" (288). In short, "poetry is an inorganic activity" (*KR* 5 [1943]: 290).

There are a few occasions where Ransom tries to escape the difficulties of his dualism. He picked up the term "icon" from Charles Morris (who in turn derived it from Charles Sanders Peirce) as an alternative to image. The term avoids the association, in English, of image with visibility, which Ransom uses even later when he says that "the artistic vision . . . makes the vast depth of natural contingency visible" (*KR* 7 [1945]: 291). "Icon" certainly emphasizes that the aesthetic sign must be a whole object. Ransom objects to Morris for considering the icon "only a medium denoting, by embodying, a value," while for Ransom "the icon is a body imitating some actual embodiment of the value" (*NC*, 289). Ransom drops the talk of value quickly, as value interests the consumer and he is concerned with "body" though he whimsically confesses that "he does not know what the body is for" (291). Morris's theory, Ransom concludes, remains "another version of affective or psychologistic theory" (289). Immediately following the account of Morris, Ransom tries, even with a diagram, to illustrate the relation between meter and meaning by a clash or struggle which seems to correct the usual irrelevance theory. "The composition of a poem is an operation in which the argument fights to displace the meter, and the meter fights to displace the argument" (295). The poet makes adaptations both of meter to meaning (introducing indeterminate sound) and of meaning to meter (introducing indeterminate meaning) (302). Some interplay, some mutual modifications are suggested. As Ransom said later, "I had the idea of a poem as a great 'paradox,' a construct looking two ways, with logic trying to dominate the metaphors, and metaphors trying to dominate the logic" to which he added meter to give the poem "the form of a trinitarian existence" (*PE*, 157). The image of head, heart, and feet also suggest such an ultimate reconciliation with organicism. In a later paper the metaphor Ransom uses of the "skeleton of summary and syntactic language" contrasted with the "flesh" of connotative poetic meaning points also to a unity of the two (*Texas Quarterly* 9 [1966]: 192).

But we must not try to assimilate Ransom to this central tradition, even when he makes concessions to it. His original insight remains the experience of the natural world as an assembly of qualities, as heterogeneity which it is the task of poetry to present to those of us who have forgotten this world of precious objects, of private experiences. Poetry thus shields us against the abstractions and exploits of science and technology which Ransom saw as destructive of the saner and happier ways of life in the South of his youth and the agrarian past of his region. As any poet-critic, Ransom writes also in defense of his own poetic craft: he obviously, like Valéry, practiced it as a balancing of sound and meaning, as a continued compromise between meter and sense, metaphor and argument. Whatever defense can be put up for organicism, for the ultimate indissolubility of content and form, of the what and the how, of style as meaning, we should grant to Ransom that there is a dichotomy, or as Roman Jakobson would say, a "binary" relation in all language utterances which, in a theory of poetry, we may rechristen theme and style, sound and meaning, and even, with Ransom's peculiar vocabulary, structure and texture. We should also grant him the merit of having revived the ancient doctrine of the imitation of nature and to have given it a new twist with his insistence on nature's particularity and heterogeneity reflected in poetry.

10: ALLEN TATE (1899–1979)

ALLEN TATE, from the very beginning of his career, is motivated by social and religious concerns. The idea that Tate or any of the New Critics uphold an art-for-art's sake theory comes from a misunderstanding of his (and their) defense of the distinctness of the aesthetic transaction, from their insight into the totality and coherence of a successful work of art. Tate (encouraged by T. S. Eliot's view of the "autotelic" nature of poetry) constantly tells us that the poem has its own integrity, that it is a whole in which the parts corroborate and modify each other. A poem, he argues, is not a statement or a communication like a tract or a sermon—all ancient motifs of any organistic aesthetics which are grossly misinterpreted if they are supposed to lead to the view that poetry is cut off from reality, is self-reflective, and hence ultimately meaningless. There are pronouncements in Tate which seem to go far in the defense of an art-for-art's-sake position, but even when he says that "there is probably nothing wrong with art for art's sake if we take the phrase seriously," he immediately adds, "and not take it to mean the kind of poetry written in England forty years ago," and explains it to mean that poetry should be considered "apart from its use (though it may be useful)" (E, 595). Poetry is removed from the "domain of practicality." A stanza from Keats's "La Belle Dame sans Merci" is "neither true nor false: it is an object that exists" (194). "It proves nothing. . . . It has no useful relation to the ordinary forms of action" (196), or phrased even more sharply, "the perfectly realized poem has no overflow of unrealized action. It does not say that men ought to be better or worse, or that they are; it has no ulterior motives" ("Poetry and the Absolute," *Sewanee Review* 35 [1927]: 44). Tate belongs to the tradition, Kantian and Schopenhauerian, which emphasizes that the "true usefulness of poetry is in its perfect inutility," in its "focus of repose for the will-driven intellect" (E, 196). Even Tate's defense of the Bollingen Award for Ezra Pound shows this basic attitude. While he approves of Pound's achievement as a poet who has "done more than any other man to regenerate the language, if

174

not the imaginative forms, of England" (512), he chides him not only for
having "thumped his tub for the Axis" but simply for being "hortatory,"
for mixing poetry and politics, a charge that Tate would also level against
the good American democrat, Archibald MacLeish. "In some Swiftian
social order we should have in fairness to provide an adjoining cell for
Mr. MacLeish" (26). Poetry, he insistently repeats, is not persuasion, is
not propaganda, is "neither religion nor social engineering" (619).

It is only an apparent contradiction when Tate ascribes the greatest
social significance to literature. "All literature has a social or moral or
religious purpose" (*E*, 133). Even the poetry of Mallarmé has "some
effect upon conduct, insofar as it affects our emotions" (27), though Tate
dismisses the inflated claims and charges about the poet's role in society.
He notes that no poet (not even Milton) ever received or exercised "com-
petently high political authority" (18) and that the burden of change in
society surely falls on others, such as statesmen and scientists, rather than
on poets, who must be concerned with a "mastery of disciplined language" (27). Tate thinks it "an irresponsible demand to ask the poet to
cease to be a poet and become the propagandist of a political ideal, even
if he himself thought it a worthy ideal" (28).

Still, we must not think that Tate's view of the poet's function is that
of having merely "immediate responsibility for the vitality of the language" (*E*, 3). Rather, Tate assigns to literature a unique function: the
purveying of a special kind of knowledge. Over and over again, Tate
says that literature provides "the special, unique and complete knowledge" (202), "knowledge of a whole object, its complete knowledge, the
full body of experience it offers us" (105). It seems, at first sight, an
obscure doctrine which sets off "poetic knowledge" from "historical documentation and information" (202) and, of course, from scientific knowledge. It may, one fears, lead to a double truth theory, an obscurantist
claim to some mystical insight. But it makes sense when we associate
Tate's knowledge with Ransom's view that poetry gives us "the world's
body," the particularity of the real world in contrast to the abstractions
of science. Knowledge means "realization," full awareness. It is an old
and respectable claim but often the meaning of "knowledge" expands
considerably in Tate's formulations. Poetry requires "powers of discrimination" which are not deductive powers, though, he admits, "they may
be aided by them: they wait rather upon the cultivation of our total
human powers" (63). "Knowledge" thus becomes the unified sensibility
of T. S. Eliot, the union of intellect and feeling achieved in poetry. It
comes about "when the will and its formulas are put back into an implicit
relation with the whole of our experience." This will-less knowledge is

"subject to no change, and therefore known with equal truth for all time" (196). Elsewhere this knowledge is identified with "a genuine knowledge of our human community" (14) and, in a crucial passage, is made to be the unique achievement of art. In the essay "The Hovering Fly" (1943), which comments on the last scene of Dostoevsky's *Idiot,* in which Myshkin and Rogozhin watch near the corpse of Nastasya Filipovna when a fly appears from nowhere, the fly is used as a symbol of the function of art. "We may *look* at the hovering fly; we can to a degree *know* the actual world. But we shall not know the actual world by looking at it; we know it by looking at the hovering fly" (*E,* 117). If I understand this correctly, Tate claims that we know the world best, at its fullest, most completely, through the symbols of art. "The buzz of the fly distends," he says fancifully, "both visually and metaphorically, the body of the girl into the world" (119). To give another example cited by Tate: Emma Bovary, at the brink of suicide in the attic of her house after receiving the cruel letter of Rodolphe, is prevented from falling out of the window by the sound of Binet's whirring lathe. "The action is not stated from the point of view of the author; it is rendered in terms of situation and scene" (139). The "correlative" sound of the lathe "gives us a direct impression of Emma's sensation" and "charges the entire scene with actuality" (140). We *know* Emma at this moment in a way which cannot be conveyed by a mere statement or an abstract analysis.

Tate himself says that he owes much to John Crowe Ransom and "I suppose I owe most of all to Coleridge, but just what it would be hard to say, beyond the general idea that poetry can be an undemonstrable form of knowledge" (*E,* xi). In the essay "Literature as Knowledge" (1941) he appeals to I. A. Richards, quoting him from *Coleridge on Imagination* (1934) as saying that "poetry is the completest mode of utterance" (*E,* 104), where, in the context of a discussion of Coleridge's metaphor of the windharp, Richards argues that "it is the privilege of poetry to preserve us from mistaking our notions either for things or for ourselves." Poetry is here simply said to speak of both reality and ourselves. Much more to the point seems Jacques Maritain's discussion of poetic knowledge in *Situation de la poésie* (1938). There he calls poetic knowledge "a knowledge which cannot be expressed in ideas and judgments, but which is rather experience than knowledge, and creative experience, because it wants to express itself and cannot be expressed except in the work." Maritain, more cautiously than Tate, recognizes that the word "knowledge" is an "analogical term." Poetry cannot be confused with metaphysics: poetry is ontology. The poet is brought back to the totality of his being. Maritain hopes for a "poetics of integrality, or rather of integration" (106, 120–22).

This is precisely what Tate hoped to establish with his theory of poetry as "tension." Tension is not simply a dynamic quality or balance but is a term formed punningly by "lopping the prefixes off the logical terms *ex*tension and *in*tension" (*E*, 64). "Good poetry is a unity of all the meanings from the furthest extremes of intension and extension" (63). The reference to the traditional meanings of extension and intension in logic is, however, misleading. It means simply the scope of a concept versus its contents. Tate's use is very different. He illustrates it by contrasting three poems representing extremes: a poem "The Vine" by James Thomson, the author of *The City of the Dreadful Night,* which has no coherent logical meaning and rather suggests only a vague mood; "A Hymn to Light" by the seventeenth-century poet Abraham Cowley, which states a bare analytical proposition; and Donne's "Valediction: Forbidding Mourning" where, in the image of the "gold to airy thinness beat," intension and extension are one and enrich each other. "Tension" turns out to be a version of Eliot's unified sensibility: feeling and intellect are reconciled in Donne's image. In an earlier attempt to classify "The Types of Poetry" (1934), the final point is identical with the argument about tension. There Tate distinguishes poetry of the practical will, which leans upon moral abstractions or allegory (like Spenser) and, in later periods, appealed to physical ideas. It is basically rhetoric, or what Tate calls oddly "positive Platonism," confidence in the limitless power of man. Allegory is condemned as "inferior poetry" (178), though an obscure exception is made for Dante. The second type is romantic poetry, poetry of emotion which strangely enough is identified with "romantic irony," disillusionment, and again called Platonism, but this time "negative Platonism" (177). Finally there is a third type which is perfect and whole, "an experienced statement" illustrated by Edgar, in *King Lear,* reflecting "Ripeness is all" (175). We are back at Tate's constant preoccupation, the vision of the whole of life, the quality of the imagination, of poetic creation, which, as he formulated it in a very early essay, "One Escape from the Dilemma" (in *Fugitive* 3 [1924]: 34), is "pure presentation of intuitions or ideas," and again and again in various vocabularies, "a permanent focus of emotional reference out of the disorder of feeling" ("Poetry and the Absolute," in *Sewanee Review* 35 [1927]: 42), or "an ordered intensification," "an absolute intensification of perception" (45, 47), or, in a terminology derived from A. N. Whitehead, "a prehensive unity of the aspects of events."[1]

Later, reading Jacques Maritain's *Dream of Descartes* (translated in 1944), Tate found a new vocabulary for his basic distinction: the contrast between the angelic and the symbolic imagination. The angelic imagination is the prehension of man and poet to become an angel, to become godlike, divorced from his body, a mere machine. Edgar Allan Poe illustrates perfectly this dualism, whereas "the symbolic imagination brings the various meanings together at a single moment of action" (*E*, 427). It conducts an action through analogy or rather a chain of analogies which lets Dante (or presumably any great poet) achieve an actual insight into "the great dilemma, eternal life or eternal death" (436), a "fullness of actuality" in "making the supra-sensible visible" (443).

The two essays, "The Angelic Imagination' and "The Symbolic Imagination" (both 1951), follow Tate's conversion to Roman Catholicism (in 1950), but they resume, with mystical overtones, the earlier sober discussion of metaphor, which is seen as the crucial strategy of poetry. Tate finds it in Aristotle's meager remarks in the "perception of similarity in dissimilars" (*E*, 489), in Longinus's analysis of Sappho's "Ode to Anactoria," which recognizes in it a "uniting of contradictions," "a clash of feelings" bound together in "one body" (482–83), and in Dr. Johnson's recognition of the *discordia concors* in metaphysical poetry. But Tate criticizes Johnson's view as static, where metaphysical and modernist poetry knows "a dynamic relation between the mind and its objects." "An essence is created by the junction of the vehicle and the tenor of the leading metaphor. It is not *in* space; it moves with experience in time" (507). Clearly this theory of metaphor anticipates the account of Dante, of his "analogical conversion of symbol" which is "constantly moving, rendered moment by moment as *action*" (440). What is achieved is "the actuality of the identity of world and mind" (460), the defeat of the Cartesian "bifurcation of nature." One cannot think of the function of poetry in more exalted terms. L'art pour l'art is left far behind. Poetry is assigned a role comparable to the imagination in Wordsworth's vision on Mount Snowdon or to the claim of Coleridge (derived from Schelling and Schiller) that art is "the mediatress between, and reconciler of nature and man."[2] Tate thus embraces finally an extreme romantic faith, though he would describe himself as an enemy of romanticism conceived of as emotional self-indulgence and utopian pretensions for mankind. Tate sounds almost like Albert Béguin: poetry is the only answer to the "elemental anguish of the creature enclosed in his temporal existence." Time and moving in time is Tate's requirement for poetry. Like Béguin and Maritain he assumes an analogical concept of the universe. "The structure of our mind and our total being and its spontaneous rhythms

are identical with the structure and the great rhythms of the universe."[3]
Poetry turns out to be, if not religion, then an analogue of religion and
a preparation for religion.

The poet works with language as his medium and he has to devise
strategies to convey his meaning in and through language. But Tate,
contrary to frequent assumptions about the New Criticism, is not convinced of the identity of language and poetry. He disapproves of the
attempt to get away from the connotative and ideational in poetry; he
rejects the idea of an abstract poetry (*LC*, 20–21) and of "pure" poetry
in the sense of Bremond or Valéry (*E*, 193). He emphatically condemned
"that idolatrous dissolution of language from the grammar of a possible
world, which results from the belief that language itself can be reality,
or by incantation can create reality: a superstition that comes down in
French from Lautréamont, Rimbaud, and Mallarmé to the Surrealists,
and in English to Hart Crane, Wallace Stevens, and Dylan Thomas"
(406). There is no prisonhouse of the language. Poetry is turned to the
world, aims at a "portrait of reality" just like philosophy, approaches an
absolute (*Sewanee Review* 35 [1927]: 43n.), is "impure," like anything human, acts on society and is acted on. The accusation of aestheticism falls
completely flat.

Nor can one suspect Tate of scientism or an advocacy of a value-free
approach to literature. Science is rather Tate's bugbear, the villain of
history which has destroyed the community of man, broken up the old
organic way of life, and paved the way to industrialism and capitalism.
Science is constantly disparaged as having "very little to say about reality"
(*LC*, 158). Science encourages utopian thinking, the false idea of the
perfectibility of man which is opposed by poetry, "the instinctive coun-
terattack of the intelligence against the dogma of future perfection" (*E*,
260), as Tate accepts the doctrine of the fall of man or, at least, of his
radical limits. Poetry is called "one of the sources of the knowledge of
evil in man," while modern social science makes "a powerful attempt to
purify ourselves of that knowledge" (29).

Mostly, in discussing methods for the study of literature, Tate equates
science with "positivism," a term he uses broadly for any kind of factualism, antiquarianism, historical determinism, and reductive explanation by sources and influences. In a witty lecture "Miss Emily and the
Bibliographer" (1940), Tate exposes the insincerity of the scholars who
profess to study literary history in preparation for literary criticism by
tracing influences conceived in terms of forces, causes, and effects, or by
biological analogies of growth and developments or by applying psychology, economics, and sociology, all in a vain attempt at imitating the

methods of science. They all shirk judgment, "the moral obligation to judge." "If we wait for history to judge," as they plead, "there will be no judgment" (*E*, 153). We must judge also the literature of our own time. The historical method, Tate said much earlier, has "disqualified our best minds from the traditional functions of criticism" (*New Republic* 49 [1927]: 330). It ignores the meaning of the destination in favor of the way one gets there. In an elaborate whimsical simile about the Smiths arriving at the Ritzfitz Hotel, the question of whether they came by car or by train is ridiculed. "There is a personal sensation along a route that never gets anywhere, in an endless stream of causes and effects" ("Confusion and Poetry," in *Sewanee Review* 38 [1930]: 139). Thus "poetry is not only quite different from science but in its essense opposed to science" (*This Quarter* 5 [1932]: 292). The union of art and science, envisaged by Edmund Wilson, is "a chimera" (*Hound and Horn* 4 [1931]: 622).

Tate would be surprised to see the method of "close reading" described as "scientific." In his own practice it has nothing to do with modern linguistics or stylistics and is never divorced from judgment or, at least, appreciation. Tate had developed his theory of poetry and his general point of view long before he engaged in anything which could be called "close reading." It is fully developed only in the essay "Narcissus as Narcissus" (1938), a commentary on his own "Ode to the Confederate Dead" (1930). There again he rejects the genetic approach. "What is the poem after it is written? That is the question. Not where it came from and why" (*E*, 594). He ridicules the idea that his poetry is "compensation," that his "one intransigent desire is to have been a Confederate general" (594). The examination of a poem apart from biography and literary history became, no doubt, an important innovation in the teaching of literature in American colleges and universities. Tate objected to the historical method, the reductionism and factualism of academic scholarship, but he always stressed the historicity of poetry. One could even argue that his theory of literature is part of a theory of history.

History is seen substantially in the terms of T. S. Eliot. There was once a perfectly ordered world which formed the background of Dante's poetry. "All that he knew came under a philosophy which was at once dramatic myth, a body of truths, and a comprehensive view of life" (*E*, 156). Donne still lived in a whole world. Bacon, Gibbon, and La Mettrie (why only these three?) are the destroyers of the magical view of the world. Tate can ask, "Will poetry survive the downfall of the myths and beliefs upon which it has been assumed to be radically based?" (*New Republic* 49 [1927]: 329–30), and, at least in the early years, Tate answered with a qualified "yes." He hoped for a reconstitution of religion and myth and hoped that some remnant of the good society could be saved, at least in the South. Tate's taking part in the agrarian movement was such an attempt: a polemic against the machine civilization, against the industrialization and urbanization of his region. But Tate was far from glorifying the Old South. While he thought it preferable to the urban commercial and industrial North, he criticized it severely for its sentimentality, rhetoric, obsession with politics, and thin religiosity. The institution of slavery damaged also the white man. "The Negro slave was a barrier between the ruling class and the soil" (*E*, 525). The South lacked a free peasantry, which, Tate believes, is the basis of a great culture. Modern civilization is seen in decay. Not surprisingly, Tate reviewed Oswald Spengler's *Decline of the West* (*Nation* 122 [1926]: 532, 534) sympathetically, though he later was repelled by the Teutonism of *Years of Decision* (*American Review* 3 [1934]: 41–47).

The disintegration of man is for Tate an incontrovertible fact, decisive also for the history of poetry. The poets who interest him most (not necessarily those he valued most highly) come at the point of the dissolution of the original unity; they dramatize the alienation of man. The early paper on Emily Dickinson (1928) sees her at the point of the dissolution of Puritanism when the "spiritual communion was breaking up" (*E*, 292), which, for Tate, is paradoxically "the perfect literary situation." Poetry "probes the deficiencies of a tradition. But it must have a tradition to probe" (293) "The poet finds himself balanced upon the moment when such a world (that of a homogeneous society) is about to fall." "The world order is assimilated, in Miss Dickinson, as medievalism was in Shakespeare, to the poetic vision" (294). Later the process of dissolution advanced much further. Hart Crane exemplifies the "disintegration of our intellectual systems" (310). His poetry vindicates Eliot's major premise "that the integrity of individual consciousness has broken down" (321). Crane's world has no center. With Crane the "disorder is original and fundamental" (310). Tate, who knew Crane intimately and admired him as a poet in spite of everything, saw him as a pathological case. He speaks of his "monstrous egoism, aggravated by homosexuality, his infantile preoccupation with himself, the sentimental conviction of the sanctity of his own experience because it was his" (*Poetry* 137: 221). Tate sees his breakdown as a personal catastrophe: Crane "would have been frustrated and destroyed in any human society that we have any record of," but nevertheless he is emblematic of the era that Tate calls "romantic," since he, with the French antiromantic critics, with T. E. Hulme and Eliot, identifies romanticism with raw emotionalism and primitivism. Crane's verse "Lie to me—dance us back our tribal norm!" is for Tate "the perfect word of romanticism in this century" (*E,* 319). Crane's "Bridge" is "an irrational symbol of the will, of conquest, of blind achievement in space" (322). "The Bridge" fails as a myth and Tate doubts even the desirability of creating a national American myth (*Bookman* 68 [1929]: 508). In spite of these severe strictures Tate puts Crane "in the first rank of American poets, living or dead" (*E,* 318).

This historical conception underlies Tate's many judgments of contemporary poets: E. A. Robinson, Thomas Hardy, Ezra Pound, W. B. Yeats, T. S. Eliot, and Archibald MacLeish, to mention only those on whom he wrote individual essays. Yeats is at the center of the tradition: nearer than Eliot or Pound. In Pound the disintegration of content and form has progressed. He has a "typically modern, rootless, and internationalized intelligence" (*E,* 368). His worship of the past is contradicted and discredited by his "crying up a rationalistic enlightenment" (371). Tate fears that the arts will become "geometrical and abstract, and destroy themselves" (351). Nowhere does Tate shirk judgment. "We must first of all decide in what respect the literary work has a specific objectivity" and attend to the "formal qualities of a poem" as "the focus of the specifically critical judgment because they partake of an objectivity that the subject matter, abstracted from the form, wholly lacks" (149). But he sees the poems always within history, in tradition or, as he formulated it early (1927), echoing T. S. Eliot's "Tradition and the Individual Talent": "My attempt is to see the present from the past, yet remain immersed in the present and committed to it" (*LC,* 189). The role of criticism seems great both for the health of poetry and ultimately for that of society.

Tate incessantly tried to set off his own point of view from that of other critics. One can sketch a history of criticism from his writings. I have alluded to his interest in the anticipations of the organic point of view in Longinus or the reconciliation of opposites in Dr. Johnson. Tate criticizes Coleridge's definition of poetry in the fourteenth chapter of *Biographia Litteraria,* acutely showing that "Coleridge diverts attention from the poem to the effect of poetry, to psychology." "He [Coleridge] cannot make up his mind whether the specifically poetic element is an objective feature of the poem, or is distinguishable only as a subjective effect" (*E,* 95), a formula which well describes Coleridge's vacillation between Kantian idealism and British empiricism. Tate deplores Coleridge's failure to escape "the dilemma of Intellect-or-Feeling" and his emphasis on pleasure as the effect of poetry, with the result that the scheme of Coleridge became gradually extinct in "the terminology of experimental psychology" (96–97). Tate of course has I. A. Richards in mind, whose psychological theories of the effect of poetry he rejects as lacking in evidence and as coming out of the "demireligion of positivism." Richards indulges in a "hocus-pocus of impulses, stimuli and responses" (203). "Poetry had been absorbed into a pseudo-scientific jargon" (100). But Tate carefully restricts his rejection of I. A. Richards to his early stage. Tate praises Richards for having "with the candor of a generous spirit repudiated his early scientism" (204). He sees Richards converted to his own view of poetic knowledge (104) and finds a repudiation of all Richards's earlier views in the statement from *The Philosophy of Rhetoric* (1936) that "language is no mere signalling system" (100). Tate did not see then that Richards had given up some of his neurological and behaviorist terminology but never changed his basic position. His later writings such as *Speculative Instruments* show that there is no question of a conversion and that Richards remained a utilitarian (see this *History*, vol. 5, ch. 7).

Tate classed Richards earlier with John Dewey, who pictures the artist as saying, "Society is disorganized. Lo! I will unify it by art." But this seems to Tate "nonsense" and Dewey ultimately appears to him a "fake mystic."[4] A fortiori, Tate must reject the later developments of semantics propounded by Charles Morris. "There is an uneasy piety in the extravagant claim that poetry is the realm of values: and there is no way, I think, to get around the conclusion that, since the values are not attached to reality, they are irresponsible feelings" (*E*, 91). Morris and Richards reduce poetry to "either nonsense or hortatory rhetoric" (90). The common view that the New Criticism grows out of a synthesis of Richards and Eliot fails in the case of Tate completely.

All of Tate's sympathies are with T. S. Eliot, whom, at least in early letters, he considered "a greater critic than poet" and whom he admired as "the most intelligent man alive" (*LC*, 36, 141). What impressed him particularly was the "restoration of the integral activity of emotion and intellect" (*LC*, 140), the impersonal theory of poetry and the concept of tradition. His influence (as Tate himself admits [*E*, xi]) is so pervasive that it would be difficult to imagine Tate's criticism without Eliot's model. Tate sympathizes with T. E. Hulme's views but thinks that he "lacks feeling for literature" and believed only in "perception," imagism (*Sewanee Review* 35 [1927]: 49–50). Surprisingly Tate praises Herbert Read in the highest terms as "one of the best critics in English, not only now but of any age" (*E*, 377). He approves of his synthesis of Coleridge and Jung and his defense of organistic aesthetics, apparently unperturbed by Read's romantic irrationalism but puzzled by his advocacy of abstract art (379).

For years Tate was a journalist immersed in the American critical debates. He had little concern for the critics he considered romantics: Van Wyck Brooks, Lewis Mumford, and William Carlos Williams. "They are dominated by a thirst for more life" (*Sewanee Review* 38 [1930]: 130), he says, curtly dismissing them. But he became engaged in polemics with the new humanists, Irving Babbitt, Paul Elmer More, and the younger Norman Foerster and Robert Shafer, who around 1930 made a considerable impression. Tate wrote for Eliot's *Criterion* 8 [1929]: 661–81, reprinted in *MO*) a paper entitled "The Fallacy of Humanism," which argued that humanism is not only defective in an aesthetic sense but is simply a version of naturalism. He recommends even then, years before his conversion, an "objective religion, a universal scheme of reference" and finds humanism not enough. Tate objects to Babbitt's attack on aesthetics, which he believes to be merely a trivial decoration of moral doctrine. Yet, Tate argues, the aesthetic approach is necessarily the philosophical approach in literature (182). Babbitt's salutary requirement of judging is, he says elsewhere, mistaken, for "the moral obligation to judge does not necessarily obligate us to make a moral judgment" (*E*, 148). More's criticism is dismissed summarily for the "poor quality of his literary judgments." "In the name of restraint More is able to evoke the limit of his personal distastes" (*MO*, 187).

The humanist movement collapsed quickly under the impact of the Depression. Social and specifically Marxist criticism dominated the thirties. Tate admires Edmund Wilson, though he thinks him "bad on poetry" (*LC*, 210) and *Axel's Castle* "written on the assumption that all poetry is only an inferior kind of social will" (*E*, 186). But Wilson of course cannot be simply classed as a Marxist. In general, Tate opposed economic determinism of any kind, the view that "all art is primarily an apology for institutions and classes" (187), and rejects Marxist criticism as a revival of moralistic allegorism, as a crude didacticism for which "the arts have always been fundamentally propaganda" (*New Republic* 75 [1933]: 308). A review of Louis MacNeice's *Modern Poetry* (*New Republic* 100 [1939]: 52–53) rejects his view that the writer is obligated to get into the "forces which at the moment make for progress." Tate also argues against David Daiches's view in *The Novel and the Modern World*, "one of the few good books on contemporary fiction" (*E*, 206), that literature is to be understood "chiefly as part of the historical process" and is to be judged by its "historical relevance" (209). His own view of the historicity of poetry is apparently different: literature does not, as Daiches demands, have to be subjected to the test of truth to reality. Daiches's attempt to put the stigma of "formalism" on any unhistorical study of literature is rejected. "There may have been critics like Mr. Daiches's formalist monster, but I have never seen one, and I doubt that Mr. Daiches himself, on second thought, would believe he exists" (208). Tate defends the study of literature outside of history, in a direct engagement with the text, but obviously could not and would not restrict it to anything which could be called "form."

Tate's sympathies for his fellow champions of the New Criticism need not be rehearsed. Tate disagreed with Ransom about T. S. Eliot and very early argued against his view of the dual role of words (*Fugitive* 3 [1924]: 35), but his relation to his teacher was far too close and his admiration for his poetry and much of his criticism far too genuine to allow him to make their disagreements public. Cleanth Brooks and Robert Penn Warren are always treated as allies. The more distantly related R. P. Blackmur is greatly admired as "the best reader of poetic texts in the United States" (*Partisan Review* 8 [1941]: 68), and his essay on Emily Dickinson is called "one of the great critical essays of our time" (*Kenyon Review* [1939]: 203). Tate is impressed by Blackmur's "almost puritanical heroism in rejecting the so-called, merely book sciences ending in *logy* (psychology, anthropology, sociology)" (*E*, 171) but complains that Blackmur uses an undigested philosophical vocabulary. His philosophizing is "amateurish, eclectic" and derivative of Santayana (*Partisan Review* 8 [1941]: 68). Kenneth Burke, admired for his "intellectual ability and terminological inventiveness" (*E*, ix), is seen distantly as a "systematic thinker" whose *Grammar of Motives* is compared to Robert Burton's *Anatomy of Melancholy* (170), a farrago of obsolete learning. "I cannot think it important for literary criticism" (274–75). But Tate admits that "it would be worse than folly to argue that the whole task of criticism must stop short of its philosophical implications or of the philosophical implications of the literary work. Any criticism that increases our knowledge of literature has its place" (171–72).

It thus comes as a surprise that in Tate's late essays the role of criticism is minimized. In "The Man of Letters in the Modern World" (1952), a fervent speech asking the man of letters to "recreate the image of man" (*E*, 3), the critic is reduced to the job of "preserving the integrity, the purity and the reality of language against the corruptions of the mass media" (14). Critics and criticism are relegated to a nook and cranny of the intellectual universe. Tate disparages his own criticism as that of a "casual essayist of whom little consistency can be expected," writing from a "mere point of view which, however, must not be considered 'relative' " (625). He concludes that as a "literary critic one knows virtually nothing" (626). Another essay, "Is Literary Criticism Possible?" (1951), denies that we shall ever know this. He discusses there first the teaching of criticism

in the university. Tate hands over literary history and sociology to the
social sciences and leaves criticism in the university with only one task:
the rhetorical study of language. He decides that one cannot teach students to "evaluate" works of literature, though this may be "not less
absurd than to try to evaluate them oneself " (36). Even the other possible
task of criticism, the communication of insights, is declared to be impossible to teach to others. "It can only be exhibited" (37) is Tate's odd
conclusion—odd since it is hard to see why the "exhibition" of insights
should not communicate them and thus teach them to the right students.
In the second part of the essay Tate ignores the separate question of
pedagogy in the American university and confronts the aims of literary
criticism in the abstract. In a scrappy and dense list of problems he says
mostly negative things about criticism. Criticism is always inferior to creation. "It is lays *about* something else" (40). It is parasitic and "perpetually
obsolescent and replaceable"—a view that can be upheld only if we think
of daily reviewing but that is obviously false if we have theory, poetics,
and history in mind. Tate recognizes, of course, that there is more systematic and methodical criticism which "tends more and more to *sound*
like philosophical discourse" (40). He distinguishes three methods: aesthetics, which he dismisses curtly, "From its point of view it is difficult
to say anything about literature that is not merely pretentious" (41). Then
Tate allows "stylistics," with its narrow limits, and historical reconstruc-
tion, which is not criticism proper. In a subsequent congested paragraph,
Tate objects to philosophical criticism: criticism which appeals to a philosophical authority in which the critic does not believe. But no evidence
is presented for why the critic could not believe in a philosopher and use
him for his purposes. We are warned that "the language of criticism had
better not, then try to be univocal" (51). There is, at last, one type of
criticism which finds favor in Tate's eye, though he asks only tentatively:
"What is the primary office of criticism? Is it to expound and to elucidate,
with as little distortion as possible, the knowledge of life contained by
the novel or the play? What critic has ever done this?" (42). One would
think that all moral and social critics were doing nothing else for centuries, but apparently Tate means something very different from what
is usually called knowledge of life. Finally he asks, "Is literary criticism
possible without a criterion of absolute truth? Would a criterion of absolute truth make literary criticism as we know it unnecessary?" (44).
Knowing Tate's convictions, an affirmative answer is required. In the
light of the truth of Revelation, criticism is unnecessary, although immediately afterward Tate declares it "perpetually necessary and in the
very nature of its middle position between imagination and philosophy,

perpetually impossible" (44). Tate must have been deeply disillusioned by his teaching of criticism, over many years, in several colleges and universities, and he must have come to these skeptical conclusions as to the ultimate value of criticism with a mind preoccupied with more important things: the fate of man and the message of religion. The similarity with the development of T. S. Eliot is striking: he also disparaged criticism and his own share in it in his last pronouncements. In the interest of criticism one cannot help deploring this turn, however satisfying it may have been to the minds and souls of these two men.

CLEANTH BROOKS is usually identified with one method, "close reading," and with a search for such devices as paradox and irony in English poetry from Shakespeare to Yeats. He has been accused of "critical monism" by R. S. Crane in an article included in the Chicago symposium, *Critics and Criticism.*[1] If one looks for a theoretical defense of his point of view, one frequently will be disappointed by his deliberate, sometimes sudden dropping of the issues by quoting and analyzing a poem. Thus Brooks's article "Literary Criticism" soon becomes a discussion of Andrew Marvell's "Horatian Ode."[2] The piece "The New Criticism and Scholarship" turns into an interpretation of Bishop Corbet's "The Fairies Farewell."[3] The address "The Quick and the Dead: A Comment on Humanistic Studies" revolves around a poem "The Fall" by Sir Richard Fanshawe.[4] The paper "Literary Criticism: Poet, Poem, and Reader" treats us to an analysis of "The Grasshopper" of Sir Richard Lovelace.[5]

Still, focusing on Cleanth Brooks's brilliant and sensitive close readings, most easily accessible in his two best-known books, *Modern Poetry and the Tradition* (1939) and *The Well-Wrought Urn* (1947), does grave injustice to the totality of his work. I can only allude to his early study *The Relation of the Alabama-Georgia Dialect to the Provincial Dialects of Great Britain* (1935) and to his editing of the multivolume *Correspondence of Thomas Percy,*[6] which shows his competence as an antiquarian eighteenth-century scholar. I shall barely refer to *William Faulkner: The Yoknapatawpha Country* (163), which studies the fictional world of William Faulkner very closely. Cleanth Brooks is also a historian of criticism, a critic of critics. His comments on criticism constitute an extensive part of his work that has not received the attention it deserves. It includes not only the 166 pages in the collaborative *Literary Criticism: A Short History* (1957) with William K. Wimsatt, in which Brooks took it upon himself to discuss the major English and American critics of the twentieth century from A. C. Bradley to Northrop Frye, but also many scattered essays and reviews, as well as passages in his books commenting on almost all prominent figures in the history of English and American criticism.

While Brooks's reputation rests largely on his interpretations of individual poems, on his "close readings," the theory—though sometimes only implied—is far more coherent than the frequent criticisms admit. Brooks has become the main target of attacks launched against the New Criticism in general. For instance, the title of his most widely known book, *The Well-Wrought Urn,* has been used to accuse Brooks and his friends of conceiving the work of art as an artifact, like a piece of sculpture, as "something static, shaped and rigid" (*Southern Review* 87 [1979]: 592). In a somewhat rueful late defense Brooks grants that a poem is "fluid, dynamic, a transaction between poet and reader." He asks "what has happened to the reader's metaphorical sense if an obviously figurative title, borrowed from one of the poems discussed in the book (Donne's "Canonization") has to be frozen into a literal application? I thought that for a book which sought to find a structure common to all genuine poetry, Donne's praise of a well-made object, however small, was apt. After all, what he sets as its opposite is the vulgarly ostentatious 'half-acre tomb.' " As a further defense Brooks cites Wordsworth comparing the body of his poetry to a "Gothic cathedral, with its 'ante-chapel,' and the 'little cells,' oratories and sepulchral recesses, ordinarily included in these edifices" (ibid.). Brooks may have added that at that time publishers were looking for striking titles with phrases from great writers: G. Wilson Knight's *Wheel of Fire* or Philip Wheelwright's *Burning Fountain* or Joseph Frank's *Widening Gyre.* Brooks cannot be accused of conceiving of a work of art as an inert artifact. Rather he often speaks of a poem "like a little drama" (Z, 730), as "resembling a play" (*WU,* 186), and sees a poem as a miniature play, pressing the analogy rather far, saying even "the statements made 'in a poem' are to be read as if they were speeches in a drama" (Z, 731). In a note he expressed agreement with Kenneth Burke's view of the poem as a "mode of action" (*WU,* 186).

The work of art is rather conceived by Brooks as "a struggle of attitudes, evaluations and interpretations." The principle of unity seems to be "the balancing and harmonizing connotations, attitudes and meanings" (*WU,* 178). A final harmony is achieved but all of Brooks's working terms "ambiguity," "paradox," "complex of attitudes," "irony" imply tension, conflicts, oppositions, contrasts within a work of art and in the experience of the reader. "The work of art," he says, "is a pattern of resolutions, and balances and harmonizations, developed through a temporal scheme" (186). Brooks hesitates sometimes about his terms, saying that he has "no brief for them" (179), and one must admit that it is sometimes unclear whether he refers to the events in the author's mind or to the experience of the reader or to an observable trait in the poem. He seems to me most persuasive when he strips terms such as "attitude," "tone," "irony," which he derives from I. A. Richards, of their psychological reference and makes them mean something in the text. They are chosen by him in order to avoid what he considers the main obstacle to an understanding of poetry, the tendency to identify poetry with "message," with rational propositions, with its truth, with statements. Poetry is not philosophy, is not moralizing, and is not propaganda. What Brooks is trying constantly to drive home is a realization that poetry is neither a statement of a truth nor simply beautiful sound- and word-play. At times he appears as if he were accepting Richards's dualism of emotional and rational languages, the emotional language being poetical language with the consequence that the effect of poetry would be reduced to its therapeutic values as it is in I. A. Richards. But Brooks wisely balks at this conclusion (191) and advocates rather the view that poetry gives knowledge but a special kind of knowledge which is not that of science. This is a difficult concept similar to Croce's view that poetry and art are cognitive—but intuitive cognition rather than conceptual. Brooks develops this to mean that poetry conveys a knowledge of the particularity and fullness of the world superior to the abstract and generalizing aims of science. The knowledge given by poetry is "complete knowledge": certainly more complete than scientific knowledge, as it comes not only from the intellect and the senses but from the mind in its totality, from the "unified sensibility" which Eliot stated was "a good deal more than the heart. One must look into the cerebral cortex, the nervous system, and the digestive tract."[7] In the early Eliot this unified sensibility is quite secular. In Brooks it occasionally assumes a religious coloring. Poetry gives us not only "a unique and formed intelligence of the world" (a quotation from Tate, WU, 236) but is "revelatory." Its main device is metaphor and symbol. Organized systematic symbols constitute a mythology which for Brooks is Christianity. Sometimes Brooks sees the dangerous implications of this claim: he criticizes Wilbur Urban's Language and Reality (a book which mediated some of Croce's ideas) for considering poetry an "ultimately distorted and imperfect philosophy" (WU, 233). But most frequently he endorses Tate's view that "poetry is neither religion nor social engineering."[8] A more modest claim for the function of poetry seems to him convincing. Literature is not as Auden argued in a moment of despair completely "frivolous" but, as Brooks comments, gives us a "knowledge of a value-structured world" (SJ, 11). This implies the hope for a "restoration of order" (27), a recognition of an "intelligible world" (the title of one of Urban's books), an "emblem of the kind of harmony that ought to obtain in wider realms—in the just society and in the true community" (51) with hints of a social utopia. But in more general terms Brooks says the poem, if it be a true poem, is "a simulacrum of reality,—in this sense at least, it is an 'imitation'—by being an experience rather than any mere statement about experience or any mere abstraction from experience" (*WU*, 194). This appeal to the oldest Aristotelian concept of mimesis refutes the odd view that Brooks and his friends would have ever thought of poetry as cut off from reality, as a meaningless play of words. Brooks develops this emphasis on reality in many ways. "A poem," he can say, is "a portion of reality viewed and valued by a human being. It is rendered coherent through a perspective of valuing." Precisely the "coherence of the parts in a literary work depends upon our belief in this plausibility of certain human actions and reactions, responses and valuations." We must believe in them, otherwise "the work of art is indeed incredible and monstrous." Still, "the correspondence to reality that a poem achieves is mediated through a special kind of structure" (*WU*, 194; "Implications of an Organic Theory of Poetry," 68, 71). Brooks quotes W. K. Wimsatt on art as "refraction" and his statement that "the refraction itself is a kind of reality" (*LC*, 737–38).

Reality means social reality and of course history. Brooks is possibly of all Southern critics the one who is most conscious of the immersion of poetry in history. The frequent accusation of "ahistoricity," even of enmity toward history, is based on Brooks's early polemics against literary history as taught in American colleges. Literary history meant simply a recital of names, titles, and dates and possibly information about the lives and the social circumstances of the writers. But the students, he soon discovered, were for the most part woefully incapable not only of evaluating poetry, discriminating between the good and the bad, but of simply understanding its literal sense and enjoying it. Brooks's first book-length publications, *The Approach to Literature* (with Purser and R. P. Warren) and *Understanding Poetry* (1938), were textbooks which after a very slow start revolutionized the teaching of English literature in American colleges. *Understanding Poetry* is deliberately designed to make the student focus on the bare text of the poem. It thus says hardly anything about biography or history except when it seemed necessary to clarify the meaning. The book is constructed in order to lead into poetry by stages, beginning with simple narratives and descriptions and continuing to poems which require attention to imagery, tone, and attitude. Off and on, in asides, comments are made to disparage poor popular poems;

Longfellow's "Psalm of Life," called "a very bad poem" (ix), Joyce Kilmer's "Trees" (307), criticized for confused imagery, or Shelley's "Indian Serenade" (319), known as an example of sentimentality. Mostly beauties and striking features are pointed out, explained, and appreciated. The anthology is actually far from revolutionary, though it does comment on a few poems by Donne and T. S. Eliot. The poet most fully represented is Robert Frost, with eleven poems, one five pages long, and there are many romantic poems which are highly valued: Wordsworth, Coleridge, and Keats in particular. The later editions of the anthology expanded its range but also diluted its lesson. The last edition, the fourth (1976), makes many concessions to recent fashions, prints trivial and commonplace stuff and much without comment and discrimination. It has become simply a large anthology mainly arranged by themes: "The False Love," "The Indifferent Lover," "The Poet Looks at a Bird," "The Breakup of Civilization," and so on.

Brooks's first book of essays, *Modern Poetry and Tradition* (1939), proposes rather a radical revision of the then current history of English poetry. In a remarkable chapter, modestly entitled "Notes for a Revised History of English Poetry," Brooks sketches a history of English poetry very much in the taste of T. S. Eliot. It was almost the first attempt; only Leavis's *Revaluation* preceded it. Brooks emphasizes the tradition of wit in English poetry of the seventeenth century: the school of Donne, Ben Jonson, and the cavalier poets all belong to it and Sir Thomas Browne joins them as a prose-writer of wit "displaying the various levels of seriousness and complexity of attitude which are to be found in the witty poetry of the time" (222). Also the best of Pope and Swift reveals a system of contrasts and tensions in such different works as *The Rape of the Lock* and *A Modest Proposal*. *The Beggar's Opera* appears as a parallel to *A Modest Proposal*. Brooks draws here on Empson's discussion of the play in *Some Versions of Pastoral* as a pastoral and at the same time a parody of the heroic. Brooks is very discriminating and sensitive in his comments on the eighteenth-century poets, whom surprisingly he is quite willing to consider as "pre-romantics." Burns is valued as a "satirist and writer of light verse" (234), and Blake appears as a "metaphysical poet." He is the first poet in that century who uses "the metaphor to define and carry the idea. It represents a fusion of image and idea" (235). The discussion of the romantic poets is highly critical, as their distrust of the intellect and their cult of simplicity violates Brooks's idea of poetry. Shelley in particular is disparaged for poor craftsmanship: for "slovenly riming, loosely decorative and sometimes too gaudy metaphor," for "confusion of abstract generalization with symbol and confusion of propaganda with

imaginative insight" (257). The lines "I die, I faint, I fall" and "I fall
upon the thorns of life. I bleed!" are singled out as embarrassing sen-
timentalities without allowing for the poem being a dramatic monologue,
"An Indian Serenade," the speech of a yearning oriental lover. Victorian
poetry is then seen as impaled on one of the two horns of the dilemma:
poetry with a message, the supposed philosophy of Tennyson and
Browning, the attempt to substitute poetry for religion, or, on the other,
pure poetry, art for art's sake (239). Brooks exempts only Emily Dickinson and Gerard Manley Hopkins and sees Thomas Hardy as the last
great poet (243) before the advent of the moderns: Yeats, Eliot, and
Auden. Especially Brooks's interpretation of *The Waste Land* is justly admired as possibly the first which made us see its coherence and overall
meaning.

Brooks's second book, *The Well Wrought Urn* (1947), is then a demonstration that his concept of poetry is not merely applicable to the poetry
of wit, to Donne and contemporaries, but also to the most diverse English
poets: Shakespeare, Milton, Herrick, Pope, Gray, Wordsworth, Keats,
Tennyson, and Yeats. Some of these essays made a deep impression. "The
Naked Babe and the Cloak of Manliness" persuasively traces the sequences of child and clothes images through *Macbeth*. I remember that
I called that year on E. E. Stoll at the University of Minnesota and was
confronted with his view that Brooks's essay is a mere subjective fantasy,
as for Stoll the meaning of Shakespeare was confined to what would have
been understood by an Elizabethan theater audience. I refused to accept
this choice. If the sequence of images can be shown to be present in the
text, the assumption that it could not and was not noticed by a contemporary audience is irrelevant. Besides, we may very well underrate the
abilities of an Elizabethan audience (or at least a part of it) to follow
sequences of intricate metaphors. At least some of those who sat in the
audience of Shakespeare's plays sat through the long sermons of John
Donne and other preachers who required a kind of attention to figures
which no contemporary congregation could master. The text is a text
and later generations have the right to discover new meanings in it, if
they can be shown to be there. Unfortunately much recent criticism ignores this condition and indulges in totally arbitrary misreadings, "mis-
prisions," and even defends complete liberty of interpretation with the
result that today anarchy and chaos have come to reign in much literary
study.

Brooks insists that a proper poem is a totality, a contextual unity, a
whole. Thus a reduction of a poem to its prose content is rejected as the
"heresy of paraphrase." I wish Brooks had avoided the stigma of "her-

esy," as paraphrase obviously is a legitimate pedagogical device (used also by Brooks) as long as we are aware that paraphrase cannot replace the actual text. But one misunderstands Brooks's term "organic unity" (derived from Coleridge) if one accuses him of considering the poem a biological organism and sees a contradiction between this organicity and modern concepts of the poem as an intentional object, a linguistic construct. "Organic" comes from Plato and Aristotle and was revived by the Germans at the turn of the eighteenth to the nineteenth century. There, one should admit, the analogy between a work of art and a living being is sometimes wrongly exploited. Goethe, for instance, compares a poor work of art with a diseased body or rotting plant. Some recent German theorists (Günther Müller is the best known) make literary scholarship almost a branch of biology. They speak, for instance, of the time-scheme of a novel as if it were the skeleton of an animal. But Brooks never succumbs to the false biological analogy. Organic form means simply totality, gestalt, wholeness, the whole which is more than the sum of its parts and where the parts function purposefully. In a lecture "The Poem as Organism"[9] Brooks voices misgivings about the metaphor. "My title is obviously a metaphor and it may be thought a superficial and trifling one—a metaphor contrived with an eye cocked in the direction of the biological sciences, and therefore in common with most attempts to ape the sciences legitimately suspect. On reconsideration I am not sure that the title is an apt one but it is not an attempt at a faddish modernity. The conception of poetry which the title of this paper would suggest is not modern." At that time Brooks did not know the phenomenological terminology and only in a note to *The Well-Wrought Urn* did he refer to my essay on "The Mode of Existence of the Literary Work of Art," which had appeared in the last number of the old *Southern Review* in 1941. There he says, "For those who cannot be content with metaphors (or with the particular metaphors which I can give) I recommend René Wellek's essay. I believe that the generalizations about poetry outlined here can be thoroughly accommodated to the position which his essay sets forth" (*WU*, 186n.). The attack on Brooks's view (very generally formulated, mainly as criticism of I. A. Richards in Paul de Man's French essay in *Critique* and in the chapter "Form and Intent in the American New Criticism" in *Blindness and Insight* [1971; 2nd ed., 1983]) is based on a confusion between the phenomenological and existentialist concept of intent and Wimsatt's and Beardsley's "Intentional Fallacy," which Brooks endorsed. The two concepts are quite different. It is simply not true that "the rejection of the principle of intentionality, dismissed as fallacious, prevented the integration of these discoveries (of distinct structures of literary language such as ambiguity and irony) into a truly coherent theory of literary form" (32). By intention Wimsatt and Beardsley meant conscious, formulated purpose and they seem to me entirely right in saying that, to quote Wimsatt's later cautious formula, the "intention of a literary artist *qua* intention is neither a valid ground for arguing the quality or meaning in a given instance of his literary work nor a valid criterion for judging the value of that work" (*Day of the Leopards* [1976], 12). This seems to me a perfectly reasonable position if one merely thinks of the many misstatements writers have made about their original intentions.

Brooks's theoretical framework is perfectly coherent and adequate to his purpose of interpreting and evaluating English poetry. One should grant to Brooks's severest and acutest critic, R. S. Crane, that his theory is insufficient to account for all the varieties of poetry and that it is a "critical monism" which imposes a limited number of criteria on a phenomenon far too diversified to be fully accounted for in his few terms.

It will be best to survey Brooks's views of other critics, in order to define his position more clearly. Much of Brooks's comment on other critics is, no doubt, self-defense, *apologia pro domo sua*. He knows that criticism is, as Benedetto Croce knew and so said repeatedly, "criticism of criticism."[10] In criticizing others, Cleanth Brooks defines his own position, sometimes clarifying or modifying it in the context of the history of criticism or with rival currents of literary theory in this century. But his criticism of criticism is not only an attempt at self-definition. It has, predominantly, an objective aim and value, taking "objective" to mean Brooks's success as an expositor of ideas often alien to his own way of thinking. Brooks is an eminently fair-minded, text-oriented, conscientious examiner of ideas who is rarely openly polemical. After all, motivation in self-defense and self-definition does not dispose of the validity of arguments. Although we are all "situated" in history, in a specific time and place, we can reach out into the realm of ideas which—without any Platonic implications—we should recognize as timeless or at least constant in the sense of their being with us throughout recorded history, debated and debatable perennially.

Something like a general history of criticism emerges from Cleanth Brooks's writings, though the emphasis is comprehensibly on the situation of his own time.

Aristotle, undeniably the fountainhead of literary theory for centuries, is not in the center of Cleanth Brooks's interest. But Brooks appeals to his example on one crucial point: he sees Aristotle as the prototype of a critic concerned with the technical analysis of works of literary art who at the same time is, in his other writings, overwhelmingly concerned with moral, political, and metaphysical issues.[11] Brooks approves of this division because he is convinced that the amalgamation and confusion of literary theory with morals, politics, and religion has been at the root of many difficulties of critical theory. He insists on a clear distinction between poetry and religion. Aristotle is thus upheld as a model of a great and exemplary man who implicitly denies Matthew Arnold's prophecy that "most of what now passes with us for religion and philosophy will be replaced by poetry."[12] Brooks confesses, "I am not one of those people who believe that man can live by poetry alone." The Arnoldian promise of a fusion of poetry and religion leads to a "real distortion of poetry and to nothing better than an *ersatz* religion."[13] He insists that "precisely those critics who, by and large, manifest a deep concern for religion are also concerned to maintain the independence of literature and its distinction from religion." He rejects the view that science has disposed of religion and that the values of religion have to find refuge in poetry. Literature would then become "the rhetorical garb for truthful propositions which are to be derived from science or philosophy."[14] The artist would be "a kind of super-advertising man—a specialist in arousing sympathetic emotions for the propositions he elected to present. In this scheme of things, poetics disappears into rhetoric." He suggests, "The shadow of Matthew Arnold still rests heavily upon our era."[15]

The American new humanists are, in Cleanth Brooks's eyes, a brand of Arnoldians. Brooks has not commented in extenso on either Irving Babbitt or Paul Elmer More. He praises Prosser Frye's *Romance and Tragedy* (1922) as "one of the ablest documents produced by the New Humanists" but remarks that Frye "out-Hegels Hegel in the sternness of his ethical demands." "As in so much of the work of this group there is a certain note of desperation. . . . He gloomily notes that almost from the very birth of tragedy there has been a falling off, with no real recoveries. . . . Frye is carrying on a stubborn rear-guard action" (*LC*, 560). This is also what Brooks thinks of Douglas Bush and his Christian humanism when he casts doubts on Bush's hope that literature can be "put to work to save the situation."[16]

Though Brooks can appeal to Aristotle's separation of poetics and ethics, he cannot relish the peculiar reinterpretation of Aristotle's poetic theories in the Chicago group. This is due not only to a reaction against the sharp criticism of R. S. Crane, whom he has singled out as a "good example" of "elaborate system building, admirable as a display of sheer dialectic, almost for its own sake."[17] Rather there is a fundamental disagreement about the role of language in poetry. The Chicago group,

Cleanth Brooks asserts, has a false view of language as "a mere phonetic protoplasm without inherent character," as the inert "material" of poetry.[18] These critics overemphasize plot and construe a theory of genres that leads to their indefensible proliferation (*LC,* 694n.). Somewhat slyly, he draws a parallel to the conflict between John Dryden and Thomas Rymer with Rymer cast as "the worthy champion of plot" (*LC,* 687n.). We may remember that T. B. Macaulay called Rymer "the worst critic that ever lived."

Aristotle as a theorist plays no prominent role in Cleanth Brooks's ancestry; one must assume that he sympathizes with John Crowe Ransom's dictum that "Aristotle does handsomely by the plot, and has nothing very impressive to say for the poetry."[19] Brooks, in any case, is not particularly interested in drama as stagecraft and plotting.

Samuel Taylor Coleridge's saying (derived from Goethe) that men are either Aristotelians or Platonists has been quoted ad nauseam. It does not apply in the case of Cleanth Brooks. I am not aware of any comment on Plato beyond a few casual allusions, but Brooks is undoubtedly indebted to Coleridge, who can be described (and has described himself) as belonging to the Platonic tradition. Brooks, however, completely cuts off Coleridge's thought from its metaphysical roots. He does not bother about the dialectics of subject and object, about the reconciliation of man and nature, the distinction between poetry and poem. He rather singles out the definition of imagination as the reconciliation of opposites and quotes it in several contexts, as T. S. Eliot has also done. The passage is used as if it were merely an endorsement of Dr. Johnson's characterization of metaphysical poetry as using "heterogeneous ideas yoked by violence together" deprived of any pejorative implication or else a definition of the "poetry of inclusion" or synthesis Brooks knows from George Santayana and I. A. Richards.

Coleridge is an authority for the view that a work of art is a totality, a unity in multiplicity, an organism. Brooks stresses that this multiplicity can be and should be contradictory, should be a multiplicity of tensions. He expressly disapproves of what he considers the romantic perversion of the organic concept of poetry to a mystical unity.[20] He has no use for Coleridge's distinction of imagination and fancy. "It lapses," he says, "in Shakespeare." Coleridge wrongly devalues fancy and wit and thus reintroduces a ranking of poetic subjects, a depreciation of the witty and low in favor of the serious and sublime. It is an inheritance of the eighteenth century or rather of the neoclassical doctrine of the levels of style. Cleanth Brooks also objects to Coleridge's suspicion against the share of intellect in poetry, to his defense of inspiration and even divine madness.

The view of poetry of Coleridge (and many other romantics) as "reve-lation of the Divine" is merely "a restatement of the didactic conception which remained to confuse critical theory" (*MPT*, 26, 6–7, 19, 52). The attempts of some recent commentators such as Richard Foster to derive the New Criticism from Coleridge, and hence to claim the New Critics as romantics despite their antiromantic professions, clearly fail in the case of Cleanth Brooks. He sees Coleridge through the lenses of Rich-ards's interpretation of Coleridge: Richards expressly declared that he was writing on Coleridge "as a Materialist trying to interpret . . . the utterances of an extreme Idealist." Brooks thus can accept Richards's interpretation of the comment by Coleridge on a passage from *Venus and Adonis* which reduces Coleridge's distinction between "esemplastic imag-ination" and "associative fancy" to a purely descriptive and even quan-tifiable typology of metaphors. Brooks's review of Richards's *Coleridge on Imagination* completely ignores Richards's attempt to resuscitate the Fichte-Schelling dialectic used by Coleridge.

In commenting on Ralph Waldo Emerson—who could be considered *the* Neoplatonist among philosophers of art—Brooks dismisses his "co-alescence of man with nature," criticizes his "symbolistic monism" and states, "There are no fixities and definites at all but only symbolic flu-idity." Coleridge's terms for fancy are invoked against Emerson's imag-ination. "If all the cards in the deck are 'wild' and can be counted as belonging to whatever suite and constituting whatever value we care to assign to them, then the game ends," comments Brooks, apparently un-aware of Emerson's own saying: "In the transmission of the heavenly waters, every hose fits every hydrant."[23] Edgar Allan Poe is grouped by Brooks with the transcendentalists and criticized for his occult and mag-ical views. "Things and thoughts are made to lie down beside each other as if any invidious distinction between them had been obliterated" (*LC*, 590).

In short, Cleanth Brooks is no idealist. He inherited from Coleridge (and his sources, Kant and August Wilhelm Schlegel) the concept of organism and with it all the difficulties raised by a view which seems to make the work of art self-enclosed and to make criticism, in Eliot's term, "autotelic." But Brooks never embraced the identification of a work of art with a biological organism, or even analogue to God's creation, but picked the term "organism" to mean "organization," ordering, coherent design. It is used as a defense of the inseparability of content and form, as a term implying a rejection of the reduction of a work of poetry to a disguised statement of philosophical truth or an immediate appeal to the reader's beliefs and convictions. It serves as an equivalent of illusion, semblance, *Schein,* or generally art as distinguished from reality, but it is not and could not mean "aestheticism" or "formalism" or even an isolation of the work of art from everything outside itself. Brooks tirelessly argues that language itself carries us outside of the poem: that the very words can be understood only in the context of an inherited language and that their meaning is circumscribed by external reality. He has, on many occasions and with many examples, combated the misunderstanding that he would want to interpret poems in a historical vacuum. He has picked poems such as Marvell's "Horatian Ode" to demonstrate the relevance of understanding a specific historical situation for a proper interpretation of a poem, and he has never been a "formalist" in the sense in which the term has been used by the opponents of the New Criticism. A formalist of the Russian persuasion could rather complain that Brooks rarely discusses form apart from meaning. He does—in the textbook *Understanding Poetry* and elsewhere—pay attention to metrics but always in order to show that prosody is not independent of meaning. Mostly, he is concerned with themes, with motifs, with tone and attitude, with what would be called "content" in older aesthetics, though Brooks of course considers themes as functioning in a whole, as cooperating even in contradiction, as working toward a unified structure which is far from being merely formal but is not merely raw, extraliterary, unshaped content.

We are back at the old problem of "versimilitude." It sounds commonplace but is a simple recognition that literature interprets reality existing outside the mind of man. Brooks is not a critic à la Georges Poulet or Northrop Frye, who believes that "there is nothing outside the mind of man," that "literature exists in its own universe containing life and reality in a system of verbal relationships."[24] Brooks, especially in his books on Faulkner, discusses the relationship between the "truth of reference" and the "truth of coherence," which he sees as complex but real. "The reader must be able to sense what is typical and what is exceptional, what is normal and what is an aberration" in Faulkner's picture of his South. Brooks emphasizes that Faulkner is writing fiction and not sociology or history but still compares his fictional picture with reality and concludes, for instance, that it is accurate when Faulkner describes the yeoman farmer or the poor white. The historian David Potter is quoted to support Brooks's view that Faulkner in the figure Gavin Stevens in *Intruder in the Dust* depicts actual attitudes held in life by real people.[25]

Brooks's main theoretical interests converge on twentieth-century English and American critics: Eliot, Richards, William Empson, Ransom, and Allen Tate. Older views are sometimes rejected but rarely discussed in extenso. Thus A. E. Housman's lecture "The Name and Nature of Poetry" is quoted several times for saying "metaphor and simile are inessential in poetry" and for the well-known passage naming "the chill down our spine" as a criterion of good poetry.[26] Both these conceptions run counter to everything Brooks could conceive to be the essence and test of poetry. Housman's views disturb him the more because he admires Housman as a metaphysical and intellectual poet. F. L. Lucas, "a late and decadent Romantic," is dismissed for his harsh comments on Richards and Coleridge.[27] Max Eastman is chided for his crude theories about "heightened consciousness" induced by literature and for his ridicule of the cult of unintelligibility. So is John Sparrow, as an enemy of modern art for his book *Sense and Poetry* (1934).[28]

Brooks is singularly indifferent to Marxist literary theory. He dismisses it as a revival of the didactic heresy. He protests Alfred Kazin's attack on the new formalists in *On Native Grounds*.[29] In a review of Kazin's *The Inmost Leaf*, he complains of "loose opinions" and doubts that Kazin's question of what a work of art "can mean to our living" concerns anyone except an eastern liberal. The only close attention to a Marxist text is to E. B. Burgum's article, "The Cult of the Complex in Poetry," which, Brooks shows, treats William Wordsworth's poem "She Dwelt Among the Untrodden Ways" merely as a "document of manners, morals, and value judgments of its age."[30] It is the familiar charge against historical relativism, which few Marxists could or would want to reject.

Among the modern American critics, Edmund Wilson seems to Brooks "the most old fashioned." He talks "sensitively, intelligently, and learnedly, but not too learnedly, about a wide variety of topics." He enjoys "the great advantage of sharing not only the positive views and values of the typical American intellectual, but the prejudices and blind sides as well." Brooks thinks that "Wilson has been wrong on almost all the big issues of the past," as has the typical intellectual. He marvels at Wilson's new jingoistic Americanism, quoting his paean to the American bathroom in preference to the cathedrals of Europe.[31] He rejects the reading of *The Waste Land* as a statement of despair and Wilson's interpretation of Faulkner's *Intruder in the Dust*.[32] The book is a novel and not a tract as Wilson would have it. The views expressed by the lawyer Gavin Stevens are not necessarily Faulkner's. "Stevens occupies no privileged position in Faulkner's novel: sometimes he talks sense and sometimes he talks nonsense."[33] Earlier Brooks took issue with Wilson's discussion of symbolism in *Axel's Castle*. He rejects the view that symbolism is decadent romanticism. Wilson's attempt to connect classicism with science, opposing to these "the poetic-romantic," seems to him gratuitous and confusing. He argues that the symbolist's detachment, his lack of propagandist intent, and his fidelity to the subject at hand place symbolist poetry far closer to the spirit of science. Brooks also emphasizes the differences within the French symbolist groups. Tristan Corbière and Jules Laforgue are witty and ironical: they are models of the early T. S. Eliot. Wilson wrongly ascribes the serious aesthetic tradition to all of symbolism and thus manages to identify Eliot with romantic escapism.[34] The last point seems well taken though one can hardly doubt the continuity of French symbolism with romanticism. One needs only to steer away from the facile concept of decadence which Baudelaire and others touted as a hallmark of sophistication.

Ezra Pound, the immediate predecessor of Eliot (who paid homage to Pound also as a critic), does not much interest Brooks in that function. He questions whether "in any language the discrete elements could retain so much of their original integrity as Pound claimed for Chinese ideograms." Brooks would have had the strong support of George Kennedy, the Chinese scholar who, in a little-known article, cogently demolished these fancies derived from Ernest Fenollosa.[35]

T. E. Hulme is seen by Brooks as a forerunner of Eliot, though their agreement can be largely explained by common sources in French criticism. Brooks praises him for valuing metaphor and for embracing "the doctrine of original sin." His classicism is a form of objectivism since Hulme "much more cleanly than Coleridge" stresses the art object. But Hulme is guilty of romantic clichés about "sincerity" and zest which go into poetic activity.[36] Brooks's sympathy with Hulme is obviously partial.

Cleanth Brooks's main admiration goes to T. S. Eliot as a poet, as a thinker on culture and religion, and as a literary critic. The experience of Eliot's poetry must have profoundly shaped Brooks's taste. He is in the company of Allen Tate rather than his teacher John Crowe Ransom, who had criticized *The Waste Land* severely when it appeared. The influence of I. A. Richards—important for Brooks's vocabulary and critical practice—came later. Brooks says himself that he "must have read *Principles of Literary Criticism* through fifteen times in the early thirties," and he read Empson's *Seven Types of Ambiguity* in 1938 (it was first published in 1930).[37] Brooks has always felt that there is no radical difference between the concepts of poetry of Eliot and Richards. Eliot, Tate, Ransom, and Richards, "employing diverse terminologies and approaches, corroborate each other emphatically," said Brooks in his first book, *Modern Poetry and the Tradition* (1939), and he repeats in 1956, "Unless one recognizes the amount of agreement between Richards and Eliot, one will find it difficult to understand the relative ease with which Richards' influence upon criticism has merged with that of Eliot." Not that Brooks did not see their differences. Especially later he recognized that "Eliot stands by his bold assertion that a poem is a *fusion* of thought and feeling." Richards, on the other hand, "from the first has endeavored to maintain a careful distinction between the emotional state produced in the reader (the balance of impulses or the state of synaesthesis) and the means to produce this emotional state" (*MPT,* 70; *LC,* 623).

In general, Eliot is invoked on central points of Brooks's concern: Brooks quotes Eliot's "Tradition and the Individual Talent" prominently and describes tradition in Eliot's terms in an article for a dictionary. Elsewhere he says, "In a time of disorder, Eliot moved toward a restoration of order."[38] He quotes him on true originality and approves of his concept of poetry as a synthesis of intellect and feeling, a fusion of opposites, with all its consequences: the recovery of the metaphysicals who combine wit and seriousness not only as a rehabilitation of neglected poets but also as a definition of the very nature of poetry (*MPT,* 70, 39; *SJ,* 39). It implies also the minimizing of the difference between imagination and fancy and, at least in principle, an acceptance of Eliot's basic scheme of the history of English poetry: the "dissociation of sensibility" in the seventeenth century.[39] Whereas Eliot's statements are more cautious, Brooks makes much of the "deadening" influence of Thomas Hobbes, a singling out of a figure who could not have played such a decisive role in a deep change pervading all Europe. Brooks also endorses Eliot's view of poetic language: the poet "dislocates ordinary language into meaning" or at the very least slightly alters it.[40] He also agrees with Eliot's views on poetic beliefs: the mind of the reader must be able, Eliot argued, to accept them as "coherent, mature, and founded on the facts of experience."[41]

On some points Brooks has disagreements with Eliot and some misgivings about his theories. He recognizes that Eliot is sometimes inconsistent, that there is much psychologism left in Eliot's concept of synaesthesis, and he is impressed by Eliseo Vivas's destructive analysis of the concept of the "objective correlative" and even agrees with Vivas's rejection of Eliot's analysis of *Hamlet.*[42] But, in general, Brooks shares Eliot's critical doctrines: the impersonal theory, the poetry of synaesthesis, the dissociation of sensibility, the view of tradition. Brooks also, in a rather lukewarm review of *The Use of Poetry and the Use of Criticism* (1933), defends Eliot's method of careful qualification, complaining of Edmund Wilson's parody in *Axel's Castle* of Eliot's critical style.[43]

Eliot's influence merged with that of Richards. Brooks is particularly impressed by the "all-important" chapter 32, "The Imagination," in *Prin-*

ciples of Literary Criticism, which distinguishes two types of poetry: a poetry which excludes the opposite and discordant qualities of experience and one which synthesizes the heterogeneity of the distinguishable impulses and thus will bear ironical contemplation.[44] Irony in this wide sense of detachment and awareness of the inclusiveness of experience became Brooks's main standard of good poetry. It hardly differs from paradox and the more limited verbal ambiguity. The terms have been often misunderstood; they are used not in the usual senses in which irony implies the opposite of the literal sense and paradox implies a proposition contrary to received opinion. Irony, in Brooks's best-known formulation, is "the *obvious* warping of a statement by the context." It is "a general term for the kind of qualification which the various elements in a context receive from a context" (*Z*, 730; *WU*, 191). It is simply the "interanimation of words," the "transaction between contexts," the principle which Richards expounded in *The Philosophy of Rhetoric* (1936), which Brooks singles out as one of Richards's "best books."[45] Brooks's method is an examination of the interanimation not only of words but of motifs, themes, metaphors, and symbols. Brooks does this by inspecting the poem's text, though particularly in his early work he often uses misleadingly the psychological vocabulary of Richards. Conceit, for instance, is defined as an "instrument" to bring "the counter-impulses into momentary conflict with the primary impulses." Later Brooks recognized that Richards's psychological vocabulary "evaporates when we get ready to use it," but he insists that we need not accept his "particular psychological theory" to agree with his theory of criticism.[46] I. A. Richards, "even while arguing that the value of a poem was to be sought, not in its makeup, but in the psychological reaction of its reader, was actually directing our attention to the subtle interconnections of the structure of poetic meaning."[47]

Brooks defends himself against the charge of denying any value to simplicity, which seems to follow from his praise of "complexity." But he does not approach it directly, deflecting attention to E. B. Burgum's idiosyncratic disposal of simplicity and suspecting defenders of simplicity of doubting that the complexities and ironies discovered in (and not merely read into) the poems discussed were not and could not have been consciously in the poets' minds. Brooks, then, argues convincingly that a bare statement such as "ripeness is all" assumes its meaning only in the context of *King Lear* and that an apparently simple lyric such as "western wind, when wilt thou blow" is not really simple at all (*LG*, 648–50; cf. *Z*, 730). But one can hardly deny that Brooks's taste and preference, as well as his theory, work against wide varieties of the world's poetry: folk poetry, narrative poetry, poetry of statement, romantic mood poetry, poetry with no metaphors. He must define "the principle task of criticism—perhaps *the* task of criticism—as making explicit the implicit manifold of meanings" (*LC*, 652). Brooks feels acutely the need of making a case for complexity to readers brought up with a taste for romantic poetry. The showpieces of Brooks's close readings are inevitably instances which allow him to reveal undervalued or unsuspected complexity. Texts which are transparent at first sight have not tempted him, though on occasion he grants their appeal and value.

Richards also taught Brooks to dismiss the old criterion of the visual vividness of metaphor and to see the need of metaphor for the expression of subtler states or emotion as well as the lack of poetic effect of mere sound divorced from meaning (*LS*, 642, 644; *UP* [1938], 230; *WU*, 9). Brooks approves and quotes Richards on many issues; I have mentioned the remarks on Coleridge's comments on *Venus and Adonis* and may add Richards's discussion of "intrinsicate" and *Antony and Cleopatra* or of the telescoped conceits in John Donne.[48] Brooks praises Richards for focusing attention upon the problem of discriminating good art from bad—alluding presumably to the chapter "Badness in Poetry" in *Principles of Literary Criticism*—though a few pages before Brooks admits that Richards's distinction between defectiveness of communication and the worthlessness of experience communicated (illustrated by poems of H. D. and Ella Wheeler Wilcox) cannot be maintained (*LC*, 632, 624).

In general Cleanth Brooks approves of Richards's concept of poetry and of his defense of myth. He quotes Richards's saying, "Without mythologies man is only a cruel animal," and refers to a passage to suggest that the study of poetry "would amount to a study of metaphysics." He is, however, convinced that "a metaphysics approached from a new angle" would be more than a study of the "resourcefulness of words," Richards's new term by which he attempted to replace the "evil-sounding name 'ambiguity.'"[49] Brooks likes Richards's raising of the problem but cannot agree with his positivistic solution: he speaks of the "debonair ruthlessness of his [Richards's] original treatment of the problem." The poet, in Richards's earlier formulations, makes pseudostatements, is not concerned with truth at all. "His task was rather to furnish therapeutic exercise for the reader's neural system and thus promote his mental health." According to Richards, "Poetry is nonsense but a valuable nonsense." Brooks professes to find "reservations and refinements" in the later Richards and sees a shift of emphasis in *The Philosophy of Rhetoric*. Here Richards, Brooks believes, "laid aside the distinction between the referential and emotive aspects of language," a change for which I do

not see any evidence. Richards's lecture at Yale in 1946 was rightly called
"Emotive Language Still." Cleanth Brooks is unhappy about Richards's
divorce between text and criticism and the obscurity of "the alleged
goings-on in the reader's neural system"[50] and at least once openly states
his disagreement. Richards, says Brooks, "puts a burden on poetry as an
activity which poetry does not need to assume and which it probably
cannot assume" (WU, 231). We are back at Brooks's objection to Matthew
Arnold.

In his public pronouncements, at least, Cleanth Brooks avoids con-
fronting the fact that Richards is and remains a behaviorist, a positivist
who considers poetry, metaphysics, and religion "nonsense," whatever
social utility he might ascribe to them. There is a basic misunderstanding
in Brooks's allegiance to Richards; it is due to the feeling of gratitude
for the formulas and techniques of analysis he has learned from him. It
conceals the gulf between Richards's scientism and Brooks's religious
commitment.

Brooks, on this point, resembles William Empson, who also learned
much from Richards but came to distrust his emotive theory. But Empson, of course, did not embrace a religious solution. Brooks's review of
English Pastoral Poetry (the American title of Some Versions of Pastoral)
praises Empson for the light he sheds on the nature of language structure, for his conception of metaphor as functional in a context, and for
the poem as dynamic structure, as the fulfillment of a total process.
Brooks admires Empson's "racoon-like curiosity."[51] In other contexts, he
quotes Empson approvingly on several occasions, often at length. See,
for instance, the comments on Pope's "mighty maze," on John Gay's
Beggar's Opera, and on Thomas Gray's Elegy.[52] English Pastoral Poetry is
highly praised as a "sampling of the ironic mode" with wide implications
for a revision of English literary history. But Brooks has serious reservations about Seven Types of Ambiguity. The term "ambiguity" is a concession to a rationalist prejudice: the phenomenon should be called rather
"plurisignation," a term derived from Philip Wheelwright. "The seven
types overlap, and at points the definitions are highly arbitrary." Empson
should not have bothered about categories and simply given readings of
the poems with no generalizations. Tellingly, Brooks criticizes Empson's
argument that there may be a type of ambiguity which "works well if it
is never discovered." Brooks objects that this would make poetry hocus-
pocus, white magic. He sees also that Empson's method can be applied
with equal success to bad poetry, that it does not and cannot lead to
critical conclusions.[53]

A later review of Empson's Structure of Complex Words shows Brooks still of two minds about Empson's methods and results. He admires the analysis of the term "wit" in Alexander Pope's *Essay on Criticism* as "a fine instance of historical recovery," and he endorses Empson's solution of the problem of belief as "admirably sensible." We imagine "some other person to hold the beliefs" we do not share in reading a poet. Brooks suggests that much of *The Structure of Complex Words* could be contained in *Seven Types of Ambiguity*; Empson's new distinction between ambiguity and "equation" is untenable. Ambiguity, in Empson, assumes the willing by a single poet; equation is caused by the historically conditioned language. But surely, Brooks argues, the poet using ambiguity is exploiting the resources of the historical language. The two claims do not cancel each other. Brooks dislikes the cumbrous mathematical notations and makes many objections to individual points. Empson is often "highly impressionistic or eccentric or just plain wrong." He interprets, for instance, the first line of the fourth stanza of the "Ode on a Grecian Urn" as making the poet "see new victims approaching." Empson says that "none of them will ever go home again," though it is obvious that the only victim will be the sacrificial heifer and that the town is empty only because everybody went out to witness the ceremony of the sacrifice. Empson, Brooks concludes, works with the most diverse approaches, such as author's psychology or audience response or lexical analysis, without much sense of distinction. He never faces the problem of relevance. "He is an incorrigible amateur." *The Structure of Complex Words* is "provocative and seminal . . . but it is also, much more than the earlier books, a kind of ragbag."[54]

Brooks's relation to the other New Critics (he has always deplored the term) is far from one of simple allegiance. He admires his teacher John Crowe Ransom as a poet and critic. He expounds the contents of *The New Criticism* in an encyclopedia and quotes *God without Thunder* about the conflict of poetry, of Hobbes, and of sound symbolism approvingly, and he praises Ransom specifically for considering myths the greatest radical metaphors.[55] But this praise should not hide the deep disagreements between pupil and teacher. Brooks is upset by Ransom's low view of the role of paradox, irony, and wit in poetry. He must criticize Ransom for his advocacy of a structure-texture dichotomy which he sees as "ominously like the old content-form dualism"[56] He suggests that Ransom did not really mean that "irrelevant texture" is "irrelevant." Ransom can distinguish between "irrelevance which is really irrelevant and irrelevance which is actually highly relevant to the goodness of the poem." Brooks predicts that Ransom "would return to a theory of functional metaphor. With regard to his theory of 'structure' and 'texture,' even if one concedes that it is a valuable metaphor which accounts for the surprise that the practicing poet may feel at finding that his digressions from the theme (forced upon him by metaphor and meter) actually enrich the theme, still I believe that he would discover that it is only a partial metaphor after all."57 Elsewhere, Brooks describes what he calls a "bifocal" cognitive theory. "Poetry gives us through its structure and texture, respectively, knowledge of universals, and knowledge of particulars. . . . Ransom hands over the realm of universals to science, and in effect retains for poetry no more than an apprehension of particulars." Brooks draws a parallel between Ransom's and Eastman's view that poetry is "heightened consciousness." Ransom, Brooks notes with some surprise, adopted Freudian psychology on this point. "Poetry ministers to the health of the mind, and Ransom's later position tends to approximate in some features the earlier position of Richards." Brooks thinks that both Richards's and Ransom's theories run into difficulties because they both begin by "slicing apart value and knowledge" (LC, 67, 630).

Cleanth Brooks is clearly much more in sympathy with Allen Tate and repeatedly endorses his formula: "Poetry is neither religion nor social engineering." Like Tate, he argues that the poem is an object and that "specific moral problems are the subject matter of literature, but that the purpose of literature is not to point a moral."58 Brooks emphatically agrees with Tate that "form is meaning" and that "poetry is complete knowledge," a somewhat obscure statement which Brooks interprets to mean the knowledge that science leaves out, presumably the knowledge of qualities claimed by Ransom as the special domain of poetry. Brooks defends Tate against the charge of formalism. Tate deals, Brooks says, rather with social history, with politics, and with the cultural situation. His strength is in his belief in a traditional society and a "coherent metaphysics,"59 an allusion presumably to Tate's proximity to Roman Catholicism. Tate joined the Church in 1950, a year after Brooks's review.

The other New Critics, only loosely related to the Southern group, have elicited less comment from Cleanth Brooks. He has written little on Kenneth Burke, though he praises the essay on the "Ode on a Grecian Urn" as corroborating his own reading. Brooks is even convinced by Burke's seeing a pun on "breed" in a line by Keats: "with brede of marble men and maidens overwrought." In a theoretical context, Brooks agrees with Burke that a poem is a "mode of action" but alludes to "several rather important reservations with respect to Mr. Burke's position" (WU, 139n., 186n.). But Brooks does not state them.

R. P. Blackmur concurs with Burke's view that a poem is a mode of action. Brooks finds an area of agreement with Blackmur's concept of "gesture," the "outward and dramatic play of inward and imagined meaning." Later, in an omnibus review of recent criticism, Brooks criticizes *Anni Mirabiles* as "a series of dark sayings," "perversely whimsical," a "personal monologue" in a "congested and involved style." Brooks asks the pertinent question whether the audience of these lectures could possibly have followed them.[60]

Yvor Winters is appreciated for his "corrective value." Brooks says that he consistently overrates conscious intention. In making poetry "a moral judgment" Winters extends the meaning of "moral" to include any and all value judgments (*LC*, 673; *WU*, 216). His theory reintroduces a dualism of intellect and emotion, denotation and connotation, with Winters always coming down heavily in favor of intellect and denotation, but Brooks would argue for a view of poetry that would deny any cleavage between intellect and emotion, denotation and connotation. In Brooks's most elaborate discussion of Winters, he is characterized as "not amiable, not charming, obviously very earnest." Winters "exhibits all the rancor of a man . . . who knows that he is right. He is perhaps our most logically rigorous critic; he is certainly one of our most intelligent; and he is undoubtedly the most cantankerous." Brooks complains about his "obtuseness" toward T. S. Eliot. The charge of "romantic mysticism" is quite unjustified. Winters is something of a stoic, insisting on man's free will and thus suspicious of any concession a poet may make to his environment. "The form of the poem must confront the chaos of a world in flux: the judgment on that world must be unequivocal; the author must know precisely what he is doing, and act with firmness and decision." Brooks protests against Winters's view of Eliot's "spiritual limpness" and argues that Winters is wrong about *The Waste Land*; it does judge modern civilization rather than "yielding" to it as Winters would have it. Once Brooks, irritated by Winters's charge of "automatism" in Eliot, speaks of him as a "moral cop, in his most vindictive mood."[61] But elsewhere Brooks endorses Winters's argument for the independence of poetry from its age and praises him for proposing "the fallacy of expressive form," the mistaken view that poets have to write chaotic poetry in a chaotic age. Brooks, however, does not share Winters's extreme unhistorical indeterminism. In agreeing, for instance, with Tate's diagnosis of cultural decay and his seeing Emily Dickinson and Hart Crane reflecting the difficulties of their respective historical positions, Brooks accepts some concept of Zeitgeist, a determinism violently rejected by Winters, who considers it predestinarianism, disguised Calvinism, or simply "obscurantism." Finally, Brooks must disagree with Winters's suspicion of the dramatic and ironic but turns the tables on him by asserting that Winters's concept of poetry really centers on "plot" and is thus "ultimately dramatic" (*LC*, 670, 674, 676). Still, the main disagreement with the rationalism and stoicism of Winters persists.

The parallel philosophical endeavors to restate aesthetics in symbolic terms excited some rather casual comment. Brooks sees that Ernst Cassirer's theory of symbolic forms (which he knows from the *Essay on Man*) exalts science and that Cassirer is vague about the relation among the symbolic forms of language, myth, art, and philosophy. Susanne K. Langer, usually labeled a follower of Cassirer, is in Brooks's interpretation rather an advocate of the view that art is a "life of sentience." She resembles Max Eastman, and her symbolism is completely random in the manner of Emerson (*LC*, 700–13).

Brooks is greatly impressed by Wilbur Urban's *Language and Reality.* He quotes the book on aesthetic intuition, on the symbol, on metaphor as symbol, on myth as dramatic language, on art as the revelation of man, and on art as the realm of values, but recognizes that Urban considers all poetry covert metaphysics or imperfect philosophy.[62] Urban belongs with Cassirer.

The new myth criticism derives from Carl Jung. Brooks sympathizes with Jung's general outlook, which he sees as parallel to the symbolist movement, but he accepts Jung's own disclaimer that his method was meant to be "a substitute for literary criticism." Jung, as far as I am aware, is only once used to explain a detail in Faulkner's *As I Lay Dying* (*LC*, 717, 719; *WF*, 399). But the flourishing American myth criticism was received by Brooks with less than enthusiasm. He agrees with Harry Levin's view that the new symbol-mongering is really "a cold-blooded seeking out of mechanical allegories." Brooks criticizes in detail the heavy-handed symbolist interpretations common in Faulkner criticism. When Leslie Fiedler advocates a concern for archetypes, he is, Brooks argues, substantially defending "a privileged poetic subject matter in disguise."[63] Equality of subject matter whether high or low is one of Brooks's basic convictions which serves to rehabilitate the metaphysicals and to recommend the poetry of T. S. Eliot.

Brooks reviews Northrop Frye sympathetically as an ingenious classifier and definer of new genres. But Brooks must disapprove of his dismissal of all value judgment and all judicial criticism as it would lead to a new historicism and relativism. He sees Frye's dilemma between a scheme which would make literature autonomous and, at the same time, fruitful for the human enterprise. Frye, like Arnold, is in danger of making literature a substitute religion—a prophetic observation if we know Frye's later writings about a "myth of concern." Myth criticism, Cleanth Brooks concludes, "provides no way of circumventing the basic problems of traditional criticism."[64]

Actually, Brooks's most sympathetic accounts of myth and archetypal criticism are devoted to the two modern poets whom he admires besides T. S. Eliot: W. B. Yeats and W. H. Auden. Every one of Brooks's books, except the books on Faulkner, contains a chapter on Yeats. Yeats's critical and theoretical writings are constantly referred to and expounded since they serve as a commentary on and support for the interpretation of Yeats's poems and the myth behind them, which is one of Brooks's major concerns. Since Yeats's most extravagant schemes of history and of psychological types or his most preposterous pronouncements upon occult phenomena and the transmigration of souls may serve to elucidate a poem, Brooks is extremely indulgent of their truth claims. Yeats's *Vision* is considered "one of the most remarkable books of the last hundred years," and its "framework is elaborate and complex: the concrete detail constitutes some of the finest prose and poetry of our time." Only rarely does Brooks demur at Yeats's occultism and allude to Yeats's "life-long interest in table-rapping, spirit mediums, and clair-voyants" (*MPT,* 173; *LC,* 600). *A Vision* is later called "that rich, confused, and baffling book." Brooks feels that a poet has his privileges and tries, sometimes forcing the texts a little, to make acceptable sense out of Yeats's pronouncements, which, restated in cooler terms, often can be made to agree with much of what Brooks accepts and approves. Thus Yeats's view of history appeals to him because of its rejection of progress and of the benefits of science. Brooks can quote Yeats on "Descartes, Locke, and Newton," who "took away the world and gave us its excrement instead," as corroborating Eliot's "dissociation of sensibility" and his own view of the "deadening" influence of Hobbes. He can expound Yeats's phases of the moon as a typology of characters since the idea of the antiself supports his impersonal concept of poetry; and he can take seriously even the weird pronouncements on Christ and Christianity as Yeats "goes far to restore to Christianity its proper dimension of awe and dread." Still, Brooks arrives at the right conclusion that Yeats was not a Christian but that he "found his imagination gripped by the great Christian symbols."[65]

Brooks's interest in Yeats's theories is also focused on the literary theories and criticism proper. He expounds Yeats's early essay "The Symbolism of Poetry" (1900) and uses his example from Robert Burns also in *Understanding Poetry.* He quotes Yeats on the "one great memory" as an "anticipation of Carl Jung's doctrine of the collective unconscious" (*LC,* 598, 599; *UP* [1950], 20), an unnecessary claim since Yeats's concept resembles rather Eduard von Hartmann's or F. W. J. Schelling's or even Emerson's and goes back to the mystic tradition (as does Jung's). In an essay "W. B. Yeats as a Literary Critic" (1963) Brooks admits at the outset that Yeats as a critic "was often cranky and perverse. His *Oxford Book of Modern Verse* is a monument to an arbitrary taste." But then Brooks collects perceptive and brilliantly phrased opinions on Walt Whitman, Keats, J. M. Synge, Byron, Pope, and Wordsworth before giving a careful account of Yeats's conception of the creative process: the recourse to the buried self. The saying, "We make out of the quarrel with others, rhetoric, but out of the quarrel with ourselves, poetry,"[66] prepares us for Yeats's concept of the true poet, distinct from the rhetorician and the sentimentalist. Brooks again expounds Yeats's scheme of the original unity of culture, the community illustrated by the Canterbury pilgrims, broken by abstraction, by Descartes's dream of a mathematical universe, and by the spinning jenny, modern physics, and technology. Brooks illustrates Yeats's concept of the rhetorician by Yeats's opinions about Bernard Shaw and discusses Yeats's attitude toward Oscar Wilde. Yeats characterized him implicitly as lacking in "true personality," as "artificial, abstract, fragmentary, and dramatic." But the dramatic is also Yeats's own concern. The poet must not be a mirror but must meditate upon a mask. Brooks is very careful to define Yeats's rejection of both anarchic subjectivity and the naturalistic recoil from it. The poet for Yeats is a maker who "has been reborn as an idea, something intended, complete." Art is, despite Yeats's own self-dramatization, ultimately impersonal. Brooks concludes by quoting Yeats on the artist's "shaping joy" which "has kept the sorrow pure, as it had kept it were the emotion love or hate, for the nobleness of the arts is in the mingling of contraries."[67] *A Shaping Joy* serves as title for Brooks's 1971 collection of essays. "The mingling of contraries" could be called the best definition of Brooks's own concept of poetry.

W. H. Auden deserves the same indulgence as Yeats for his opinions, though Auden spoke condescendingly of Yeats's superstitions. Auden's often whimsical views serve, as do Yeats's, as a commentary on the poetry. But Auden's criticism appeals to Brooks also for quite objective reasons. In a special essay, "W. H. Auden as a Literary Critic," Brooks describes and characterizes Auden's "zest for classification," his search for patterns of motifs when he discusses the master-servant relationship in literature, and his interest in symbolic clusters which can be regarded as a form of archetypal criticism. Brooks does not conceal some misgivings. "The Guilty Vicarage: Notes on the Detective Story, by an Addict" seems "Auden at his weakest and most absurd" and "at his most special, limited and eccentric."[68] Brooks admires the introduction to *A Selection from the Poems of Alfred Lord Tennyson* (1947). There Auden called Tennyson "the great poet of the Nursery" and compared him with Baudelaire. Baudelaire had a first-rate critical intelligence, but Tennyson was "a fool to try to write a poetry which would teach the Ideal." We have returned again to Brooks's central concern, the "error to make a religion of the aesthetic." Brooks shares Auden's view that art has only a limited role in history and quotes him to the effect that "if not a poem had been written, not a picture painted, not a bar of music composed, the history of man would be materially unchanged." Brooks seems even to agree with Auden's view that art is "in the profoundest sense frivolous"—frivolous apparently in the sense in which Søren Kierkegaard disparaged the aesthetic compared to the ethical and religious stage—and that art must not be misused as magic or prophecy. Brooks quotes Auden as saying that Shelley's claim that the poets are "the unacknowledged legislators of the world" is "the silliest remark ever made about poets." An endorsement of Auden's view would put Brooks into the opposite camp from that of I. A. Richards, who felt aggrieved when I argued against Shelley's grandiose phrase.[69] Auden is thus left with an aestheticism which, in an essay "Nature, History, and Poetry" (1950), he tried to rescue from frivolity or mere game playing by defining the subject matter of the poet as "a crowd of historic occasions of feeling in the past. . . . The poet accepts this crowd as real and attempts to transform it into a community." With this sociological terminology which seems to derive from Ferdinand Tönnies's distinction between *Gesellschaft* and *Gemeinschaft* Auden restates what Brooks usually formulated in the terminology of organic aesthetics. "Community" seems here another term for organism. The basic task of criticism, says Brooks, is "discovering whether the poem is truly unified or chaotic, whether it embodies order or is rent apart by disorder." The central poetic problem for both Brooks and Auden is "the problem of securing unity," which is inclusive in fitting the disparate and recalcitrant into the poem and exclusive in rejecting what cannot be fitted. Brooks is pleased that Auden—a serious moralist with clear religious convictions—holds "what amounts to a formalist conception of poetry" and states, "The assumption that poetry must be either an escape from life or else the blueprint for a better life is obviously oversimple" (*SJ*, 138–40). Brooks does not seem to notice the contradiction of Auden's view of a fallen but redeemable world he had quoted before, of which the poem provides an analogue. "Analogue" differs little from blueprint: poetry, in Auden, does provide a plan for redemption.

Auden's difficulty runs through Brooks's criticism. Aristotle's distinction between poetics and politics, ethics and metaphysics links up with Auden's separation of Christian faith from "frivolous" art. Brooks must sympathize with this view because he distrusts the confusion of realms: the Arnoldian (and Richardsian) view of poetry as ersatz for religion. But Brooks cannot honestly accept the view that art is frivolous (though he seems to do so in this essay, possibly with an undertone of despair at the ineffectiveness of high art to provide a proper discipline for the moral life). But actually, as all his writings show, Brooks cannot surrender the claim that literature gives us knowledge, "knowledge of a value-structured world." The adjective goes beyond the claims for the truth of literature, for the value of imitation, or for awareness of the world's concrete particularity as formulated by Ransom. "Value-structured" implies the task which Brooks ascribes to T. S. Eliot: "the restoration of order," a recognition of an "intelligible world," an "emblem of the kind of harmony that ought to obtain in wider realms—in the just society and in the true community" (SJ, 11, 37, 51), or as the passage about a "simulacrum of reality" quoted before says, in more general terms, a world "rendered coherent through a perspective of valuing."[70] Though Brooks holds fast to the distinctions among poetry, politics, and religion, poetry is for him ultimately a way to truth, a way to religion. The charge of "formalism" falls flat. It would be correct only if formalism means simply a grasp of the aesthetic fact, an insight into the difference between art and statement, art and persuasion, art and propaganda. Brooks's analyses of poems show this amply. But they show also that he believes in a meaning of art which transcends hedonism, play, harmony, and joy. Poetry for Brooks is "a special kind of knowledge. Through poetry, man comes to know himself in relation to reality, and thus attains wisdom" (LC, 601). Brooks is defining the view of his favorite poet Yeats, but he could be speaking of his own.

12: ROBERT PENN WARREN (1905–)

ROBERT PENN WARREN, like Cleanth Brooks a student of John Crowe Ransom at Vanderbilt, collaborated in Brooks's anthologies *Understanding Poetry* (1938), *Understanding Fiction* (1943), and *Modern Rhetoric* (1949) so closely that it is impossible to distinguish between the shares of the two authors. They were then both young professors at the Louisiana State University at Baton Rouge and together founded and edited *The Southern Review* from its inception in 1935 to its demise during the war in 1942. Warren concentrated his enormous energies more and more on fiction and poetry, and achieved a well-deserved fame. Criticism with him became a sideline, mostly confined to the editing and elucidation of American poets and novelists in a pedagogical context. In a late interview (*A Conversation with Robert Penn Warren,* ed. Frank Gado, 1972), Warren says expressly that criticism is "an extension of teaching—even conversation. There is something about a poem or a novel that you've perceived, and you try to explain it, to bring it to clarity. That's what the critical act basically is, I suppose" (8).

Compared to Brooks, Tate, and Ransom, Warren shies away from theory and praises the old virtues: "intelligence, tact, discipline, honesty, sensitivity" (*Selected Essays,* 1958, xii). He does not believe in a single methodology or critical strategy, and he emphasizes that the New Criticism has no consistent doctrine. "Let's name some of them—Richards, Eliot, Tate, Blackmur, Winters, Brooks, Leavis (I guess). How in God's name can you get that gang into the same bed? There is no bed big enough and no blanket would stay tucked" (*Paris Review* interview, reprinted in *Robert Penn Warren: A Collection of Critical Essays,* ed. John L. Longley, Jr., 1965, 26). Warren ridicules the idea that there was "a dark conspiracy supposed to be the New Criticism" (*A Plea for Mitigation: Modern Poetry and the End of an Era,* 1966, 10) and at most grants that they have "enemies in common" (*SE,* xii). In 1966 the New Criticism appears to him "a closed chapter," as something "temporarily useful" (*A Plea,* 10).

Most of Warren's criticism collected in *Selected Essays* consists in characterizations of authors, retellings of their lives, judgments of characters, situations, and plots in novels or themes in poems, leading usually to some consideration of the social and philosophical attitude of the author discussed. Warren was an early admirer of Faulkner, on whom he wrote several essays, always stressing his "ethical center" (*SE*, 67) and explaining and defending his attitude toward the Negro. Slavery is for Faulkner "a particular Southern curse" (60) but also an allegory of the human lot. Faulkner's work is a great "rebuke" to our technological civilization. He succeeds to do what Stephen Dedalus wanted for Ireland, "to forge the conscience of his race." Faulkner "stayed in his native spot, and, in his soul, in vice and in virtue, reenacted the history of that race" (*Faulkner, A Collection of Critical Essays*, ed. R. P. Warren, 1966, 271). Piety is thus the key to Faulkner's work (ibid., 269).

Faulkner is for Warren the greatest American writer of his time, comparable to Melville and Henry James. Hemingway, though judged sympathetically, seems to him more narrow, suffering from "monotony and self-imitation" (*SE*, 105). Still, *A Farewell to Arms* is praised as "a religious book" (107) because of the concept of unselfish love implied and formulated by Frederick.

In contrast, Thomas Wolfe is downgraded as wholly autobiographical, self-indulgent. "Shakespeare wrote *Hamlet*; he was not Hamlet" (*SE*, 183). The novelist whom Warren admires most in Europe is Conrad. A highly appreciative essay on *Nostromo* calls it his "supreme effort" (327) and exalts it as proof that Conrad was a "philosophical novelist," "one for whom the documentation of the world is constantly striving to rise to the level of generalization about values, for whom the image strives to rise to symbol, for whom images always fall into a dialectical configuration, for whom the urgency of experience, no matter how vividly and strongly experience may enchant, is the urgency to know the meaning of experience" (58). Warren is describing here his own ambition.

The essay on "The Themes of Robert Frost" is also concerned with the question of how ideas "are operative in the poems themselves" (*SE*, 119). He knows that a poem "is a controlled focus of experience" to which not any response is appropriate (120). He gives faithful readings of some of the most well-known poems, rising to a generalization about the nature of poetry which requires the fusion of man and nature accomplished in Frost's poetry (135). Warren finds a similar "depth, complexity, and shadowy interfusion of values" in the poetry of Herman Melville (*Selected Poems of Herman Melville*, ed. R. P. Warren, 1970, viii). He shows the "astonishing continuity" (*SE*, 198) between the early *Battle*

Pieces and the neglected long poem *Clarel,* which he expounded and anthologized.

In other commentaries Warren's interest shifted to a study of the social picture and the biographical background. *John Greenleaf Whittier's Poetry* (1971) contains mainly a retelling of his life and his part in the Abolitionist movement. It recognizes that his poetry "lacks inwardness or organic quality" (24) though Warren comments admiringly on "Ichabod," the poem on the lost leader Daniel Webster. Also *Homage to Theodore Dreiser* (1971) is mainly a biography which draws a psychological profile of the writer, retells the novels in relation to Dreiser's life, and judges them extremely favorably, glossing over their failings. Even the novels of the trilogy—*The Financier, The Titan, The "Genius"*—are defended, although Warren knows very well that "form is meaning." But he admires Dreiser's "massive and passionate daydream of power" (*Homage,* 87) and is deeply stirred particularly by *An American Tragedy.* Faulkner's rebuke to America seems to him repeated in spite of all the crude philosophizing surrounding powerful scenes and dialogues.

Two early essays make theoretical pronouncements and have attracted most attention. "Pure and Impure Poetry" (1942) is ostensibly a paradoxical plea for "impure poetry" when the polemic about pure poetry was still in the air. Actually the essay is a defense of what Santayana and I. A. Richards called "inclusive poetry," poetry that juxtaposes contrasting moods as Romeo and Juliet are flanked by Mercutio and the Nurse, poetry that undercuts a dominant solemn theme with irony. Thus in Landor's "Rose Aylmer" a "soft" subject, the mourning of a dead woman, is undercut by the poet promising to "consecrate a night of memories and sighs" to her—one single night, as Warren reads it. Warren develops this theme to state that "the poet proves his vision by submitting it to the fires of irony" (*SE,* 7) and uses this argument then against the wartime demands for patriotic and optimistic writing. Van Wyck Brooks must have been in his mind. It is an effective, even brilliant piece combining topicality and close reading with an insight into the nature of poetry as neither effusion of sentiment nor ideological pleading.

Warren's most sustained excursion into scholarly research and interpretation is a study of Coleridge's *Rime of the Ancient Mariner,* "A Poem of Pure Imagination: An Experiment in Reading" (1946). Warren has little trouble rejecting interpretations which consider the poem simply a fantastic yarn with a crude moral message tagged on. He argues well for the significance of the killing of the albatross as a gratuitous act, a sin of pride against Nature. The Mariner's redemption starting with his blessing of the watersnakes "unawares" is seen as a recognition of the

"One-Life," of the identity of man and nature. This reasonable conception of the main action is crossed by an attempt to argue that the other
theme of the poem is "imagination." The moon and the sun are symbolic
clusters: the sun of death, the "bloody sun," is interpreted as a "fable of
the Enlightenment and the Age of Reason whose fair promise had wound
up in the blood-bath of the end of the century" (*SE,* 241) while "the
moon of imagination" is the "adored, the guiding, the presiding power"
(247). Without trying to enter the endless controversies about the poem
(well summarized in *The English Romantic Poets: A Review of Research and
Criticism,* ed. Frank Jordan, Jr., 3rd ed., 1972), I must express my doubts
that the poem created by imagination for which Coleridge much later
elaborated a theory, well rehearsed by Warren, is *about* imagination at
all. I do not see why and how the sun can be pressed to be a symbol of
the eighteenth century or how the scene in the homeport with the ser-
aph-men standing next to the corpses of the mariners is supposed to be
the "final fusion of the imagination and the sacramental vision" (248).
While Warren rightly rejects the biographical and psychoanalytical readings propounded by Kenneth Burke and others, his own interpretation
is an early example of symbol-hunting and forcing which, for a time,
became the bane of American criticism.

A FRIEND of R. P. Blackmur told me that one of Blackmur's favorite passages came from Donne's third *Satire*:

> On a high hill
> Ragged and steep, Truth dwells, and he that will
> Reach it, about must and about must go.

"Going about and about" seems an accurate description of Blackmur's critical method: the groping, painful struggle to describe, by circumlocution or metaphorical analogue, the experience of poetry which, he feels, is always beyond the reach of ordinary rational discourse. "There is," he says bluntly, "finally, as much difference between words used about a poem and the poem as there is between words used about a painting and the painting. The gap is absolute" (*LG,* 381). If this were true, Blackmur would have to conclude that descriptive criticism is a failure. Analysis cannot touch a poem; all the critic can do is "to set up clues," as there always remains a "territory of the poem which we cannot name or handle but only envisage" (264).

Still, provisionally, Blackmur defends and defines the task and limits of criticism much more coherently than his sense of the ultimate irrationality and obscurity of poetry would suggest. "Any rational approach is valid to literature and may be properly called critical which fastens at any point upon the work itself " (*LG,* 379) is a statement which implies an acceptance of the emphasis of the New Criticism on the text, of what I have called, after Manfred Kridl, "the ergocentric view." Clearly, Blackmur draws the consequences when he rejects the methods of extrinsic criticism: biography, psychology, Marxism, and academic historical scholarship. Blackmur had no academic education (he did not even graduate from high school) and uncertain scholarly attainments (his knowledge of the classical and foreign languages, at least, was very limited), but he had—in difference, for example, from Allen Tate—no resentment or violent feelings against the English Department Establishment on public record. Actually he became a Professor of English at Princeton University by an unorthodox route, the writing program then in vogue. "Scholarship," he says, "is *about* literature," it is "without the work" (*LH,* 180–81). It is useful in supplying us with facts but becomes obnoxious when it "believes it has made an interpretation by surrounding the work with facts" (181).

Marxism also remains on the periphery. Its economic insights "offer only a limited field of interest and enliven an irrelevant purpose" (*LG,* 374). Granville Hicks's Marxist history of American literature, *The Great Tradition,* is not "criticism at all."

Blackmur consistently has little use for the psychological schemes of Richards or Kenneth Burke. Blackmur admired Richards personally as "a warm and passionate man and a lover of poetry" (*PI,* 76) and grants that Richards's writings are "a preparatory school to good criticism," an "excellent aid to the understanding of poetry and its criticism" (*HH* 3:453), but that ultimately "he ought not be called a literary critic at all" (*LG,* 387). "A literal adoption of Mr. Richards' approach to literary criticism would stultify the very power it was aimed to enhance—the power of imaginative apprehension, of imaginative coordination of varied and separate elements" (389). Blackmur admired Richards's *Coleridge on Imagination* for its passionate declaration of faith in poetic imagination but felt that "he has exaggerated the bearing of his concept and made it paramount beyond practical possibility" (*Nation* 146: 423–24).

Kenneth Burke, whose indebtedness to Richards is obvious to Blackmur (*LG,* 391), is "only a literary critic in unguarded moments, when rhetoric nods" (*LH,* 392). His method, Blackmur observes acutely, "could be applied with equal fruitfulness either to Shakespeare, Dashiell Hammett, or Marie Corelli" (393). But he moves on a plane of abstract rhetoric which absorbs everything in a "methodology."

The rejection of the critical value of biography is equally emphatic. Biographical knowledge "cannot affect the poetry or our understanding of it as poetry. . . . The more life or mind, the more extraneous material of any sort, you introduce into the study of a poem as belonging to it, the more you violate the poem as such, and the more you render it a mere document of personal expression" (*KR* 1:97). But this of course is not a condemnation of biography as a genre: actually Blackmur devoted a lifelong effort to an intellectual biography of Henry Adams.

Eliot was clearly the greatest influence on Blackmur. In his first early essay on Eliot, Blackmur defines "the quality which makes Eliot almost unique as a critic" as "the purity of his interest in literature as literature—as art autonomous and complete" (*HH* :292). This, he argues, is not sterile aestheticism. Criticism focused on the work "without a vitiating bias away from the subject at hand" (293) is the right kind of criticism. "Eliot's most remarkable criticism and his most trivial equally carry that mysterious weight of authority—which is only the weight of intelligence" (317). Blackmur really drew from Eliot not only the emphasis on the autonomy of literature and the impersonality of art but also accepted most of his decisions on matters of taste: the selection from the past, the antiromanticism, the interest in Dante and in symbolism. But Blackmur's reservations become articulate with Eliot's shift toward a criticism by religious criteria. "We cannot follow him" (*DA*, 177), he states bluntly in reviewing *After Strange Gods* in 1935. "It Is Later Than He Thinks" is the heading for a review of *The Idea of a Christian Society* (*KR* 2:235–38; also in *EG*). "We are not able; it will not happen. Mr. Eliot's ideal of a Christian society . . . cannot be realised in this world and I should imagine would be unsuitable in any probable world" (*EG*, 241). In a later article, "In the Hope of Straightening Things Out" (1951), Blackmur reviews appreciatively Eliot's key concepts of feeling, emotion, sensibility, and impersonality but ridicules some of the effects of Eliot's criticism: Milton, Shelley, and Swinburne are not read any more. A whole literary generation sprang up whose only knowledge of Christianity was what they got by reading Eliot, and "a 'cult' for Dante spread through Bloomsbury and Cape Cod" (*LH*, 167). Eliot became a critical dictator unexampled in our time but actually failed to enforce his preferences for Ben Jonson, Dryden, and Dr. Johnson. Blackmur approves of Eliot's later religious turn only insofar as it recognized that "poetry saves nobody, but shows rather the actual world from which to be saved or not" (175). The "adventure of incarnating religion in poetry[,] . . . what Eliot has been up to all along" (174), failed and had to fail.

Among the Southern critics, Allen Tate is the only one with whom Blackmur sympathizes. He agrees with Tate's "battle against the Richards ideas, against any ideas not found directly in poetry itself, and in the particular poem itself, and against any positive or organized theory of literature . . . allied to one or another branch of systematic philosophy" (*PI*, 166). The salute to Tate ends in an oddly noncommittal recitation of Tate's main notions of Incarnation, Order, Experience, Prejudice, Historical Imagination, Will, Communion, and Love, calling the list "Diplomacy on the high scale" (176). One wonders whether the term should not be applied to Blackmur's own essay.

Inevitably Blackmur discusses Ransom along with Tate. Earlier, Blackmur had seen Ransom only as a rhetorician, working with the terms "tenor," "vehicle," and "texture," ignoring, in his analysis of *Lycidas*, "the intellectual and poetic subject of the poem" (*LH*, 192); while, in the late essay on Tate, Ransom is criticized rather for concentrating his attention "almost exclusively on the problem of knowledge," on "epistemology and ontology." Blackmur sees Ransom as "the solipsist trying to find out how he knows the only thing he can trust in the world he creates—the formal aspects in which it appears" (*PI*, 169). Ontology, Blackmur knows, means a "science of Being," but he still sees Ransom as concerned only with a form and relation, not with reality. He seems, however, right in pointing to Ransom's restless experimentation: "He creates the scaffold of system after system for Tate to see through and beyond" (170), a strangely phrased conclusion which makes the teacher somehow serve the disciple.

The attitude toward Cleanth Brooks is even more negative: he "has made . . . a rhetoric of Irony and Paradox, with sub-types of Ambiguity, Attitude, Tone, and Belief." Blackmur endorses Ronald Crane's attack on Brooks's "Critical Monism." The New Criticism seems to him "impossible with Milton or Shakespeare" (*LH*, 192), though he recognizes the illumination of its method if applied within limits and not overruled by a thesis, "a set of principles" which, in his view, mars Brooks's *Modern Poetry and the Tradition* (*MLN* 65:388–90).

Blackmur, with the years, set himself increasingly against the New Criticism. It "has dealt almost exclusively either with the executive technique of poetry (and only with a part of that) or with the general verbal techniques of language" (*LH*, 206). It seems to him "useless for Dante, Chaucer, Goethe, or Racine. Applied to drama it is disfiguring, as it is to the late seventeenth- and all the eighteenth-century poetry" (207). It has become a "methodology," a "rebirth of the old rhetoric" (189). "There was," however, "never a coherent critical position, certainly never a uniform practice" (191).

The vehemence and, I think, the injustice of these later pronouncements must be due to Blackmur's reaction to his own past. Blackmur made his early reputation with analyses of modern poetry: of the techniques, forms, and meaning of Thomas Hardy, Ezra Pound, T. S. Eliot, Hart Crane, Wallace Stevens, E. E. Cummings, and Marianne Moore. He himself recognized that the accusation of criticism for criticism's sake may with point be applied to himself. But one cannot say that he recanted. If we examine his theory of criticism in its early stages we have to acknowledge a consistency throughout his career, even though his interests perceptively shifted and widened from a dominant concern with modern poetry to the novel, from purely American topics to foreign writers such as Flaubert, Thomas Mann, Tolstoy, and Dostoevsky, and finally to more general topics beyond the province of literary criticism proper: to a view of our culture, to the differences between America and Europe, and even to the meaning of history and religion.

Still, the basic insight remained the same: a recognition of the central obscurity in poetry, in literature, and in life, which becomes, in the operation of the intellect, skepticism, an "unindoctrinated thinking" that harkens back to the "early Plato and the whole Montaigne" (*LG,* 375). He objects, for example, to the rationalism of Mortimer Adler, his ignoring of "the realm of anterior conviction" (*KR* 2:355), and he violently rejects the teaching of the American neohumanists, who at the beginning of his career dominated the critical scene. In 1930, Blackmur contributed to C. Hartley Grattan's symposium, *A Critique of Humanism,* condemning its censorious attitude toward modern literature, its rigid body of arbitrary doctrine, its conception of a tradition so static and self-imitating that "they can admire only Sophocles, Dante, and Racine" (*CH,* 251). A later essay, "Humanism and Symbolic Imagination" (1941, in *LH,* 145–61), is possibly even harsher. "Babbitt's mind," we are told, "operated by rote." He suffered from "some deep privation of imagination, some paucity of sympathy, some racking poverty of sensibility. . . . He never took account of the chthonic underside of things." He "was interested only in the abstractable elements of literature" (146–48). Blackmur expands his criticism to condemn the whole "history of ideas" approach to literature: "To deal with literature as a current of ideas is about as rewarding . . . as dealing with the plays of Shakespeare as the current of the plots which he begged, borrowed, or invented" (159). We could reach, in that way, only "the intellectually formulable order" and not the "intimate [actual] orders" which may not be "susceptible of verbalization on the intellectual level" (159). Intellect in general is disparaged. "[It] is but the manners of the mind, and the Humanist who inadvertently makes himself, as Babbitt did, all intellect, is all manners and no man" (161).

Intellect with Blackmur is not, of course, equated with reason. He even emphatically proposed in 1948 to "evangelize in the arts . . . rational intent, rational statement, and rational technique; and I want to do it through technical judgment, clarifying judgment, and the judgment of discovery, which together I call rational judgment" (*LH,* 212). "Reason" is here used in a special sense as a faculty distinct from the intellect in about the way Coleridge distinguished between reason and understanding in a loose parallel to Kant's use. Psychology and semantics are dismissed by Blackmur as "trouble-makers" which "lead to the proliferation of a sequence of insoluble and irrelevant problems so far as the critic of literature is concerned." Aesthetics is also unhelpful, as it "comprises the study of superficial and mechanical executive techniques, partly in them-

selves, but also and mainly in relation to the ulterior techniques of conceptual form and of symbolic form" (209). The distinctions and unusual
terms are somewhat clarified by what follows. "Executive techniques" are,
for example, metrical schemes or narrative or dramatic modes. "Conceptual techniques" are illustrated by examples: Dostoevsky's Double,
the Homeric pattern in Joyce's *Ulysses,* the phases of the moon in the
later poetry of Yeats, the pattern of Christian rebirth, conversion, or
change of heart in the modern novel. Blackmur defines "symbolic technique" rather obscurely as "invokable forces, or raw forces, the force of
reality": it includes the creation of memorable characters such as Hamlet,
Lear, Emma Bovary, and the brothers Karamazov. Blackmur conceives
of these techniques as collaborating rationally: the logic, the rhetoric,
and the poetic form an oddly arranged triad in which the "executive
technique" is aligned with logic, "conceptual technique" with rhetoric,
and "symbolic technique" with poetry. The arts "make a rationale for
discovering life. . . . Through the aesthetic experience . . . we discover,
and discover again, what life is, . . . we also discover what our culture is"
(211). We now understand the sentence about the different kinds of
judgment: the technical judgment will refer to the executive technique,
to logic; the clarifying judgment to conceptual techniques, to rhetoric;
and the judgment of discovery to symbolic technique, to poetry.

A slightly different classification appears in "Notes on Four Categories
in Criticism" (1946). The first is that of "superficial techniques"; the
second of "linguistic technique," images and tropes, as well as "idiom"
which seems another term for style. The third category is "the ulterior
technique of the imagination: how the mind makes its discourse in images . . . as meaningful as the original parallel experiences . . . in life"
(*LH,* 218). Here the history of ideas, the Freudian approach, and any
deterministic method as well as historical criticism belong—all considered
inevitable but inadequate. Blackmur argues, in a tortuous page, that the
arts exemplify the "actual," the concrete, through which the "real" shines
only fitfully, as "human kind cannot *know* very much reality" (221). The
theme of ultimate obscurity recurs. The artist can illuminate the mystery
by the "symbolic imagination," the fourth and final category, which is
exemplified only by a little scene from *Madame Bovary*: Emma on the
farm, before her marriage, offering a cordial to Dr. Bovary, herself stick-
ing her tongue into the narrow glass.

Symbolism is Blackmur's central critical concept which he tries to explain on several occasions. In the paper "Language as Gesture" (1942),
which serves as the title of the third collection of his essays, all the arts
are derived from a prime "gesture," a term used so broadly that it allows

him to speak of gesture in architecture. A spire, a bridge, a dome, a crypt make gestures. Even sculpture is somehow "gesture": "man breeding shapes out of his brooding" (*LG*, 7); painting, dancing, and music derive from gesture. In poetry gesture is used as the meaning of words—the rhythm, cadence, and interval not conveyed in ordinary pedestrian writing. It appears also in repetition and culminates in symbol. "A symbol," Blackmur formulates, "is what we use to express meaningfulness in a permanent way which cannot be expressed in direct words or formulas of words with any completeness; a symbol is a cumulus of meaning" (16). The examples which follow range widely: from pithy sayings in Shakespeare such as "The rest is silence" or "Ripeness is all" to puns, synaesthesia, onomatopoeia, meter, and refrain—all instances of poetic devices which abandon the traditional idea of symbol to return to "gesture," a term which seems to mean little more than any contextual meaning, any device of language deviating from the normal.

Criticism is thus for Blackmur not a science. The attempt to make it a science fails, as it "can handle only the language and its words and cannot touch—except by assertion—the imaginative product of the words, which is poetry; which in turn is the object revealed or elucidated by criticisms. Criticism must be concerned, first and last—whatever comes between—with the poem as it is read and as what it represents is felt" (*LG*, 390), and "no amount of linguistic analysis can explain the *feeling* or existence of a poem." Nor does philosophy help: it "gives criticism no power over the substance (the felt life, the behavior) which it reflects and orders" (*LH*, 291). Criticism ultimately leaves the reader "with the poem, with the real work yet to do" (*LG*, 396). Thus Blackmur can come to a modest view of criticism. It is a regrettable necessity. "Critic and scholar are go-betweens and should disappear when the couple are gotten together, when indeed there is no room left for them. That is why there are no statues to critics and scholars. That is why there is nothing deader than dead criticism and scholarship" (*LH*, 184). This is the reason Blackmur called his second volume *The Expense of Greatness*, though only an essay on Henry Adams discusses the theme: "Failure is the expense of greatness." Criticism is ultimately a failure. Blackmur had great ambitions and real talent as a poet, and he seemed to have felt his critical writing as a *pis-aller*. But in difference from those who wrote criticism as artists *manqués*, such as Pater or Wilde, Blackmur did not want to write "creative" criticism aiming at rivaling or replacing another work of art. Rather, he modestly conceives of the "burden of criticism" as a making of bridges between society and the arts, as "the audience needs [today] instruction in the lost skill of symbolic thinking" (*LH*, 206). With a

slightly different emphasis Blackmur phrases the perennial task of criticism as "bringing the work of art to the condition of performance" (290),
where performance, if I understand him rightly, must mean something
like the "concretization," the right response of the reader. Criticism has
a strictly mediatory task, a removal of obstacles to the wedding of reader
and work—a narrow conception which forgets not only about theory but
about judging and ranking.

Judging and ranking was, however, the main preoccupation of Blackmur's early articles on modern poetry. "Notes on E. E. Cummings' Language" (1930) criticizes Cummings for "romantic egoism," for his dogma
that "whatever I experience is real and final" or, in somewhat different
terms, for "emotion which existed before the poem began and is the
result of the poet's private life" (LG, 319). Blackmur charges Cummings
with sentimentality which he defines by using Eliot's distinction of emotion and feeling: "the use of emotion in excess of its impetus in the feelings" (332) or for "accepting every fragment of experience as final" (318).
Blackmur condemns reverie, dreaming, mere "private musing" (325),
which leads to unintelligibility. Cummings's language shows a lack of
"communicable precision" (330). It is abstract and at the same time
vague, while poetry should be "concrete, qualified, permanent, and public" (339), "solid, definite" (325). Cummings lacks "fidelity to his words
as living things" (338), "an entire submission to his words" (324) which
seems a variant for concreteness. The abstract, the "idea" is disapproved
of. Thus the term "flower," a favorite of Cummings, is said to "be dead-
ened to an idea" (324). Cummings's poetry "ends in ideas about things"
(334).

The insistence on impersonality, objectivity, concreteness, and intelli-
gibility is central also to other essays of the thirties. "D. H. Lawrence and
Expressive Form" (1935) criticizes Lawrence's poetry for existing "only
at the minimum level of self-expression" (LG, 288), for depending "entirely upon the demon of inspiration, the inner voice, the inner light"
(289) which, later in the essay, Blackmur wants to rename "hysteria,"
"disproportionate reactions to the shock of experience" (295). Blackmur
recognizes Lawrence's "furious honesty of observation" (297) and makes
"no objections to the view of life involved" (287) but considers Lawrence's
poetry radically vitiated by "the plague of expressive form . . . the fallacy
that if a thing is only intensely enough felt its mere expression in words
will give it satisfactory form" (288–89). Lawrence's poetry lacks in "the
devices which make a poem cohere, move, and shine apart" (288). Blackmur upholds an objective order. "The chaos of private experience cannot
be known or understood until it is projected and ordered in a form

external to the consciousness that entertained it in flux" (295). In Lawrence "the disorder alone prevailed" (300).

Such a very different poet as Emily Dickinson is judged and downgraded by the very same standards. Blackmur recognizes "her aptitude
for language" but criticizes her "frantic strain toward meaning—a strain
so frantic that all responsibility toward the shapes and primary significance of words was ignored" (LG, 42). Her poems remain—like
Lawrence's and Cummings's—"exercises in self-expression" (40), "un-
composed disorder" because "written automatically" (41). In a satirical
conclusion, Blackmur calls her "neither a professional poet nor an amateur: she was a private poet who wrote indefatigably as some women
cook or knit. Her gift for words and the cultural predicament of her
time drove her to poetry instead of antimacassars" (49). Inflated claims
for "the greatest woman poet of all time" (27) offended Blackmur's sense
of proportion and blinded him to her genuine originality and finesse.

The discussions of Pound and Wallace Stevens imply slightly different
standards. Pound, Blackmur decides, is "at his best a maker of great
verse rather than a great poet" (LG, 124), a distinction then renovated
by Eliot. He is "all surface and articulation" (125). His best work is in
his translations, as he lacks "sufficient substance of his own" (136). The
Cantos, though they contain "passages of extraordinary beauty and clarity" (152), are a helter-skelter chaos. "Confusion is a deliberate element
of procedure" (145). It does not help the poetry.

Blackmur early recognized Wallace Stevens as a "genuine poet" who
has "created a surface, a texture, a rhetoric in which his feelings and
thoughts are preserved in what amounts to a new sensibility" (LG, 249).
Blackmur sees his preciosity and comments on his odd and outlandish
words, his wit, elegance, and obscurity, approving of his "writing an
existing language as if it were his own invention" (221). "Nature becomes
nothing but words and to a poet words are everything" (249). But later
Blackmur doubted Stevens's "speculative imagination" (252). Stevens lacks
the power of the " 'received,' objective and authoritative imagination"
(253). He became "prolix," engaged in hocus-pocus, euphuism, and dan-
dyism saved from triviality only by its undertone of desperation.

Blackmur reached a similar conclusion about Marianne Moore. She is
an "idiosyncratic poet" who does not attempt "major poetry." Blackmur,
in an analytical mood, describes her technique sympathetically: rhyme,
the use of punctuation, the whole attempt to evoke a "physiognomy, an
object with surfaces and signs" (LG, 270). But Marianne Moore, like
Emily Dickinson, remains for him something of an oddity.

Among older poets Blackmur admired Thomas Hardy but also judged him by the standard of the Eliotic theory of objective, impersonal, and, at the same time, concretely emotional poetry. In a reversal of Eliot's aphorism about Henry James having so fine a mind that no idea could violate it, Blackmur displays Hardy as "the great example of a sensibility violated by ideas" (*LG*, 79): the ideas of nineteenth-century evolutionism, atheism, and pessimism. Hardy's poetry "fails to reach the condition of anonymity," a term presumably synonymous with impersonality: "For it is a curious thing that when the author pokes his head in so does the reader, and straightway there is no room for the poem" (65). On occasion, in a few poems, Hardy overcame these handicaps.

Yeats like Hardy was addicted to his own set of ideas—magic and a private symbolism—but he succeeded in "representing their emotional or dramatic equivalents" (*LG*, 90) in great poetry. Blackmur does not hide his misgivings about the supernatural, occult, and magic view implied in Yeats's poetry. "Magic promises precisely matters which it cannot perform—at least in poetry" (93); but Blackmur admits that "magic may be a feature of a rational imagination" (103), that in Yeats's successful poems (all belonging to his later period) "the machinery is fused in the dramatized symbol" (118). Mostly, Yeats "hovered between myth and philosophy, except for transcending flashes, which is why he is not one of the greatest poets" (122). This hovering seems to describe not only Yeats's inability "more than half the time" to believe in his own system (117), but rather a vacillation between myth incarnated in poetry, which Blackmur approves of, and "philosophy," a merely stated belief which Blackmur considers unpoetic. Surprisingly and somewhat illogically, Yeats is called "the greatest poet in English since the seventeenth century" (123), which puts him above Pope and all the romantics and Victorians; though, Blackmur tells us, Yeats "could not create, except in fragments, the actuality of his age, as we can see Joyce and Mann and it may be Eliot, in equal rebellion, nevertheless doing" (122). A double standard is implied: poetry as an autonomous, "unaccountable fact of creation" (110); and poetry creating the "actuality" of an age, poetry as mimesis.

While Blackmur ranked Yeats most highly among modern poets, Eliot has been the earliest and most intense subject of his preoccupation. The essay in *Hound & Horn* (1927), never reprinted, and those included in *Language as Gesture* (1952) and *The Lion and the Honeycomb* (1955) provide a commentary reaching from the early poetry to *Four Quartets*. Blackmur's first essay makes great claims for Eliot changing the sensibility of the age, which is, in Blackmur's view, "equivalent to a change in identity, a change in soul" (*HH* 1:187). It does not, however, become clear of what precisely this change of soul is supposed to consist. Blackmur rather

defines poetry and Eliot's poetry in terms derived from Eliot's own theory: "Poetry is not thought, nor theology, nor science" (188). Poetry must
lack bias, must make no assertions, should be primarily moved by the
intelligence. "Eliot's poems are an extreme illustration of the presence
of intelligence making good poetry" (189). Intelligence is used here in
opposition to intellect and to simple sensation. But the distinctions remain vague. Blackmur admits that "none is more confused on this matter
than myself " and concludes that it is "impossible to define the new way
of feeling, the new forms for the combination of feelings of which
Mr. Eliot is the creator" (200). Still, in reference to specific poems Blackmur makes critical distinctions. "Gerontion" fails in the issue of sensibility. Obviously exciting and pungent, it is "not accomplished, not
articulated" (202), while "The Hollow Men" is "a complete success" (213).
"Whispers of Immortality" is most original. Blackmur sees Eliot's "self-
mockery" and "the great feat and peculiar quality" of these poems in
"presenting certain perspectives of the soul with the comic force of the
immediate" (212). Eliot is a "classical" poet who, in this early essay, is
chided for "perhaps not having risked failure enough" (210). Blackmur
asks boldness of Eliot, an expansion which he saw accomplished in the
later poetry, from "Ash Wednesday" to *Four Quartets*. But then Blackmur—who had agreed with Richards's view of *The Waste Land* as a poetry
without beliefs—confronts Eliot's turn to religion with misgivings. He
knows that Eliot's poetry is not devotional like Hopkins's or Crashaw's
but religious "in the sense that Mr. Eliot believes the poetry of Villon
and Baudelaire to be religious—only an educated Villon and a healthy
Baudelaire" (*LG*, 168); but he questions "the moral and technical validity
of Mr. Eliot's Christianity as it labors to seize the actual for representation
in his poetry" (165). He is unconvinced by "The Rock" and *Murder in
the Cathedral* but deeply impressed by *Four Quartets*. Blackmur comments
on Eliot's images and individual words such as "peregrine," the working
of "analogy," and the circular pattern. Blackmur formulates the doctrine
implied: "The purgation destroys that which was to have been purged,
and that refinement is into nothingness" (217–18). *Four Quartets* are
"court poetry without the operative aid of a court; religious poetry without the operative aid of a church; classical poetry without the effective
presence of the classics" (203).

These insights are, however, overlaid by ruminations which, stripped
of their pretentious vocabulary, amount to saying that a poem has a
beginning and an end and is a sequence in time, or that a poem imposes
some order on reality which Blackmur calls "behavior," possibly in order
to restrict reality to human actions (*LG*, 192). Blackmur, in several vari-

ations, repeats that the *Quartets,* "having the *dogma* of the real, are an exemplary *vade mecum* for Eliot's pilgrimage toward the *emotion* of reality: or we can put it the other way round, that in these poems the actual is the riddle of the real, where the riddle is not so much for solution as for redemption" (201). If we disentangle Blackmur's metaphors and restate them in public language, we have to conclude that he said merely that in poetry only the emotion of reality, not reality itself, can be represented. Eliot knows dogmatically what reality is like. Using the Platonic distinction between the "actual" and "the real" derived from Santayana, Blackmur says that, for Eliot, "actuality" or ordinary reality is a riddle, a mystery, hinting at a higher reality. The riddle for Eliot cannot be solved: the mystery, however, serves redemption; for example, salvation by faith. There are dozens of passages in this essay that yield some vague general sense in almost any situation. "Nobody can tell honestly what is lost of the real when it gets into the actual" (204); or "man dwells in the actual, between the real and the real" (205); or general statements of sheer verbal self-indulgence: "The menace and caress of wave that breaks on water; for does not a menace caress? does not a caress menace?" (204). A writer as perceptive and acute as Blackmur, who was able to describe events and characters very clearly and to formulate his observations and judgments often with pungent epigrammatic wit, should be given the benefit of doubt. But on occasion one cannot avoid the suspicion that he is engaging in deliberate obfuscation, in verbal jugglery and even charlatanry. Though there are amazingly fuzzy pieces earlier, and the first essay on Eliot is honestly groping and obscure, the deterioration seems to set in about the year 1950.

By that time Blackmur had shifted his interest to the novel. Not that he had not cared for it before. Henry James was his early love, and his introduction to the *Critical Prefaces* of Henry James (1934) made an excellent and rightly influential systematization of James's theories as well as a nice demonstration of the application of these theories in *The Ambassadors.* In a tortuous essay on *The Sacred Fount* (in *KR* 4:328–52), in an unusually lucid account of James's stories about artists ("In the Country of the Blue," 1943), in a broad survey for Spiller-Thorp-Johnson's cooperative *Literary History of the United States* (1946), and, most impressively, in "The Loose and Baggy Monsters of Henry James" (1951), Blackmur came to grips not only with the problem of the novel as form but with the moral issues and events in James's fiction. Blackmur greatly admired James's theory of the novel, and the exposition he gave of it in his edition of the prefaces to the New York edition called *The Art of the Novel* (1934) must have greatly enhanced its authority. Blackmur, however, soon saw that even James's own novels cannot be judged by the standards of the well-made, objective, dramatic novel James advocated in theory. In the last essay, Blackmur turns James's description of Tolstoy's and Dostoevsky's novels as "loose and baggy monsters" against James himself. He interprets James's three last novels (*The Ambassadors, The Golden Bowl,* and *The Wings of the Dove*) not on the pattern of James's own concern for the central observer but in terms of the "Christian pattern of rebirth, the fresh start, the change of life or heart" (*LH,* 276), as "educational novels" in the German sense. Technical form is only a means of conveying the feeling of life, the "struggle between manners and behavior, between the ideal in sight and the actual momentum in which the form of life is found" (268). Blackmur, however, does not allegorize them as many have done before and since. He sees their position in a history of ideas and society: the art-for-art's-sake movement, the late nineteenth-century individualism, with its sense of the "incommunicable, the purely expressive, the fatally private, . . . and [the] ambition . . . to make the individual *feeling* of life the supreme heroism" (285).

Earlier Blackmur had judged Melville with the standard of a Jamesian novel: "He added," Blackmur complains, "nothing to the novel as a form" (*LH,* 125), as his novels suffer from technical defects and move within "conventions of character and form" which even Melville did not believe in (129). The allegory—which Blackmur considers an inferior method, in which things are *said* but need not be *shown*—"in *Moby Dick* broke down again and again" (131). The single consciousness of Ishmael is often abandoned without sense of inconsistency. Melville's sensibility is rather Gothic and Elizabethan: he failed "because of his radical inability to master a technique—that of the novel—radically foreign to his sensibility" (144).

Such formal considerations recede in Blackmur's later writings: he becomes frankly a moralist and possibly a somewhat shamefaced theologian. "The novel is ethics in action" (*LH,* 289) and "literature is our theoretic struggle with behavior" (305) are statements announcing the point of view of *Eleven Essays in the European Novel* (1964). They concern the main novels which have attracted critical attention in the United States: Flaubert's *Madame Bovary,* Tolstoy's *Anna Karenina,* Joyce's *Ulysses,* and Mann's *Magic Mountain* and *Doctor Faustus*; and in a second part Dostoevsky's *Crime and Punishment, The Idiot, The Possessed,* and *The Brothers Karamazov.* To judge by the prefatory note, Blackmur now uses Aristotelian categories. Long before, he had proclaimed his ambition to reconcile Coleridge and Aristotle—Coleridge here meaning the concern for language and imagination, Aristotle the concern for mimesis and catharsis. In the *Essays* the concern for language disappears almost completely, possibly because Blackmur had to read his Continental novels in translation. Even *Madame Bovary* is read in the Marx-Aveling translation and the two remarks on French terms are oddly mistaken. The concern for plot, *mythos,* and character, *ethos,* is proclaimed supreme.

The essays vary greatly in closeness to their text. In some the loss of contact with the work is so extreme that one could read whole pages without knowing to what book they refer. In others, Blackmur makes acute observations on the characters and events of the story; in still others or even in the same essays he indulges more than ever in vague speculative remarks or in metaphorical fancies which seem almost devoid of concrete meanings. For example, the essay on *Anna Karenina,* which is called "The Dialectic of Incarnation," opens with a quotation from Carl Jung's *Psychology and Religion* about the "terrible ambiguity of an immediate experience" and asserts that Tolstoy exposes his men and women to it and expresses their reactions and responses to that experience. This allows him to speak of a "dialectic of incarnation, . . . the bodying forth in aesthetic form by contrasted human spirits of 'the terrible ambiguity of an immediate experience' through their reactions and responses to it" (*EE,* 3–4). For two pages Blackmur has not said anything which would not be true of any novelist and, critically, he has not arrived at anything more than the trivial distinction between passive (reacting) and active (responding) characters.

The essay on *Madame Bovary* starts with the portentous declaration that "it is a novel which is the shape of a life which is the shape of a woman which is the shape of a desire" (*EE,* 48), a sentence which yields no more rational meaning than that the book is the story of a woman full of desire. Not much can be made of a sentence such as "Emma's body sweeps us through Charles right into her arms" (55). After the clubfoot operation, we are told, "the author is only one of the obstacles she [Emma] has to overcome in running her course and finding her fate" (62). How a fictional figure can find an obstacle in its own author is beyond comprehension: it can at most mean that Flaubert did not succeed in the second half of the novel—a judgment which seems quite unjustified and which is in no way argued by Blackmur.

There is much verbiage of this sort in the essays, but occasionally there are perceptive remarks of a psychological nature: for example, on Stiva's and Anna's "less than honesty" (*EE,* 9), on Madame Bovary's decline—

"She is inside herself a haggard witch" (69)—on the "incredible" Svidrigailov (136), on the "unsmirchable" prostitute Sonya Marmeladov (134), or on the Idiot as the living image of primitive Christianity (148).

Rather rarely, remarks of a more strictly critical nature are interspersed among psychological and ethical comments. Thus in *Ulysses* "the overt orders of the book—homeric, organic, stylistic—make obstacles, provoke challenges, not all of which are overcome; and also serve to get around (by forcing overflows, damming power) such psycho-ethical matters as motive in character, meaning in action, and purpose in sequence" (*EE,* 32). In the essay on *The Idiot* some critical judgments are made: Blackmur singles out the first five chapters of the second part for praise and complains that "both women [Natasya and Aglaia] rage too much" (162). The role of parody in *Doctor Faustus* is brought out well and the parallel between Anna Karenina and Vronsky's horse is cleverly elaborated, though the original suggestion belongs to Merezhkovsky.

The *Essays* deviate at many points into meditations on the fate of our culture, the role of the artist in society, or the relation of art to religion. "The Legend of the Grand Inquisitor" affords a perfect occasion. Blackmur, however, misinterprets Dostoevsky when he asserts that "the Grand Inquisitor turns his omnicompetent power into love" (*EE,* 210), or when he labors the view that Ivan's, like Smerdyakov's, guilt is childish, as "it is in the nature of guilt to be childish" (232–33). The Grand Inquisitor is forgiven by Christ for his loveless lust for power and Ivan's guilt is rational, speculative, and far from childish.

One should recognize Blackmur's concern for the unity of "poetry and religion" which "rise through us from a deeper and earlier source than any theology or any church—any prosody or any rule of genre" (*EE,* 217). Though Blackmur had dismissed Matthew Arnold's hope for the substitution of poetry for religion and saw the fallacy of Richards's idea that poetic therapy could replace religion, Blackmur, possibly as early as 1940, accepted the view that the poet discovers or creates religion as an aesthetic experience: "The poet has to put his religion itself into his poetry along with his experience of it" (*LH,* 202). He felt the attraction of the Latin and Roman Catholic tradition—though always from the distance of "northerner"—and "the everlasting and vital predicament" of the human condition which, he thinks, is in our time mainly acknowledged in works of art: in Dostoevsky, in Mann, and in Joyce in particular. Still Blackmur's own position did not go beyond such an acknowledgment. He remained, while conscious of the Christian tradition and its historical role, outside the Church or any church. At least in his printed writings there is no evidence of Blackmur's "prophecy," for the kind of theological or philosophical role assigned to him in the essays of his friends, R. W.B. Lewis ("Casella as Critic," in *KR* 13:473–74) and Joseph Frank (in *The Widening Gyre*, 1963). He remained of the family of Montaigne or Marcus Aurelius, whom Henry Adams accepted as guides in later years, as Blackmur tells us in an essay rightly put at the end of a posthumous collection which is not unaptly called *A Primer of Ignorance*.

Blackmur's biography of Henry Adams which was unearthed and published only in 1980 does not change this picture at all. Adams, Blackmur says again, was "intellectually a twentieth century skeptic" (319) and so was apparently Blackmur. Some of the posthumous book reprints published accounts but a long chapter, "The Virgin and the Dynamo," a retelling of *The Education of Henry Adams* using letters and scattered writings, and a section, "King Richard's Prison Song," are substantially new. They narrate and comment lucidly and even movingly on Adams's life and doctrines with emphasis on his philosophy of history. The section on the last years when Adams was preoccupied with twelfth-century French poetry and songs is held together by Adams's memory of his grandfather remembering after his defeat by Andrew Jackson the song from Grétry's opera "O Richard! O mon Richard! L'Univers t'abandonne." Richard Blackmur felt then like Adams abandoned, deserted, a failure, "the expense of greatness." The whole book is permeated with a sense of identification with a man one would think to be as far removed from Blackmur in social standing, experience, and the manner of writing as possible. But this attachment and personal involvement carried Blackmur through many years of labor and resulted in an admirable biography which is his greatest single achievement, though it is not and does not pretend to be primarily literary criticism. Still there are passages which should be singled out as criticism: for instance, the acute analysis of the two sonnets Adams sent to Spring Rice, the British Ambassador, in 1917 a few months before his death (332–34) and the contrast and parallel drawn between Adams and Henry James. It is based on the insight that Adams used a "set of intellectual instruments" which "*predicted* what he would discover while James resorted to instruments only to ascertain what his sensibility had *already* discovered," a rephrasing of the old contraries of deduction and induction. Surprisingly Blackmur speaks of "the thinness" in James which "comes from excess of feeling; in Adams thinness comes not from a want of feeling, but from an excess of consideration" (315–16). In spite of their thinness Henry James and Henry Adams were and remained the central figures of Blackmur's intellectual life. Only T. S. Eliot could rival them.

Blackmur's later preoccupations were not always with ultimate questions. Rather, growing out of his concern for James and his experience of the American in Europe, Blackmur studied, in exceptionally lucid essays, "The American Literary Expatriate" (1944, in *LH*, 61–78), "The Economy of the American Writer" (1945, in *LH*, 51–60), and, after a prolonged trip to Europe and Asia, the differences between the main civilizations. Some of these late essays (collected in *PI*) reflect sensibly on the role of the American intellectual at home and abroad, while others are travel impressions. Whimsicalities about St. Peter's being the "Via Veneto of the Cross," pronouncements such as "I do not like Santa Sophia" or "I adore Ravenna," do not encourage one to take the generalizations about American, Russian, and German national characteristics drawn from comparisons between ballet companies very seriously. The fine-spun fuzziness, the "cobwebbing" in a style which imitates the late stage of Henry James assumes sometimes an air of sheer whimsicality and even sheer fakery. One must not take Blackmur literally, but he said that "*Felix Krull* is in effect a marvelous and heightened version of my own autobiography" (*PI*, 29) He seemed, however ironically, to have recognized the streak of the imposter or confidence man in himself. But this streak should not make us forget or undervalue the criticism, particularly of his early and middle years. It is even then permeated by a sense of its ultimate failure. Failure and a final mystery, or simply opacity, is the special attraction which men like Henry Adams and T. E. Lawrence held for Blackmur, and failure, or rather an insight into human insufficiency and into the ultimate obscurity of life, death, and art, seems also his last word. He found only an "irregular metaphysics," "the great grasp of unreason"—titles of two chapters of his opaque lectures on the literature of the twenties, *Anni mirabiles* (1956)—in modern literature. He seems to have shared them himself.

14: KENNETH BURKE (1897–)

KENNETH BURKE stands apart from New Critics, though he is often classed with them and in Stanley Edgar Hyman's *Armed Vision* (1948) was hailed as the man who "will build the most all-embracing system ever" (394), with criticism "almost unequalled for power, lucidity, depth and brilliance of perception." He has since been called "the foremost critic of our age and perhaps the greatest critic since Coleridge" (again by Hyman, in *Perspectives by Incongruity*, vii), but he has also been dismissed as a "Yankee crank," "a crackpot with a panacea," "a circus-rider, indulging in intellectual capering and larking" (Rueckert, *Kenneth Burke*, 6). I prefer to argue that Burke is not primarily a literary critic at all but a philosopher who devised an all-embracing scheme of human motivation and linguistic action in books which contain well over five million words and cover every endeavor of mankind from physiology to religion. Burke says it himself: "Sometimes literary critics have quarreled with the author for neglecting the problems of literary criticism proper" (*CS*, 219) and defends the neglect by saying that "no other course was open to him," as he wanted to discuss "symbolic motivations and linguistic action in general." He knows that this enormous project takes him often "outside the realm of literary criticism proper" (*LSA*, 494). This is surely no sin and may be a virtue. Still, it absolves the historian of literary criticism from discussing Burke's system, his peculiar combination of psychoanalysis, Marxism, semantics, and pragmatism, just as the historian of criticism has no obligation to discuss Kant's *Critique of Pure Reason* and Hegel's *Logic* as such. We have, besides, at least two competent books, William H. Rueckert's *Kenneth Burke and the Drama of Human Relations* and Arnim Paul Frank's *Kenneth Burke*, which give sympathetic and coherent accounts of his thought in its totality.

For our purposes strictly limited to the literary criticism it seems appropriate to distinguish between the early writings of Burke, of which the first collection, *Counter-Statement* (1931), established his reputation as a literary critic while the two following books, *Permanence and Change*

(1935) and *Attitudes toward History* (1937), are largely devoted to speculations about history and society in a Marxist vein. In the later thirties,
with the essays collected as *The Philosophy of Literary Form* (1941), Burke
returned to more strictly literary concerns, which he then again subordinated to the elaboration of his general system expounded in *A Grammar
of Motives* (1945) and *A Rhetoric of Motives* (1950). A later volume, *Language as Symbolic Action* (1966), which collects essays from the fifties and
sixties, constitutes a partial return to literary criticism. It seems best to
discuss all the later critical writings together as they show no radical shifts
in basic positions, and to give, first, an account of the early books, *Counter-Statement, Permanence and Change*, and *Attitudes toward History.*

Counter-Statement, while it foreshadows some of Burke's later preoccupations far removed from literary concerns, contains not only essays on
literary figures—Flaubert, Pater, Remy de Gourmont, Thomas Mann,
and Gide—but sketches a theory of literature. It is substantially a view
of art and literature as rhetoric: the emphasis is on the effect of literature
on the audience. Form is called "the psychology of the audience": it is
"the creation of an appetite in the mind of the auditor and the adequate
satisfying of that appetite" (*CS*, 31), or stated differently, "Form is an
arousing and fulfillment of desires" (124). Burke can even say, "Form,
psychology and eloquence are synonymous terms" (40). "Eloquence is
simply the end of art, and is thus its essence" (41). Burke plays down the
author and the expressive function and rejects the aesthetic sense (63).
Beauty is merely "the term we apply to the poet's success in evoking our
emotions" (58). Literature is "designed for the express purpose of arousing emotions" (123). It is a theory of effect similar to Tolstoy's idea of
"infection" and to I. A. Richards's view, though Burke does not limit the
emotions to good emotions as Tolstoy did and does not describe the effect
of art merely as patterning, tranquilizing, inducing a mental equilibrium
as Richards did. Burke seems to hold, at this stage of his career, the view
that art is there to stimulate and to surprise, to make us see things in a
new light, for which he invented the striking term "perspective by incongruity." Burke, however, refuses to see art as definite propaganda for
a specific cause. "The artist—qua artist—is not generally concerned with
specific political issues" (113). Art, he says, hesitatingly, "may be of value
purely through preventing a society from becoming too assertively, too
hopelessly, itself " (105). Literature "may assist a reader to clarify his
dislike of the environment in which he is placed." "The artist can become
'subversive' by merely singing in all innocence of respite by the Mississippi" (119). Burke also rejects quite definitely the view that art is caused
by the social context. "The theory of economic causation seems to rest

upon the assumption that there is only one possible aesthetic response to a given situation and that this situation is an economic one" (81). Though Marxism is not mentioned by name and seems here rejected, Burke accepts some general "economic determinism" (81) deeply impressed by Oswald Spengler's *Untergang des Abendlandes*. If art is not persuasion to specific action and serves merely the exciting of emotions, we must still face the question of truth or simply of knowledge conveyed by art. Information is one of the functions of art, Burke admits, modifying the emotional theory of Richards. It cannot, he recognizes, be neutral for long, as it conveys "ideology," which Burke calls "the nodus of beliefs and judgments" (161) which "contributed to the formation of attitudes and thus to the determining of conduct" (163). Realism is rejected: it seems to Burke "one of the diseases of form." It "originated to mere formal requirements (the introduction of life-like details to make outlandish plots plausible)," and "became an end in itself " (144). Art "is not the discovery of fact, not an addition to human knowledge in the scientific sense of the word. It is rather the exercise of human propriety, the formulation of symbols which rigidify our sense of poise and rhythm. Artistic truth is the externalization of taste" (42). This obscure formulation (how can taste be externalized? If it merely means expressed in works of art, the concept of truth evaporates) allows Burke to develop what amounts to a symbolist concept where "the symbol is the verbal parallel to a pattern of experience" (152), not only of the author but of the "submerged patterns of the reader" (155). Eloquence—and we heard that it is a synonym for literature—is "a frequency of Symbols and formal effects" (165). In a section called "Lexicon Rhetoricae" Burke attempts to distinguish between universal and permanent symbols on the one hand and the remoteness of patterns, the divergence of modes, the degree of familiarity in order to distinguish among the reactions of readers as either "commonsense," detached, will-less, "going to art for nothing but art itself " (100). The other type Burke calls "hysteric." He expects the symbol to be "medicinal" to his situation. Its appeal will depend upon the reader's previous experience, a circumstance which apparently earns him the term "hysteric" (180).

Burke makes an attempt to list the various kinds of form, which requires "no other terms in an analysis of formal functionings" (*CS*, 129). But he only can list, sometimes with new names, familiar and even obvious distinctions. "Syllogistic progression" is simply a coherent plot, as in a mystery story; "qualitative progression" is based on sudden contrasts, as the Porter's speech in *Macbeth* or the quotation from Ophelia saying "Goodnight, ladies, goodnight, sweet ladies," in Eliot's *Waste Land*: the "repetitive form" is a term so wide as to include any rhythmic pattern or rhyme scheme; "conventional form" is simply any established genre or subgenre such as the sonnet and "minor or incidental form" is used as a catchall for all kinds of tropes: metaphor, paradox, and even the monologue. Burke shows that these forms can interrelate and overlap. In Othello's last suicide speech we find all six varieties. The classifications and the examples are often striking and witty but also indulge in deliberate pointless paradoxes, as when we are told that "classicism is the flowering of romantic excess" (187).

Fortunately the book contains essays which are straightforward characterizations and comparisons, especially the fine essay on "Thomas Mann and André Gide." It first contrasts the two as conscientiousness and solitude versus novelty, vice, and art and then corrects the contrast by emphasizing Gide's ethical preoccupations and Mann's sympathy for the abyss. Both try to "humanize the state of doubt, try to make us at home in indecision" (CS, 105). "What Mann does with irony, Gide parallels with experimentalism, with curiosity" (103). None of the other essays and incidental comments come up to this standard. The elaborate discussion of *Hamlet*, quite consciously derivative from Eliot's essay, has nothing new to say on the playwright's supposed "confusions" (197).

In the light of Burke's later thinking the rejection of Marxism and psychoanalysis is surprising. Psychoanalysis is criticized for exploiting the method "Heads I win, tails you lose." "If the art follows the same pattern as the psychosis, they can explain it as consistent—but if it does not follow this pattern, they account for it as 'sublimation' or 'compensatory' " (CS, 74). Burke seems not to have remembered his own argument in later years, as he seems to have forgotten that he rejected the interpretation of art as a dream-life or escape as avoidance of some other activity. Still, the whole scheme of eloquence anticipates his later speculations and has already the implication that literature and art have nothing specific and are immeasurably inferior to "life." "The meanest life is so overwhelmingly superior to the noblest poem that illiteracy becomes almost a moral obligation" (x) is one of Burke's outrageous paradoxes. Still, the earliest essays show some sympathy for the art-for-art's-sake movement, as Burke seems to believe in the ineffectiveness of art as experience. Art seems futile indeed if the appeal of art as method is eliminated and art is reduced to its effect on experience. Burke himself says "by making art and experience synonymous, a critic provides an unanswerable reason why a man of spirit should renounce art for ever" (77). Burke faces a self-created dilemma: either art as method, form, technique or no art at

all. He more and more chose the second alternative. Art then serves only
as a document for some problems of life from child abuse to religion. It
had to happen as Burke has little aesthetic sense. He does not or does
not want to discriminate between great art and ephemeral writing: he
moves from Shakespeare to Odets, from Tolstoy to the *Early History of a
Sewing Machine Operator* without qualms, as everything is grist for his mill
pouring out theories of human behavior, motivations, and aims.

Permanence and Change (1935) is hardly a book of literary criticism
though it contains many remarks on writers and writings and develops
ideas which Burke applied to literature. But the main concern of the
book is political: a glorification of Communism as "the only coherent and
organized movement for the subjection of the technological genius of
humane ends." "For though Communism is generally put forward on a
purely technological basis, in accordance with the strategy of recommendation advisable in a scientific era, we must realize the highly humanistic or poetic nature of its fundamental criteria" (*PC*, 93). These
criteria are seen by Burke as community and communication. He hopes
"for a restoration of homogeneity in the means of communication in the
Marxian emphasis upon one unifying ideology that will inform the Marxian culture" (94). Poetry is then conceived as "the concentration of human desires" (92) and style is "ingratiation. It is an attempt to gain favor
by the hypnotic or suggestive process of 'saying the right thing' " (71).
This is illustrated by the "style" of approaching a drunkard, by Cordelia,
"both well meaning and misunderstood," and by the Porter in *Macbeth*
"objectifying something so private as the hard knock of conscience" (74).
Throughout the book we are told that "life itself is a poem" (326), that
"all action is poetic" (275), though "some people write their poems on
paper, and others carve theirs out of jugular veins" (102). If killing is a
poetic act, "poetry" with Burke becomes thus a catchall term which loses
all connection with its traditional meaning. But then, Burke tells us himself, he is "deliberately indiscriminate in scrambling magical, religious,
poetic, philosophical, mystical and scientific lore" (207) and we are ad-
vised "to study one's dog for *Napoleonic* qualities or observe mosquitoes
for signs of wisdom" (158).

Burke follows Richards in the emphasis on the metaphorical nature
of language. He must have derived from him the erroneous information
that "Bentham discovered that poetry is implicit in our very speech"
(*PC*, 101) as they, at that time at least, had not heard of Vico, Hamann,
and Herder. Poets, according to Burke, "show signs of a unified attitude
precisely such as may be summed up in one metaphor: He calls life a

dream . . . or a pilgrimage . . . a carnival . . . or a labyrinth" (127) as "the ultimate metaphor for discussing the universe must be the poetic or dramatic metaphor" (338).

With Richards, Burke shares the concern for the effect of poetry. "A persuasive work of art is nothing else than 'homeopathic magic' " (*PC*, 276). Burke expounds and endorses Richards's defense of D. H. Lawrence's *Fantasia of the Unconscious*. While condemning Lawrence's science he approves his fantasies as fostering an attitude, "an incipient plan of action" (324). Burke would extend Richards's "pseudo-statements" to life experience or action, abolish the distinctions between the real and the make-believe, between acting and play-acting (327). He uses Henley's poem as an example: "A man can extract courage by reading that he is captain of his soul; he can reenforce this statement mimetically by walking down the street as vigorously as though he were the captain of his soul or he can translate the mood into a more complex set of relationships by greeting an acquaintance as one captain-of-the-soul to another, and the two of them can embark upon such a project as two captains-of-their-souls might embark upon" (327). Thus any mood of elation or depression can be ascribed to poetry and developed in a life-situation. Poetry literally dissolves into life for which Burke finds a "master purpose in a Communist movement" (324n.), as "Communism is humanistic as poetry is" (344). One can hardly imagine anything more divorced from historical reality, even at that time.

The two volumes of *Attitudes toward History* (1937) are of much greater interest for the literary critic. The first volume attempts a psychology of poetic categories: a genre theory which combines distinctions in the attitude toward life, "the frame of acceptance or rejection," with some historical and Marxist explanations of genres. Burke illustrates "frames of acceptance" by discriminating between the attitudes of William James, Whitman, and Emerson. James appears as neither a pessimist nor an optimist but as a meliorist. Whitman accepts the universe in toto. Emerson sees that everything has two sides and thus learned to be content. Burke contrasts these American writers with the rejectionists: Marx, Machiavelli, Hobbes, Byron, the futurists, Marinetti, "a cruel caricature of Whitman" (*AH*, 33), glorifying war.

The genre theory is then based on this scheme. Genres are divided between those of acceptance (epic, tragedy, comedy, humor) and those of rejection (elegy or plaint, satire, burlesque, and the grotesque). None of these poetic categories are discussed in formal terms: they are considered rather attitudes like Schiller's in *Naive und sentimentalische Dichtung*. Occasionally the comment focuses on actual works. The epic is described as fostering an attitude of resignation with the glorification of the hero. "The social values of such a pattern resides in its ability to make humility and self-glorification work together" (*AH*, 36). Virgil is interpreted as "writing to celebrate the close of commercial freedom" (35), merely because he praised Augustus.

Tragedy is seen as another frame of acceptance: "orthodox, conservative, reactionary" as it makes pride, hubris, the basic sin and welcomes it by tragic ambiguity, surrounding it with the connotations of crime (*AH*, 39). Usually tragedy deals sympathetically with crime but Burke draws on Caroline Spurgeon's *Shakespeare's Imagery* to suggest that the "ill-fitting clothes" imagery in *Macbeth* suggests that the "weight of stylistic admonitions against his [Macbeth's] crime is stronger than in most cases of tragic sympathy with crime" (40n.). An obscure link between tragedy and the rise of commerce is suggested as well as a connection with the "proliferation of the forensic" while "the magical concepts of fatalism remain" (38).

In comedy and humor, two other frames of acceptance, the emphasis shifts from pride and crime to stupidity. People are shown not as vicious but as mistaken, necessarily mistaken, exposed to situations in which they must act as fools (*AH*, 41). Comedy deals with man in society, tragedy with the cosmic man (42). Humor is the opposite of the heroic. "It dwarfs the situation, it converts downwards"; and hence it does not "make for so completely wellrounded a frame of acceptance as comedy, as it tends to gauge the situation falsely. In this respect it is close to sentimentality" (43). While all this may be suggestive, the economic remarks seem mistaken. Why should Samuel Johnson have "purveyed a comic humanism of the sort desired by his employers which led him to misgauge the significance of incoming romanticism" (41)? Why is Johnson's humanism "comic," we might ask, and who were his employers and what could Johnson know about romanticism, unless Burke simply alludes to Johnson's critical view of Thomas Gray and William Collins, who could be described as preromantic?

The rejection of reality dominates the elegy or plaint, satire, burlesque, and the grotesque. Burke endorses Empson's concept of the pastoral which seems "to fall on the bias across the categories of humor and elegy" (*AH*, 47), and he admires the analysis of Gray's *Elegy* as the right kind of Marxist criticism (49). In a digression about homeopathy and allopathy, we are told that Shakespeare "evolved a set of solaces that 'made the best of things,' as in his 'Sweet are the uses of adversity' (from *As You Like It* II, i, 12) formula, the formula we consider as the 'essence' of the feudal Shakespeare" (46n.).

The satirist is said to "attack in others the weakness and temptations that are really within himself " (*AH,* 49), a generalization which could hardly withstand examination. Burlesque, we are told, is purely external, detached, while the grotesque focuses on mysticism (57). It is "the cult of incongruity without the laughter" (58). We hear of Ibsen's *When We Dead Awaken.* Rusbeck, who sculpted portraits with disguised animal features, suggests to Burke that Ibsen must have felt that he is himself a Rusbeck (67). Associations crowd each other without rhyme or reason. We hear of Joyce misquoting "Brightness falls from the air" (59), of the motives of an electrician which might have made him choose his trade (60), about homosexuals and hermaphrodites (61), about poets "clambering over 'mother-mountains' " or being drawn to magnetic mountains (62), about the dinner conversations of the elder Henry James (62–63n.), about the Joseph novel of Thomas Mann (64), about the titles of the novels of Huysmans (64), all in a few pages, presumably to illustrate the method "by interacting associations, to fuse symbols logically at odd: life, death, eternity, mother, sexual desire, castration, health, disease, art, forests or the sea, all linked indiscriminately together so that he [the poet] can only talk of one by talking of the others" (64). Burke suggests an "analysis of associational clusters or constellations," "a *phenomenological* science of psychology" (68).

For some obscure reasons the argument, if it can be called that, jumps to considerations about monasticism and to the category of the didactic, which is oddly enough identified with theory. Theories follow practice. Aristotle comes after Greek tragedy; Adam Smith after the "imaginative symbolization of enterprise in Bunyan, Defoe, and Swift," and Symbolism as a literary movement preceded psychoanalysis. Hence, Burke agrees, Trotsky is probably right in denying the possibility of a proletarian literature, as the process would be reversed there. Revolutionary literature was rather anticipated by Dostoevsky, an odd view apparently supported by simply assimilating Dostoevsky to the cult of Stalin: his supposed identification of the Czar with the Russian people is like the official glorification of Stalin (*AH,* 77). Didacticism is headed toward allegory as it divides people into friend and enemy, black and white, and thus risks sentimentality, a willed simplification, by the division of people into classes. Sentimentality is transcended by the process of Hegelian "Aufheben" which Burke finds, quite arbitrarily, allied to Goethe's "Entsagen" (80). This strange argument is then supported by a speculative interpretation of Hesiod and a reading of Eliot's *Murder in the Cathedral.* It makes a clumsy attempt at a psychology of the author who abandoned "the inelegance of Missouri for the elegance of upperclass England" and then discovers that England is moving toward Saint Louis. "England is not elegant enough. And eventually the poet meditates upon God, the only symbol elegant enough" (84). Eliot however knows that he must get to God in humbleness, that he must "transcend his elegance" (84). The play is allegorized to fit his pattern of "negating the negation." The stylistic changes in *Murder in the Cathedral* from poetry to polemic prose and back to poetry is seen as a parallel to the poet who "each morning will arise, will slay himself, the critic will step forth, towards nightfall the Phoenix-poet will rise again," the procession continuing indefinitely and thus ending in Goethean resignation (85–86). A note draws a parallel to Milton's poetic development: the poetry of *Lycidas* was followed by the polemic prose with a return to poetry with *Paradise Lost*. But why this obvious periodization of Milton's career has anything to do with the alternation of poetry, prose, poetry in Eliot's play remains as obscure as the other examples of transcendence, a heterogeneous group consisting of the Greek philosopher Thales, Lola Ridge, and Wagner's *Tristan and Isolde*. Wagner's "Liebestod" illustrates the equations: love-life, love-death, and life-death (89–90). It all is supposed to illustrate Hegelian and Marxist dialectics, the final acceptance or resignation which is not, however, passive. Comedy, of all the poetic categories, comes nearest to this process. "Whatever poetry may be, criticism had best be comic" (107) is the conclusion where "comic" must mean reconciling antitheses, charity, even irony and playfulness.

The next section, "The Curve of History," is a capsule history of Europe since antiquity, indulging in broad generalizations about the Middle Ages, the "Protestant transition" to naive capitalism, culminating in "emergent collectivism," condemning in the messianic tone of a believing Marxist "a history of the past" as "worthless except as a documented way of talking about the future" (*AH,* 159).

A third part, "Analysis of Symbolic Structure," moves back to considerations more directly related to literature. In discussing the "General Nature of Ritual" (*AH,* 179) Burke endorses Richards's view that literature makes order out of chaos but disapproves of a "purely sanitary view of the function of literature." The Soviet criticism of Shostakovich's opera *Lady Macbeth of Mzensk* is used as an example of blindness. The section "The Tracking Down of Symbols" stresses again the evidential value of "gratuitous, irrelevant metaphors" (195), for instance, Housman's preoccupation with death. The ritual of death and rebirth is seen everywhere: it even explains Goethe's "shifting allegiances to different women" (198n.). Art is considered "the dial on which fundamental psychological processes of living are recorded" (202).

Burke would like to give us a "Dictionary of pivotal Terms" (*AH,* 216), but he has not the historical erudition to trace these. Thus "Alienation" is supposed to have been derived by Hegel from Diderot, though Hegel used the old term from theology long before he knew *Le Neveu de Rameau* (216). Burke again indulges in his love of puns. Desdemona is "death" and "moan" (205), though the name is clearly Greek, "bureaucratization" has something to do with Burke, and Kenneth Burke does not mind the association with the Edinburgh Burke who stole corpses to sell them to doctors and suggested the verb "to burke" (238). The speech of Jaques about the Seven Ages of Man is used to tell us that Shakespeare, on the contrary, does not recognize such sharp distinctions between the ages, that "the strategy of transition forms the essence of Shakespeare's work" (241). In an odd aside, Burke approves of the Greek word *mimesis* because it acts out, with the two *m*'s, the food and mother category (243). It sanctions an artistic process as "adult breastfeeding" while the English translation "imitation" is "not half a meal" (243). *M*emory is the essential word of poets, says Burke, but does not ask about *Erinnerung,* and the other *m*-less words in many languages. Burke agrees with Dewey that the poet is not holding up the mirror to nature but imitates when he reproduces the cultural norms of the group (245).

Burke is on the lookout for "self-defeating emphasis" (*AH,* 259) almost like the much later deconstructionists. He admires Caroline Spurgeon's *Shakespeare's Imagery* (273), accepting the view that a writer gives himself away in imagery. He admits, however, that a consciousness of the advice "watch your metaphor" may lead to deliberate emphases on noble metaphors (274–75n.).

Shakespeare is constantly drawn on, often to fit a Marxist scheme: thus Richard II is said to "become the true king only as he approaches the deposition, thereby revealing Shakespeare's basic affinity with the churchly 'prosperity of poverty,' threatened by the incoming bourgeois morality of acquisition" (*AH,* 277n.). A curve of Shakespeare's development is traced somehow parallel to historical processes. The earlier plays are feudal (278). *Hamlet* is seen as confessional, showing Shakespeare threatened with loss of his essential identity. In *The Tempest* Shakespeare overcame the crisis. The title of *A Winter's Tale* "attests to connotation of subsistence." Shakespeare's "dramatic philosophy is rounded out by his somewhat pantheistic sense of 'universal undulation' in which all spiritual and bodily movements are subtly merged" (281). "Universal undulation" seems to be a conclusion from Florizel's wishing Perdita to be "a wave of the sea," a passage quoted earlier (278).

Burke admits that he cannot make "a complete schematization of symbolic ingredients" (*AH,* 285) as his basic principle in that "all symbolism can be treated as the ritualistic naming and changing of identity" (285). Still, he tries to distinguish three kinds of imagery from these rituals of change or "purification": by ice, by fire, or by decay. Trial by fire suggests "incest-awe" as fire is feminine. Siegfried freeing Brunhilde from the fire encircling her supposedly proves this (285). A passage from a forgotten book, Nathan and Charles Reznikoff's *Early History of a Sewing Machine Operator,* is then interpreted in psychoanalytic terms. Barrels of whiskey are seen as the woman made pregnant and offered for sale (287). But it remains a mystery why this interpretation should have such an "epitomizing effect."

Burke's program as a literary critic is to "integrate technical criticism with social criticism (propaganda, didactic) by taking the allegiance to the symbol of authority as the symbol" (*AH,* 331) but it remains unclear what this technical criticism could be except what he calls "verbal atom-cracking." "You wrench a word loose and metaphorically apply it to a different category" (308). Words contain programs of action. Burke distinguishes three levels: the mimetic, the intimate, and the abstract, which, mingling, are named "character-building by secular prayer" (341). The social aspect of language is "reason" which comes into focus in "symbols of authority" (343). In a new formulation of the varieties of human motivation (in an appendix dating from 1958), seven offices are ascribed to literature: to govern, to serve (materially), to defend, to teach, to entertain, to cure, and to pontificate (minister in terms of a "beyond") (359). The function of literature is seen as threefold: teaching, pleasing, and moving. Pleasing means also entertaining, moving means also governing. Hence Burke can subscribe to Shelley's pronouncement that "poets are the unacknowledged legislators of the world" (362) or in more humble terms that "the future is disclosed by finding out what people can sing about" (335). Still, Burke is a skeptic about language. "Words are a mediatory realm, that joins us with wordless nature while at the same time standing between us and wordless nature" (373). The critic is an ironist, or, in his terms, he must look at everything from a "comic" perspective. "However 'tragic' tragedy may be in itself, the critical analysis of 'tragic' motives is in essence 'comic' " (348–49) is restated in the afterword to the second edition (1939) of *Attitudes toward History.* But then skepticism is far from complete. Accurate naming is seen as a moral act (341). With that exclusively linguistic marvel, the Negative, "conscience" is born (374) and with conscience the feeling for our fellow man, the social hope which Burke at that time sees in his peculiar version of Communism.

Only after the three early books, *Counter-Statement, Permanence and*

Change and *Attitudes toward History,* did Burke develop his whole philosophical system of dramatism, his curious attempt at a synthesis of semantics, Marxism, and psychoanalysis. Only late did he return to the
question of strictly literary criticism.

In commenting on Cleanth Brooks's critical "credo" Burke professes
agreement with his main position: the emphasis on the description and
evaluation of a work of art, on the value Brooks ascribes to unity and
coherence, rejecting any divorce between content and form, and between
form and meaning, and the emphasis on literature as "ultimately metaphorical and symbolic," and on its aiming at the general and universal
through the concrete and particular. But Burke's endorsement is either
lip-service, due to a desire for conciliation, or a profound misunderstanding. Nowhere in Burke is there an awareness of the normative nature of
the criteria proposed by the New Criticism, nor is there any attempt to
grasp the coherence and integrity of an individual work of art or to see
the unity of form and content. Nor is Burke's interest in metaphor and
symbol at all the same as that of Brooks or Wimsatt. With them metaphor
and symbol are conceived as functioning within a work of art and also
within a fundamentally religious view of the world. Burke concludes only
that formalist criticism "is not enough" (*LSA,* 485) and that Brooks himself in his later book on Faulkner makes comments which "could be called
'sociological,' and maybe even 'Marxist' " (*LSA,* 499). But the New Critics,
particularly the Southern critics, were never formalists in any sense which
would exclude content and meaning, and they always had social concerns,
as witness the Southern agrarians, who were always non-Marxist or even
clearly anti-Marxist.

In theory, Burke advocates a critical pluralism. "The main ideal of
criticism, as I conceive it, is to use all that there is to use" (*PLF,* 23); or,
in a later formulation, "All kinds of approaches are needed, to throw
full light upon the objects of our study" (*LSA,* 36). Criticism focused on
the object has to be supplemented by two other considerations: the events
in the poet's mind—the "processes of poetry" which, Burke recognizes,
"interest [him] often more than the poetry itself " (336)—and the effect
of poetry on the readers, the neglect of which he particularly objects to
in the "formalist" position which he ascribes to Brooks (488). The effect
of literature is, for him, both psychological and social. It cannot be understood without an examination of language both as individual symbolic
action and as a collective enterprise.

Burke, who has read Freud diligently, found him "suggestive almost
to the point of bewilderment" (*PLF,* 256). He uses him everywhere: in
the conception of the poems as dream, in the persistent interest in the

concealed or latent meaning of puns and ambiguities, in his preoccupation with the sexual basis of the poet's motivation, and particularly in adapting to literary contexts the "free association" method which Freud used in treating patients. By examining imagery and particularly "clusters" of imagery, the critic, Burke believes, can discover the "motive" of a work (269). But Burke is not simply a Freudian: he objects to Freud's emphasis on the patriarchal pattern, the Oedipus complex, which he would replace by a matriarchal pattern, the desire to return to the womb, to be reborn. This to Burke would seem to be the main motive of every human being and the central motive of all art. Freud seems to Burke "handicapped by the aesthetic" of his time: the excessive emphasis on art as self-expression, on art as "blurting out," as "catharsis by secretion" (281). Freud does not see that art may also be what Burke calls "prayer," that is, persuasion or, in reverse, invective, indictment, curse (281). Nor does Freud properly recognize that art is also what Burke calls "chart," an attempt to map out reality and to come to terms with it. But Burke defends Freud against the Marxist charge of irrationalism: there is "nothing more rational than the systematic recognition of irrational and nonrational factors" (290). A reconciliation of Freud and Marx is Burke's ideal, or, rather, a fitting of Freud "into the Marxist perspective" (296). Freud, in Burke's recent writings, is found also to be deficient in stressing the other two members of what Burke calls the "Demonic Trinity." Burke would want to have the excremental side of man, elimination and urination, emphasized more than the strictly sexual. This is Burke's later obsessive concern, which he considers a rectification of Freud's doctrine rather than an attack on him (LSA, 953).

Whatever Burke's reservations, his basic approach to literature has been psychoanalytical and has become more exclusively so in his recent practice. Years ago he recognized that the Freudian method uses a "Heads I win, tails you lose" mechanism (CS, 74n.), but in later writings Burke uses the "free-association" method without restraint as "a truly liquid attitude towards speech" (AH, 231). This allows him to equate almost everything with everything else, to transform any word into any other on the basis of the most tenuous phonetic resemblance, and thus to reduce any meaning to a latent unconscious meaning largely scatological. Literary criticism with Burke becomes often a game which he himself calls "joycing," a word which contains an allusion not only to Joyce but apparently also to a translation of "Freude."

To give a conspicuous example: Keats's statement "Beauty is truth, truth beauty," concluding the "Ode on a Grecian Urn," is "joyced" to mean "Body is Turd, Turd Body" (RM, 204). It seems hard to believe and impossible to prove that this substitution could have occurred to Keats. The line, though considered "enigmatic" by Burke, is perfectly comprehensible and is clearly related to what precedes. Art is perception of truth. Everything real (and thus true) is beautiful. The identification of beauty with body and truth with turd cannot even be assumed to be present in the pattern of the language. It requires a forcing both of phonemic resemblances (truth and turd are far apart) and of conceptual analogies which strains all credulity. Even if Burke were able to establish the possibility of such punning, it would still remain unclear what would be achieved for criticism of the interpretation of a poem the general theme of which is totally unrelated to such idiosyncratic association.

Even in the essay on *Kubla Khan,* which makes reasonable suggestions on the progression of the poem and argues for its completeness, the psychoanalytic obsession with punning intrudes. "Loud" music suggests "lewd" music (*LSA,* 215). The mention of "forests" is interpreted as implying "wood" which in turn suggests "matter" and "mother" (206). The "sunless sea" is called "the womb-heaven of the amniotic fluid by which the fetus was once 'girdled round' in Edenic comfort" (206). In a very different poem, "Christabel," Geraldine is said to have a "stately neck," and this detail has a bearing on "a stately pleasure-dome" decreed by Kubla Khan. Burke consults a concordance and assumes that every word must be related to every other word of either the same sound or a similar sound, and that all words are cryptic. As he says, "Cryptology is all" (132).

The search for puns and hidden symbolism is not the only Freudian motif in Burke. Even more insistently he argues that the critic must "try to discover what the poem is doing for the poet" (*PLF,* 73). The "doing" is not simple satisfaction in making nor simple self-expression. Burke assumes that all men have guilt-feelings and try to get rid of them. The poet does so by writing, which somehow purifies him and thus changes his identity. This purification is not a direct act of confession of his guilt but a personal catharsis through the invention of a symbolism which is taken to be a code, a cryptogram which the critic must decipher. Thus *The Ancient Mariner* is conceived of as a "ritual for the redemption of his [Coleridge's] drug" (*PLF,* 96) and the albatross as "a synecdochic representative of Sarah [Coleridge's wife]" (72), even though there is no evidence that Coleridge in 1798, the time of the composition of the poem, had been taking laudanum excessively enough to have feelings of guilt or that these feelings could be redeemed in a poem (as they obviously were not). Why should Sarah be identified with the albatross killed in a wanton act? Burke makes an attempt to connect the albatross and Sarah by pointing out that the albatross came through the fog "as if it had been a Christian soul," while in another poem, "The Eolian Harp," Sarah is called a "Meek Daughter in the family of Christ." But obviously this "parallel" (71) will not stand inspection: the albatross is welcomed by the crew as something alive in the desolate waste of the sea, while the poet's wife, in a totally different context, is mildly chided for her pietistic objections to Coleridge's preoccupation with poetry. The two passages have nothing in common except the reference to Christianity. Nor can one see why the word "silly" in the phrase "silly buckets" filled with rain should foreshadow the fate that befell the pilot's boy who did "crazy go" merely because the adjective "silly" today suggests the word "crazy." Burke need not have "pondered for years" (287) the reference to "silly buckets." "Silly" means here, as a glance at the *NED* shows, "plain, homely" and has nothing to do with the mental state of buckets and even less with the mental state of the boy. The poem, a ballad, is simply misread.

Burke's earlier, "decorous" interpretation of Keats's "Ode on a Grecian Urn" is another unconvincing example of this method. There "Beauty is truth, truth beauty" is equated with "Act is scene, scene act," though Burke modifies this assertion by drawing on the phrase "fair attitude" to reflect that "act" is, rather, an incipient act. But the identification of "beauty" with "act" seems completely arbitrary. Beauty is represented by the urn as inactive and still, as a "silent form," a "cold pastoral." Nor is a preceding shift of interpreting "beauty" to equal "poetry" and "truth" to equal "science" accurate, as the beauty on and of the urn is not primarily poetry at all. It is the beauty of the sculptured urn and of the scenes on it and possibly the beauty of the maidens. Truth in Keats's poem is not, as Burke asserts, that of modern science, of utility and business, of "technological accuracy, accountancy, statistics, actuarial tables" (*GM*, 859). There is thus no shred of evidence for his conclusion: "It was gratifying to have the oracle proclaim the unity of poetry and science because the values of technology and business were causing them to be at odds" (462).

Nor is the elaborate love-death equation (used in Keats's letters) needed for the interpretation of the poem. Burke himself remarks that the poem speaks "not of love and *death*, but of love *for ever*" (*LSA*, 856). Transient human love is contrasted, in this poem, with the unchangeable but also unconsummated love depicted on the urn. Immortal love is envied because of its unchangeability, but it is surely also distanced and put in its place as unfulfilled, unreal, static, and cold. It seems to me totally unnecessary to see the identification of death and sexual love as "particularly representative of romanticism that was the reflex of business" and to note "the part that capitalist individualism plays in sharpening this consummation" (*GM*, 450). Precapitalist civilization knew of the affinity of love and death, as the medieval Tristan story testifies. Burke himself often refers to the seventeenth-century use of the word "dying" to mean "orgasm." Nor was Keats's individualism "capitalist" in any concrete sense. His conscious political sympathies were "liberal." Hazlitt and Leigh Hunt were his friends. There is even an anticapitalist passage in *Isabella* which drew extravagant praise from G. B. Shaw. With his usual sleight of hand Burke brings in the "unimpeachable authority" of Shakespeare, quoting from "The Phoenix and the Turtle": "Property was thus appall'd / That the self was not the same" (451). But "property" here has nothing to do with physical possessions or with capitalism. "Property" here can mean only the characteristic quality, the nature of the thing. Burke's wide range of quotations from Shelley, Shakespeare, Coleridge, Donne, Yeats, and the references to Richard Wagner, D. H. Lawrence, Leo Spitzer, and Ernst Kretschmer (449–63) should not conceal the fact that they throw no light whatever on the poem itself or on Burke's argument about "an abolishing of romanticism through romanticism" (447) or on the theological parallel about "God [willing] the good *because* it is good" (455), which has no relevance to anything in the text. A poem which both expresses envy for the eternity of art and knows that this eternity is purchased at the price of life and has the urn proclaim the old Platonic identity of beauty and truth is distorted, misread by Burke's method, which compounds arbitrary allegorizing with misconstrued psychoanalysis and far-fetched Marxist analogizing.

Burke is possibly even more interested in what a poem does to the audience and hence to society. "Many of the things that a poet's work does for *him* are not things that the same work does to *us*" (73). In practice Burke is, however, unable to distinguish between the satisfaction of the poet and that of the audience. The poet's unburdening, his act of purification, his "expiatory strategy," is shared by the audience, and, in sharing, the audience purifies itself (*LSA*, 188). A version of the Aristotelian catharsis understood as medical purgation is basic to Burke's view of the effect of art. Burke takes tragedy to be the basic genre and generalizes from it to all verbal art, to all linguistic expressions, and even to all human behavior. This is why he calls his philosophy "Dramatism." In criticism it has a certain plausibility for tragedy, but it is forced and strained when made to account for other genres.

Burke's reading of *Antony and Cleopatra* is a favorable example of his method. The audience, we are told, identifies with the lovers: it feels itself "ennobled" (*LSA,* 102) in their grandeur. The "global" aspects of the love affair, the stage-setting, love in terms of politics, all serve as "means of amplification" (103). Somehow, Burke assumes, the plot "flatters each customer's sense of the aggrandizement associated with courtship" (105), which Burke, in order to bring in some sociopolitical aspect, considers as "assisted, or prodded, by [the] emergent imperialism" of the English in the early seventeenth century. Even the eunuchs in Shakespeare's play serve this function. With the "many telling references to eunuchs' shortcomings," the drama sets up a "situation implying that practically all the men in the audience were *in the same class* with Antony. Such classification-by-contrast enabled Shakespeare to accentuate Antony's exceptional amative prowess without risk that persons of more moderate resources in this regard might lose their sense of 'identification' with him" (105–06). But this "ostentation of . . . love" is excessive: the lovers perish. "Along with sympathetic involvement in the two grandiloquent suicides (each by definition an act of *self*-abuse), there are the conditions for a purge. The humble and moderate can thank God that they personally are not driven by this excessiveness" (108). Burke sees in this "punishment" of excess an "incipiently Puritan" (108) outlook, ignoring its being a fact of history which was narrated by Plutarch and is paralleled in most tragedies of other ages. The coming of "puritanism" ("incipient" in Shakespeare or in the audience?) is irrelevant to the play. The whole speculation about the presumed effect on the Elizabethan audience is quite tenuous: it ignores the characterization of Cleopatra as a willful coquette and of Antony as a fool of love. Only in the last scenes do they rise to heroic grandeur. Cleopatra is negotiating with Augustus up to the very end.

The principle of audience identification can be applied elsewhere in Shakespeare only by considerable stretching. Coriolanus is a victim, a "sacrifice that will permit the purging of the audience" (*LSA,* 87), but Burke has difficulties in showing that we ever could identify with him or what we are supposed to be purged from. He argues that social divisiveness, "the delights of faction," is the guilt from which we suffer and that we are cleansed of it "thanks to his overstating of our case" (89). Burke tries to fortify this view by looking for a divisive historical situation at the time the play was performed, and he finds it in the riots caused by the enclosure acts, which set landowners against peasants (82). One may doubt, however, whether the London audience could identify the conflict between the overbearing and insulting individual Coriolanus, "the lonely dragon," and the Roman mob with a situation in contemporary rural England. Burke disparages Coriolanus; he resembles "a char-

acter in a satyr play" (92), he is a "railer," a "master of vituperation."
This allows Burke to exploit his obsession: invective is "fecal" and Coriolanus is rightly named Corio*lanus* (96). The purgation theory seems
strained to the bursting point.

The essay on *Othello* culminates also in a description of the "ritual of
riddance," that is, purgation, which the last act is supposed to accomplish.
"It is a requiem in which we participate at the ceremonious death of a
portion of ourselves. . . . It permits us the great privilege of being present
at our own funeral. For though we be lowly and humiliated, we can tell
ourselves at least that, as a corpse, if the usual rituals are abided by, we
are assured of an ultimate dignity, that all men must pay us tribute
insofar as they act properly, and that a sermon doing the best possible
by us is in order" (*PI*, 167). It remains, however, unclear why this feeling
is in any way peculiar to the conclusion of *Othello* or even appropriate to
it: Desdemona lies strangled on her bed, Emilia is stabbed to death,
Othello has committed suicide, and Iago is taken away to torture. Nor
can I see how Burke can speak of "the ultimate interchangeability of
Othello and Iago" (193), which seems to be a restatement of an earlier
comment on the scene in which Iago and Othello are "kneeling together,
and well they should, for they are but two parts of a single motive—
related not as the halves of a sphere, but each implicit in the other"
(186). At that moment, on a highly generalized level, Othello and Iago
share in the desire for revenge (though from very different motives), but
their characters could not be more diverse. The scheming villain Iago is
not "implicit" in Othello, nor is the trusting, somewhat obtuse Moor
implicit in Iago. Burke must drag in economic history: the tragedy is
one of "ownership," of "possession, possessor, and estrangement (threat
of loss)" (154). "There were the enclosure acts, whereby the common
lands were made private; here [in *Othello*] is the analogue, in the realm
of human affinity, an act of spiritual enclosure. And might the final
choking be also the ritually displaced effort to close a thoroughfare, as
our hero fears lest this virgin soil that he had opened up become a
settlement?" (156). But it is obvious that the Moor's possessiveness is in
no way analogous to the English enclosure acts, since it is given in the
Italian source and is surely paralleled in many civilizations of all ages
and climes which treat or have treated women as chattels and considered
unchastity as punishable by death.

Often the idea of audience response is generalized into a social situation seen largely in Marxist terms. Burke indulges in an allegorizing of
poetry according to which a "hidden realm," a "mystery," is discovered
in the plainest text (*RM*, 219). Thus Shakespeare's *Venus and Adonis* is

treated as an allegory in which Venus represents nobility, Adonis the middle class, and the boar the lower classes. Venus, Burke argues, "is not a 'goddess' is any devout sense. She is a distinguished person compelled to demean herself by begging favors of an inferior" (215). But it remains unclear why that noble beast, the "boar" (cf. the crest of Richard III), should represent the lower classes, and why the poem should "disclose . . . a variant of revolutionary challenge" (217). Nor does the introduction of psychoanalysis help. Venus is supposed to be "mother," and Adonis's relation to the boar homosexual, though only "vaguely" so (214). The poem, a witty and erotic virtuoso piece, is completely distorted to serve a "socioanagogic" interpretation, the purpose of which remains obscure.

The paper on Goethe's *Faust I* is another example of social allegorizing which seems to me completely mistaken. Burke assumes that *Faust* translates Goethe as the "elderly statesman," his "courtly situation," and his fear of the French Revolution into sexual equivalents. The courting (a pun on "court") and the seduction of Gretchen are, Burke tells us, more of an "allegory" than are the "supernatural" or "preternatural" episodes. "Gretchen's seduction becomes an imaginal substitute for the principle of riot (and of precisely such riot as a court minister, *né* romantic poet, would basically distrust if it were expressed politically)" (*LSA*, 150). All this is perverse in a literal sense. Goethe wrote the original version of *Faust*, which centers on the "*Gretchentragödie*," before he ever went to Weimar in 1776, before he knew a court, and long before the French Revolution. Apart from historical impossibilities, any person with a feeling for poetry must consider the allegorizing of the Gretchen tragedy as defying all immediate evidence. The Gretchen scenes are vivid poetry, lyrical and dramatic, and quite possibly reflect Goethe's sense of guilt in forsaking Friederike Brion, and most certainly his compassionate interest in the cruel punishment of infanticide which was a public issue of the 1770s. They surely are not allegorical. The supernatural episodes, the Prologue in Heaven and the Walpurgis Night, were added much later to impose a unifying frame. I will not even try to refute the grossly unfair and absurdly farfetched passage in which Goethe is said to have "anticipated Hegel and thereby anticipated both communism and nazism":

> When Gretchen, accosted by her seducer on the street, first refuses to be *led by him* (she will go home *ungeleitet*), we are helped to be modest in hindsight prognosis here by the fact that the word for street in this text is *Strasse*. Otherwise, when the becoming has been reduced to sex and flower, and the internal conditions call for a meeting on the street, we might be tempted to say that Gretchen's

first intuition had been correct when she rejected what was, in sexual
disguise, the political seductiveness of a *Gauleiter*! (*LSA*, 155).

Any use of the word "leiten" would thus somehow anticipate Nazism,
and any "Strasse" would allude presumably to the forgotten Gauleiter
Gregor Strasser.

The discussion of *Faust II* is less disastrous: it circles around key terms
which Burke looked up in Paul Fischer's *Goethe-Wortschatz* (*LSA*, 174). But
I am puzzled by the completely unjustified identification of Doctor Marianus with Faust (182–83)—Doctor Marianus alludes, rather, to
St. Bernard in Dante's *Paradiso*—and by the stodgy interpretation of the
concluding line, "Das Ewig-Weibliche / Zieht uns hinan." Supposedly it
proclaims "irresolution." "I'd translate the 'ewig' (eternal) as meaning:
Given the kind of merger that goes perfectly with the *Ur-Geist-Streben*
nexus, the problem of ultimate motivation, as personalized in sexual
terms, necessarily remains unresolved. It has the 'eternal' quality of the
essentially unending" (184). *Ewig*, however, means here the "ideally feminine" as represented by the Virgin Mary, the principle of forgiveness
through love. It has nothing to do with "unending" and does not point
to any "irresolution."

The allegorical method which dominates Burke's practical criticism is
the consequence of a basic doctrine which he has stated clearly in a paper,
"What Are the Signs of What?" (*LSA*, 359ff.). It amounts to a realism in
the medieval sense. Things are the signs of words (361). Language is a
kind of action, symbolic action. The referential aspect does not enter.
Rather, the analysis of language starts with the problem of catharsis
(367). Nature becomes "a fantastic pageantry, a parade of masques and
costumes and guildlike mysteries." "Nature gleams secretly with a most
fantastic shimmer of words and social relationship" (379). In an earlier
discussion of imagination Burke had definitely rejected the view that
poetry gives us any kind of truth or knowledge (*GM*, 225). Aesthetics is
dismissed as a typical product of modern idealistic philosophies, and the
earlier underestimation of "imagination" is endorsed. Romantic theories
of imagination "took a momentous step away from the understanding of
art as action and towards a lame attempt to pit art against science as a
'truer kind of truth'" (226). Art with Burke cannot be distinguished
from persuasion, from rhetoric, and has really no relation to reality. It
is the invention of a system of symbolism, a view which seems similar to
Ernst Cassirer's concept expounded in *The Philosophy of Symbolic Forms*.
But Burke himself remarks on the difference between his and Cassirer's
view: Cassirer's is epistemic, "scientific"—Cassirer thinks of symbolic

myth, language, and the categories of the mind as instruments of knowledge, while Burke returns to an older tradition in which things and
words are identified (*LSA*, 23). This is further clarified in a paper, "A
Dramatic View of the Origins of Language," where the "negative" is
considered a "peculiarly linguistic resource" (419). One remains unconvinced if one reflects that a suckling at his mother's breast refusing further milk can make a prelinguistic gesture of refusal, can say "no"
without the use of language. The linguistic realism taught by Burke
implies also skepticism, probabilism, relativism, or what he calls "perspectivism" (very different from what is meant by the term in either
Ortega y Gasset or in my own writings), which has been noted as a quality
of "imperviousness," for instance, by Benjamin De Mott (in Rueckert,
Critical Responses, 361). I shall not, however, doubt Burke's strong commitment to social and political causes, nor his intense sense of the biological foundations of human life, even though they are most frequently
in his writings absorbed into a language system seen allegorically and
punningly. But Burke's perspectivism, or "comic frame" (a version of
"romantic irony" mediated by Thomas Mann, whom Burke translated
and greatly admired), leads to an occasionalism which denies causality
and attacks the scientific world order. It leads to his denial of any sense
of the correctness of interpretation, to his advocacy of a complete liberty
of interpretation, to the acceptance of a universal symbolism in which,
as in Emerson's or Carlyle's kindred versions, "every hose fits every hydrant" (W3:37; W4:121). It must lead also to an indifference to strictly
aesthetic values and hierarchies as well as to an unhistorical view of
literature, which is treated as existing simultaneously, outside of time, in
spite of some excursions into Marxist or Spenglerian periodizations.
Blackmur's charge that Burke's method can "be applied with equal fruitfulness to Shakespeare, Dashiell Hammett, or Marie Corelli" (*Language
as Gesture* [1982], 393) was admitted by Burke to be true, though he
defended his procedure by saying that "you can't properly put Marie
Corelli and Shakespeare apart until you have first put them together"
(*PLF*, 302), a good defense of a general theory of literary creation which
would be valid if Burke would ever put Shakespeare and Marie Corelli
apart. But he has no interest in doing so: he equalizes texts of the most
diverse aesthetic value and historical provenience, flitting without a sense
of distinction from Aeschylus to Odets, from Shakespeare to William
Carlos Williams, using texts as pretexts for his speculations. In his theory,
literature becomes absorbed into a scheme of linguistic action or rhetoric
so all-embracing and all-absorbing that poetry as an art is lost sight of
and the work of art is spun into a network of allusions, puns, and clusters

of images without any regard for its wholeness or unity. Art perishes and one wonders what the grand drama is for. By an odd reversal Burke can disparage language and literature: he can say, on the one hand, that "the mind is largely a linguistic product" (*PLF,* 163), that "life is a poem" (*SC,* 254), but, on the other hand, he can tell us that a "headache is more 'authentic' than a great tragedy" (76–77), or that "the meanest life is superior to the noblest poem" (x). In Burke extremes meet easily. All distinctions fall. The laws of evidence have ceased to function. He moves in a self-created verbal universe where everything may mean everything else.

15: YVOR WINTERS (1900–1968)

YVOR WINTERS tells us, in his last and longest book, *Forms of Discovery* (1967), that "the time has come when my faithful reader may as well face certain facts, no matter how painful the experience: namely, that I know a great deal about the art of poetry, theoretically, historically, and practically" (*FD*, 346). We should grant this without feeling pain. Winters has for decades propounded a view of poetry which can be described easily, for he has stated it repeatedly in clear terms. Poetry is "a statement in words about a human experience" (*DR*, 11). It is a rational statement, for words are concepts, but it differs from a statement of a purely philosophical or theoretical nature in having "a controlled content of feeling" (363). Each word, besides its conceptual content, has a feeling-content which the poet manipulates by adjusting concept to feeling, or, as Winters formulates it, "motive" to "emotion" (365). Translated into more familiar terms, also used by Winters on occasion, poetry uses denotative words, concepts, and arguments in order to generate connotations which induce feelings, attitudes, and ultimately elicit judgments. Stated in this manner, the theory amounts to something well known: art, while making a statement about reality, true or false, embodies and induces an emotion which is "specific and unparaphrasable" (*CH*, 305 = *DR*, 20 "particular and unparaphrasable"). But unlike similar theories such as Eliot's or Coleridge's about a unity of thought and feeling, Winters insists that this unity is achieved by an act of moral judgment (*DR*, 370) and not by an act of the imagination. Winters tells us over and over again that "ethical interest is the only poetic interest, for the reason that all poetry deals with one kind or another of human experience and is valuable in proportion to the justice with which it evaluates that experience" (505). Winters calls this theory "for lack of a better term ... moralistic" (3). This moralism, however, is not ordinary didacticism. "Moral" is used by him in a very wide sense: often it means discrimination, a sense of truth and falsehood and not only a sense of right and wrong. Poetry is thus a "technique of contemplation" [or "an act of meditation" (491)] which should "increase the intelligence and strengthen the moral temper" (*CH*, 317 = *DR*, 29). In 1929 Winters went so far as to say that "the basis of Evil is in emotion; Good rests in the power of rational selection in action." He agrees with the Stoics that the end of man is a "controlled and harmonious life," that the "greatest possible degree of consciousness" is desirable, and that the arts provide "a profoundly difficult emotional discipline" (*UER*, 221–23).

Criticism is a judgment of the judgment pronounced by the poem. It will and must appeal to constant principles, to some fundamental concept of good and evil. In 1929 he stated that "the belief that such a concept can rest only on divine revelation seems to me unfounded." An ethic "not parasitic on religion" was, after all, elaborated by Aristotle, and if this is naturalism, so be it (*UER*, 220). But later, in the foreword to *In Defense of Reason* (1947), Winters recognized that "my absolutism implies a theistic position, unfortunate as this admission may be" (*DR*, 14). "The primary function of criticism is" thus "evaluation." "Unless criticism succeeds in providing a usable system of evaluation it is worth very little" (*FC*, 17). Not only can we state the difference between art and non-art but within the canon the critic must be able to decide that this poem is better than that one, that this stanza, this line, this metaphor, and even this word is better than an alternative. Ranking is Winters's main and, among American critics, almost unique preoccupation. The law is laid down with a tone of finality. No appeal is possible, though once Winters makes a modest disclaimer that he "personally has free access to these absolutes and that his own judgments are final" (*DR*, 10). Once also he doubts that the verdict of the critic can be "communicated precisely, since it consists in receiving from the poet his own final and unique judgment of his matter and in judging that judgment" (372). But usually there are no such reservations. Still, Winters tries to buttress his view with arguments: by setting them off from other theories, by illustrating them with examples, and by an elaborate scheme of a history of English poetry.

Winters defends his theory against obvious alternatives. He rejects ordinary didacticism on the grounds that "the paraphrasable content of the work is never equal to the work" (*DR*, 4) and that a moral can be stated much better in straightforward prose. For instance, he chides Vernon L. Parrington for "neglecting the quality of feeling with which the paraphrasable content is stated . . . neglecting, that is, the final and irreducible act of judgment which gives the poem its essential poetic identity" (559–60). American humanism is considered a version of didacticism which fails to see that "the *poetic* content inheres in the feeling, the style, the untranslatable, and can be reduced to no formula save itself " (*UER*, 224).

Winters also rejects hedonism, the view that art is pleasure or gives intensity to our experience, and he has no use for the theory he considers specifically romantic: the view that art is self-expression. "The poet, in creating, must lose himself in his object" (*UER*, 198). He must be impersonal, for indulgence in personal emotion leads to mannerism, to subservience to every impulse, and finally to automatism and even madness: all vices which Winters considers inherent in romanticism. With equal ease Winters disposes of mimesis. The "doctrine of imitation unmistakably collapses, for poetry is composed of words, which are primarily abstractions" (*DR*, 522), an objection which hardly touches the problem of the representation of reality in literature, which is done, admittedly, by words. Similarly, Winters disposes of catharsis: in the interpretation of Ransom (which is that of Bernays) catharsis would make poetry "contemptible," make it "an obscure form of self-indulgence." Aristotle, we are told, "should have done better" (553).

Elsewhere, however, Winters proclaims his adherence to the Aristotelian ethical tradition (*UER*, 222), particularly as restated by Thomas Aquinas, who, according to Winters, has "composed . . . the most thorough and defensible moral and philosophical system, in all likelihood, that the world has known" (*DR*, 374–75). But we must not label Winters an Aristotelian or Thomist. He expressly tells us that he is not a "Christian" (408), and he voices sharp disagreement with the aesthetics of such Neo-Thomists as Maritain and Gilson (*FD*, xii).

In practice Winters cannot avoid the pitfalls against which he has warned. He constantly discusses the paraphrasable content of a poem, he cannot avoid drawing inferences from the character of the poetry to that of the poet, and he must refer to the reality represented in poetry, judging, for instance, the accuracy of an image or a description, often very acutely (for example, the remarks on Tate's jaguar [*DR*, 530–31] or the rattlesnake in a poem by Alan Stephens [*FD*, 341]. But Winters always objects to a deterministic view of the relations between work and author, author and time. He coined the term "the fallacy of expressive, or imitative, form" (*DR*, 41) for the view that a chaotic life must be expressed in chaotic form or that a chaotic subject or a chaotic time requires correspondingly chaotic poetry. Winters traces this view to a saying of Henry Adams (414, also 497n.), but he knows that it is implied in the notion of *Zeitgeist*. He considers it a consequence of the doctrine of organic form (453), which he equates with determinism à la Taine (482) and with "the notion that the subject, or the language, or the oversoul, or something else operates freely through the poet, who is merely a passive medium" (585), surely a misunderstanding of the original idea derived from Aristotle.

Nowhere does Winters consider more sophisticated theories of the function of art: he seems entirely ignorant of the main, largely German tradition of modern aesthetics, partly because he simply dismisses the problem of a common core of the arts (*DR*, 518; *FD*, xii) and partly because he misunderstands the argument of aesthetics as an argument for "art for art's sake," for pure hedonism. He refuses to see the problem of "semblance," "illusion," "aesthetic distance," or whatever we may call it: he comments on Eliot's term "autotelic" (*DR*, 461ff.) and on Ransom's distinction (derived from Croce) between "a practical and an aesthetic stage" (508) so obtusely that one must conclude him unaware of the whole issue.

Still, whatever the limitations of the theory, it allows Winters to make distinctions of critical value. Particularly in his first book, *Primitivism and Decadence* (1937), Winters attempts a classification and ranking of types of poetry by an acute analysis of techniques. He draws the distinctions from Kenneth Burke's *Counter-Statement* but uses them for his purposes of evaluation, while Burke, as Winters immediately recognized, has lost "the power of judgment" and ends in complete relativism (*DR*, 74). Winters distinguishes several methods or techniques of poetry: the method of repetition, condemned; the logical and the narrative method, both approved; the method of "pseudo-reference," for example, the reference to a nonexistent plot (46), or to a nonexistent symbolic value (47), or a nonexistent or obscure principle of motivation (51). A fifth type is called "qualitative progression," by which Winters (and Burke) mean mere associative sequences, for instance, the stream of consciousness. And finally the "Double Mood," which includes anticlimax and romantic irony. The latter confess a "state of moral insecurity" (70) and hence are a "vice of feeling" (88).

This classification allows Winters to assign modern, English, and American poets to different types and evaluate them according to one standard: does the poem make a rational statement, convey its meaning with feeling, and judge it as a moral experience (not, of course, as "an abstraction from experience but a concentration of experience")? "The universality of its scale of emotional reference is," Winters assumes, "pretty much in proportion to the degree in which one *cannot* draw from it abstract conclusions" (*UER*, 264). A distinction between the category of universality, which remains concrete as in Hegel, and generality, which is abstract, is drawn here, though hardly ever properly defended and elaborated. As the poem is conceived as a statement of the author, responsible, direct, and serious, Winters objects to everything "dramatic," that is, to any imitation of a different or inferior intelligence than the author's. In discussing fiction he argues—long before Wayne Booth's *Rhetoric of Fiction*—against the theory of the novel propounded by Flaubert and Henry James that "the author should write wholly from within the minds of his characters" (*DR*, 38). Winters considers this a "superstition" which he feels is reduced to absurdity in Hemingway's short stories about prizefighters and bullfighters, though he admits that the damage is mitigated in Flaubert by the subtlety of his style, and in James by the high development of the characters, who become all but indistinguishable from the author himself (39).

Winters comments perceptively on James's acute moral sense, which James tests in situations that give his characters the greatest possible freedom: a justification for James's preference for millionaires and princes. But Winters finds in James a central obscurity, a "development of the feeling in excess of the motive" (*DR*, 327), and objects to James's ambiguity. Our final attitude toward Chad Newsome in *The Ambassadors* and to Owen Gareth in *The Spoils of Poynton* remains unresolved. "This," he comments strikingly, "may not be untrue to life, but it is untrue to art, for a work of art is an evaluation, a judgment, of an experience" (334). In short, we are told, James "had too much moral sense, but was insufficiently a moralist." Still, Winters considers him "the greatest novelist in English" (336).

In spite of the lavish praise for James's power of characterization, "the vast crowd of unforgettable human beings whom he created" (*DR*, 342), Winters concludes surprisingly by exalting Edith Wharton's *Age of Innocence* as "the finest single flower of Jamesian art" and *The Valley of Decision* as "superior to any single work by James" (342), making it by implication the greatest work of English fiction. Edith Wharton appeals to Winters because she "gives greater precision to her moral issues than James is able to achieve" (310), though, with the exception of the two novels praised, he finds her "mediocre when she is not worse" (342). The earnest Winters simply disapproves of any ambiguity, irony, and obscurity in motivation and moral judgment, and even of anything dramatic if it means representing a mentality inferior to the author's.

This is apparently the main objection to drama itself. One has the impression that Winters did not care for the theater at all. He disparages actors and acting with comic violence (*FC*, 85; *FD*, 127): "In general I think the world would be well enough off without actors." He discusses

Macbeth, "the greatest play with which I am acquainted and a great work of literature" (*FC,* 55), to show that the flaws of the play are due to the medium. In depicting Macbeth's crime and his growing realization of its consequences, Shakespeare is compelled to have Macbeth speak in stages of obtuseness and unawareness, of imperfect intelligence, and thus to write inferior poetry, rising to great poetry only in the speech beginning "Tomorrow, and tomorrow, and tomorrow" (27–28). Winters can assert, with some complacency, that "the novel in our time is nearly dead" and that the drama is so completely (39). As the epic is a dead form which will never be revived (46), only the lyric or, as he prefers to call it, "the short poem" survives and has a future. "This form is the greatest form" (74), Winters declares. Next to it, Winters admires "literary" historiography because it narrates and judges morally: Hume, Gibbon, Macaulay above all, and the Americans Motley, Prescott, Parkman, and Henry Adams's *History of the United States during the Administration of Thomas Jefferson and James Madison.* Winters dismisses Carlyle: "the less said about Carlyle the better" (*DR,* 422n.) and never even alludes to any historian writing in another language. Winters has some shrewd things to say about his favorite historians, and the praise of Adams is generous even though it seems doubtful that he "introduces a new style and an entirely new conception of historiography" (422) or that the *History* could be ranked "the greatest historical work in English" (415). Adams's "curiosity about psychological motives" (422), his skill of portraiture, was hardly a novelty in the 1880s.

Winters's main interest is, however, lyrical poetry in England and America from Wyatt to his own disciples. Besides, he was greatly interested in French poetry from Baudelaire to Valéry. Baudelaire is praised early (1930) as "beyond much doubt, one of the two or three chief sources of a truly humane discipline to be found in the last two centuries" (*CH,* 330). Winters deplores the survival of romanticism in Baudelaire but thinks that precisely "his knowledge of the essential viciousness of Romanticism, combined with whatever he retained of his Catholic training, seems to have given him the extraordinary insight into tragic weakness which is the matter of his great poems. Whatever the flaws of the book [*Les Fleurs du mal*] as a whole, it is a great book; and it contains some of the greatest poems ever written" (*FC,* 63). Winters is willing to name them: they are "Les Petites Vieilles," "Le Goût du néant," and "Le Mort joyeux" (*FD,* 188). Winters praises also Rimbaud and Mallarmé as "far more talented poets than Blake" (*FC,* 68). The only extended comment on a poem is a discussion of Mallarmé's "L'Après-Midi d'un faune" as an example of change of method by the use of "two distinct sets of

alternating movements" (*UER*, 255–56). But Winters reserved his greatest praise for Valéry, particularly "Le Cimetière marin" and "Ebauche
d'un serpent," which seem to him "the two greatest short poems ever
written" (*FC*, 63). Winters prefers the second poem and makes a careful
paraphrase of its argument, though one may doubt whether one can
state the theme as the "most inclusive of tragic themes: one might describe it as the theme of tragedy" (65). Allen Tate is clearly right when
he objects that "what Winters describes as the theme of tragedy seems
to me to be merely the historic paradox of imperfection and evil" (*Memoirs
and Opinions* [1975], 137). "Ebauche d'un serpent" borrows "something
from the dramatic method and something from the associationists, without sacrificing the essential form of the short poem, that of exposition,
or its essential virtue, the most intelligent writing possible" (*FC*, 66).
"Ebauche d'un serpent," he concludes, is "in my opinion . . . the greatest
poem which I have ever read, regardless of kind" (74). One wonders at
this certainty.

Winters never discusses any German, Italian, Spanish, or Russian poet
or novelist, unless we take seriously his easy dismissal of Goethe and all
German poetry by quoting two lines—"O Erd! O Sonne! O Glück! O
Lust!"—from "Mailied," a very early poem dating from 1771, as "suffi-
ciently typical of a race, but as poetry . . . negligible" (*UER*, 193). Once
he disparages the allegory of the panther in the first canto of Dante's
Inferno (*FC*, 45) as "a very mild embodiment of lust." The remark appears
in the context of a wholesale rejection of allegory, particularly of *The
Faerie Queene* (44), while elsewhere the allegorizing of Hawthorne and
Melville is considered a fault of these otherwise admired writers. *Moby
Dick*, we are told, is rather an epic poem than a novel (*DR*, 219), surprising praise from Winters, who otherwise dismisses the epic: neither
the *Cid* nor the *Song of Roland* nor even the *Aeneid* and the *Iliad* impress
him (*FC*, 41–42), and *Paradise Lost* is several times disparaged. "It requires more than a willing suspension of disbelief to read most of Milton:
it requires a willing suspension of intelligence" (43).

By far the bulk of Winters's writing is devoted to the lyric and to a
history of the lyric in England and the United States. It is critical history,
most fully (though also most dogmatically) stated in his last book, *Forms
of Discovery*, but sketched out very early. Winters aims at a complete trans-
valuation of values buttressed by a theory of intellectual history. It will
be best to give a survey of Winters's view following the chronology of
English and American poetry. Winters only alludes to Chaucer and other
medieval poets. He has no admiration for medieval society in spite of
his interest in Thomas Aquinas. He criticizes Henry Adams's glorifica-

tion of the thirteenth century as "merely a version of the Romantic Golden Age" (*DR*, 411). He rejects the whole idea of a *Zeitgeist,* of the representativeness of great minds for a period. Selecting Dante and Thomas Aquinas is as false as selecting Dewey and Bertrand Russell for ours: we could choose Gilson, Maillol, and Valéry and would come up with a very different spirit (487). Thus Winters's history of English poetry moves, at first at least, *in vacuo*: it is a series of comments on individual authors and poems. Winters requires that a historian of poetry should be able to find "the best poems" (*FC*, 197) and goes resolutely about to do so.

The story begins with Thomas Wyatt, who established the tradition of the English short poem in plain style: often proverbial, logical, expository, aphoristic (*FD*, 3). Winters sees Wyatt as reacting against the "courtly, ornate, aureate, sugared, or Petrarchan" style (8), though one could argue that much of Wyatt consists in free paraphrases from Petrarch and his Italian and French followers. According to Winters the early plain style culminates in George Gascoigne. Gascoigne's "Woodmanship" is his greatest poem (17), but also Sir Walter Raleigh and Thomas Nashe belong to this plain tradition, which Winters considers greatly superior to the Petrarchan movement leading up to Sidney and Spenser. In a review of C. S. Lewis's *English Literature in the Sixteenth Century,* Winters chides Lewis for underrating the poetry Lewis had labelled "Drab." "Lewis simply has not discovered what poetry is" (*FC,* 197). He "sees the entire poetry of the period in terms of a Romantic prejudice: he likes the pretty so profoundly that he overlooks the serious" (195). Sidney and Spenser are the "pretty" poets: "their sensitivity to language is greatly in excess of their moral intelligence" (*FD*, 28). They suffer from "the taint of decadence, of decoration, of means in excess of matter" (28). Spenser's "Epithalamium"—"the only one of his poems that appears in any measure to justify his reputation"—"lacks weight and intellectual concentration, and it has little of the moral grandeur, the grandeur of intellectual substance and personal character to be found in Gascoigne and Raleigh" (29). Winters simply detests what Pound called the *fioritura* of the Elizabethans. Only short "airs" are exempt, though they are slight and trivial. The plain style, in the later Elizabethan age, culminates in Fulke Greville and Ben Jonson. They are the two greatest masters of the short poem in the Renaissance (44). Winters sees "a greater density of intellectual content in [Greville's] work than in the work of any other poet of the Renaissance" (52). Ben Jonson is the master stylist of the plain tradition, a "classicist in the best sense" (63), in whom he finds "an exact correlation between motive and feeling," an integrity and nobility unmatched elsewhere (64).

Compared with Greville and Jonson, Shakespeare in his *Sonnets* and Donne seem eccentrics to Winters. Shakespeare succumbed to excessive and uncontrolled sensibility. Donne had a sophisticated ingenuity which Winters dislikes. Like Ransom, Winters dissects some of Shakespeare's sonnets and finds them obscure, sentimental, full of vague feeling, while Donne's poems suffer from naive violence and purely arbitrary decoration, which puts them rather in the tradition of Sidney than in the anti-Petrarchan movement which Donne is usually considered to head. The metaphysical conceit is seen as an outgrowth of Petrarchism. But Winters has no sympathy for Donne's sensibility: he calls him "a man of harsh and often of imperceptive temperament. He is given to overdramatizing himself, even to the point of dismal melodrama. He is oversexed, neurotically so" (*FD*, 74). Winters ridicules "The Canonization" for its extravagant figures and comments: "I am not interested in the petulant conversation of Donne or of any other man, and I see no reason why Donne should have to inflict his on me in order to prove his sincerity" (76). Winters forgets that he is dealing with a poem and not with the record of a conversation. Mysteriously, Donne is still considered a great poet.

Winters deals more briefly with the other seventeenth-century poets: he prefers Edward Lord Herbert of Cherbury to his brother George. "Church Monuments" is the one poem of George Herbert that he admires greatly, but otherwise he finds him marred by "a cloying and almost infantile pietism" (*FD*, 88). Crashaw is distasteful. Winters detests the confusion of religiosity and sexuality, particularly in the "greatly overestimated" "Hymn to Saint Teresa" (92). In Vaughan, Winters admires two poems, "The Lamp" and "To His Books." "The last eleven and a half lines" of this poem, Winters declares with his usual assurance, "are certainly among the greatest in our poetry" (102), but "The Retreat" remains "a kind of sentimental fantasy" (103). Surprisingly, Winters is cool to Marvell: "The Horatian Ode" is "a kind of newsletter for the year" (103). "To His Coy Mistress" is "an exceptionally brilliant academic exercise on a set theme, but it is no more than that" (104). Only "The Garden" is praised, though the supposed pantheism puzzles Winters, who has no use for nature-worship.

This leaves Winters with Milton. "L'Allegro" and "Il Penseroso" are full of platitudes, and proceed by "lazy associationism" (*FD*, 119), and in *Lycidas* the rational structure is decaying toward association. Milton—

though Winters recognizes that the doctrine was not yet current (123)—
prepares the fatal turn of English poetry: the surrender to associationism
and sentimentalism.

Up to the end of the seventeenth century, Winters proceeds strictly by
his method of anthologizing, which suffices to define two main poetic
traditions: the plain style and the ornate style. While he recognizes some
crossings and combinations (FD, 123), Winters, in general, downgrades
the ornate "Italian" tradition, Sidney, Spenser, and Milton, in favor of
the tradition of the plain style extending from Wyatt to Dryden. At this
point in history Winters shifts ground and propounds a historical explanation for the decline of English poetry in the eighteenth and nineteenth
centuries. Unlike Eliot's "dissociation of sensibility" or the theories of the
baleful influence of scientism and rationalism, Winters ascribes the decline to two definite causes: associationism, which destroyed the earlier
rational structure of poetry, and sentimentalism, which treated "impulse
. . . with respect" and "reason with suspicion" (124). This doctrine "de-
prives the poet at a stroke of his proper subject matter, which is the
understanding of human nature." "More than two thousand years of
ethical and psychological study were thrown away" (124). The view then
prevailed "that ideas can be expressed in sense-perceptions" (125). The
natural object becomes the adequate poetic symbol. Associationism necessarily dissolves the structure of poetry. "One can scarcely depend
wholly on imagery without employing the structure of revery" (125).
Hence the term "Age of Reason" is a gross misnomer: "The reasoning
of the Age of Reason was very largely directed toward the destruction
of the authority of Reason" (DR, 450–51). Eighteenth-century poetry is
not "bad because too intellectual"; "in reality, eighteenth-century poetry
is commonly good and is often great but displays defects which are primarily due to intellectual deficiency" (451). Pope, however, is praised as
"one of the most exquisitely finished, as well as one of the most profoundly moving, poets in English" (138), though the Essay on Man contains "nonsense and sentimentalism" (451n.), "inept deism," and displays
only an "inability to think" (488). Winters loves to make discoveries.
Charles Churchill, though not totally unknown, is his for the eighteenth
century. The "Dedication to Bishop Warburton" is proclaimed "the
greatest English poem of the eighteenth century and one of the greatest
in our language" (FD, 145), praise that even the detailed comment cannot
quite make comprehensible. It is purely personal and very local, as is the
other poem, The Candidate, admired by Winters (DR, 139; also FD, 130).
The associative method expressly defended by Churchill in an admiring
reference to Sterne's doctrine of digression (quoted by Winters, FD, 128–

29) should presumably be counted against him, but his moral indigna-
tion, his "exhibition of the psychology of evil" (*FD*, 144) overrides all
other considerations.

Dr. Johnson's imitations of Juvenal are dismissed as "very dull reading"
(*FD*, 151) but the prologues to *Comus* and to *A Word to the Wise* are praised
highly. Winters knows that Johnson "had nothing but contempt for
deism, yet his style," he assserts, "shows the influence of deism" (*DR*,
451). "These poems are the work of a great genius employing a decadent
language" (451), "decadent" apparently meaning here "stereotyped" and
"sentimental," qualities considered the effect of deism, which is, by definition, sentimental and abstract.

The decadence is clearly evident in Collins and Gray. Winters criticizes
the "Ode to Evening" for bad syntax, soft clichés, and an unconvincing
moral (*FD*, 152–53). Gray's "Elegy" is trounced for monotony and sentimentality and the bad writing of the epitaph. "The sentimental and
conceited poet, the affected dandy, is an intrusion" (156; cf. *FC*, 21).

Winters sees no radical break with the coming of romanticism: it grows
out of the sentimentalism and associationism of the eighteenth century.
"Blake and Wordsworth broke the somewhat narrow frame of this early
romanticism by freeing new emotions, mainly the obscurely prophetic"
(*DR*, 452). Blake, however, is a false prophet: "his beliefs [are] so foolish
that I could not be moved by any statement of them" (*FD*, 161). "The
Tyger" is "a remarkable fusion of genius and foolishness; it is astonishing
but is not great." "We have, in brief, a great deal of tiger, with no explanation of why he is there" (162). The "Introduction" to *The Songs of
Experience* is an "invitation to humanity to throw off the shackles of intellect and law, and to free the true God," but it rests "on a precise
inversion not only of Christian mythology, which perhaps does not matter,
but of Christian morality as well" (*DR*, 178). It is "an exhortation to what
for most of us is vicious nonsense" (*FD*, 163). "London" implies the same
creed of anarchy. Thus "it is foolish to speak of Blake as a great poet;
he is a talented poet who wasted his talent on his delusions of grandeur"
(167).

Wordsworth does not come off any better. "He is a very bad poet who
nevertheless wrote a few good lines" (*FD*, 167). As Winters had no use
for pantheism or nature-worship or prophecy or for Miltonic grandilo-
quence, nothing remains for praise except an isolated verse such as "the
unimaginable touch of Time" (169–70). Winters cannot believe that
"Wordsworth's passions were charmed away by a look at the daffodils"
(*DR*, 369). "The evening is not like a nun" (*FD*, 168), he protests, and
the river Thames "does not glide at its own sweet will, and this is very

fortunate for London; the river glides according to the law of gravita-
tion." "Insufferably pretentious," "arrant nonsense," "pompous pseudo-
piety" are some of the epithets hurled at Wordsworth in a chapter which
culminates in calling Wordsworth "a comical figure except for the appalling fact that he has been preserved in amber (or something) by (and
with) a good many scholars and critics for more than a century" (172).

Coleridge, we shall not be surprised to hear, is "merely one of the
indistinguishably bad poets of an unfortunate period" (*FD*, 175). *The
Rime of the Ancient Mariner* is "a story for children with a Sunday-School
moral attached" (173). Attempts to read into it profundities are mistaken.
Kubla Khan glorifies the idea of the poet as an inspired madman. "It is
a foolish idea: if poets have any value, it is because of their superior
intelligence, not because of their flashing eyes and floating hair" (174).

In Shelley "one can find no single poem that is not weak or worse in
conception and predominantly bad in execution" (*FD*, 178). Winters cannot believe that Shelley's "passions . . . were aroused by the sight of the
leaves blown about in the autumn wind" (*DR*, 369). Keats fares no better.
"There is almost no intellect in or behind the poems; the poems are
adolescent in every respect" (*FD*, 179). The "Ode on a Grecian Urn"
"ends in magniloquent nonsense" (180). Byron is dismissed as "amusing
but shallow" (172–73). Winters dislikes the destruction of a mood by
anticlimax, of which Byron was the first popular practitioner (*DR*, 65).
For Winters poetry must come straight.

The condemnation of the English romantic poets is violent but perfunctory. The case against their American contemporaries is argued
more closely and seriously. Emerson is Winters's main *bête noire*: he takes
the place of Babbitt's Rousseau. Winters considers his doctrines the acme
of romantic foolishness. His doctrine of submission to emotion, his idea
of equivalence which renders man an automaton and paralyzes genuine
action, is considered "romantic amoralism" (*DR*, 267–68) which corrupted the whole course of American civilization and poetry. Winters
selects passages from the essays and poems which he interprets as defense
of complete caprice, thoroughgoing relativism, and foolish optimism
(578ff.). Emerson's poetry "deals not with the experience, but with his
own theory of the experience: it is not mystical poetry but gnomic, or
didactic, poetry, and as the ideas expounded will not stand inspection,
the poetry is ultimately poor in spite of a good deal of vigorous phrasing"
(279).

The onslaught on Edgar Allan Poe as a "bad writer accidentally and
temporarily popular" (*DR*, 234) follows as a matter of course. Winters

scores Poe's ignorance and vulgar sentimentality. The critical doctrine is easily refuted, though Winters overshoots the mark when he accuses Poe of reducing poetry to a "position of triviality" (241). In intention at least, Poe's notion of "supernal beauty" is far from trivial. "The Philosophy of Composition" is "a singularly shocking document." It is "an effort to establish the rules for a species of incantation, of witchcraft" (248). We need not rehearse Winters's view of Poe's poetry. Only "The City in the Sea" escapes condemnation (251, 253). Winters's conclusion that "Poe is no more a mystic than a moralist; he is an excited sentimentalist" or, better, "an explicit obscurantist" (246) is predictable.

It seems hardly worthwhile to repeat what Winters has to say about the best-known English and American poets of the second half of the century. Tennyson "has nothing to say, and his style is insipid" (FD, 181); Browning is "fresh, brisk, shallow, and journalistic" (182); Arnold "sentimental to the point of being lachrymose" (183). Swinburne wrote "no poems that will endure serious reading" (185). In America, Whitman is condemned as "utterly lacking in literary talent" (315). He illustrates the fallacy of expressive form. He tried "to express a loose America by writing loose poetry" (DR, 62). "He had no capacity for any feeling save of the cloudiest and most general kind" (91) and he is, of course, derived from Emerson (578).

Of all the later nineteenth-century poets only Gerard Manley Hopkins receives separate treatment and close reading. Winters is interested in the theory of sprung rhythm but decides after some discussion that it is "quite foolish" and that it led to "deformations of language which are nearly unpronounceable and are often ridiculous" (FC, 123). Hopkins's spiritual struggle remains obscure: "There is in a large portion of his verse an element of emotional violence which is neither understood nor controlled" (136). Though Winters admires many poems, he considers Hopkins as "very often an immoral poet" (141), apparently because he wanted to express his individuality and indulged in what Winters considers meaningless emotion. Discussing "The Windhover" and the diverse possible meanings of the key word "buckle," Winters concludes: "To describe a bird, however beautifully, and to imply that Christ is like him but greater, is to do very little toward indicating the greatness of Christ" (133). In an oddly personal passage, Winters speaks of his breeding of airedales and states his preference for a dog over a bird, brushing aside any "Romantic and sentimental feeling attached to birds as symbols of the free and unrestrained spirit" or any appeal to a "sacramental view of nature," which seems to him "merely foolish" (133–34). One must object that birds such as eagles and falcons antedate romanticism considerably as symbols of power and grace. Hopkins, Winters concludes, is overrated. He is a minor good poet.

Winters exhumed two American poets for whom he makes great claims, Jones Very, a mystic, and Fredrick Goddard Tuckerman. Very is pronounced to be as excellent as Blake, or Traherne, or George Herbert (*DR*, 269). His genuine mysticism and moralism is set against Emerson's sentimentalism (279). The enthusiasm for Tuckerman focuses on one poem, "The Cricket," which Winters declares "the greatest poem in English of the century, and one of the greatest in English" (*FD*, 263). It reminds him of Baudelaire; it is "a greater poem than [Wallace Stevens's] *Sunday Morning*" (259). The lines:

> Behold! the autumn goes,
> The shadow grows,
> The moments take hold of eternity,

are called "one of the greatest passages in our poetry" (262), though, to my ear, they sound like derivative Wordsworth, and the whole poem like an inferior "Ode to a Nightingale." It is not clear why Tuckerman's sensibility is supposed to be "related to that of Valéry" (261).

"The eighteenth and nineteenth centuries were low periods in the history of English poetry" is Winters's conviction. A turn for the better came, however, in the later part; in France, with Baudelaire, and independently in America and England. Emily Dickinson is the admired herald, the greatest American writer except Melville: "one of the greatest lyric poets of all time" (*DR*, 299). Not that Winters does not see her faults: "silly playfulness" (284), "obscurity" (287), "brisk facility" (296), lack of "taste" (298), and lack of contact with educated "tradition." "She was almost purely a primitive—not as the American Indians are primitives, but as Grandma Moses was a primitive" (*FD*, 266). Winters selects a few poems conveying nostalgia or suggesting the experience of dying for their "intense strangeness" (*DR*, 293ff.) but emphasizes that she was not a mystic nor did she think of herself as one (288). Using Eliot's formula, Winters thinks that "in the best lines sense-perception and concept are simultaneous; there is neither ornament nor explanation, and neither is needed" (*FD*, 270).

Thomas Hardy is compared to Emily Dickinson: he is essentially naive, a primitive of remarkable genius (*FD*, 189). Winters obviously does not care for his doctrines and must disapprove of his determinism, which he considers "mythic and animistic" rather than scientific (*DR*, 27).

Two English poets of the turn of the century are in Winters's view the inheritors of the great tradition: Robert Bridges and T. Sturge Moore. Bridges's "best poems display a kind of passionate intellectuality, comparable to nothing else in English so much as the great poems of Fulke Greville, Ben Jonson, and George Herbert" (*FD,* 194). The poem "Low Barometer" is praised with superlatives which seem to cancel themselves. "In my opinion there is nothing greater in English poetry and there is little as great" (197). Winters prefers the poem even to his favorites in Greville and Jonson: it is not dependent on Christianity and is hence "more nearly universal" (198). But the selection from Bridges made by Winters is very small. The bulk of his poetry seems to him "corrupted by the facile diction of the nineteenth century" (194). He disapproves of his metrical theories and considers the meter of *The Testament of Beauty* monotonous (*DR,* 146–47). Bridges represents for Winters "that type of poetry which displays at one and the same time the greatest possible distinction with the fewest possible characteristics recognizable as the marks of any particular school, period, or man; as, in brief, that type of poetry which displays the greatest polish of style and the smallest trace of mannerism" (82–83). One could call this neoclassicism, and Bridges and Moore are academic literary neoclassicists. Particularly Moore's *Daimonassa,* a blood-curdling play on a Greek theme which Winters calls "one of the greatest works in English" (*FD,* 239), and his poem "From Titian's Bacchanal in the Prado at Madrid," quoted in full by Winters (247–48), seem to me ultra-academic performances, mere poetic antiquarianism. Winters, however, reflects complacently: "If Bridges survives, he will have my talent to thank as well as his own, and I might never have been born" (324).

Winters speaks of all modern poetry as "post-Symbolist," presumably because he reserves the term "symbolist" for the French. He expressly denies it to W. B. Yeats: he doubts that Yeats had a sufficient command of French to read the prose of Mallarmé, let alone his verse (*FD,* 233), ignoring the intermediary Arthur Symons. Winters like Auden and Eliot is greatly bothered by the truth-value of Yeats's philosophical and political views. "The better one understands him, the harder it is to take him seriously" (205), Winters begins his devastating essay, which reviles the absurdity of Yeats's historical and psychological notions and ridicules his politics. Yeats wanted a "pseudo-18th century Ireland," with a landed gentry, reckless horsemen, gracious ladies, peasants staying in their place, and picturesque beggars (207–08). In discussing "Leda and the Swan" Winters raises common sense objections: he does not believe that sexual union is a form of mystical experience, nor that history proceeds in cycles of two thousand years, nor that the rape of Leda inaugurated a new cycle. "But no one save Yeats has ever believed these things, and we are not sure that Yeats really believed them" (212). Besides, "a question, if it is really a question, is a weak way in which to end a poem, for it leaves the subject of the poem unjudged" (211). "The Second Coming," Winters argues, approves of the beast and thus of brutality. "Among Schoolchildren" is ridiculed for its conclusion: "How can we know the dancer from the dance?" "If the dancer and the dance could not be discriminated in fact, the dancer could never have learned the dance" (220). Winters finds some merit in lesser-known poems but concludes that "it is impossible to believe that foolishness is greatness." Yeats's self-assertion, the bardic tone, the anti-intellectual drift of his work, its emotional heat, account for his success (234).

Winters launched a somewhat similar attack against the poetry of Robert Frost. Frost is "an Emersonian Romantic" (*FC*, 159), a "spiritual drifter" (the title of the essay, also 163) who believes in impulse and relativism, which has "resulted mainly in ill-natured eccentricity and in increasing melancholy" (162). Winters detests *The Masque of Reason*: he is appalled at Frost's "willful ignorance, at his smug stupidity" (176). He salvages a few poems but objects to whimsicality on the ground that "most of the world's great poetry has had to do with serious steps seriously taken, and when the seriousness goes from life, it goes from poetry" (166).

Seriousness, moral earnestness, is what appealed to Winters in Edward Arlington Robinson, to whom he devoted a small book (1946) and his very first essay for *Poetry* in 1922 (*UER*, 3–10). Winters deplores Robinson's Emersonian heritage but sees that the moralistic strain inherited from his New England background predominates (*R*, 18). He discusses Robinson's relations to Browning, Tennyson, and Praed, and deplores the prolixity and dryness of his longer poems. But Robinson's virtues—his "plain style, the rational statement, the psychological insight, the subdued irony, the high seriousness and the stubborn persistence"—particularly in some of the shorter poems, which Winters enumerates and grades with his usual assurance—"outweigh his defects" (146). Winters admires "the crisp meter of didactic poetry and the structure of formal exposition" in Robinson's best poems (21) as much as the implied view of the world: that "life is a very trying experience, to be endured only with pain and to be understood only with difficulty" (31). "The Wandering Jew" is praised because it is "rational in general structure, packed with thought in its detail, perfectly clear in its meaning and development, and nearly free from sensory imagery." It is "one of the great poems not only of our time but of our language" (37).

Winters calls Pound, Eliot, Wallace Stevens, William Carlos Williams, and Marianne Moore "the Experimental Generation" (DR, 104n.). He is highly critical of Pound. The Cantos proceed "from image to image wholly through the coherence of feeling" (57); they are "a blur of revery" (59), "wandering conversation" (145). Pound is "a sensibility without a mind, or with as little mind as is well possible" (496). Pound is "a man who is deeply moved by the sound of his own voice" (FD, 317). Winters acknowledges the charm of some details in the early Cantos but finds the bulk "insufferably dull." But Pound is "among the very few great translators in English" (DR, 494). Objections to the accuracy of his imitations do not disturb him (see FD, 352–54). But his relation to tradition remains whimsical: "that of one who has abandoned its method and pillaged its details—he is merely a barbarian on the loose in a museum" (DR, 480).

Eliot seems to Winters "inferior to Pound" as "Pound has a much better ear" (FD, 321). The early poems do not appeal to Winters, who dislikes all irony (DR, 88, 496). The Waste Land is Baudelairian, but Baudelaire controls his subject matter, whereas Eliot surrenders his form to his subject (497). The result is "confusion and journalistic reproduction of detail" (499). "Gerontion" seems to Winters Eliot's best poem (492); he sees it as "the most skillful modern poem in English to employ any large measure of pseudo reference" (87), ambiguous praise which implies the charge of obscurity due to "perhaps, the fallacy of imitative form: the attempt to express a state of uncertainty by uncertainty of expression" (87). Of the later poems only "Burnt Norton" is criticized. The first ten lines "are simple-minded profundities; then we come to the sad little clichés about the rose-garden, the rose-leaves, and the door never opened. . . . The language is that of discreet journalistic cliché and sentimentality. . . . The treatment is lazy and diffuse" (FD, 321). Quite gratuitously Winters considers Eliot's conversion "to have been merely nominal; at least, so far as one can judge from what Eliot has written, it really meant nothing at all" (DR, 501). This was published in 1943 when plenty of evidence to the contrary was available. But Winters then considered Eliot "the least interesting of the poets" of his generation (FD, 322).

Winters valued Wallace Stevens most highly of all recent American poets. In his very first essay on Robinson, Winters called Stevens "this greatest of living and of American poets" (UER, 10), at a time when Stevens had not yet published a single collection of poems. In Primitivism and Decadence (1937), Stevens is called "probably the greatest poet of his generation" (DR, 70), and in the long essay devoted to him in The Anatomy of Nonsense (1943), Winters calls "Sunday Morning" "probably the greatest

American poem of the twentieth century" and "certainly one of the greatest contemplative poems in English" (*DR*, 433, cf. 447). In *Forms of Discovery* the praise of his mastery of diction and meter is even greater: "In these respects, [Stevens is] fully the equal of Ben Jonson and the superior of Donne, Sidney, or the Shakespeare of the sonnets" (*FD*, 274). But this praise extends only to a few poems: "Sunday Morning," "The Course of a Particular," "Of the Manner of Addressing Clouds," and a few others. In the long essay and more succinctly in the section on Stevens in *Forms of Discovery*, Winters argues that Stevens was a hedonist, that hedonism leads to ennui, to romantic irony, to "laborious foolishness" and even to "willful nonsense" (*DR*, 445–46). Stevens is "released from all the restraints of Christianity, and is encouraged by all the modern orthodoxy of Romanticism: his hedonism is so fused with Romanticism as to be merely an elegant variation of that somewhat inelegant System of Thoughtlessness" (459). Winters is unimpressed by Stevens's doctrine of the imagination, borrowed from Coleridge. He points to the crucial difference: in Coleridge imagination is a link to transcendental reality, whereas in Stevens it is only a principle of order arbitrarily imposed by the poet (*FD*, 273). The later poetry of Stevens, almost everything after *Harmonium* (1931), seems to Winters inferior: he speaks of "the rapid and tragic decay of the poet's style" (*DR*, 433). Winters sympathizes with Stevens's central theme: "that there is no life after death, that man is isolated in time and space but in a universe of magnificent beauty" (*FD*, 273), though he refuses to draw Stevens's consequences, which seem to him, at most, a recommendation of art for art's sake, or worse, of self-indulgence, pleasure and play for their own sake.

William Carlos Williams elicited often contradictory opinions over the years. There is an early, rather ambiguous review of *Sour Grapes* in *Poetry* (1922; *UER*, 13–15), and in 1929 Williams is called "the most magnificent master of English and of human emotions since Thomas Hardy" (55). He has "a surer feeling for language than any other poet of his generation, save, perhaps, Stevens at his best" (*DR*, 93). He is "an experimental poet by virtue of his meter" but "in other qualities of his language one of the most richly traditional poets of the past hundred and fifty years," comparable, in this respect, to Hardy and Bridges (84). But in other contexts Winters comments harshly on Williams's encouraging "in his juniors . . . a sentimental debauchery of self-indulgence" (55). The late comments in *Forms of Discovery* are extremely hostile: Williams was "an uncompromising romantic" who believed in the surrender to emotion and to instinct. He believed in "organic form"—"a poem moves as a crab moves or grows as a cabbage grows" (*FD*, 318–19). "It is foolish to think of Williams as a great poet; the bulk of his work is not even readable. He is not even an anti-intellectual poet in any intelligible sense of the term, for he did not know what the intellect is. He was a foolish and ignorant man, but at moments a fine stylist" (319). Winters would want to salvage a few poems and surprisingly enough admired *The Destruction of Tenochtitlan*, a prose piece that he considers "superior to the prose of *Anabase* and of *Anna Livia Plurabelle*," "superior in all likelihood to nearly any other prose of our time and to most of the verse" (*DR*, 63, cf. 93–94). Williams's expository writing is, however, "largely incomprehensible" (93).

In the classification by generations of twentieth-century poets made by Winters (*DR*, 104n.), Hart Crane is listed with the last, "The Reactionary Generation," to which he belongs "solely by virtue of his dates, personal affiliations, and inability to write or understand free verse." Winters knew Crane, mainly in 1927, and corresponded with him for four years before a break caused by Winters's partly unfavorable review of *The Bridge* in *Poetry* in 1930 (36:153–65; reprinted in *UER*, 73–82). Winters admired Crane greatly but considered him the prime example of the corrupting influence of Emerson and Whitman logically leading to madness and suicide. Winters, in his usual anthologizing manner, isolates some lines of *The Bridge* as "the most magnificent passages of Romantic poetry in our language." The second of "The Voyages," Crane's "greatest poem" (*DR*, 92), seems to him "one of the most powerful and one of the most nearly perfect poems of the past two hundred years" (598). But Crane might be called "a saint of the wrong religion" (602), "a poet of great genius, who ruined his life and his talent by living and writing as the two greatest religious teachers of our nation [Emerson and Whitman] recommended" (598). Winters deplores his "intellectual confusion" (22), his vague mysticism, an appeal to "some vaguely apprehended but ecstatically asserted existence of a superior sort" (27), his identification of extinction and beatitude (45), and his reliance not on myth but on a feeling of "mythicalness" (52). Winters dislikes his dealing with death and immortality by calling the soil Pocahontas or "mistaking the Mississippi Valley for God" (592–93). Winters often finds Crane deliberately obscure, though in one case he misunderstood a passage flagrantly (42–43) and had to correct himself in the preface to *Maule's Curse* (153–55).

After Crane, who was Winters's contemporary, few poets elicit considered comments from Winters, though he likes to point out unknown or little regarded poets and to shower them with superlatives. The only recent English poet he admires is Elizabeth Daryush, the daughter of Robert Bridges. He introduced a small selection of her poems (*Selected*

Poems, 1948). She is to him "the finest British poet since T. Sturge Moore" (*DR*, 105n.), and "at her best she is a good deal better than Landor" (*FD*, 347). He concludes that "England has not given us much notable poetry in the past two hundred and fifty years" (347), a statement which dates the end of the great age about 1715.

There is no dearth of praiseworthy Americans. Adelaide Crapsey, we hear with some surprise, is "certainly an immortal poet" (*DR*, 568). She wrote little poems in the Japanese manner of which Winters thinks very highly (*FD*, 329). Another favorite is J. V. Cunningham, whom Winters, in 1943, considered "the best scholar and critic among the younger Americans" as well as potentially "the best [poet] of his generation" (Cunningham was born in 1911; *DR*, 574). The discussion in *Forms of Discovery*, though more detailed, voices, however, many reservations. Cunningham is Winters's most distinguished pupil: he lists him first among the six or seven former students of his he considers "among the best poets of this century" (*FD*, 346). We can dispense with the list, for Winters dismissed as unworthy of discussion Sandburg, and Vachel Lindsay, E. E. Cummings (chided elsewhere for "trickery": *UER*, 252), Archibald MacLeish, W. H. Auden, Dylan Thomas, and Robert Lowell (*FD*, 359). Winters must have forgotten the highly laudatory review of MacLeish's *Streets in the Moon* (1927) in which he speaks of MacLeish as one who "can rightly take a place beside the most distinguished poets of the preceding generation" (*UER*, 46).

Winters has, one should grant, an almost heroic courage with which he declares his impatience with everything and everybody that runs counter to his idea of poetry. He rejects all emotionalism, mysticism, obscurantism, asking constantly for a reasonable statement, a moral judgment of man's predicament in a language charged with emotion, but with an emotion which must be adequate to the motive, to the "idea." This idea seems to me mainly that of the transience of life, of the uncertainty and obscurity of man's fate. He likes poets "on whom the black ox has trod" (*FD*, 70, a quotation from Greville's *Life of Sir Philip Sidney*, *FD*, 52). His selections resemble oddly Arnold's touchstones in tone and mood: gloomy, resigned, and proud.

Almost independently of theme and diction—though Winters would plead for interdependence—poetry must be metrical. Winters writes much about meter, scans many poems, worries about free verse, sprung rhythm, and the proper recitation of poetry (see *FC*, 79ff.). Though he shows sensitivity to subtle effects, scans persuasively, and makes good objections to the theories of Poe, Bridges, and Hopkins, his own contribution to prosodic theory seems to me negligible, for he has no concept of modern phonemics and is unable to analyze free verse.

Winters's whole critical attitude implies a lack of sympathy with the then-ruling historical scholarship in the American academe. He rejects the superstition of value-free literary history. "Every writer that the scholar studies comes to him as the result of a critical judgment" (*FC*, 24). "It is hard to see how our scholar will be able to write the history of poetry, let us say, when he does not know what a poem is or how it functions" (24). But he does not, by any means, advocate abolishing literary history: he wants a union of criticism and history. "The critical and the historical understanding are merely aspects of a single process" (*DR*, 565). Winters recognizes that the situation in American universities has greatly improved in recent decades. "The quality of traditional scholarship has improved as well, and I believe that the improvement is due in a considerable measure to the critics on the faculties" (*FC*, 13). He defended eloquently his own choice of teaching against a rather silly attack. Teaching forced him to clarify his ideas about literature. "Had it not been for my academic career, it is quite possible that I should still be a minor disciple of W. C. Williams, doing little impressionistic notes on landscapes" (*UER*, 308). Surprisingly, if one considers Winters's long uphill struggle for academic recognition, he puts his trust in the university, which is still "the intellectual and spiritual center of our world." One wonders whether he could have said today that it is a "concrete embodiment . . . of the belief in absolute truth . . . of intellectual freedom and integrity" (*DR*, 569).

Winters's relationship to the critical movements which brought about the change he welcomed is, however, often ambivalent and even hostile. At times he sounds like Irving Babbitt: he shares his antiromantic views, and the ethical emphasis as well as the rationalism seem similar. But he later declared emphatically: "I do not consider myself one of the Humanists: I disagree with Babbitt on too many counts to do so, though I admire him and have learned a good deal from him" (*DR*, 569). Winters had contributed to C. Hartley Grattan's symposium *The Critique of Humanism* (1930) an essay which consists, in part, of an early statement of his view of poetry and, in part, of comparatively mild criticism of Paul Elmer More and incidentally of Babbitt. Then Winters preferred More to Babbitt as a critic and reflected that the moral doctrine advocated by the new humanists is that being advocated from "our better Presbyterian pulpits" (*CH*, 330) and concludes that "there is probably little in their philosophy that could not be extracted, and in a richer form, from Matthew Arnold" (332). He sees that Babbitt is "obviously imperceptive in writing about poetry" (*FC*, 11) and he chides More and Babbitt together for their dislike of Baudelaire (*CH*, 330).

Winters kept also his distance from the New Critics, though he says himself, "I am sometimes reputed to be one" (*FC*, 81). He thought that there is "nearly nothing" in the thought of Allen Tate or of R. P. Blackmur "which is not to be found in Eliot and Ransom" (*DR*, 556), and he suspects Blackmur of being "a relativist," "unwilling to commit himself to any principles" (*FC*, 17). The references to Cleanth Brooks, a "master of paraphrase" (*FD*, 31, 75), are tinged with some irony. Brooks sees poetry purely as structure and does not notice stylistic defects (*FC*, 16). Ransom's criticism is the subject of a long essay, which is, in part, a reply to Ransom's own dissection of Winters in *The New Criticism* (1941) and therefore a defense of his own position. He criticizes Ransom mainly for nominalism and hedonism, doubts that art is imitation or cognition of concrete qualities, and objects to Ransom's dichotomy of structure and texture as well as to his views of meter and metaphor. Poetry for Ransom, he concludes, "is an obscure form of self-indulgence, a search for excitement by ways that Ransom cannot define" (*DR*, 553). It seems a pity that Winters often misinterprets Ransom's meaning, for Winters does not understand or want to understand the traditional problems of aesthetics. He can conclude much later that "Ransom is dated, in his style and in his ideas" (*FD*, 334). Still, he recognizes the triumph of criticism in the academy to be the effect of "a handful of men of my generation" who "bore the brunt of it: Ransom, Tate, Brooks, Blackmur, and myself " (*FC*, 13).

Winters was for a time at least impressed by the Chicago Aristotelians, particularly by the learning and acumen of Ronald S. Crane, though as a critic he is rather a "scholarly amateur; he knows no more about criticism than Tate, Ransom, and their agrarian friends of twenty years ago knew about farming" (*FC*, 22). More convincingly he notes that Crane "seems . . . to have come to poetry through an interest in criticism" (22) and that his advocacy of critical pluralism is "relativism in theory" but "irresponsible personal dogmatism in fact" (23).

Winters, I believe, never refers to F. R. Leavis, with whom he shares a concern for the moral meaning of poetry and an antiromantic taste: the rejection of Milton and the downgrading of English poetry roughly between Pope and Ezra Pound. But they also differ profoundly: Winters could not possibly have joined in Leavis's exaltation of D. H. Lawrence or even the early admiration for T. S. Eliot both as critic and as poet. The similarity is obviously due rather to common sources: to Babbitt,

Arnold, and the French antiromantic critics. In spite of all sharp disagreements there is also an affinity between Winters and Pound as critics. They share the same tastes and distastes in the history of English poetry: the liking for the "Drab" style, the aversion to Elizabethan *fioritura*, Milton, and romantic poetry, and they share something less amiable: the strident tone, the violence, and often the comic violence of pronouncements—the deliberate use of superlatives, positive and negative, the obvious desire to shock not so much the bourgeois as the conventional academic professor. Winters considers Pound "the most influential critic in American letters" for "about fifteen years," for he "could show us poems and passages which were genuinely fine" (*FC*, 12). Winters thinks that "a great critic, indeed, is the rarest of all literary geniuses" and that "perhaps the only critic in English who deserves the epithet is Samuel Johnson" (*DR*, 565). Winters shares his moralism and certainty, his melancholia and "private bitterness" (138); he has, I think, learned from him his method of puncturing metaphors by an appeal to common sense so literal that it reminds one of the satirical techniques of Voltaire or Thomas Rymer, but Winters lacks, of course, Johnson's hold on the classical tradition and his secure relation to everyday life. Compared to him Winters is alone, eccentric, and willful. Whatever the skill with which Winters quotes, however clearly he tells us that this idea or statement is good or bad or that this piece of writing, line by line, is precise or shoddy, this or that image accurate or blurred, we always run up against a final obscurity: the *ipse dixit* of Winters, the appeal to "the taste which enables a reader to recognize a good poem among fifteen hundred or more pages of bad" (*FD*, 324). The criteria in the judgment of older poetry seem clear enough: Winters wants a reasoned statement, preferably about an important topic, but with modern poetry the criteria shift. Winters admires writing which must seem obscure and difficult to anybody trained in the classical or romantic tradition: symbolist writing like Valéry's two poems, or Wallace Stevens, and, with reservations, Hart Crane, three of the most obscure poets of the century. But often Winters favors the antiquarians over the innovators, Bridges and Sturge Moore over Yeats and Eliot. Winters prefers symbolist, or, as he calls it, post-symbolist poetry even to his Drab Elizabethans. "The controlled association offers the possibility, at least, of greater flexibility and greater inclusiveness of matter (and without confusion) than we can find in the Renaissance structures; the post-Symbolist imagery provides a greater range of thinking and perceiving than we have ever had before. The method, I believe, is potentially the richest method to appear. In fact, I will go farther: I believe that the greatest poems employing this method are the greatest poems that we have, and furthermore that the group of poets whom I shall now discuss are, *as a group*, the most impressive group in English" (253). But we are let down when we read the names in the group, which seem to have little or nothing in common: F. G. Tuckerman, Emily Dickinson, Wallace Stevens, Louise Bogan, Edgar Bowers, N. Scott Momaday—the last two, pupils of Yvor Winters. It is an arbitrary, willfully selected group. We cannot, finally, believe in Winters's rewriting of the history of English poetry and thus accept his contradictory concept of poetry. Winters does not reconcile his moralism and rationalism with his actual taste. It remains a purely "subjective evaluation of a body of experience" which Winters had demanded of Paul Elmer More in his early antihumanist essay. "Unfortunately," he admits, "that is the only kind of evaluation of experience, literary or non-literary, that is ultimately possible, and one has to have the training as well as the courage to make it" (*CH*, 320). Winters surely had the courage: he presented us with a massive body of evaluations, with a definition of his taste, and thus raised again the constantly disputed question about the possibility of agreement and the validity of any critical judgment and ranking. He also resolutely faced the question of the truth-value of poetry. He saw that it cannot be dismissed by theories such as I. A. Richards's "pseudo-statements." He knew that poetry can be preserved in our time only if it has something to say about man and his condition, something that can be judged by a simple appeal to a concept of truth. Winters did not quite face the difficulties of this concept, but he stated or rather restated a position which needs to be reasserted in the critical debate of our time.

16: WILLIAM K. WIMSATT (1907–1975)

I HAVE left the discussion of William Wimsatt to this last chapter partly because he is the youngest of the American critics treated at some length and partly because I consider him as the critic who best summarized and formulated a revised position related closely to the New Criticism, even though he early disavowed being "an advanced Ricardian or Ransomite" (*University Review* 9 [1942]: 139). When he died in December 1975, the obituaries praised him, rightly, as an eminent scholar of English eighteenth-century literature. His books on Dr. Johnson's style and vocabulary, his edition of one of the volumes in the Yale Boswell papers, and his acute and sensitive articles on Alexander Pope (skillfully summarized in the introduction to *Selected Poetry and Prose,* 1972), to which we should add the wide-ranging studies of the development of English poetry from the Augustan mode through the revivals of older poetry in the later eighteenth century to romantic nature imagery, would be enough for a scholar's whole lifetime. But we must add the sumptuous volume on *The Portraits of Alexander Pope* (1966), which not only collects and reproduces all the known portraits of the first English poet of whom we have a full pictorial record but also examines the relationship between poet and painters and traces the archetypes of the portraits so meticulously that the method can serve as a model for similar investigations into the history of portrait painting and of sculpture.

Still, he will be mainly remembered as a theorist of literature. More radically than any other reputable critic, Wimsatt asserted "objectivism," the focus on the work of art itself as the central concern of literary criticism. Since his first widely noticed theoretical paper, "The Intentional Fallacy" (1946, in collaboration with Monroe C. Beardsley), Wimsatt rejected the approach to literature through its genesis either in the mind of the author or in its historical and social antecedents. The early, somewhat disjointed article was largely directed against the view that the "design or intention of the author is either available or desirable as a standard for judging the success of a work of literary art" (*VI,* 3), while later, in many contexts, most prominently in "Genesis: An Argument Resumed" (1968, in *DL*), intention served as a focal point for a criticism of standards derived from ideas such as "inspiration, expression, authenticity, sincerity, purpose and the like" (*DL*, 35). This view implies a criticism of the expressionist theory of Croce (though Croce also rejected overt intention as a criterion of value); it implies a rejection of Freudianism and its variants; of the Geneva school's search for the "cogito" behind the author's work; and, of course, of the usual search for biographical information, extending even to brothers, sisters, and ancestors of the poet, as advocated by Sainte-Beuve; and finally it extends to any historical determinism: Marxist, which is summarily dismissed, or simply positivistic and historic. A work of art cannot be explained by the conditions of the time or its genesis.

The work of art is independent not only of its origins but also of its effects on audience or reader. The second paper with Monroe C. Beardsley, "The Affective Fallacy" (1949), argues against the "emotive" theory of I. A. Richards as well as against impressionism in criticism and the resultant relativism in which "the poem itself, as an object of specifically critical judgment, tends to disappear" (*VI*, 21). Again in later contexts the focus on Richards widens to an examination of the whole tradition descending from Longinus of such concepts as "rapture," "the sublime," "the grand style," and the like. "A poetry of pure emotion is an illusion" (37). Catharsis, which in Aristotle seems to mean only "a sounder sleep when we get home," is a concept rather "in the realm of experimental psychology than in that of literary criticism" (*LC*, 37).

If we eliminate the author and the audience from our critical concerns we focus on the work itself, which is conceived as existing somehow "out there," "objectively," or at least "hypostatized as an object, and metaphorically as a spatial object" (*DL*, 194–95). The figure of the urn or the icon is defended. Not every kind of space, Wimsatt argues, is visual. "Some kinds of order and concept are neither visual nor spatial. The current simple dichotomy between temporal dynamics and the spatial rigidity is a complacent vulgar error" (*LC*, 194n.). This objectivism has earned Wimsatt the sobriquet of "Yale formalist," an imaginary group which includes Cleanth Brooks and myself. But Wimsatt is no formalist in any conceivable sense of the word, for he sees the work of art steadily as a union of content and form, sound and meaning (*DL*, 118). He constantly asserts the "organic unity" of a work of art, though in a late article, "Organic Form: Some Questions about a Metaphor" (1971, in *DL*), he warns against the extremes to which the biological metaphor has been pushed. He must approve of "organicity" because it means a rejection of atomistic ideas of composition; but he cannot accept it if it means total unity, which would lead to indiscriminate uniformity. Rather Wimsatt asserts the coincidence of opposites, an idea that filters down from the Middle Ages through Coleridge. The work of art is a whole, individual and unique. The whole is prior to the parts, the parts are interdependent with each other and with the whole (DL, 214–15). An "intimate, manifold (and hence dramatic and imaginative) "interinanimation' of parts in a poem, must surely be one of the modern critic's most carefully defended doctrines" (220). But the analogy to a living organism obscures the fact that a poem is "all knowable; it is all knowledge, through and through" (216). The power of the human mind to revise and to recast itself (211) refutes the idea that poems are literally organisms.

Poems are, first of all, made out of words. Wimsatt, particularly in his practical criticism, is a resolutely verbal critic. His acute papers on English meter and rhyme, while attentive to what has been called the sound-stratum of a work of art, see meter and rhyme always implicated in meaning. For instance, the essay "One Relation of Rhyme to Reason" argues persuasively that to speak of Alexander Pope's "poverty of rhyme" is a mistake that springs "only from a limited view of rhyme as a form of phonetic harmony," to be appraised "in terms of phonetic accuracy, complexity, and variety—in other words, from a failure to connect rhyme with reason" (VI, 163). Reason is "meaning," the contrast of different parts of speech or of different functions of the same part of speech, the surprise of confrontations, serious or comic, which is not "euphony." "The music of spoken words in itself is meager," for "the art of words is an intellectual art" (165). With many concrete examples Wimsatt illustrates the role of such figures as zeugma, parallelisms, and puns, which could be called "counterlogical," as well as that of logical devices such as repetition, elegant variation, or jingles, which we class as faults (207). Wimsatt's dissertation, The Prose Style of Samuel Johnson (1941), has a first chapter entitled "Style as Meaning." While the book necessarily pays attention to formal devices such as parallelism, antithesis, and sentence structure, Wimsatt never forgets that words point to something outside their verbal context. One would totally misunderstand him if one thought of him as believing in the "prison-house of language" of the French structuralists or in Northrop Frye's "verbal universe." He constantly emphasizes that "all our verbal knowledge is to some extent also bound to be a knowledge of things." Poetry is then "a type of discourse where a certain kind of thing knowledge is intimately dependent on word knowledge, and compressed into it" (HC, 70). Words in poetry are not any more merely statements, signs, or pointers, but they "present the things which language is otherwise occupied in designating." The sign becomes a symbol, or, as he prefers to say (in order to avoid the ambiguity of that term), an icon. Icon is a word derived from Charles Sanders Peirce via Charles Morris and means, according to Wimsatt's note on the title of *The Verbal Icon,* his first collection of essays, a "verbal sign which somehow shares the properties of, or resembles, the objects which it denotes. . . . It is not merely a 'bright picture,' but also an interpretation of reality in its metaphoric and symbolic dimension" (*VI,* x). Thus Wimsatt believes that language is not merely *thesei* (by agreement) but also *physei* (by nature), a problem debated since Plato's *Cratylus,* decided by Saussure in favor of the complete conventionality of language but reopened by Roman Jakobson, Beneviste, Genette, and others. Wimsatt's last paper, "In Search of Verbal Mimesis" (1975), assembles arguments ranging from concrete poetry through onomatopoeia, root-forming morphemes, and sound symbolism to diagrams, in order to convince us that "words really do embody reasons for meaning what they mean" (*DL,* 73).

Still, metaphor is for Wimsatt the main bridge between the poem and reality. *Literary Criticism: A Short History* (Wimsatt's longest sustained book: 554 pages out of 755 are his) concludes with a veritable hymn to metaphor as "in a broad sense the principle of all poetry" (*LC,* 750). It combines "concreteness and significance" (753): it allows us to incorporate mimesis into a theory of poetry. Mimesis is not a "mirroring of reality" as Marxist critics parrot incessantly but a creative principle, almost the imagination in the sense in which Coleridge used it. But one has to say "almost" since Wimsatt has misgivings about the truth of all idealist theory of art from Plotinus to Croce and Susanne Langer. "It may be doubted," he says, "if the theory succeeds in making the transition from general epistemology to poetics without a leap that largely abandons the epistemology as a formal principle" (399). Wimsatt cannot, in the last analysis, believe in the identity of subject and object, art and nature postulated by the romantics, and concludes that we have there only "a theory of 'animating' imagery, of romantic anthropomorphism" (400). Poetry can offer only "truth of 'coherence' rather than truth of 'correspondence.' " But in poetry "the dimension of coherence is by various techniques of implication greatly enhanced and thus generates an extra dimension of correspondence to reality, the symbolic or analogical. But all this structure of meaning rises upon a certain element of unavoidably direct reference to outside reality and a minimal truth of such reference" (*VI,* 241). He thus can approve of Sidney's saying: "The poet nothing affirmeth, and therefore never lieth" (*LC,* 748) but, I think, cannot do so fully, because for him the "conception of truth is a thing beyond language" (*VI*, 279) and the work of art does say something about reality in its totality. Thus Wimsatt revived the Hegelian formula of the "concrete universal" (as Josiah Royce and Bernard Bosanquet tried before him). The poem appears as "a tacit larger metaphor or symbol of other areas of reality than those explicitly mentioned in the poem" (*LC*, 256). Poetry and presumably all art is treated as a single metaphor of the world. In the epilogue to *Literary Criticism* Wimsatt draws a surprisingly specific lesson from poetry about the nature of the world. Poetry cannot fit into a Platonic or Gnostic monism, nor within a Manichaean dualism. The "dogma of the Incarnation" provides the orientation within poetry, for poetry supports this view of the world, an "optimism within the vision of suffering," or, more obscurely phrased, "not simply a complicated correspondence, a method of alternation, now sad, now happy . . . but the oblique glance, the vertical unification of the metaphoric smile" (746). Wit "generates a certain mimicry of substance which is poetry." "Irony may be usefully taken rather as a cognitive principle which shades off through paradox into the general principle of metaphor and metaphoric structure—the tension which is always present when words are used in vitally new ways" (747). Here the key words of the New Criticism—irony, paradox, wit—are assembled under the domain of metaphor, and the metaphor somehow suggests the nature of the world.

Wimsatt refuses to go beyond this. Myth, which can be conceived as growing out of metaphor, according to Vico's saying that "every metaphor is a short myth," is looked upon with suspicion as the "hugest cloudy symbol," myth criticism as "antiverbal poetics," as a variety of didacticism (*LC*, 733–35). Northrop Frye is elaborately criticized for his reliance on the quest myth as the source of all literary genres. "Such a coherent, cyclic, and encyclopedic system, such a monomyth, cannot be shown ever to have evolved actually, either from or with ritual, anywhere in the world" (*DL*, 88). Frye's all-inclusive claims for myth offend Wimsatt's firm belief in the separation of poetry from religion and philosophy. The myth critics "want a new myth when the main thing alleged against the old myth is that it *was* a myth" (*VI*, 278).

Wimsatt finds Matthew Arnold's prophecy that poetry will supplant religion simply "appalling" (*LC*, 448). He also condemns Irving Babbitt's "purity of withdrawal from revealed religion" as "surpassing even the cultural dreams of Arnold" (451). Nor can he sympathize with Shelley's grandiose proclamation about the poets as the "unacknowledged legislators of the world" (421–23).

It is sometimes difficult to see what the function of poetry could be in Wimsatt's scheme. Metaphor is a "holding together of oppositions." "And through this tension poetry gives a fresh vision of reality, a fullness, completeness, concreteness of experience" (*HC*, 41)—a rephrasing of Ransom's idea of the "World's Body," which itself descends from empiricist theories of particularity. But literature also offers ethical guidance, models of behavior, of attitudes which must not, however, be confused with straight didacticism or propaganda art. Wimsatt has his difficulties with morality in art. Thus he condemns *Antony and Cleopatra* as "immoral" (*VI*, 96) and becomes indignant at "the silly ideas" of Blake's "depraved" poem "London" (*DL*, 32–33). Religious and moral standards are imposed on literature and may conflict with aesthetic standards: Wimsatt recognizes that *Antony and Cleopatra* is a "great" play. He can declare that "there is a certain sense in which religion is the only theme of important poetry" (*HC*, 39), forgetting his concern with poetry as play or game (*DL*, 99), which fits with the analogy he draws between poetry and chess and with his absorbing interest in comedy and laughter. But literature must never usurp the function of religion or of a specific philosophy. Literature remains a panorama of not fully reconcilable worldviews: Homer, Greek tragedy, Lucretius, Dante, Shakespeare, Milton, Wordsworth, Baudelaire present "a widely heterogeneous concreteness" (*VI*, 89). The "Christian critic" (and Wimsatt calls himself one) will keep his standards apart and aloof.

Hitherto we have spoken of poetry or imaginative literature as if it were something distinct and uniform, general and particular, present though past. Wimsatt cannot accept any subdivision of poetry into genres except as a descriptive convenience. He objects to the Chicago Aristotelians sharply because they deny that any generalization about poetry is possible which does not pass into the realm of psychology. In a passage of metaphorical wit characteristic of his best writing, he ridicules their view that "you have to divide [a topic such as poetry] into its parts or species in order to remain objective. If you try to pick up a pie whole, it will melt into a plan for a pie or the taste of a pie. If you cut it into slices, it will remain pie and *whole* pie" (*VI*, 57). The cumulative experience of literary criticism testifies against the genre theory. E. D. Hirsch's attempt to make interpretation depend on knowing the genre fails. "We discover the genre of a work by being able to read it, and not vice versa" (*DL*, 191).

Poetry, or rather imaginative literature, is a single concept clearly set off from the other arts. Wimsatt distrusts general aesthetics as "centered on sensationalism" which may not provide "adequate prescriptions for the *literary* critic (*JEGP* 52 [1953]: 586n.), and does not believe that there is an "aesthetic component in literature," at least in the sense of "a thing which inheres there but is not involved with the ideas and life concerns which are also present" (*JEGP* 53 [1954]: 270). A paper entitled "Laokoön: An Oracle Reconsulted" (*DL*, 50ff.) concludes that "a really formal, stylistic, or aesthetic dependence of one art upon another is not possible." Croce's attempt to abolish the distinctions between the arts fails because there is an insurmountable difference between a poem composed in the mind, a verbal construct, and a painting or a piece of sculpture elaborated only in the process of making. Poetry, he says strikingly, is "a bird in the hand," the painting in the mind of the painter "a bird in the bush" (*LC*, 403). Literature differs from the other arts because "the intellectual character of language makes literature difficult for the aesthetician" (*VI*, 230). In a late review of F. E. Sparshott's *Structure of Aesthetics,* Wimsatt even came to the surprising conclusion that among the three key concepts of aesthetics, representation, form, and expression, he would have to choose expression as the one applicable to all the arts. Representation is "all but undetectable in music," and form "in any purified or technical sense might be at its best only in certain kinds of very cold music or in certain sheer kinds of mathematical painting or sculpture." Expression is thus the master concept in general aesthetics, but expression is "not really separable from anything that is either represented or formed in any kind of art." Expression is not so much connected with biography or the poet but is instead conceived as "articulation, abstraction, symbolization, significance 'incarnate' in a form" (*Review of Metaphysics* 20 [1966]: 82, 85). Representation, mimesis, dominates literature; form and expression are presumably less important.

Literature is felt as an immediate presence in the sense in which T. S. Eliot defined tradition. Tradition and history are seen as a seamless web. "I do not accept a view of literature as essentially a rebellion" (*DL*, 117). Particularly the continuity with antiquity is felt very strongly: Plato, Aristotle, Horace, and Longinus are argued with as if they had written yesterday. They offer prototypes of concepts for today. Thus Wimsatt does not believe in the historian's demand that we must judge purely in terms of the time in which an author wrote. It seems absurd to say that "all critical insights about Shakespeare stopped shortly after the time of Shakespeare" (*VI*, 56). Rather, "Shakespeare has more meaning and more value now than he had in his own day. There is a sense in which even Homer, though we construe his language with pain and are not sure how many persons he was, has more meaning and is more valuable today than ever before" (*DL*, 39). There is thus an accrual of meaning in history or at least in the history of criticism which seems to run counter to Wimsatt's general view of the disintegration of the Western mind.

Wimsatt speaks of "modern man's three-century decline from the pinnacles of theology and metaphysics" (*DL*, 161): he believes in the dissociation of sensibility, a catastrophe that occurred in England in the seventeenth century. "Both feeling and the act of valuing," he says rather awkwardly, "were theoretically detached from a certain something—an Aristotelian structure of ideas, a substantive belief about God, man, and the universe" (*LC*, 253), or, more clearly, "a dissociation of the feeling and responding side of human consciousness from the side of knowing and rational valuing" worked in two directions, "toward the inspirations of the author of poetry, and toward the responses of his audience" (284). Dissociation here means then a trend away from the "objectivism" to the "intentional" and "affective fallacy," views which are as old as antiquity and can hardly be called inventions of the seventeenth century.

Literary criticism, for Wimsatt, begins with a commentary, allows a neutral description of the traits of a work of art, rises slowly to an explication of the implied meaning, a demonstration, for instance, of the unity and coherence of a poem, and thus naturally gives rise to value judgment. "Our main critical problem is always how to push both understanding and value as far as possible in union, or how to make our understanding evaluative" (*VI*, 251). Valuation, Wimsatt argues, is not purely subjective. He is a "believer in real values and a hierarchy of values" (*JEGP* 52 [1958]: 585). Criticism becomes "objective and absolute, as distinguished from the relative criticism of idiom and period"; Wimsatt believes in the universal nature of man and in a moral realm that allows us to consider human actions as good or bad and a poem as mature, complex, rich, and deep, or shallow and thin (*VI*, 82). But whereas judgment can be absolute, criticism always runs up against a final mystery. Saying that "in each poem there is something (an individual intuition—or a concept) which can never be expressed in other terms" (83) might be only a version of the "heresy of the paraphrase." But it is more than that: it is a recognition of the limits of criticism. A poem is like the square root of two or like *pi*. "There is the knowable yet indefinable individuality of the poem and the unknowable and incommunicable mystery of the poet's inspiration" (*LC*, 53). There is "a certain nuclear area of the indefinable [which] will never be reduced by the theory" (25). It is precisely because Wimsatt allows for this ultimate mystery that he disapproves of the Catholic writers such as Bremond, Péguy, and the later Maritain, who speak of prayer, trance, and ecstasy in order to develop a mystical poetics. Wimsatt confesses to being "an invincible

Ramist and visualist" who maintains that "as theorists we can make no progress unless in the direction of clarity" (*HC,* 35). Wimsatt loves to illustrate his arguments with diagrams, with visual metaphors, convinced that criticism must progress by rational generalizations, by theoretical reflection which may leave mysteries alone but cannot condone the new anti-intellectualism. He deplores "the boundless expansions of the school of 'consciousness,'" the self-justifying apparatuses of transformational grammar, the neutralisms of historical hermeneutics, the despairs of the trope of 'silence,' the 'aleatory' assemblage of *textes* from newspaper, dictionary, or telephone directory, the celebrations of the 'death of literature,' the various other attempts to play midwife to the 'post-modern imagination' " (*DI,* 248).

Hitherto I have tried to give a conspectus of Wimsatt's theories suggesting something like a loosely held system in his mind. Only incidentally did I hint at some disagreements, though in the very process of exposition I had to make choices and put on accents which may seem misplaced from a different point of view. I must be guilty of what Wimsatt calls "the idolatrous assumption that a given author's mind or vision during his whole career is necessarily a coherent whole or a dialectic development, as good an entity as, or better than, any one of his works" (*DL,* 37). Still, this exposition shows, I hope, that one can hardly refuse to recognize the consistency, coherence, and clarity of his views throughout a writing career of some thirty-five years, from his early articles demolishing some of the claims made for Edgar Allan Poe's intellectual prowess to his last speculations on verbal mimesis included in the posthumous volume, *Day of the Leopards: Essays in Defense of Poems* (1976). Small shifts of emphasis, no doubt, occurred, and often later formulations improve or clarify an earlier text. The "Intentional Fallacy" in particular gave rise to many misunderstandings and to long, often quibbling debates. Wimsatt tried to take them into account in his late paper "Genesis: An Argument Resumed" (1968). A whole volume, *On Literary Intention* (edited by David Newton-De Molina, 1976), collected some of the major contributions to this discussion, slanting it sharply in the direction of the defenders of the role of intention in criticism. But most of the attacks on Wimsatt's position seem to me directed against a straw man. Wimsatt could never have doubted that "the words of a poem come out of a head, not out of a hat," as he himself quotes E. E. Stoll (*VI,* 4). He merely insisted, to cite the later, more careful formula, that the "intention of a literary artist *qua* intention is neither a valid ground for arguing the quality of meaning in a given instance of his literary work nor a valid criterion for judging the value of that work" (*DL*, 12), a perfectly reasonable position if one merely thinks of the many misstatements writers have made about their original intentions. The much wider and more debatable question of the relevance of personality, biography, and generally historical and social antecedents is also misstated if it imputes to Wimsatt a wholesale dismissal of these questions. Actually Wimsatt had an absorbing interest in biography and literary history. He makes many declarations recognizing the historical determinants of the meaning of words or the impact of social situations. To quote a few: "Meaning lies outside the words in their whole history and the contexts in which they have been used. The author's experience of the words and their associations for him form a part of their history" (*University Review* 9 [1942]: 141), or "Words, the medium of literature, have to be understood, and understanding is derived at least in part from historical documents" (*VI*, 254). He says expressly that "historical causes enter in a pronounced way into the very meaning of literary works" (254), and, in commenting on Pope's and his contemporaries' cultivation of aristocratic friends, he goes so far as to say that "this fact was not merely a social and economic cause of literature, it entered into the very mind of the writer and gave him a certain kind of matter and cast of mind" (Pope, *Selected Poetry and Prose*, xxii). Still, Wimsatt insists on the distinction between genetic and descriptive accounts of literature, a distinction which seems as clear as that elaborated by Saussure between synchronics and diachronics in linguistics. It is a question of methodology which has led to enormous advances in descriptive linguistics but has, in recent decades, been combated by arguments in favor of the indivisibility of historical and descriptive study. Wimsatt's view has helped to turn attention to the analysis and evaluation of actual texts and has cast doubts on such standards of traditional criticism as sincerity, spontaneity, authenticity, and "lived experience." It has helped to reject the extremes of social and historical determinism in which a work of art is reduced to a symptom of an age or even a class situation. Wimsatt cannot question the context of poetry in biography and history but asks, as does Hillis Miller, "Where does the context of a poem stop?" (*DL*, 196), and must answer that there are limits to the regress in genesis.

Also Wimsatt's attack on the "Affective Fallacy" can be defended if it is understood as a rejection of vague emoting about poetry or of the mysterious "balancing of impulses" of I. A. Richards. One can understand that Wimsatt does not think that the exact nature of the aesthetic emotion is a problem for literary criticism, for he has doubts about the whole idea of a specific aesthetic response and the traditional concept of beauty, at least in regard to literature. "This correct response will have to take care of itself " (LC, 740). But Wimsatt's "ergocentric" view (a good term, derived from Manfred Kridl, which has not caught on because it is often misprinted as "egocentric") cannot be refuted by Eliseo Vivas's true observation that "to grasp the poem itself is to ask [the reader] to talk about a poem he has neither heard nor seen" (The Artistic Transaction, 224). Wimsatt constantly discussed the effects of literature, particularly in his effort to unravel the theories of comedy. Laughter, Hobbes's "sudden glory," disillusionment are necessarily affective concepts. Wimsatt on occasion speaks even of a "particular listener [who] has a great deal to do with determining a certain kind of style, a certain kind of structure, a certain kind of metaphor. Other poems we may conceive as poems for a sex, a caste, a party. The Rape of the Lock is addressed, immediately, to a more squeamish audience than The Dunciad." Saying that "at the fully cognitive level of appreciation we unite in our own minds both speaker and audience" (VI, xvi), Wimsatt seems to anticipate the "fusion of horizons" propounded by the German advocates of Rezeptionsästhetik. Actually, however, he is wary of attempts like those of F. W. Bateson to decide "the validity of the literary work by its measure of conformity to the understanding of some historically specific audience." Wimsatt sensibly concludes that "a critic ought to have in mind not just any response of a contemporary reader, or the average response, or even the response of any elite group, but in a more generally human sense an 'ideal response.' And in this of course we refuse the question, taking the onus off the shoulders of any empirically identifiable audience and placing it on the 'meaning' of the poem itself " (LC, 546–47).

The meaning of the poem is Wimsatt's central concern. He made excellent acute analyses not only of its devices—meter, euphony, rhyme—but above all of style conceived of as a relation of name and sense. He eloquently and consistently defended the unity of form and content, the organicity of the work of art, which he saw as unity in diversity, as a union of opposites which he called "tensional," to distinguish it from the purely formal or stylistic and the contentual or didactic view (HC, 36). But he is, besides, and that is one of the peculiarities of his position, greatly concerned with the relation of poetry to reality. He has found for poetry the striking term "the verbal icon," which, he argues, describes the nature of poetry best, suggesting a representation and interpretation of reality in its very medium. Wimsatt is acutely aware of the difficulty into which a purely "autotelic" concept of literature must run. How can a poem be self-enclosed, preserve its individuality and cohesion, if it is considered as simply an utterance about reality? The concept of the icon, developed and varied in such terms as the concrete universal, metaphor, and symbol, and finally in the attempts to document verbal mimesis, serves as a bridge to link poetry to reality. One may agree that a poem "has a kind of rounded being or substance and a metaphoric relation to reality" (*VI*, 217). In ever new variations, Wimsatt celebrates "the thickening of the medium," the solidity and density of the poem, "the fullness of actually presented meaning" (231). But Wimsatt has to assume an ultimately mystical view of the universe, one that sees analogies and metaphors in reality, a language of meanings in nature and society "incarnate" in poetry. This is the *signatura rerum,* embraced by a Crashaw or even by the Schlegels, Novalis, and Coleridge, but it seems unacceptable in the present situation of thinking about such matters. I am far from underrating the role of metaphor in poetry but consider it a figure that has its important function of inducing a kind of stereoscopic effect in making us see two things from two sides and still as one. Metaphors of language do not, however, represent analogies, correspondences, and similarities which are given in the order of existence or in our thinking. A phenomenological approach derived from Husserl, as developed by Roman Ingarden or Mikel Dufrenne, or the compatible semiotic theory expounded in the writings of Roman Jakobson and Jan Mukařovský, would obviate an appeal to the mystery of Incarnation and an emblematic view of the universe. But this is an ultimate philosophical or religious decision. An answer differing from Wimsatt's should not, however, obscure the value of his literary theory: its focus on the object, his analyses of its features, his polemical successes against fashionable rival views such as the Chicago Aristotelians or the myth critics, his excursions into the history of poetry and criticism, his resolute defense of evaluation in criticism, and his never-misplaced plea for the meaning of literature as "being" something in its own right but also "saying" something about man and the universe, in many and often discordant voices.

POSTSCRIPT

IN 1950, T. S. Eliot and F. R. Leavis dominated the critical scene in England and the New Criticism in America. The two conflicting doctrines of the end of the nineteenth century—aestheticism and naturalism—had been rejected and replaced by a recognition of the old doctrine that form and content are indissoluble and even identical. The idea goes back to Aristotle, but in the English-speaking world it was memorably reformulated by Coleridge, who added creative imagination, the reconciliation of opposites, the poem as an organic whole, symbol in contrast to allegory to the common parlance of criticism, however differently used. T. E. Hulme and T. S. Eliot professed classicism, I. A. Richards translated Coleridge into the terms of behaviorism, Herbert Read read poetry romantically as "the true voice of feeling." Whatever the objections and reservations against the organic analogy, the idea of the whole, of *Gestalt*, configuration or structure permeated criticism in the early twentieth century. A central insight, often quite unformulated, into the "aesthetic" quality of a work of literature and the experience of its readers was, in spite of all the diversities and disagreements, preserved. Almost all the prominent critics had a grasp of literature as art. They understood that the critic's task is to distinguish between art and what is not art, to select and appraise the great works, past and present, and thus to establish a canon, a tradition, a set of models or classics.

Both in England and in America most critics agreed that the merely impressionistic appreciation inherited from the nineteenth century was not enough and that much closer analysis was required to justify the critical act. Attention to the language of literature became for most critics of diverse professions the primary concern. It focused mostly on poetic diction: images, metaphors, and symbols. At that time most critics had, however, no use for technical linguistics in literary studies, and even a general concern for language was dismissed by the Chicago Aristotelians preoccupied with plot and genre. The old division between those who saw literature as a purely secular art and those who agreed with Kant that art was a symbol of morality and finally a form of philosophy and religion persisted. The disagreement ran the gamut from those who thought of poetry as presenting a simulacrum of the real and ideal worlds to those who looked for a mystery behind the surface: for philosophical, religious, or even occult meanings. Equally deep ran the division between those who focused on the work with methods I have called "intrinsic" and those who brought "extrinsic" methods to bear on the study of literature. Genetic criteria, focusing on the biographical and psychological conditions of writers, and social criteria, which ask us to judge the accuracy of the social picture and its implications for social attitudes and actions, absorbed the concerns of many critics.

In about 1950 the interest in literature's derivation from and affinity to the basic myths of mankind, as studied by the new anthropology, began to dominate criticism. The work of G. Wilson Knight (discussed at length in volume 5) and R. P. Warren's symbolic interpretation of *The Ancient Mariner* pointed the way, prepared by the practice of T. S. Eliot and James Joyce. Northrop Frye interpreted in *Fearful Symmetry* (1947) Blake's prophetic books as a system of coherent myths, and Richard Chase in *The Quest for Myth* (1949) identified all good literature simply with myth. This turn was a reaction against the supposed formalism of the New Critics, who actually themselves thought of myth as a central device of poetry, a turn toward plot, theme, or simply content. Any story could be treated as myth: Huck Finn floating down the Mississippi became a myth. Often the new myth criticism was straight allegorizing or an attempt to discover a primitive myth or ritual behind a work, as in Philip Wheelwright's sensitive readings of the *Oresteia* and *The Waste Land* in his *Burning Fountain* (1954) or in Francis Fergusson's *Idea of a Theater* (1949) searching for the ritual behind dramas from Sophocles to Chekhov and T. S. Eliot. Much of the myth criticism wandered far off from literature. Wheelwright considered "aesthetic contemplation" as a "halfway house to mysticism" and buttressed it with Buddhist lore and emblems.

Myth criticism was "recuperated" for literary theory by Northrop Frye in his *Anatomy of Criticism* (1957). Frye, on quite different premises, anticipated the new version of structuralism, since he conceived of literature as "existing in its own universe, no longer a commentary on life and reality, but containing life and reality in a system of verbal relationships." He devised an intricate system of modes, symbols, and myths for which the Jungian archetypes are the basic assumption though Frye professes no interest in genetic explanation by the collective unconscious. His was a synchronic theory of genres where comedy, romance, tragedy, and satire are made to correspond to the rhythm of nature, to the four seasons, spring, summer, autumn, and winter. All manner of substitutions, condensations, and identifications are made as Frye defends his scheme by the perilous plea that "the literary universe is a universe in which everything is potentially identical with everything else." In such a scheme all distinctions of artistic value disappear: the simplest folktale will fit just as well as *Hamlet*. In his "Polemical Introduction" Frye excludes value judgment from his concept of criticism, which should, he hopes, "show a steady advance toward undiscriminating catholicity." Frye, a Canadian, has not been influential in England. Rather, Frank Kermode, in his *Romantic Image* (1957) argued against the whole tradition of Imagism and Symbolism and doubted the supposed inevitable consequence of the alienation of the artist and his exaltation to a prophet and seer.

In the United States, partly under the impact of Frye, the reaction in favor of the Romantic prophets and seers was strong. Meyer Abrams's learned and penetrating expositions of Romantic criticism and philosophy in *The Mirror and the Lamp* (1953) and *Natural Supernaturalism* (1971) laid the foundation. Geoffrey Hartman in *The Unmediated Vision* (1954) and *Wordsworth's Poetry* (1964) reinterpreted Wordsworth's poetry as a conflict between consciousness and nature, and Harold Bloom elevated *The Visionary Company* (1961) of the English romantic poets, contrasting the line from Blake to Yeats and Wallace Stevens with Eliot's tradition from the Metaphysicals to the Symbolists.

The critical atmosphere changed in the United States with the importation of French structuralism, signaled by a conference at Johns Hopkins University in 1966 attended by French scholars. Actually the influence of recent French criticism was felt earlier. Hartman had read Maurice Blanchot. Phenomenology as propounded by Georges Poulet and the Geneva group called "Critics of Consciousness" soon found an adherent in J. Hillis Miller, whose books on *Dickens* (1958) and English and American writers of the nineteenth and twentieth centuries (*The Disappearance of God*, 1963; *Poets of Reality*, 1965) describe the inner landscape of the writers by building a mosaic of quotations drawn from every jotting, deliberately ignoring the integrity of a work of art. The aim is to identify with the "cogito," the person behind the work. The method leads to philosophical and religious answers about time and space, the human condition, and God's disappearance.

French structuralism is inspired by the linguistics of Saussure and Roman Jakobson and the anthropology of Claude Lévi-Strauss. In the United States it found adherents and excellent expositors of its theories

in Robert Scholes and Jonathan Culler but produced little original criticism except in "narratology," the new name for the study of the technique of fiction. Studies of this sort cannot, however, compare with the
work of Gérard Genette or Tzvetan Todorov in France. What has been
successful in the United States was rather "post-structuralism" or "deconstructionism," stimulated by Jacques Derrida and practiced by Paul
de Man and J. Hillis Miller, who repudiated his own earlier writings.
"Deconstruction" leads to complete skepticism and even nihilism quite
foreign to mainline structuralism, a scientifically inspired movement
flourishing at least since its formulation by the Prague Linguistic Circle
around 1929. Still, deconstruction develops some of the assumptions of
structuralism: the view that language is a self-enclosed system in no relation to reality. We live, they teach, in a prison-house of language (the
title of Fredric Jameson's Marxist analysis, 1972): a word refers only to
another word, and so ad infinitum. "There is nothing but text." The
death of the author, even the end of man as an individuality, is complacently proclaimed.

But literature is not simply language: it is an art like painting, sculpture, and music, and thus a theme of aesthetics. Yet "deconstructionism"
denies simply the aesthetic experience as it has been in the past denied,
for instance, by I. A. Richards. With this denial any difference between
literature as imaginative fiction and any other writing, now called "écriture" or "text," is abolished. Criticism becomes fiction. Critics can display
their hangups, paradoxically aspire to be artists while denying the very
possibility of aesthetic experience. If art is abolished as a category, literature is too: we can study any kind of writing—expository, argumentative, rhetorical. Value criteria disappear. Kitsch, colportage, become
favorite topics, defensible as a study of popular taste and basic literary
devices but subversive of any scale of values. Leslie Fiedler, in a book
What Was Literature? (1982), dismissed as "elitist" and even oppressive all
the literature he had formerly admired—T. S. Eliot, Joyce, and others—
in favor of pulp science fiction, hardcore pornography, and "novelists
never accepted into the canon of o.k. art": *Gone With the Wind,* Jack
London, and the Leatherstocking Tales.

If there is no qualitative difference among texts, they obviously have
no authority of any kind, do not challenge the reader and interpreter,
have no "structure of determination." Complete liberty of interpretation
has been advocated long ago: I. A. Richards, Kenneth Burke, and William Empson lent it support. But if interpretation is left completely to
the caprice of the reader and critic, if every text is ambiguous, polysemic,
"undecidable" we arrive at the end of scholarship, at a frankly nihilistic

conclusion. J. Hillis Miller pressed the words "parasite" and "host" as parallel to the relation of interpretation and text to arrive at the conclusion that all texts are "unreadable" if readable means "open to a definite univocal interpretation." "Nihilism is," he states, "an inalienable presence within Occidental metaphysics, both in poems and in the criticism of poems." A passage in Nietzsche, who has suddenly become a great authority, which asserts that truth "is a mobile army of metaphors, metonymies, anthropomorphisms" and that "we have nothing but metaphors of things which in no way correspond to the original entities" is quoted as gospel truth. Thus the late Paul de Man, in *Blindness and Insight* (1971), elaborates the view that poetry only "names the void, asserts itself as pure nothingness" and in *Allegories of Reading* (1979) tries to return literary study to rhetoric as a study of tropes, contradictions, "aporia," as he calls them. Rhetoric is a text, "in that it allows for two incompatible, mutually self-destructive points of view and therefore puts an insurmountable obstacle in the way of any reading or understanding." Hopelessness seems the only way out. W. H. Auden's famous pronouncement in 1939 that "if no poem had been written, not a picture painted, nor a bar of music composed, the history of man would be materially unchanged" is endorsed. No wonder students stay away from the study of literature, self-proclaimed to be futile.

I would not, however, wish to lament the decline of literary criticism and scholarship. Titles such as "The Death of Literature," "The Prison house of Language," "A Map of Misreading," "What Was Literature?" seem to summarize the situation and certainly indicate a prevailing mood. But extreme skepticism is also a device of avoiding a confrontation with hard and ultimate questions. Despair can hide an escape into an ivory tower. If all literature is only a language game, we can still study rhetoric, tropes, ambiguities, "undecidables," and do not have to commit ourselves to any literary value judgments and any specific view of the world and society. Marxists in their polemics against these theories can easily score points against the denial of reality and history without persuading to their specific version. At least something is saved: rhetoric means new close reading, attention to the minutiae of texts. The emphasis on "intertextuality" and "contextuality" revives source studies in a more sophisticated version. The new attention to reader response allows us to study old book-reviews, to cultivate the history of criticism, and to study devices such as parody and imitation. The rejection of the canon encourages the study of subliterature. Feminist criticism stimulates the unearthing of unknown or neglected women writers and the study of social attitudes toward women, their social position, their grievances and achievements. Psychoanalysis, which flourishes on the margin of literary studies, makes us study biographies, and autobiographies in particular, in order to interpret the intimate and sexual life of writers. The new interest and sympathy for the so-called third world encourages attention to little-known literatures and texts, allows an enormous expansion of comparative literature into fields hitherto neglected by European-centered traditional literary history. Even the denial of any authority to the text may in some cases be a valuable stimulus to fantasize, to spin webs of personal associations, to meditations, however remote from a rational study of literature, on all the problems of our common culture.

This sketch of some recent trends in American criticism should not conceal that England has been almost immune to the allurements of recent French criticism. When David Lodge, in *Working with Structuralism* (1981), seemed to proclaim his collaboration with the French movement, he actually only used Jakobson's distinction between metaphor and metonymy to study modern fiction. Geoffrey Strickland, in *Structuralism or Criticism?* (1981), votes loudly and clearly for criticism understood in the terms of Leavis's almost instinctive judgments and condemns structuralism particularly for its ambition to describe all literature as a closed system of signs. Iain McGilchrist, in *Against Criticism* (1982), proclaims again an English tradition of enmity to theory. "The only genuine critical theory is that of non-theory, the only applicable abstraction the rejection of abstraction," but then goes on to expound and endorse the main doctrines of organistic aesthetics: the wholeness of a work of art, the inseparability of form and content, the unity of opposites, and so as if he himself had discovered them.

In England a new Marxism offered the only alternative. It has its master in Raymond Williams, whose many books leading up to *Marxism and Literature* (1977) have studied sensitively the social implications and effects of literature without ignoring the aesthetic function even though he rejects it as a category, while younger propagandists such as Terry Eagleton in *Literary Theory* (1983) are completely committed to the Marxist dogmatism.

This sketch of the newest trends in literary theory in the United States and England is, I fear, loaded in favor the new and thus startling. The majority of teachers and researchers in the profession remain untouched by the newest fashions. They continue interpreting texts, believing that their interpretations are better, or at least correct. They continue to edit and annotate texts, to search for sources, to dig for biographical and bibliographical facts, to study the social and historical background in order to elucidate a work of literature; to fulfill one of the main functions of criticism: to preserve the past, to transmit the heritage of great literature in an age of technological civilization. In short, much of the old factualism and positivism (if not in any strict sense of adherence to its doctrines) survives. While the whole twentieth century, as these volumes have shown, revolted against the obvious limitations of positivism, it may be time to defend a proper respect for facts, for evidence, for established values and traditions and simply for commonsense and rational approaches to the study of literature. Some correction is needed to the excesses of recent varieties of skepticism which, if its teachings should be generally accepted, would lead literally not only to the "deconstruction" but to the destruction of all literary criticism and scholarship. But this plea for a return to sanity must not be understood as advocating the abandonment of the great task of a theory of literature which has been built up in continuous efforts and debates since the time of Plato and Aristotle. With philosophical aesthetics, art history, and musicology, a theory of literature—poetics—is one of man's main attempts to understand his own creations.

BIBLIOGRAPHIES AND NOTES

SELECT BIBLIOGRAPHY:
CRITICISM BEFORE THE NEW CRITICISM

NATURALISTS, SYMBOLISTS, AND IMPRESSIONISTS

Bernard Smith. *Forces in American Criticism* (1939). Often perceptive despite its Marxist assumptions.

Robert E. Spiller, Willard Thorp, et al., eds. *Literary History of the United States,* 3 vols. (1948). Contains relevant chapters, "The Discovery of Bohemia," by Harry Levin and "The Battle of the Books," by Robert E. Spiller, and full bibliographies in vol. 3.

Morton D. Zabel, ed. *Literary Opinion in America,* rev. ed. (1951). Has a good introduction.

William Van O'Connor. *The Age of Criticism, 1900–1950* (1952).

Clarence Arthur Brown. *The Achievement of American Criticism* (1954). Prints out-of-the-way texts.

Floyd Stovall, ed. *The Development of American Literary Criticism* (1955). Contains essays on this time by Robert P. Falk and John H. Raleigh.

John Paul Pritchard. *Criticism in America* (1956). Inferior but has good bibliographies.

Hans-Joachim Lang. *Studien zur Entstehung der neueren amerikanischen Literaturkritik* (1961). Valuable, firsthand study of many minor figures.

Arnold T. Schwab. *James Gibbon Huneker: Critic of the Seven Arts* (1963). An ample life and account of his work.

Walter Sutton. *Modern American Literary Criticism* (1963). Perfunctory on this period.

Richard Ruland. *The Rediscovery of American Literature: Premises of Critical Taste, 1900–1940* (1967). A general account of the revival of interest in early American literature.

NOTES TO PAGES 1–3

1. Quoted by Harry Levin in Spiller, *Literary History,* 1075.
2. Wilson, *Classics and Commercials,* 114; *Shores of Light,* 713.

H. L. MENCKEN

A Book of Prefaces (1917). Cited as *BP.*

Prejudices: First Series (1919). Cited as *PFS*.
Prejudices: Second Series (1920). Cited as *PSS*.
Prejudices: Third Series (1922). Cited as *PTS*.
Prejudices: Fourth Series (1924). Cited as *PFthS*.

H. L. Mencken's Smart Set Criticism, ed. Wiliam H. Nolte (1968). Reprints selections from that journal.
Betty Adler and Jane Wilhelm, eds. *H. L. Mencken: A Bibliography* (1961). Lists thousands of items.
William H. Nolte. *H. L. Mencken: Literary Critic* (1967). Most useful.
Douglas C. Stenerson. *H. L. Mencken: Iconoclast from Baltimore* (1971). A good general account.
Carl Bode, ed. *The Young Mencken* (1973). Reprints the early work in selection.

NOTES TO PAGES 3–10

1. Isaac Goldberg. *The Man Mencken* (1925), 91.
2. Wilson, *Shores of Light,* 486.
3. *A Mencken Chrestomathy* (1944), 501–05, originally in *American Mercury* (1926).

VAN WYCK BROOKS

F. R. Leavis. "The Americanness of Van Wyck Brooks," in *Anna Karenina and Other Essays* (1967).
James R. Vitelli. *Van Wyck Brooks* (1969).
Robert E. Spiller, ed. *The Van Wyck Brooks–Lewis Mumford Letters: The Record of a Literary Friendship, 1921–1963* (1970).
William Wasserstrom. *The Legacy of Van Wyck Brooks* (1971). Reprints fugitive pieces in the appendix.
James Hoopes. *Van Wyck Brooks* (1977). The fullest account based on manuscript sources.
William Wasserstrom, ed. *Van Wyck Brooks: The Critic and His Critics* (1979). Reprints periodical criticism, including my essay, "Van Wyck Brooks and a National Literature," originally in *American Prefaces* 8 (1942): 292–306.
Raymond Nelson. *Van Wyck Brooks: A Writer's Life* (1981). A well-told biography but hardly containing anything new.

SELECT BIBLIOGRAPHY: THE NEW HUMANISTS

IRVING BABBITT

Literature and the American College (1908). Cited as *LC*.
The New Laokoon (1910). Cited as *NL*.
The Masters of Modern French Criticism (1912). Cited as *MFC*.
Rousseau and Romanticism (1919). Cited as *RR*.
Democracy and Leadership (1924). Cited as *DL*.
On Being Creative and Other Essays (1932). Cited as *BC*.
Spanish Character and Other Essays (1940). Contains a bibliography of Babbitt's writings and an index to the books. Cited as *SC*.

PAUL ELMER MORE

Shelburne Essays, 11 vols. (1904–21). Cited as *SE*. A convenient reprint is *Shelburne Essays on American Literature,* ed. Daniel Aaron (1963).
New Shelburne Essays, 3 vols. (1928–36). Cited as *NSE*.
A Paul Elmer More Miscellany, ed. A. H. Dakin (1950). Reprints odds and ends and lists 600 anonymous items.
The Essential Paul Elmer More, ed. Byson C. Lambert (1972). An anthology containing a preface by Russell Kirk.

BABBITT AND MORE

Louis J. A. Mercier. *Le Mouvement humaniste aux Etats-Unis: W. C. Brownell, Irving Babbitt, Paul Elmer More* (1928). The first book-length study.
Norman Foerster, ed. *Humanism and America: Essays on the Outlook of Modern Civilization* (1930).
———. *Toward Standards: A Study of the Present Critical Movement in American Letters* (1930).
C. Hartley Grattan, ed. *The Critique of Humanism: A Symposium* (1930).
Francis Elmer McMahon. *The Humanism of Irving Babbitt* (1931).
T. S. Eliot. "The Humanism of Irving Babbitt" (1927) and "Second Thoughts about Humanism" (1929), in *Selected Essays, 1917–1932* (1932).
Louis J. A. Mercier. *The Challenge of Humanism: An Essay in Comparative Criticism* (1933).
Robert Shafer. *Paul Elmer More and American Criticism* (1935).
Folke Leander. *Humanism and Naturalism: A Comparative Study of Ernest Seillière, Irving Babbitt and Paul Elmer More* (1937).
Victor Lange and Hermann Boeschenstein. *Kulturkritik und Literaturbetrachtung in Amerika* (1938).

Frederick A. Manchester and Odell Shepard, eds. *Irving Babbitt: Man and Teacher* (1941).

Malcolm Young. *Paul Elmer More: A Bibliography* (1941). Most useful.

Austin Warren. "Irving Babbitt," in *New England Saints* (1956), pp. 143–64.

Robert M. Davies. *The Humanism of Paul Elmer More* (1958).

Arthur Hazard Dakin. *Paul Elmer More* (1960).

Harry Levin. *Irving Babbitt and the Teaching of Literature* (1961).

Francis X. Duggan. *Paul Elmer More* (1966).

Austin Warren. "Paul Elmer More," in *Connections* (1970), pp. 129–51.

J. David Hoeveler. *The New Humanism: A Critique of Modern America, 1900–1940* (1976).

Thomas R. Nevin. *Irving Babbitt: An Intellectual Study* (1984). Bibliography.

NOTES TO PAGES 17–35

1. *Humanism and America: Essays on the Outlook of Modern Civilization,* ed. Norman Foerster, and *The Critique of Humanism,* ed. C. Hartley Grattan.

2. *Saturday Review,* November 12, 1932; reprinted in *Designed for Reading,* ed. H. S. Canby (1934), pp. 333–38.

3. Oscar Cargill, *Intellectual America* (1941), 530.

4. In Manchester and Shepard, *Irving Babbitt: Man and Teacher,* 235.

5. Francis X. Duggan, quoting a letter in *American Literature* 35 (1963): 554.

6. Foerster, *Humanism and America,* viii.

7. Russell Kirk, in *The Essential Paul Elmer More,* ed. Byson C. Lambert, 9.

SELECT BIBLIOGRAPHY: OUTSIDERS

JOHN JAY CHAPMAN

John Jay Chapman. *Emerson and Other Essays* (1898). Cited as *E.*

———. *Selected Writings,* ed. Jacques Barzun (1957).

M. A. De Wolfe Howe. *John Jay Chapman and His Letters* (1937).

Richard Bennet Hovey. *John Jay Chapman: An American Mind* (1959).

Melvin Herbert Bernstein. *John Jay Chapman* (1964).

W. C. BROWNELL

Victorian Prose Masters (1901). Cited as *VPM.*

American Prose Masters (1909). Cited as *APM*.
Criticism (1914). Cited as *C*.
Standards (1917).
The Genius of Style (1924).

GEORGE SANTAYANA

The Sense of Beauty (1896). Cited as *SB*.
Interpretations of Poetry and Religion (1900). Harper Torchbooks ed. (1957), cited as *IPR*.
Reason in Art (1905). Vol. 4, Triton ed. of *The Works* (1936), cited as *RA*.
Three Philosophical Poets: Lucretius, Dante and Goethe (1910). Cambridge ed. (1944), cited as *TPP*.
Winds of Doctrine and Platonism and the Spiritual Life (1913). Gloucester ed. (1971), cited as *WD*.
Egotism in German Philosophy (1915). Vol. 6, Triton ed. of *The Works* (1936).
The Genteel Tradition at Bay (1931).
Obiter Scripta (1936). Cited as *OS*.
The Letters, ed. Daniel Cory (1955). Cited as *L*.
Essays in Literary Criticism, ed. Irving Singer (1956). Cited as *ELC*. The most convenient collection.

George Washburn Howgate. *George Santayana* (1938). Contains a chapter on "Critic and Essayist."
Paul Arthur Schilpp, ed. *The Philosophy of George Santayana* (1940). Contains "Apologia pro mente sua" and essays by George Boas, "Santayana and the Arts," and Philip Blair Rice, "The Philosopher as Poet and Critic," explicitly concerned with literary criticism.
Jacques Duron. *La Pensée de George Santayana: Santayana en Amérique* (1950). A diffuse French thèse.
Daniel Cory. *Santayana: The Later Years* (1963). Contains more letters.
Myron Simon and Thornton H. Parsons, eds. *Transcendentalism and Its Legacy* (1969). Contains an essay by Joe Lee Davis on "Santayana as a Critic of Transcendentalism."

NOTES TO PAGES 47–58

1. Van Meter Ames, *Proust and Santayana* (1937); in Gladys Dudley Lindner, *Marcel Proust* (1942), 235.

2. See Maurice Brown, ed., *Emerson Society Quarterly* (1964), no. 37, part 2: 60–70.

3. Printed in the *Boston Daily Advertiser,* quoted by Joe L. Davis in Simon and Parsons, *Transcendentalism and Its Legacy,* 170.

SELECT BIBLIOGRAPHY: ACADEMIC CRITICISM

J. E. SPINGARN

J. E. Spingarn. *Creative Criticism* (1917). Reprint ed. (1931), cited as *CC*. Marshal Van Deusen, *J. E. Spingarn* (1971).

NOTES TO PAGES 61–63

1. First published in *Columbia University Faculty Lectures in Literature,* 1911, but more widely known since its reprint in Spingarn's *Creative Criticism* (1917).
2. In *English Association Essays and Studies* 4 (1913); reprinted in *Creative Criticism.*
3. See Mencken, "Criticism of Criticism of Criticism," in *Prejudices: First Series* (1919).

THE CHICAGO ARISTOTELIANS

R. S. Crane, ed. *Critics and Criticism* (1952). Cited as *CC*.
————. *The Language of Criticism and the Structure of Poetry* (1953). Cited as *LCSP.*
————. *The Idea of Humanities and Other Essays,* 2 vols. (1967). Cited as *IH*.
J. C. Ransom. "Humanism at Chicago," *Kenyon Review* 14 (1952).
Eliseo Vivas. "The NeoAristotelians of Chicago," *Sewanee Review* 61 (1953); reprinted in *The Artistic Transaction and Essays on the Theory of Literature* (1963).
René Wellek. "Literary Scholarship," in *American Scholarship in the Twentieth Century,* ed. Merle Curti (1953), pp. 110–45.
Willliam K. Wimsatt. "The Chicago Critics: The Fallacy of Neoclassic Species," in *The Verbal Icon: Studies in the Meaning of Poetry* (1953), pp. 41–65. A witty, devastating attack.
John Holloway. "The New and the Newer Critics," in *The Charted Mirror: Literary and Critical Essays* (1960), pp. 187–203.
Lee J. Lemon. *The Partial Critics* (1965), pp. 150–55.
Walter S. Davis. *The Act of Interpretation* (1978). Applies Crane's method to interpret Faulkner's "The Bear."

MORE SCHOLAR-CRITICS

ARTHUR LOVEJOY AND VERNON PARRINGTON

Vernon L. Parrington. *Main Currents of American Thought,* 3 vols. (1927–30). Cited as *MC.*

Arthur O. Lovejoy. *The Great Chain of Being* (1936). Cited as *GCB.*

———. *Essays in the History of Ideas* (1948). Cited as *EHI.*

Lionel Trilling. "Parrington, Mr. Smith and Reality," *Partisan Review* 8 (1940): 24–40; a shorter version, "Reality in America," in *The Liberal Imagination* (1950).

Yvor Winters. *The Anatomy of Nonsense* (1943), pp. 556–64; reprinted in *In Defense of Reason* (1947).

Robert Allen Skotheim. *American Intellectual Histories and Historians* (1966), pp. 124–48.

Richard Hofstadter. *The Progressive Historians: Turner, Beard, Parrington* (1969).

F. O. MATTHIESSEN

American Renaissance (1941). Cited as *AR.*

Henry James: The Major Phase (1944). Cited as *HJ.*

The Responsibilities of the Critic: Essays and Reviews, ed. John Rackliffe (1952). Cited as *R.*

George Abbott White. "Ideology and Literature: *American Renaissance* and F. O. Matthiessen," in *Literature and Revolution,* ed. G. A. White and Charles Newman (1972), pp. 430–500.

Giles Gunn. *F. O. Matthiessen: The Critical Achievement* (1975).

Fredrick C. Stern. *F. O. Matthiessen: Christian Socialist as Critic* (1981).

STANLEY HYMAN

Howard Nemorov. "A Survey of Criticism," in *Poetry and Fiction: Essays* (1963).

NOTES TO PAGES 68–88

1. See *Style, Rhetoric and Rhythm,* ed. J. Max Patrick and Robert O. Evans (1966).

2. In *Comparative Literature* 1 (1949): 1–23, 147–72; reprinted in *Concepts of Criticism* (1963), 128–98, with a supplement, "Romanticism Reexamined," 199–221.

3. "The Painter's Sponge and the Varnish Bottle," *American Bookman*
1 (1944): 49–80; reprinted as appendix in *HJ*, 152–86.

4. *Faulkner,* ed. R. P. Warren (1966), 15.

SELECT BIBLIOGRAPHY: MARXIST CRITICISM

Max Eastman. *The Enjoyment of Poetry* (1931). Reprint ed. (1939), cited
as *EP.*
———. *The Literary Mind: Its Place in an Age of Science* (1932). Cited as
LM.
Granville Hicks. *The Great Tradition: An Interpretation of American Literature
since the Civil War* (1933). Reprint ed. with afterword by Hicks (1969),
cited as *GT.*
Max Eastman. *Artists in Uniform: A Study of Literature and Bureaucratism*
(1934).
James T. Farrell. *A Note on Literary Criticism* (1936). Cited as *NLC.*
Michael Gold [Irwin Granich]. *Mike Gold: A Literary Anthology,* ed. Michael
Folsom (1972). Cited as *MG.*
Philip Rahv. *Image and Idea* (1949). Cited as *II.*
———. *The Myth and the Powerhouse* (1965). Cited as *MP.*
———. *Literature and the Sixth Sense* (1969). Cited as *LSS.*
———. *Essays on Literature and Politics, 1932–1972,* ed. Arabel J. Porter
and Andrew J. Dvosin, with a memoir by Mary McCarthy (1978). Cited
as *ELP.*

All histories of American criticism contain sections on the Marxist group.
I know of no substantial discussion of Philip Rahv beyond the little memoir of Mary McCarthy reprinted in *Essays on Literature and Politics.*

Granville Hicks et al., eds. *Proletarian Literature in the United States: An
Anthology,* with introduction by Joseph Freeman (1935). Contains a
section on criticism.
Daniel Aaron. *Writers on the Left* (1961). The best history that I know of.
David Madden, ed. *Proletarian Writers of the Thirties,* with preface by
Harry T. Moore (1968). Contains several essays touching on criticism.
Milton Cantor. *Max Eastman* (1970). A survey with some attention to the
criticism.
Martin Christadler and Olaf Hansen, eds. *Marxistische Literaturkritik in
Amerika* (1982). An excellent new anthology (in English) of the main
texts.

SELECT BIBLIOGRAPHY: EDMUND WILSON

Axel's Castle (1931). Reprint ed. (1945), cited as *AC*.
The Triple Thinkers (1938). Revised and enlarged ed. (1948), cited as *TT.*
To the Finland Station (1940). Anchor Book ed. (1953), cited as *FS*.
The Wound and the Bow (1941). Cited as *WB*.
Classics and Commercials (1950). Cited as *CC*.
The Shores of Light (1952). Cited as *SL*.
Red, Black, Blond and Olive (1956). Cited as *RB*.
Patriotic Gore (1962). Cited as *PG*.
The Bit Between My Teeth (1965). Cited as *BBT.*
A Window on Russia (1972).
The Devils and Canon Barham, foreword by Leon Edel (1973). Cited as *DCB*.
The Twenties: From Notebooks and Diaries of the Period, ed. Leon Edel (1975). Cited as *TW.*
Letters on Literature and Politics: 1912–1972, ed. (1977).
The Thirties: From Notebooks and Diaries of the Period, ed. Leon Edel (1982).
The Forties: From Notebooks and Diaries of the Period, ed. Leon Edel (1983).

Alfred Kazin. *On Native Grounds* (1942), pp. 446–52.
Robert B. Heilman. "The Freudian Reading of *The Turn of the Screw,*" *Modern Language Notes* 62 (1947): 433–45.
Stanley Edgar Hyman. *The Armed Vision* (1948), pp. 19–48. Highly unfavorable.
John Farrelly. *Scrutiny* 18 (1951–52): 229–33.
Alfred Kazin. *The Inmost Leaf* (1955), pp. 93–97.
———. *Contemporaries* (1962), pp. 405–11.
Frank Kermode. *Puzzles and Epiphanies* (1962), pp. 55–63.
John Wain. *Essays on Literature and Ideas* (1963), pp. 141–45.
Norman Podhoretz. *Doings and Undoings* (1964), pp. 30–50.
Sherman Paul. *Edmund Wilson: A Study of Literary Vocation in Our Time* (1965).
Richard Gilman. "E. Wilson: Then and Now," *New Republic* 155 (July 2, 1966): 23–28.
Frank Kermode. *Encounter* 26 (1966): 61–66, 68, 70.
Werner Berthoff. *Edmund Wilson* (1968). Critical.
Charles P. Frank. *Edmund Wilson* (1970). Has a good chapter on literary criticism.
Delmore Schwartz. *Selected Essays* (1970), pp. 360–74.
Leonard Kriegel. *Edmund Wilson* (1971).

Richard David Ramsey. *Edmund Wilson: A Bibliography* (1971). Indispensable for a list of scattered essays and reviews and a list of articles and reviews about Wilson.

Leon Edel. "A Portrait of Edmund Wilson," in *The Twenties* (1975), pp. xvii–xlvi.

NOTES TO PAGES 99–122

1. Henry Brandon, "We don't know where we are." A conversation with Edmund Wilson in *New Republic,* March 30, 1959, pp. 13–14.

2. See Johann Peter Eckermann, *Gespräche mit Goethe,* ed. H. H. Houben (1948), 480 (March 28, 1827).

3. Quoted by Kriegel, *Edmund Wilson,* 9.

4. *A Prelude* (1967), 62.

5. *The Papers of Christian Gauss,* ed. Katherine Gauss Jackson and Hiram Haydn (1957) and his other published writings do not bear out his eminence as a critic and literary historian.

6. *The American Jitters* (1932; rpt. 1968), 307. This chapter was dropped from the reprint in *The American Earthquake* (1958). A similar passage in *A Prelude,* 227.

7. *A Piece of My Mind* (1956). Anchor ed. (1958), 59, 232.

8. Beerbohm belongs to the "cultivated merchant class" (*TT,* 224 on Johnson's background).

9. Wilson quotes Arthur Schlesinger. In *PG,* 35.

10. In "Modern Literature: Between the Whirlpool and the Rock," *New Republic* 48 (November 2, 1926): 296–97.

11. In preface to Emeric Fiser's *L'Esthétique de Marcel Proust* (1933).

12. *New Republic* 58 (March 20, 1929): 134–35, and *New Republic* 62 (February 26, 1930): 34–40, (March 5, 1930): 69–73.

13. Note that this passage comes from the "Einführung zur Kritik der politischen Ökonomie" (1857), a manuscript that was abandoned and was published in an obscure journal in 1903, *Die Neue Zeit* 21 (1903): 710–18, 741–45, 772–81.

14. "Are Artists People?" *New Masses* 3 (1927): 5–9.

15. "The Progress of Psychoanalysis: The Importance of the Discovery, by Dr. Sigmund Freud, of the Subconscious Self," *Vanity Fair* 14 (1920): 41, 86, 88.

16. A. E. Dyson, *The Inimitable Dickens* (1970), rejects Wilson's view, but Angus Wilson accepts it, with some hesitation. See introduction to Penguin edition of *The Mystery of Edwin Drood* (1974), 23.

17. *The Notebooks,* ed. F. O. Matthiessen and K. Murdock (1947),

pp. 178–79. I quote the refutation by F. R. Leavis in *Scrutiny* 18 (1950): 117. There is an incredibly inflated literature on this story.

18. *Nassau Literary Magazine* 70 (1914): 286–95.

19. "Is Verse a Dying Technique?" in *TT*, 15–30. Originally as "The Canons of Poetry" in *Atlantic Monthly* 153 (1934): 455–62.

20. "Meditations on Dostoevsky," *New Republic* 56 (October 24, 1928): 274–76. Note that *TW*, 312, has entry: "All of literature gives a false view of life." In the novel *I Thought of Daisy* (1929), 174–76, the sentiments of the Dostoevsky article are repeated, sometimes verbatim.

21. But Wilson wrote an introduction to the Borzoi edition of Rousseau's *Confessions* (1923) which sees its importance as "the first real romantic autobiography."

22. Professor Grosbeake in *I Thought of Daisy* expounds Whitehead in these terms (226). Wilson defended Whitehead against P. E. More (*SL*, 465).

SELECT BIBLIOGRAPHY: LIONEL TRILLING

Matthew Arnold (1939). Cited as *A*.
E. M. Forster (1943). 2nd ed. (1964), cited as *F*.
The Liberal Imagination (1950). Cited as *LI*.
The Opposing Self (1955). Cited as *OS*.
Gathering of Fugitives (1956). Cited as *GF*.
Beyond Culture (1960). Cited as *BC*.
The Experience of Literature (1967). Cited as *EL*.
Literary Criticism (1970). Cited as *LC*.
Sincerity and Authenticity (1972). Cited as *SA*.

Periodicals are cited with the following abbreviations: *Kenyon Review* (*KR*); *Mid-Century Review* (*MCR*); *Partisan Review* (*PR*); *Sewanee Review* (*SR*).

Joseph Frank. "Lionel Trilling and the Conservative Imagination," in *The Widening Gyre: Crisis and Mastery in Modern Literature* (1963), pp. 253–74. First printed in *Sewanee Review*, 1956, and reprinted in *Salmagundi* 41 (1978), with new appendix.

Roger Sale. "Lionel Trilling," *Hudson Review* 26 (1973).

Nathan A. Scott, Jr. *Three American Moralists: Mailer, Bellow, Trilling* (1973).

Marianne Gilbert Barnaby. Bibliography in *Bulletin of Bibliography* 31 (1974): 37–44. Invaluable list of Trilling's scattered writings.

Robert Boyers. *Lionel Trilling: Negative Capability and the Wisdom of Avoidance* (1977).

William M. Chace. *Lionel Trilling: Criticism and Politics* (1980).
Philio French, ed. *Three Honest Men: Edmund Wilson, F. R. Leavis, Lionel Trilling* (1980).

NOTES TO PAGES 123–143

1. Introduction to Robert Warshow, *The Immediate Experience* (1962), 14.
2. Introduction to the reprint of *The Middle of the Journey* (1975), xv.
3. See Delmore Schwartz, "The Duchess' Red Shoes," in *Selected Essays* (1970), 212–13.
4. The view of Nathan Scott, in *Three American Moralists*, 170.
5. John O'Hara, *Selected Short Stories* (1956), xiii.

SELECT BIBLIOGRAPHY: THE NEW CRITICISM

Murray Krieger. *The New Apologists for Poetry* (1956).
John M. Bradbury. *The Fugitives: A Critical Account* (1958).
Louise Cowan. *The Fugitive Group: A Literary History* (1959).
Richard Foster. *The New Romantics: A Reappraisal of the New Criticism* (1962).
Lee J. Lemon. *The Partial Critics* (1965).
John L. Stewart. *The Burden of Time: The Fugitives and Agrarians* (1965).
Ulrich Halfmann. *Der Amerikanische "New Criticism"* (1971).
Louise Cowan. *The Southern Critics* (1972).

SELECT BIBLIOGRAPHY: J. C. RANSOM

God without Thunder (1930). Cited as *GT.*
The World's Body (1938). Cited as *WB.*
The New Criticism (1941). Cited as *NC.*
"Criticism as Pure Speculation," in *The Intent of the Critic,* ed. Donald A. Stauffer (1941). Cited as *IC.*
"The Literary Criticism of Aristotle," in *Lectures in Criticism: The Johns Hopkins University,* ed. Huntington Cairns (1949). Cited as *LC.*
Poems and Essays (1955). Cited as *PE.*
Beating the Bushes: Selected Essays 1941–1970 (1972).

Periodicals are cited with the following abbreviations: *Kenyon Review* (KR); *Saturday Review of Literature* (Sat R); *Sewanee Review* (SR); *Southern Review* (So R).

Thomas Daniel Young, ed. *John Crowe Ransom: Critical Essays and a Bibliography* (1968). Indispensable for its list both of Ransom's articles and reviews and of comments on Ransom's criticism.

James E. Manger, Jr. *John Crowe Ransom: Critical Principles and Preoccupations* (1971). Deserves attention.

Thomas Daniel Young. *Gentleman in Dustcoat: A Biography of John Crowe Ransom* (1976).

————. "John Crowe Ransom: A Checklist, 1967–76," *Mississippi Quarterly* 30 (1976–77).

NOTES TO PAGES 159–173

1. *Die Phänomenologie des Geistes*, ed. Georg Lasson (1928), 91–92, 145, 257, 264, 407.

2. *Vorträge und Aufsätze* (1954), 2:42–43.

3. "The lie of Unity, the lie of thinginess, of substance, of duration" (*Werke* [1919], 8:77).

4. "We have on the model of the subject, invented thinginess and interpreted it into the chaos of sensations" (*Werke*, 16:55).

5. "Peeperkorn's desire for thinginess had other reasons" (*Die Zauberberg* [rpt. 1966], 820).

6. "Thinginess and unthinginess of the subject-matter" (*System der Aesthetik* [1925], 3:421)

7. "Sketch of a phenomenology of thinginess and particularly of spatiality." See Walter Bienel, "Einleitung," in *Der Idee der Phänomenologie* (1950), xi.

8. In *Situations I* (1947), 245–93.

9. A review of *Beyond the Pleasure Principle*, in *Sat R*, October 4, 1924, 161–62.

SELECT BIBLIOGRAPHY: ALLEN TATE

Essays of Four Decades (1968). Cited as *E*.

The Literary Correspondence of Donald Davidson and Allen Tate, ed. John Tyree Fain and Thomas Daniel Young (1973). Cited as *LC*.

Memoirs and Opinions, 1926–1974 (1975). Cited as *MO*.

Monroe K. Spears. "The Criticism of Allen Tate," *Sewanee Review* 57 (1949): 317–34; reprinted in Squires, *Allen Tate and His Work*.

R. K. Meiners. *The Last Alternatives: A Study of the Works of Allen Tate* (1963).

Ferman Bishop. *Allen Tate* (1967).

Marshall Fallwell, Jr. *Allen Tate: A Bibliography* (1969). Invaluable for lo-
cating Tate's scattered writings.
Radcliffe Squires. *Allen Tate: A Literary Biography* (1971).
———, ed. *Allen Tate and His Work: Critical Evaluations* (1972). Reprints
most worthwhile periodical articles.

NOTES TO PAGES 174–187

1. Letter to Mark Van Doren, April 11, 1926, quoted in Squires,
Allen Tate, 65.
2. See S. T. Coleridge, *Biographia Litteraria*, ed. J. Shawcross (1908),
2:254–55.
3. In *L'Ame romantique et le rêve* (1946), 400–01.
4. See "The Aesthetic Emotion as Useful," *This Quarter* 5 (1932): 295,
303.

SELECT BIBLIOGRAPHY: CLEANTH BROOKS

Understanding Poetry, with Robert Penn Warren (1938). Rev. ed. (1950).
  Cited as *UP.*
Modern Poetry and the Tradition (1939). Cited as *MPT.*
The Well-Wrought Urn (1947). Cited as *WU.*
Literary Criticism: A Short History, with William K. Wimsatt, Jr. (1957).
  Cited as *LC.*
The Hidden God: Studies in Hemingway, Faulkner, Eliot, and Warren (1963).
William Faulkner: The Yoknapatawpha Country (1963). Cited as *WF.*
A Shaping Joy: Studies in the Writer's Craft (1971). Cited as *SJ.*
"Irony as a Principle of Structure," in *Literary Opinion in America*, ed.
  Morton D. Zabel, rev. ed. (1951). A revision of "Irony and Ironic Po-
  etry," *College English* 9 (1948): 231–37. Cited as *Z.*
William Faulkner: Toward Yoknapatawpha and Beyond (1978).

Lewis P. Simpson, ed. *The Possibilities of Order: Cleanth Brooks and His Work*
  (1976).

NOTES TO PAGES 188–213

1. "The Critical Monism of Cleanth Brooks," in R. S. Crane, ed.,
Critics and Criticism: Ancient and Modern (1952), 83–107.
2. In *English Institute Essays, 1946* (1947), 127–58.
3. In W. S. Knickerbocker, ed., *Twentieth-Century English* (1946), 371–
83.

4. In Julian Harris, ed., *The Humanities: An Appraisal* (1950), 1–21.

5. In Stanley Burnshaw, ed., *Varieties of Literary Experience* (1962), 95–114.

6. Six volumes of the Thomas Percy correspondence have been issued to date (1942–61) and another is being readied for publication.

7. T. S. Eliot, "Metaphysical Poets," *Selected Essays 1917–1932* (1932), 276.

8. Review of Allen Tate's *On the Limits of Poetry*, in *Hudson Review* 2 (1949): 132; "Metaphor and the Function of Criticism," in S. R. Hopper, ed., *Spiritual Problems in Contemporary Literature* (1952), 127–28.

9. "The Poem as Organism: Modern Critical Procedure," in *English Institute Annual, 1940* (1941), 20.

10. Benedetto Croce, *Poesia e non poesia* (1948), viii.

11. "Literary Criticism: Poet, Poem, and Reader," 96–97. Cf. Brooks's review of Alba Warren's *English Poetic Theory, 1825–1865,* in *American Oxonian* (1952): 52–53.

12. Matthew Arnold, *Essays in Criticism: Second Series* (1888), 2.

13. "Implications of an Organic Theory of Poetry," in M. H. Abrams, ed., *Literature and Belief: English Institute Essays, 1957* (1958), 77–78.

14. "Metaphor and the Function of Criticism," 130–31.

15. "A Note on the Limits of 'History' and the Limits of 'Criticism,' " *Sewanee Review* 61 (1953): 135.

16. Ibid., 134.

17. Review of Allen Tate's *On the Limits of Poetry*, in *Hudson Review* 2 (1949): 129.

18. "Implications of an Organic Theory of Poetry," 66.

19. John Crowe Ransom, *Poems and Essays* (1955), 97.

20. "The Poem as Organism," 27.

21. Richard Foster, *The New Romantics: A Reappraisal of the New Criticism* (1962); I. A. Richards, *Coleridge on Imagination* (1934), 19.

22. *LC,* 636–37; review in *New Republic* 85 (November 13, 1935): 26–27.

23. *LC,* 586, 708; *The Complete Works of Ralph Waldo Emerson* (1903), Edward Waldo Emerson, ed., 3:34–35.

24. *LC,* 737–38; Northrop Frye, *The Educated Imagination* (1964), 29; Northrop Frye, *The Anatomy of Criticism* (1956), 122.

25. *WF,* 6, 13, 423.

26. Review of A. E. Housman's *The Name and Nature of Poetry,* in *Southwest Review* 19 (1933): 25–26. Brooks quotes Housman in the following: "Metaphor and the Function of Criticism," 133; "Metaphor, Paradox, and Stereotype in Poetic Language," *British Journal of Aesthetics* 5 (1965):

316; "Literary Criticism: Poet, Poem, and Reader," 113; and "The Quick and the Dead," 43.

27. "The Poem as Organism," 26, 38.

28. *MPT,* 2, 59, 66. See also *WU,* 70, and "Implications of an Organic Theory of Poetry," 57.

29. *MPT,* 47; *WU,* 179–80. See also Brooks's introduction to R. W. Stallman, ed., *Critiques and Essays in Criticism* (1949), xvii.

30. Review of Alfred Kazin's *The Inmost Leaf,* in *New York Times Book Review* 7 (November 6, 1955): 40; *LC,* 649. E. B. Burgum's "The Cult of the Complex in Poetry" appears in *Science and Society* 15 (1951): 31–48.

31. Brooks, "The State of Criticism: A Sampling," *Sewanee Review* 65 (1957): 485–86.

32. *LC,* 166. Edmund Wilson's article is reprinted in his *Classics and Commercials* (1950), 460–70.

33. "The Quick and the Dead," 45. See also *WF,* 279, 281, 420–24.

34. "A Note on Symbol and Conceit," *American Review* 3 (1934): 201; reprinted in *MPT,* 54.

35. *LC,* 664; George Kennedy, "Fenollosa, Pound, and the Chinese Character," *Yale Literary Magazine* 126 (1958): 24–36.

36. "Metaphor and the Function of Criticism," 136–38; *LC,* 661–62.

37. Brooks, "Empson's Criticism," *Accent* 4 (1944): 208.

38. "The Poem as Organism," 27–29, 30; Brooks, "Tradition," in Joseph T. Shipley, ed., *Dictionary of World Literature* (1943), 585–86; *SJ,* 37.

39. *WU,* 26. See "Notes for a Revised History of English Poetry" in *MPT,* 219–44, in which Brooks does not use Eliot's term.

40. *MPT,* 235; Brooks, "The Language of Poetry: Some Problem Cases," *Archiv für das Studium der Neueren Sprachen und Literaturen* 203 (1967): 401; *UP* (1950), 587; *WU,* 192, 8.

41. *MPT,* 48; *WU,* 228; *Z,* 732. Cf. T. S. Eliot, *The Use of Poetry and the Use of Criticism* (1933), 96.

42. *LC,* 668–69, 623; Eliseo Vivas, *Creation and Discovery* (1955), 175–89.

43. In *Southwest Review* 19 (1934): 1–2. Cf. Edmund Wilson, *Axel's Castle* (1945), 124.

44. *MPT,* 41. Cf. Brooks, *The Poetry of Tension* (1972), 3–4.

45. *SJ,* 95. Cf. "The Language of Poetry," 407.

46. "A Note on Symbol and Conceit," 208; *LC,* 620; Brooks, "The Pernicious Effects of Bad Art," *Et Veritas* (1949): 14.

47. "Implications of an Organic Theory of Poetry," 63.

48. "The Poem as Organism," 23–24, 25–26. Cf. *UP* (1938), 230; *UP* (1950), 576; *WU*, 22.

49. "Metaphor and the Function of Criticism," 135; *WU*, 236, 237. See also I. A. Richards, *Speculative Instruments* (1955), 75–76.

50. "Implications of an Organic Theory of Poetry," 55, 56; *LC*, 626, 641.

51. "Empson's Criticism," 208–16; *LC*, 646.

52. "The Poem as Organism," 21–22; *UP* (1950), 514–15; *WU*, 102–03; *MPT*, 227–29.

53. "Empson's Criticism," 214, 211; *LC*, 638, 639–40.

54. Review of William Empson's *Structure of Complex Words*, in *Kenyon Review* 14 (1952): 669–78.

55. Brooks, "New Criticism," in Alex Preminger, ed., *Encyclopedia of Poetry and Poetics* (1965), 567; *MPT*, 91, 52, 46; "Implications of an Organic Theory of Poetry," 58; *UP* (1950), 244; "Metaphor and the Function of Criticism," 134.

56. *LC*, 622; "Implications of an Organic Theory of Poetry," 58.

57. Combined review of Yvor Winters's *Anatomy of Nonsense* and books by others, in *Kenyon Review* 6 (1944): 287.

58. Review of Tate's *On the Limits of Poetry*, 132; "Metaphor and the Function of Criticism," 127–28; "The Poem as Organism," 29. See also Brooks, "The Formalist Critic," *Kenyon Review* 13 (1951): 72.

59. "Literary Criticism: Poet, Poem, and Reader," 98; *WU*, 236; review of Tate's *On the Limits of Poetry*, 132.

60. *WU*, 186n.; "The State of Criticism," 492–94.

61. Review of Winters's *Anatomy of Nonsense*, 283–86; "Implications of an Organic Theory of Poetry," 61, 66; *WU*, 215–16.

62. *WU*, 182–83, 189n., 232–33, 235–36, 237n. See also "Implications of an Organic Theory of Poetry," 69.

63. "The State of Criticism," 490–91; *WF*, 6–8, 377, 380, 408–10; *LC*, 713.

64. Review of Northrop Frye's *Anatomy of Criticism*, in *Christian Scholar* 41 (1958): 172, 170, 171; *LC*, 711, 714.

65. Brooks, *The Hidden God*, 47, 53, 60; *SJ*, 111.

66. *SJ*, 102, 107. For the quotation from Yeats, see his *Mythologies* (1958), 331.

67. *SJ*, 124–25. For the quotation from Yeats, see his *Essays and Introductions* (1961), 255.

68. *SJ*, 133, 135. W. H. Auden's "The Guilty Vicarage" is in his *The Dyer's Hand* (1962).

69. *SJ*, 133, 135, 137. Cf. I. A. Richards, *So Much Nearer* (1968), 152, 179.

70. "Implications of an Organic Theory of Poetry," 51.

SELECT BIBLIOGRAPHY: ROBERT PENN WARREN

"A Poem of Pure Imagination: An Experiment in Reading" in *The Rime of the Ancient Mariner by Samuel Taylor Coleridge* (1946). Reprinted in *Selected Essays*.

Selected Essays (1958).

A Plea in Mitigation: Modern Poetry and the End of an Era. 1966.

Faulkner: A Collection of Critical Essays, ed. R. P. Warren.

Homage to Theodore Dreiser (1971).

John Greenleaf Whittier's Poetry. An Appraisal and a Selection (1971).

Selected Poems of Herman Melville (1971).

A Conversation with Robert Penn Warren, ed. Frank Gabo (1972).

Elder Olson. "A Symbolic Reading of the Ancient Mariner," in *Critics and Criticism: Ancient and Modern,* ed. R. S. Crane (1952).

Frederick P. W. McDowell. "Robert Penn Warren's Criticism," in *Accent* 15 (1955): 173–96.

Klaus Poenicke. *R. P. Warren: Kunstwerk und kritische Theorie* (1959).

John L. Longley, Jr., ed. *Robert Penn Warren: A Collection of Critical Essays* (1965).

SELECT BIBLIOGRAPHY: R. P. BLACKMUR

The Critique of Humanism, ed. C. Harley Grattan. Cited as *CH*.

The Double Agent (1935). Cited as *DA*.

The Expense of Greatness (1940). Cited as *EG*.

Language as Gesture (1952). Cited as *LG*.

The Lion and the Honeycomb (1955). Cited as *LH*.

Anni Mirabiles, 1921–1925: Reason in the Madness of Letters (1956).

Eleven Essays in the European Novel (1964). Cited as *EE*.

A Primer of Ignorance (1967). Cited as *PI*.

Henry Adams (1980).

Periodicals are cited with the following abbreviations: *Hound and Horn* (*HH*); *Kenyon Review* (*KR*); *Modern Language Notes* (*MLN*).

Delmore Schwartz. "The Critical Method of R. P. Blackmur," *Poetry* 53 (1938): 28–29.

Alfred Kazin. "Criticism and Isolation," *Virginia Quarterly Review* 17 (1942): 448–53.

R. W. B. Lewis. "Casella as Critic: A Note on R. P. Blackmur," *Kenyon Review* 13 (1951): 458–74.

Denis Donoghue. "Poetic in the Common Enterprise," *Twentieth Century* 161 (1957): 537–46.

Hugh Kenner. "Inside the Featherbed," in *Gnomon: Essays on Contemporary Literature* (1958). Satirical.

Joseph Frank. "R. P. Blackmur: The Later Phase," in *The Widening Gyre* (1963), pp. 229–50.

William H. Pritchard. "R. P. Blackmur and the Criticism of Poetry," *Massachusetts Review* 8 (1967): 633–49.

Gerald J. Pannick. "Richard Palmer Blackmur: A Bibliography," *Bulletin of Bibliography* 31 (December 1974).

Russell Fraser. *A Mingled Yarn: The Life of R. P. Blackmur* (1979). A mixture of admiring appreciation and often malicious satire.

Gerald J. Pannick. *Richard Palmer Blackmur* (1981).

René Wellek. "The Nineteenth Century Russian Novel in English and American Criticism," in John Garrard, ed., *The Russian Novel from Pushkin to Pasternak* (1983), pp. 260–71. Contains a more detailed discussion of Blackmur's essays on Tolstoy and Dostoevsky.

SELECT BIBLIOGRAPHY: KENNETH BURKE

Counter-Statement (1931). 2nd ed. (1953), cited as *CS*.
Permanence and Change (1935). Cited as *PC*.
Attitudes toward History (1937). Reprint ed. (1961), cited as *AH*.
The Philosophy of Literary Form (1941). Cited as *PLF.*
A Grammar of Motives (1945). Cited as *GM*.
A Rhetoric of Motives (1950). Cited as *RM*.
Perspectives by Incongruity, ed. Stanley E. Hyman (1964). Cited as *PI*.
Language as Symbolic Action (1966). Cited as *LSA*.

Kenneth Burke wrote a long answer to my original article "Kenneth Burke and Literary Criticism" (*Sewanee Review* 79 [1971]: 171–88), entitled "As I Was Saying," in *Michigan Quarterly Review* 40 (1972): 9–27. None of the quibbling arguments induced me to change the text here reprinted.

Austin Warren. "Kenneth Burke: His Mind and Art," *Sewanee Review* 41 (1933): 225–36, 344–64.

Sidney Hook. "The Technique of Mystification," *Partisan Review* 4 (1937): 57–64.

Bernard Duffy. "Reality as Language: Kenneth Burke's Theory of Poetry," *Western Review* 12 (1948): 132–45.

Marius Bewley. "Kenneth Burke as Literary Critic," in *The Complex Fate* (1952), pp. 211–43.

Luciano Gallino. "Kenneth Burke e la critica americana," *Studi Americani* 3 (1957): 315–46.

George Knox. *Critical Moments: Kenneth Burke's Categories and Critiques* (1957).

William Rueckert. *Kenneth Burke and the Drama of Human Relations* (1963).

———, ed. *Critical Responses to Kenneth Burke, 1924–1966* (1968). Contains bibliography of Burke's writings, writings about him, and a large selection of reviews and essays.

Arnim Paul Frank. *Kenneth Burke* (1969).

Hayden White and Margaret Brose, eds. *Representing Kenneth Burke* (1982). A collection of essays, all celebratory. Some articles concern literary criticism.

SELECT BIBLIOGRAPHY: YVOR WINTERS

The Critique of Humanism. Cited as *CH*.

Primitivism and Decadence: A Study of American Experimental Poetry (1936).

Maule's Curse: Seven Studies in American Obscurantism (1938).

The Anatomy of Nonsense (1943).

In Defense of Reason (1947), includes preceding. Cited as *DR*.

The Function of Criticism: Problems and Exercises (1957). Cited as *FC*.

On Modern Poets (1959).

The Poetry of W. B. Yeats (1960).

Forms of Discovery: Critical and Historical Essays on the Form of the Short Poem in English (1967). Cited as *FD*.

Uncollected Essays and Reviews, ed. Francis Murphy (1976). Cited as *UER*.

Kenneth A. Lohf and Eugene P. Sheehy. *Yvor Winters: A Bibliography* (1959).

Hart Crane and Yvor Winters: Their Literary Correspondence, ed. Thomas F. Parkinson (1978).

Keith McLean. *The Moral Measure of Literature* (1961).

Richard J. Sexton. *The Complex of Yvor Winters's Criticism* (1973).

W. W. Robson. "Yvor Winters: Counter-Romantic," in *The Definition of Literature and Other Essays* (1982).

Dick Davis. *Wisdom and Wilderness: The Achievement of Yvor Winters* (1983).

SELECT BIBLIOGRAPHY: WILLIAM K. WIMSATT

The Prose Style of Samuel Johnson (1941).

The Philosophic Words (1948).

The Verbal Icon: Studies in the Meaning of Poetry (1954). Cited as *VI*.

Literary Criticism: A Short History, with Cleanth Brooks (1957). Cited as *LC*.

Hateful Contraries: Studies in Literature and Criticism (1965). Cited as *HC*.

The Portraits of Alexander Pope (1965).

Day of the Leopards: Essays in Defense of Poems (1976). Cited as *DL*.

The *Journal of English and German Philology* is abbreviated as *JEGP.*

Eliseo Vivas. "Mr. Wimsatt on the Theory of Literature," in *The Artistic Transaction and Essays on Theory of Literature* (1963). Also in *Comparative Literature* 7 (1955): 344–61.

CHRONOLOGICAL TABLE
OF BOOKS

1896	G. Santayana:	*The Sense of Beauty*
1898	J. J. Chapman:	*Emerson and Other Essays*
1899	J. E. Spingarn:	*A History of Literary Criticism in the Renaissance*
1900	V. Thompson:	*French Portraits*
	G. Santayana:	*Interpretations of Poetry and Religion*
1901	W. C. Brownell:	*Victorian Prose Masters*
1903	Frank Norris:	*Responsibilities of a Novelist*
1904	P. E. More:	*Shelburne Essays: First Series*
1905	J. Huneker:	*Visionaries*
	H. L. Mencken:	*G. B. Shaw*
	G. Santayana:	*Reason in Art*
1908	H. Garland:	*The Crumbling Idols*
	H. L. Mencken:	*The Philosophy of Friedrich Nietzsche*
	Van Wyck Brooks:	*The Wine of the Puritans*
	I. Babbitt:	*Literature and the American College*
1909	W. C. Brownell:	*American Prose Masters*
1910	J. Huneker:	*Promenades of an Impressionist*
	G. Santayana:	*Three Philosophical Poets: Lucretius, Dante and Goethe*
	I. Babbitt:	*The New Laokoon*
1911	J. E. Spingarn:	*The New Criticism*
	G. Santayana:	*The Genteel Tradition in American Philosophy*
1912	I. Babbitt:	*Masters of French Criticism*

1913	Van Wyck Brooks:	*The Malady of the Ideal*
	G. Santayana:	*Winds of Doctrine*
	M. Eastman:	*The Enjoyment of Poetry*
1914	Van Wyck Brooks:	*John Addington Symonds*
	W. C. Brownell:	*Criticism*
1915	G. Santayana:	*Egotism in German Philosophy*
1916	Van Wyck Brooks:	*America's Coming of Age*
1917	H. L. Mencken:	*Book of Prefaces*
	J. E. Spingarn:	*Creative Criticism*
	W. C. Brownell:	*Standards*
1919	H. L. Mencken:	*The American Language*
	H. L. Mencken:	*Prejudices: First Series*
	I. Babbitt:	*Rousseau and Romanticism*
1920	Van Wyck Brooks:	*The Ordeal of Mark Twain*
	G. Santayana:	*Character and Opinion in the United States*
1921	H. L. Mencken:	*Prejudices: Second Series*
1922	H. L. Mencken:	*Prejudices: Third Series*
	G. Santayana:	*Soliloquies in England*
1925	Van Wyck Brooks:	*The Pilgrimage of Henry James*
1927	Van Wyck Brooks:	*Emerson and Others*
1928	P. E. More:	*New Shelburne Essays: The Demon of the Absolute*
1930	N. Foerster, ed.:	*Humanism in America*
	C. Hartley Grattan, ed.:	*The Critique of Humanism*
	J. C. Ransom:	*God Without Thunder*
1931	G. Santayana:	*The Genteel Tradition at Bay*
	Edmund Wilson:	*Axel's Castle*
	Kenneth Burke:	*Counter-Statement*
1932	M. Eastman:	*The Literary Mind*
	Van Wyck Brooks:	*Sketches in Criticism*
1933	Granville Hicks:	*The Great Tradition*
1934	M. Eastman:	*Artists in Uniform*
1935	R. P. Blackmur:	*The Double Agent*
	K. Burke:	*Permanence and Change*
	F. O. Matthiessen:	*The Achievement of T. S. Eliot*
1936	Van Wyck Brooks:	*The Flowering of New England, 1815–1865.*
	G. Santayana:	*Obiter Scripta*
	J. T. Farrell:	*A Note on Literary Criticism*

1949	F. Fergusson:	*The Idea of a Theater*
	P. Rahv:	*Image and Idea*
	R. Chase:	*Quest for Myth*
	A. Tate:	*The Hovering Fly and Other Essays*
	R. Wellek and A. Warren:	*Theory of Literature*
1950	L. Trilling:	*The Liberal Imagination*
	E. Wilson:	*Classics and Commercials*
	K. Burke:	*A Rhetoric of Motives*
1951	F. O. Matthiessen:	*Theodore Dreiser*
1952	Van Wyck Brooks:	*The Confident Years, 1885–1915*
	F. O. Matthiessen:	*The Responsibilities of a Critic*
	E. Wilson:	*The Shores of Light*
	R. P. Blackmur:	*Language as Gesture*
	R. S. Crane, ed.:	*Critics and Criticism*
1953	Van Wyck Brooks:	*The Writer in America*
	M. H. Abrams:	*The Mirror and the Lamp*
	G. Hartman:	*The Unmediated Vision*
	A. Tate:	*The Forlorn Demon*
1954	R. S. Crane:	*The Languages of Criticism and the Structure of Poetry*
	W. K. Wimsatt:	*The Verbal Icon*
1955	L. Trilling:	*The Opposing Self*
	R. P. Blackmur:	*The Lion and the Honeycomb*
	J. C. Ransom:	*Poems and Essays*
	A. Tate:	*The Man of Letters in the Modern World*
1956	M. Krieger:	*The New Apologists for Poetry*
1957	C. Brooks and W. K. Wimsatt:	*Literary Criticism: A Short History*
	Northrop Frye:	*Anatomy of Criticism*
1957	Y. Winters:	*The Function of Criticism*
1958	Van Wyck Brooks:	*The Dream of Arcadia*
	R. P. Warren:	*Selected Essays*
1959	Van Wyck Brooks:	*Howells: His Life and Work*
	Y. Winters:	*On Modern Poetry*
	A. Tate:	*Collected Essays*
1960	L. Trilling:	*Beyond Culture*
1961	H. Bloom:	*The Visionary Company*

1962	E. Wilson:	*Patriotic Gore*
1963	C. Brooks:	*William Faulkner: The Yokna-patawha Country*
	N. Frye:	*Fables of Identity*
	C. Brooks:	*The Hidden God*
1964	R. P. Blackmur:	*Eleven Essays in the European Novel*
1965	P. Rahv:	*The Myth and the Powerhouse*
	E. Wilson:	*The Bit Between My Teeth*
	W. K. Wimsatt:	*Hateful Contraries*
1966	K. Burke:	*Language as Symbolic Action*
	R. P. Warren:	*A Plea for Mitigation*
1967	R. P. Blackmur:	*A Primer of Ignorance*
	R. S. Crane:	*The Idea of Humanities*
	Y. Winters:	*Forms of Discovery*
1969	P. Rahv:	*Literature and the Sixth Sense*
1970	A. Tate:	*Essays of Four Decades*
1971	C. Brooks:	*A Shaping Joy*
	M. H. Abrams:	*Natural Supernaturalism*
	R. P. Warren:	*Homage to Theodore Dreiser*
1972	L. Trilling:	*Sincerity and Authenticity*
1973	L. Trilling:	*Mind in the Modern World*
	E. Wilson:	*A Window on Russia*
	E. Wilson:	*The Devils and Canon Barham*
1976	W. K. Wimsatt:	*Day of the Leopards: Essays in Defense of Poetry*
1978	C. Brooks:	*William Faulkner: Toward Yoknapatawpha and Beyond*
1980	R. P. Blackmur:	*Henry Adams*

INDEX OF NAMES

INDEX OF TOPICS AND TERMS